Russian Monarchy

Russian Monarchy

Eighteenth-Century

Rulers and Writers in

Political Dialogue

Cynthia Hyla Whittaker

 NORTHERN ILLINOIS UNIVERSITY PRESS

DeKalb

© 2003 by Northern Illinois University Press

Published by the Northern Illinois University Press, DeKalb, Illinois   60115

Manufactured in the United States using acid-free paper

All Rights Reserved

Design by Julia Fauci

Images are courtesy of the Slavic and Baltic Division, The New York Public Library, Astor, Lenox and Tilden Foundations.

Library of Congress Cataloging-in-Publication Data

Whittaker, Cynthia H., 1941–

Russian monarchy : eighteenth-century rulers and writers in political dialogue / Cynthia Hyla Whittaker.

   p.   cm.

Includes bibliographical references and index.

ISBN 0-87580-308-3 (alk. paper)

1. Monarchy—Russia—History—18th century. 2. Russia—Politics and government—1689–1801. 3. Russia—Intellectual life—18th century. I. Title.

JN6540.W475 2003

320.947′09′033—dc21

2002040951

To Robert L. Belknap

C O N T E N T S

ILLUSTRATIONS

ACKNOWLEDGMENTS

No book ever has a single author. The historian is nurtured not just by the texts of the past, but also by the colleagues of the present, the expertise of library staff, and the institutions that provide the time and funding to write in the midst of teaching and administrative responsibilities. Above all, I owe infinite thanks to my husband, Bob Belknap, who, with his usual combination of kindness, wisdom, and love, shared with me the joys and difficulties of scholarship; having read every draft of every chapter, he certainly deserves, at the least, having this book dedicated to him. Orest Pelech, a peerless friend and one of the field's most generous colleagues, spent hours giving the manuscript a close and careful reading. I am also very grateful to my many friends in Baruch College's Department of History and to our secretary, Jessica Gonzalez, all of whom have provided assistance and encouragement on a daily basis. While neither Marc Raeff nor Richard Wortman was directly involved in my work on this book, they both provided inspiration through our many conversations and their own scholarship. In this regard, I deeply regret that I finished the book too late to obtain a reading from Bruce Lincoln, who proved an analytical force in my previous work and whom we all miss very much.

Scholars in the field of Russian history are fortunate to have so many first-class librarians worldwide to assist us in our work. I would like to extend my gratitude for the help, friendship, and fun I have had doing research with Päivi Paloposki of the Slavonic Library of the University of Helsinki and Polina Vakhtina of the Russian National Library, St. Petersburg. Edward Kasinec and Robert Davis of the Slavic and Baltic Division of the New York Public Library gave me unstinting support at every phase in the writing of this book and in providing me with appropriate illustrations.

I have received an embarrassment of riches in funding. I began research ten years ago on a Fulbright-Hays Award to Helsinki, Finland, and that same year had the good fortune to spend a month in Bellagio, Italy, on a

Rockefeller Foundation Fellowship. Further research was sponsored by IREX, NEH, and the many funding programs of the City University of New York. During the entire decade I spent working on this study, I received generous reassigned time from the Weissman School of Liberal Arts and Sciences of Baruch College. I also express my appreciation to the University Seminars at Columbia University for their help in publication, and material in this work profited from its presentation to the University Seminar on Slavic History and Culture. Last but certainly not least, I was able to finish the book due to a glorious year I spent as a Senior Fellow at the Slavic Research Center of Hokkaido University, Japan.

A NOTE ON NAMES

Russian names will be transliterated with one exception: the more common English renditions of the names of eighteenth- and nineteenth-century Russian monarchs will be used, e.g., Peter, Catherine, and Alexander rather than Petr, Ekaterina, and Aleksandr.

*R*ussian Monarchy

Literature on Monarchy

A Supragenre

*C*onceptions of monarchy changed profoundly in eighteenth-century Russia. Petrine reforms and Enlightenment ideals awakened a widespread public dialogue that transformed political attitudes about the country's form of government. On one end of the interchange, monarchs and their entourage felt the need to justify absolute power and the right to rule. On the other end, writers among the educated elite expended their energy defining legitimate authority and advising rulers to abide by the criteria their subjects had devised. Official publications and the whole spectrum of literary genres served as the forum wherein this dialogue took place. The results revolutionized the idea of monarchy.

While many Russians, including the peasant majority, clung to traditional views, rulers and published members of the elite fashioned a model of monarchy more in tune with the aspirations of an eighteenth-century polity. Secular justification for power replaced religious sanction. Dynamic change legitimized the office rather than maintenance of stability. Rationalist arguments superseded acceptance based on custom. An elective principle coexisted with that of dynastic inheritance. Rule by law challenged the notion of a sovereign remaining above the law, and the idea of contractual obligation injected accountability into monarchical actions. As a result, the figure of the Russian ruler as the equivalent of other European absolutist monarchs supplanted the image of a despotic, isolated, and unique Orthodox tsar.

The present study will document and analyze these changes. The dialogue between monarch and writers has previously attracted little attention since it was nonconfrontational: participants worked toward a consensus that absolute monarchy remained the best form of government for Russia in the eighteenth century. Historical scholarship for over one hundred years has translated this conviction to mean the willing subjection of a slavish, passive, or mute population to a despotic regime, an attitude usually derided as "naïve monarchism."[1] A historian as eminent as Richard Pipes characterizes the Russian government of this epoch as a system in which "a citizenry . . . as such does not exist at all . . . the people is the *object* of the ruling authority."[2] With equal conviction, Soviet scholars insisted upon branding rulers as reactionary and deriding nonrevolutionary Russians as servile; they thereby created dichotomies that scoffed at political commentary, which accepted but continued to explore and develop monarchy as a viable form of government.

Similarly, influential historians of other European states, for instance, Reinhart Koselleck and Jürgen Habermas, have brushed aside as court puffery or "princepleasing" any public dialogue that takes place within a monarchical framework; they define serious eighteenth-century discourse as bourgeois literature adversarial to a ruling authority.[3] These presumptions denied the possibility of public political exchange in a monarchist Russia with virtually no bourgeoisie. The proleptic quality of much historical writing exacerbated this dismissive attitude toward nonrevolutionary opinion because of a tendency to focus on antecedents of the Russian Revolutions of 1917 or on a line of development that Russia did not follow, namely, the European "metamorphosis from absolute monarchy to democracy."[4] Beginning in the 1980s, however, historians of continental Europe began to recognize the "prejudice" and "inaccuracy" of understanding the growth of public discourse "simply as a movement of opposition to absolutism."[5] The example of Russia demonstrates just how much historical tone is lost when voices supporting, rethinking, adjusting, or reforming political institutions are ignored or marginalized.

In eighteenth-century Russia, political discourse centered on the monarchy, since it was the central institution, and support of absolute monarchy became solidified as a result of the public discussion. Although habit played its role, this position resulted from conscious choice determined through critical analysis.[6] Russian writers examined the monarchy's legitimacy, debated its feasibility, and elaborated sophisticated arguments, drawn from the arsenal of current European opinion, to arrive at rational endorsement. Throughout, the participants in this discourse, both rulers and ruled, perceived absolute monarchy as a dynamic form of government, not reactionary or even static, and therefore saw themselves as part of a progressive polity, with support of the existing political institutions acting as a source of integration and cohesion. Of equal interest, the rhythm of the discussion of monarchy became a barometer that reflected swings in public attitudes and interests and charted the penetration of Enlightenment influences into Russia.

In early modern societies, political discourse took place in print. Publications provided the primary channel for the diffusion of ideas and often the only public means for exchanging political opinion. In Russia as well, the discussion of monarchy was made possible by and was contained in printed works. Since print culture was in its infancy in the 1700s and the number of works finite, the simple methodology of *de visu* examination of the century's publications has for the most part uncovered the instances of political discourse.[7] Overall, of the ten thousand titles that appeared in the eighteenth century, roughly 10 percent provide pertinent examples. However, in the publication explosion that took place during the reign of Catherine II, the discussion of monarchy featured prominently in about 20 percent of all published belles-lettres.[8]

This rich array of printed materials provides the evidence for the ensuing analysis of how eighteenth-century Russians reconceived their central political institution. The chapters of this book that cover the first decades of the century until the 1760s focus primarily on official documents that were addressed to the general public and depict the changing self-identity and projected image of the Russian ruler. Peter the Great issued a seemingly endless stream of laws and regulations that comprised 44 percent of all publications in his reign.[9] In the post-Petrine era, the accession documents that accompanied each new ruler's ascent to power constituted an original political genre and included a trove of detailed manifestoes and proclamations. Catherine the Great's foray into political theory, her *Instruction (Nakaz) to the Legislative Commission,* created an environment that nurtured discussion of monarchy throughout her time in power.

Especially in the chapters that cover the second half of the century, this study concentrates on writers, the monarchs' partners and interlocutors in political dialogue. Their attitudes are found in a wealth of literary sources. These "explicitly produced" works or "cultural texts" offer an abundance of written evidence for reconstructing eighteenth-century concepts of monarchy and complement Richard Wortman's masterful study of "the symbolic sphere of ceremonies and imagery."[10] Valuable commentary on monarchy surfaces in every genre: 15 histories of Russia; about 100 articles in 40 journals; over 150 sermons and odes; a couple of dozen speeches, essays, and political treatises; a score of prefaces to translations; 20 biographies; 94 memoirs and diaries; about a hundred novels; two dozen plays; two dozen works of children's literature; and assorted letters and fables.[11] All in all, besides official decrees, this book cites approximately 250 authors and 500 works published in the 1700s. Nearly a century ago, a Russian scholar, V. V. Sipovskii, guessed that "political ideas and opinions in eighteenth-century Russia were infinitely more popular than has been generally supposed."[12] He was right: the theme was ubiquitous.

The political content of a wide swath of literature has escaped notice because the statements about monarchy in various texts have never been treated as a whole or in relation to each other, either in the eighteenth century or in later scholarship.[13] Some scholars flatly denied the existence of "dialogue" or "justificatory . . . abstractions" in this era.[14] And usually, when literary historians discovered a political voice in the works they were examining, they tended to label it "unique," "unusual," or a "first step."[15] But, once these disquisitions are teased out, linked together, and interwoven, the contexture reveals the richness and pattern of the theme and yields something quite new, a supragenre of literature on monarchy.

The prevalence of works in which monarchy is discussed signals a political consciousness among what is often termed the educated elite. Writers and their readers were principally drawn from the nobility residing in the capitals, although one-third of book and journal subscriptions came from people who lived in four hundred provincial towns.[16] By dint of education and some wherewithal, a few others, besides nobility, could take part in the select group whom print culture separated from the illiterate masses or even from their less enlightened brethren.[17] The ranks of this educated elite included professors, academicians, courtiers, bureaucrats, clergy, merchants, military officers, members of the free professions, and men and women of letters and of leisure; in general, in Marc Raeff's words, members comprised "those elements that participated actively in the cultural and institutional life of the country." The group was not numerous, comprising a fraction of the nobility, which itself counted less than 1 percent of a population of about forty million in 1800.[18]

By the second half of the eighteenth century, some among this educated elite saw themselves as forming what one leading man of letters, Aleksandr Sumarokov, called a *publika*, "people of knowledge and taste" who felt competent to judge cultural and then political topics in a critical manner; he excluded from that corps "the ignorant, no matter how high their rank."[19] These people did not form the type of public that Habermas admires, people who "battled with public power" and were possessed of a "common will to take clearly defined political action."[20] And yet, as Douglas Smith has argued, neither were they the pathetic group so often described: "captive to the all-powerful tsarist state, impotent and underdeveloped, a mere shadow of the 'real' publics found in more 'advanced' western European countries."[21] While the Russian educated elite may fall short of the accepted definition of a "public" and what it thought of "public opinion," its ranks counted a sizeable number of writers who possessed keen political awareness.

Those who published formed a tiny fraction of that fraction of less than 1 percent that constituted the educated elite. Their influence, though, was in inverse proportion to their numbers. Articulate and sophisticated, writers were the interlocutors with whom monarchs engaged in public dialogue via the printed word and whose publications provide the resources for this analysis of Russian conceptions of monarchy. These men and women of letters, in Gary Marker's description, thought of themselves as speaking for their readers and acting as the "conscience of the educated public" and "the herald of public opinion."[22] Of equal importance, monarchs likewise thought that writers represented the thinking of the elite, and this provided the motivation and rationale for a dialogue.

It is beyond the scope of this study to prove that writers *actually* represented the thinking of the educated elite, which indubitably varied a good deal on many issues. It would take another book to grapple with the questions of who read what in the eighteenth century and how readers reacted to or were influenced by publications. However, the type of texts that writers produced does suggest that they reflected conventional thinking about monarchy. Few of the works are formal political tracts, and few are great works of literature, since both were in short supply in this century, but mundane and unpretentious writings better expose commonplace conceptions than "'great texts' of political theory."[23] Minor texts, as Irina Reyfman has noted, tend to "echo majority opinions and set forth prevalent beliefs," because their authors are usually engrossed in parochial concerns rather than universal topics. As another author explained, what can make a group "interesting was the fact that they did *not* rise above the notions and prejudices of their own generation."[24]

Furthermore, when eighteenth-century Russian writers engaged in political discourse, they tended to lack disciplined purpose or tight coherence, so their views cannot be sanctified as ideology but more as accepted truisms or perhaps "rhetorical truth."[25] In fact, statements about monarchy often came in asides, digressions, or offhand remarks. While this "discursive formation" with its spontaneous theorizing may suffer from "enunciative poverty"—to use Michel Foucault's apt but awkward terms—those pedestrian qualities indicate the reflection of a Zeitgeist, of general attitudes rather than personal theory.[26] The regular repetition of themes and postures also carries a likelihood of their circulation among the writing and reading public and, at the same time, points to at least a vague consensus about political truths.

In contrast to the adversarial implications of the terms "public" and "public opinion," the dialogue between ruler and ruled in Russia aspired to be nonconfrontational. Writers were content to have "political issues treated indirectly by way of literature" and expected that "their socio-political aspirations could be fulfilled" through a benevolent monarch.[27] But this stance was not tantamount to selling out. Russian men and women of letters self-consciously hoped to act as a cohesive force, as mediators between the needs of the state and its subjects. The influential philosophe, Louis-Sébastien Mercier, counseled writers to "enlighten the government about its duties, its shortcomings, its true interest, about the public opinion to which it should conform."[28] In France, the philosophes operated outside the state structure. But in Russia, Mercier's tasks made double sense since the worlds of the court, the bureaucrat, the writer, and the educated elite overlapped in a multitiered service society; Russian Enlightenment figures felt a loyalty both to the monarch and to their idea of how to achieve the general welfare and found no conflict between the two.[29] It was natural, then, that writers—who at the same time might be courtiers, civil servants, or clergy—wanted to exert moral and political pressure to reform, not abolish, the government and had more opportunity to do so and less reason to turn radical than their French analogues.

No matter how nonthreatening, published political opinion challenges absolute power because it sets up an alternative authority to the monarch—no longer the sole public voice—and puts forward rationality and critical judgment as the basis for loyalty rather than unquestioning tradition.[30] Furthermore, an open dialogue about monarchy between ruler and ruled recognizes a limitation on absolute power and a desire, if not yet a demand, for some form of public participation in political life. Monarchs and their ministers throughout Europe perceived the contradiction but also the opportunity to use the new influence of print and pundits as a conservative force engendering tranquility and stability, especially in states neither despotic nor free. Jacques Necker, the great statesman, and Jacques Peuchet, a philosophe who wrote on French public administration, advised Louis XVI that public opinion was a "peaceful" force not given to "divisions and factions" or "passions." In other words, allowing a measured amount of political expression constituted a safety valve and provided a halfway house between "the spirit of obedience that must reign in a despotic state and the popular opinions that prevail in republican deliberations."[31] The French rapidly escaped the timid boundaries that Necker and Peuchet had set, but Russians remained within the limits envisioned, perhaps because the dialogue this book describes disarmed the sense of alienation and impotence. Within those confines, the political dialogue involving writers and their monarchs opened a new and prodigious chapter in the history of their relations.

Even earlier than their French counterparts, Russian monarchs had grasped the importance of print culture as a new source of support for monarchy. At the beginning of the century, Peter the Great expanded the ranks of the educated elite and invited them into a partnership aimed at achieving change and reform, including the transformation of the Russian monarch from an Orthodox upholder of the status quo into a secular force for modernization. Fifty years before the French kings, Peter used the preambles of published decrees to explain, justify, and win support for his actions and his absolute power, while at the same time ordering the publication of works designed to defuse opposition to his policies.[32] He thereby initiated the public discussion of monarchy. His subjects responded with their own opinions, and by 1730, in the midst of a succession crisis, a full-fledged debate occurred among a broad sampling of the educated elite, not just writers, over the viability of monarchy in Russia. In 1741, 1762, and 1801, monarchs were ousted from their thrones in large part because they failed to communicate with an *engagé* elite and did not meet its new and complex criteria for legitimacy. Catherine II the Great best understood the power of political dialogue. For most of her long reign, the empress encouraged the discussion of monarchy through her own writings and by eschewing any "systematic policy of censorship, indirect or otherwise," thus overseeing the blossoming of public discourse.[33]

Writings about monarchy in eighteenth-century Russia fell into two broad categories that I am calling justification literature and advice literature. Beginning with Peter, monarchs and their entourage used passages in official publications to justify absolute power, their own right to the throne, and their fitness to rule. Imperial pronouncements endeavored to provide the reasons why subjects should obey in conscience and with conviction. Writers responded with advice literature. While "mirrors" for princes are usually considered the sole example of this branch of literature, eighteenth-century Russians expanded the confines of such writing so that hortatory or didactic passages permeated nearly every genre.[34] They offered portraits of ideal or vile rulers, with a subtext to exhort reigning monarchs or their heirs to abide by the high standards described or meet a dreadful end; panegyrics offered fulsome praise for traits not possessed, with the intention of tactfully suggesting their adoption. Overall, writers explained how monarchs should behave and wield their power in order to warrant reasoned obedience.[35] There was a great deal of overlap between the genres. Catherine the Great, who ruled Russia for over three decades, was also a writer and produced both justification and advice literature, as did many of the authors who engaged in political dialogue. With all these complexities, justification and advice comprised the supragenre of literature on monarchy, and the interchange created the standards by which monarchical behavior was judged.

The dynamic, sophisticated interaction between monarchs and writers employed an arsenal of weapons drawn from every Weberian category: traditional, affectual, rational, and legal.[36] The arguments escaped becoming ritualized rhetoric since they changed with every generation in response to shifts in domestic or foreign policy, changing Enlightenment criteria for good government, recurring nostalgia for traditional practices, or alterations in public values and expectations. While the pattern is not neat, generally those who came of age in the first decades of the eighteenth century embraced Peter's image of the reforming tsar; the second generation emphasized the elective basis of sovereignty; later writers celebrated the monarch as the agent of history, the concept of rule by law, and the moral qualities expected in a good ruler. However, each new generation's argument was not substituted for the previous, but added on to it, like a palimpsest, so that layers of legitimacy underlay the institution of monarchy by the end of the century and helped ensure its viability for another one hundred years.

Peter's discourse of justification proved the most innovative and durable. He remodeled absolute monarchy to embody the bywords of the Enlightenment: secularism, progress, and rational reform. Succeeding rulers routinized that motif but placed their own personal stamp on the discourse. Works by Richard Wortman and Stephen Baehr have already described the images monarchs wanted projected in odes and the symbolic sphere; they liked to imagine themselves as godlike, foreign, or imperial.[37] In contrast, the advice literature that this study examines concentrates on the more mortal and domestic conceptions of monarchy and characterizes the monarch as parent, dynast, legislator, impartial judge, builder of consensus, virtue incarnate, and, of course, as someone who hearkens to advice. All these attributes implied constraints on willful action. Indeed, limitations are inherent in advice; the literature is based on the assumption that rulers are not free to do as they please. Thus, paradoxically, a fundamental sign of legitimacy involved absolute monarchs wielding less than absolute power, since rulers were limited de facto by expected norms of behavior. These precepts were to be self-imposed, but not trusting royal discipline, advice literature constantly counseled adherence to the code of governance writers had embraced.

Acceptance of absolute monarchy, then, did not mean defense of unlimited power and certainly not of arbitrary power. While lacking the intermediary corporate bodies that hemmed in western European rulers, Russian sovereigns faced practical, not just theoretical, limitations: "distance, diversity, and limited resources"; bureaucratic procedures; patronage networks; ecclesiastical and advisory bodies; and lack of communications technology.[38] The result was, as David Ransel laconically put it, that the "power of the Russian autocracy was in fact very narrowly circumscribed." Edward Keenan and Nancy Shields Kollman, though, have argued that "the *idea* of a strong tsar" or "the façade of autocracy" remained necessary to governmental functioning in order to preserve unity and avoid infighting.[39] At any rate, without de jure limitations it remains historically accurate, when describing the quality of power, to refer to eighteenth-century polities as absolute monarchies.

Subsequent to the eighteenth century, however, the use of "autocracy" and "absolutism" (a neologism of the 1820s) produces only misconceptions. In the nineteenth century, proponents of constitutionally limited power defined these two terms as synonymous with tyranny and, in the analysis of Nicholas Henshall, erected "into an organized system what was almost unanimously recognized before 1789 as a malfunction."[40] Similarly, Isabel de Madariaga, using linguistic evidence, suggested avoiding the designation "autocrat" *(samoderzhets/samoderzhitsa)*, since it has come to be equated with "despot."[41] In contrast, a normal eighteenth-century translation of despotism was "unlimited autocracy" *(bezpredel'noe samoderzhavie)*, which of course suggests that autocrats were at least de facto constrained in their use of power.[42] This study will avoid using the term autocrat because of its current meaning but also because it is unhistorical; in the 1700s, Russians used "autocrat" only when mentioning the ruler's official title. In the literature of the era, they referred to monarch *(monarkh/monarkhinia)*, sovereign *(gosudar'/gosudarynia)*, tsar *(tsar'/tsaritsa)*, or emperor *(imperator/imperatritsa)*.[43]

For all these reasons, eighteenth-century Russian monarchs and the writers with whom they engaged in dialogue resolutely refused to equate absolute monarch and despot, and their taboo was not based on pure mythology or wishful thinking. Nearly all absolute monarchs, according to Lord Acton's dictum, were corrupted by their absolute power and possessed some despotic features. However, because of the theoretical and practical restrictions already enumerated, few descended into tyrants who ruled in a completely arbitrary fashion, ignored divine and moral law, worked solely for their own personal gain, and disregarded the general welfare. Indeed, a time-honored defense of monarchy was that it rarely became despotic. Early in the nineteenth century, Nikolai Karamzin would look back and count only two instances of tyranny in Russian history, the sixteenth-century Ivan IV the Terrible and Paul I; at roughly the same time, Réné Chateaubriand marveled that in ten centuries the French had "thirty-three kings and not one a tyrant."[44] Despite this optimism, littérateurs who wrote about monarchy considered it their central task constantly to warn their all-too-human rulers away from the despotic path.

In contrast to the view that monarchy rarely became despotic, the literature demonstrated a firm conviction that democracy and aristocracy always did. The first secular histories of Russia appeared in the eighteenth century and sketched a grim picture of the inevitability of a tyranny of the mob or of a tyranny of oligarchs whenever the monarchical principle was weakened or abandoned. In addition, political theory throughout Europe deemed democracy and aristocracy—the only recognized alternatives to monarchy—as not only impracticable but destructive in a large state. Sweden's aristocratic Constitution of 1720 led to its loss of great power status, and Poland's "liberties" led to her extinction; the non-absolutist states of Denmark, the Netherlands, and the Ottoman Empire were all marked as declining powers; and many regarded England, because of the turbulence of the years from 1640 to 1714, as an example of a divided and unstable country.[45] Franco Venturi has noted that, in the eighteenth century, states other than absolutist were regarded as "abnormal, strange, and increasingly incomprehensible."[46]

Given the adherence of most Europeans to slow, organic development and the existence in Russia of serfdom, widespread illiteracy, and poverty, hardly anyone would dream that Russia was ready for a freer regime. Therefore, when Russians concluded that absolute monarchy was the only possible form of government for their state, they should not necessarily be regarded as passive, timid, servile, or exhibiting a failure of political imagination. In fact, the ancient institution reached its peak in the eighteenth century with the progressivism embedded in the policies of enlightened absolutist rulers. Throughout most of Europe, absolute monarchy, as defined by contemporaries, was perceived as the most successful and efficacious form of government—until the French Revolution.

Since the state possessed the same form of government as most of the rest of Europe and writers and readers among the educated elite were conversant with the aspirations of the Enlightenment, Russia in the eighteenth century was probably more Western than at any other time in her history, despite the time lag between East and West that the Germans call *west-östliches Kulturgefälle*.[47] Internally, to paraphrase Marc Raeff, this was a coherent, "well-defined" epoch to a degree unparalleled in Russian history. Rulers and their most prominent subjects breathed the same rarefied political air, spoke the same "language," and adhered to a similar value structure.[48] Martin Malia observed that Voltaire directed a chorus of philosophes in an "idealization" of this furthest outpost of "civilization." But the "golden legend of Russian monarchy" ended in 1789, when "the reforming eighteenth century . . . crossed the threshold into the revolutionary nineteenth century."[49]

As early as the 1780s, one segment of the Russian educated elite had begun what Nicholas Riasanovsky has titled a "parting of the ways"; many began to see the necessity for de jure restraints on absolute power—a trend throughout Europe—but all the tsars stubbornly resisted. They refused to go beyond the eighteenth-century political dialogue, take the next step, and institutionalize public opinion in some type of representative body; what had been transitional in the rest of Europe became a state of arrested development in Russia. Arguments validating monarchy that had resonated with hope in the eighteenth century and even in much of the nineteenth century lost their intellectual power and sounded more and more hollow as the world moved in other political directions.[50]

Intellectual residents of the twenty-first century may prejudge defenses of monarchy as hopelessly myopic, wrongheaded, and lacking in humanitarian values. But to penetrate the self-definition of the Russian eighteenth-century elite—to see them as they saw themselves—it is necessary to understand their conceptions of their basic political institution. In reminding his fellow historians how to "enter" a remote society, Sir Isaiah Berlin warned against judgments based on "the measuring-rods of our own civilization" and suggests, even when confronted with an uncongenial doctrine, endeavoring to "understand how and why it could, nevertheless, be acceptable" in another age.[51] The object of this study is not to exhume or exonerate monarchy but to understand the strength of its appeal. It is easy to itemize the reasons for the collapse of the Russian old regime in 1917, but the challenge resides in comprehending how it established and maintained enough credibility to become the "last and most durable Absolutism in Europe."[52] The cogent arguments validating monarchy that were devised in the dialogic exchange between eighteenth-century rulers and writers became absorbed into Russian political culture and certainly provided one significant cause for the longevity of the institution those men and women had defined, justified, and sought to improve.

Writing about Monarchy

A Historical Perspective

*R*ussian writing about monarchy arose as part of a ubiquitous and continuous discourse that extended from classical times to the modern era. For much of human history, monarchy reigned as the most widespread type of government. In Western civilization, its absolutist form maintained an uninterrupted existence for two millennia starting in the Greco-Roman world and continuing in the Byzantine Empire. At about the time that Constantinople fell to the Ottomans in 1453, the New Monarchs revived absolutist theory and practice in most corners of Europe, including Muscovy, and maintained a strong following until about 1800. The nineteenth and twentieth centuries—with their multitude of revolutions and evolutions that gave birth to the modern world—finally relegated the seemingly all-powerful monarch to obsolescence.

Writing about monarchy often took the form of dispassionate political treatises or heated attack. However, eighteenth-century Russian writers concentrated on justification and advice literature, and this chapter will focus on the long tradition of these genres and the eclectic way in which Russians borrowed from them. Throughout history, an "elaborate framework" of justification secured the longevity of monarchies. A veritable army of thinkers and writers, both within and outside a ruler's entourage, appealed to common sense as well as to a sense of mystery and awe to propound the benefits of monarchy in general and absolute monarchy in particular.[1] Even after the strength of custom settled in as a major validation, theorists continued to rationalize the various advantages of their central political institution. Just as frequently, many of these same writers contemplated the dangers of absolute power and advised monarchs how to avoid its abuse, but even when that occurred, defended the continuance of the existing form of government. The thrust of these arguments penetrated the *mentalité* of the humblest subjects so that the idea of the superiority of monarchy became one of the most popular beliefs in the history of humankind. In the eighteenth century, Russians made sustained and original contributions to the genres of justification and advice literature. Until then, the Russian dissection of the monarchical idea remained derivative, with writers wandering among long-established conventions.

THE CLASSIC CONVENTIONS

Europeans, Russians included, assimilated the "ideal cultural patterns" for conceptualizing monarchy that the early Greek philosophers had devised. Although constantly reworked to suit time and place, the formulations of the ancients remained preternaturally dominant and in broad outline virtually unchanged through to the eighteenth century.[2] The political doctrines of Plato and Aristotle, confirmed by Hellenistic principles of rule and Roman imperial practice, led to a fundamental "conception of kingship" that identified a monarch with absolute power. As Rudolf Vierhaus defined it:

> In theory such rule resided in the undivided and unlimited authority of an individual, who, as legislator, was not bound by the laws, who was independent of all control, and who exercised sovereignty without consulting any groups or institutions except those created by himself. But this was theory only.[3]

Because of this hallowed ideal conception, even when monarchs were circumscribed in power by magnates or representative institutions—for instance, in medieval Europe, Kievan Rus', or Muscovy—convention dictated their being described as possessing the fullness of power.

The problems inherent in conceiving a monarch as a single individual wielding absolute power gave origin to both justification and advice literature. Despotism is indefensible, but its threat is intrinsic to monocratic government; a fourth-century Greek statesman warned his emperor: "Tyranny is a neighbor, and a very near neighbor, of kingship."[4] This danger necessitated justifying why monarchy should nonetheless be preferred and advising rulers of its ever present pitfalls. Justification literature revolved around six major topics: the pragmatic idea that monarchy functioned better than other forms of government; the conception of monarchy as the most natural form of government; the establishment of the legitimacy of rulers; the erection of legal foundations for the institution; the elaboration of monarchical virtue; and the connection of monarchy with some aspect of divinity. Advice literature was less nuanced; its practitioners exhorted rulers to conform to standards of royal behavior that were set down by Greek writers in the fourth century B.C.E.

The fundamental argument in justification literature was pragmatic: monarchy worked better than democracy or aristocracy in the historical circumstances of what would now be called premodern societies. From the end of the fifth century B.C.E., when city-states began to prove unworkable, monarchy proved inevitable. Given the backdrop of external threat, internal strife, and larger states with diverse and uneducated populations, only monarchs seemed able to assure stability, political unity, military direction, the keeping of the peace, the dispensation of justice, cultural development, and an impartial voice to stand above classes and interests. As Aristotle concluded, they proved better "benefactors of the people in arts or arms."[5] Historical evidence early demonstrated the seemingly inevitable results of the alternatives. Writers beginning with Herodotus pointed out that democracy easily slid into the anarchy of mob rule. And Homer, witnessing how aristocracy ended in oligarchy, or rule by a narrow caste for its own benefit, tersely concluded: "Lordship for many is no good thing."[6] For two millennia, thinkers continued to argue that with democracy and aristocracy, "all is confusion and the state returns to anarchy." The perceived superiority of a unified supreme power and the "Manichaean-like tendency to view any alteration as totally negative" made it "clear, even obvious, that no viable alternative to monarchy was available."[7]

The empirical slant of the pragmatic justification was reinforced by the conception of monarchy as the most natural form of government, since it best resembled the order of the physical and social world. Christian writers observed that God ruled the universe like a monarch, not a democrat or aristocrat, and that a normal society was hierarchically structured, wherein the "lower serves the higher and the higher directs and guides the lower." Commonly, analogies connected royal rule with the eagle's dominion over birds, the lion over the beasts of the jungle, and the king bee over his hive (it was only in 1609 that scientists realized the correct gender).[8] Since the majority of monarchs were male, from the time of Homer writers imagined the monarch as captain, doctor, charioteer, or shepherd, besides being the "head" of the body politic. However, the most popular and inevitable analogy was that of paterfamilias. When Aristotle first described "absolute royalty" as a constitutional form of government, he used the paternal model, and *Pater patriae* became an official title in Imperial Rome, as it would later in Imperial Russia.[9]

Practicality, historical experience, and analogy provided easy evidence for the superiority of monarchy as a form of government in the premodern era, but often, establishing the legitimacy of an individual who ascended the throne proved a more daunting task. Rulers normally acquired power via conquest, election, or heredity, and justification literature addressed all three circumstances. While a forcible seizure of power was recognized as legitimate, a subsequent rule through terror was not. The Greek historian

Polybius made clear that the designation of "true kingship" could only be awarded to a "government by one man which receives the voluntary assent of its subjects and acts by persuading the judgment rather than by fear and force."[10] For this reason, election offered a clearer path to winning legitimacy. In Western civilization, the first recorded monarchs were elected, and the Romans' especial emphasis on justification by election never died out despite the ubiquity of dynasties. Even when a monarchy was not officially elective, the literature of political mythology nonetheless regularly described rulers as "elected," "chosen," or "made" by the "whole civil or mystic body of the realm," to quote a fifteenth-century French theorist.[11] A usual phrase, "by the common will of all," meant by agreement with the magnates of the realm, the "weightier part" of the people, whose support, the Carolingian writer Archbishop Hincmar of Rheims noted, a monarch needed to rule effectively.[12] Because heredity offered more stability than conquest or election, dynastic inheritance—despite the problems inherent in the luck of the genetic draw—was a practice usually victorious, although often interrupted, throughout premodern times.

Writers erected a complex of legal foundations for justifying absolute monarchy that proved just as tenacious and imaginative as the pragmatic, analogical, elective, and dynastic conventions, and the arguments became intertwined in the literature. Legal thinkers were concerned with the origin of power, the restrictions on power, and the right to resist. Some theorists conceived of power as directly handed to the monarch by God. Others, although not denying the ultimate divine source of all power, believed that it originated in the people, who then transferred the right to rule either outright or through election. The former doctrine held that the "people," at some moment in time, made an irreversible grant of full power to the monarch, who then exercised sovereignty and was owed obedience. Through this fictive contract, the ruler acquired his fundamental capacities as sole lawgiver and supreme judge. The Emperor Justinian's Code, for instance, rested the justification of imperial absolutism on this transfer.

> What the emperor ordains has the force of law, since . . . with regard to his sovereign power the people have transferred to him and bestowed upon him all their sovereignty and authority. Consequently, it is well established that whatever the emperor rules in a rescript, or decrees in judicial process, or enacts in an edict, is a law. These are what are called constitutions.[13]

The Byzantine ruler was thus conceptualized as animate law *(nomos empsychos)* or the revelation of divine and natural law in the realm and hence the fittest dispenser of infallible justice. Written or positive law, Plato's "ignorant tyrant," was considered inferior since it lacked the flexibility of a monarchical will to attend to mitigating circumstances. Whatever the variants, the concept of monarch as legislator and judge remained central in every political culture.

Although the ruler incarnated the law because of his public office, as a person he was subject to legal restrictions, a tension brilliantly described by Ernst Kantorowicz.[14] No matter how theoretically absolute the power, a monarch had to abide by customary law and those ever blurry "laws of God and nature," including the Golden Rule, the Ten Commandments, and universally accepted moral standards. The rulers of the Medes and Persians, for example, were empowered to do anything, except change an existing law. In addition, because of the contractual obligations implied in a transfer of power, the ruler could only pursue the general welfare or common good, a limitation that supposedly enabled subjects to obey and still maintain their moral freedom and dignity. Thus, when pagan or Christian theorists repeated the potent passage, "What pleases the ruler has the force of law," they envisioned a realm where "subjects are free and the whole community happy."[15] Foucault commented on these legal justifications in acerbic fashion: "The history of monarchy went hand in hand with the covering up of the facts and procedures of power by juridico-political discourse."[16]

While labored and obfuscating, the concept of legality lent assurance of the innocence of absolute power. The monarch was conceived as essentially different from a tyrant, who ruled by whim and by force and for his own benefit and thus legally violated the standards of conduct that bring legitimacy. In the fourth century B.C.E., Archytas of Tarentum rendered the categorical judgment on this issue: "But if he violates the law, the *basileus* is a tyrant, his rule incongruous, his people slaves, and the whole community unfortunate."[17] Theorists usually, albeit reluctantly, argued against the right to resist an evil monarch. Conveniently, the despotic actions of a bad ruler were almost always understood as a just punishment for the people's sins, even though the ruler's character supposedly set the moral level of his subjects. The real issue in pinning the blame on the populace and regarding the ruler's transgressions as a direct action taken by the deity was to argue in favor of the necessary continuation of obedience. Even when the ruler was held personally responsible for his evil deeds, his fate remained in the hands of the deity, not the people. In the first century, Dio of Prusa claimed that "the king receives his scepter from Zeus, and he receives it on the one condition that he should direct his counsel and care to the interests of his subjects," but, if he does not, it is "Zeus [who] thrusts him aside," while the good ruler "he brings to old age."[18] Few writers were willing to denounce an existing ruler as a despot, perhaps because of possible personal repercussions, but also because of the intrinsic reverence with which the office was held. The scholar Jean Dunbabin has pointed out that at least until the fifteenth century, no French or English king was denounced as a tyrant, although tyrannous behavior was constantly condemned.[19] Even when a despot emerged, few counseled resistance since the evildoer would eventually die, and upheaval presented a greater trauma than compliance. The agreement that despotism was exceptional and temporary contributed yet another justification of absolute monarchy.

Less complex and even more strained than the legal justification for absolute power was the habit, following once again the Greek tradition, of ascribing perfect virtue to the monarch. This passage into the realm of fiction was born of necessity. Most agreed, in the apt phrase of the medieval writer Christine de Pizan, that "untrammeled kingship is justified by the supremely virtuous character of the ruler," and more still agreed that the occurrence of virtue was rare.[20] Many writers resolved the issue by ascribing to the monarch's essential nature the attributes he ought to possess and thus allowed the fiction that his actions by necessity produced only good. Plato inaugurated this justification from virtue with his fabled abstract philosopher-king who promised an "end to the troubles of states . . . [and] of humanity itself." The Stoics followed suit by equating "true" monarchy with good government, and over a millennium later thinkers as illustrious as Thomas Aquinas and John of Salisbury still contended that since the monarch's "decision may not be at variance with the intention of equity," the ruler deserved unlimited power in order to accomplish infinite good.[21] At any rate, logical and rational justifications for an institution human beings recognize as a necessary part of their existence are rarely sufficient, and writers oblige with arguments that add mystery and awe. Part of the marvel of monarchy was that once rulers were installed, they would embody the general will and find themselves constrained to do good.

The virtue of the monarch was a significant concern since writers beginning with the ancients believed that the fate of the state resulted from the character of the royal person and that "the goodness and badnes of any realme lyeth in . . . the rulers."[22] If exemplary, a golden age would ensue under the *restitutor orbis* whose reign would bring an "abundance of corn, wine, and oil, and a wealth of all fruits." In contrast, the monarch who engaged in "royal license," cavorted with "wicked companions," and displayed an "ignorance of public affairs" doomed the state to ruin.[23] Even the ruler's tastes affected the rest of the population; in Synesius's words: "For the thing, whatever it be, in which the king rejoices, must immediately have vogue and be imitated by the majority."[24]

Monarchs, their advisors, and clerics must have recognized the difficulties of pretending "the supremely virtuous character of the ruler." A more direct way to establish the mystery and awe of absolute power was the convention of hedging the monarch about with some form of divinity, which became a "general habit," a "universal institution," and one of the most believed political myths of all times.[25] The Egyptians made their rulers gods-incarnate, the Persians bestowed a divine nimbus, the great Alexander was acclaimed a god, and the Romans officially hailed Caesar as "God manifest and general Savior of the life of mankind."[26] Napoleon is said to have quipped that when Alexander the Great declared his descent from a god, he demonstrated a sure instinct for real politics. In the Judeo-Christian tradition, biblical kings, Byzantine emperors, and medieval European monarchs figured as God's elect or vice-regent, rather than an actual deity. Anointed at coronation by a cleric, the ruler claimed to rule "by the grace of God." In fact, Marcus Aurelius first used the formula, and even Vandal chieftains ruled "by the grace of the gods."[27]

Despite the nimbleness of the foregoing justifications of absolute power, the writers of advice literature continued to believe that the human tendency to err was no small problem in rulers, whatever their connection to divinity. The conviction of the need to provide monarchs with a moral education led to a continuing stream of "mirrors for princes."[28] These books portrayed good rulers and praised the list of policies and attributes that would earn the love and adulation of their subjects. Reverse "mirrors" provided stories of evil rulers, and their despicable fates were offered as warnings. Scholars originally thought of these books as written from the ruler's point of view but now recognize them as containing both "deference and criticism" and constituting a "disguise" but not an "avoidance" of contemporary issues; certainly tales of the depositions of kings were "not concessionary." Monarchs and their heirs could hardly miss the point; the message was "recognizable."[29] Often, though, writers would be kind, even to their mediocre monarchs. An Egyptian papyrus of the first century B.C.E. concluded: "Yet they did not pursue the worse when they failed in the choice of the better."[30]

The earliest Western examples of advice literature—*Nicocles* and *Evagoras* by Isocrates and *Cyropaedia* by Xenophon—already expressed the criteria for correct monarchical behavior that would characterize the literature for the next two millennia.[31] Over the ages, pagan, Jewish, and Christian writers exhorted the monarch "to rule over his own passions," recognizing what Foucault described as the "essential relationship between dominion over others and dominion over oneself."[32] The ruler was also expected to control "his wife, his children, and his household," since all politics were "palace, even family politics."[33] The formulaic list of virtues for a ruler included piety, mercy, justice, courage, temperance, wisdom, generosity, truthfulness, patience, kindness to strangers, openness to suppliants, and an overall zeal for the welfare of the population.

In addition, writers expected monarchs to project "a solemn majesty, a gracious behavior, and a capacity to inspire awe," as well as a knowledge of how to make themselves loved.[34] The duties of rulership likewise consisted in a time-honored litany: to end civil commotion, to command armies, to cement empire, to dispense justice equally to rich and poor, to punish wrongdoers and exalt benefactors, to conform to custom and tradition, and to serve the gods. Given the humanity of the ruler and the aim of the writer, an essential trait included the willingness to listen to advice, first of all from those who authored "mirrors" for princes. In addition, the good monarch sought the counsel of magnates who served in the court; the medieval *Book of Emperors* flatly declared that the good king always reached decisions "with

the general consent of the leading nobility." Indeed, one of the most compelling monarchical images was "the ideal of a king governing personally in
conjunction with his councils" and, writers might add, in keeping with
their advice.[35]

Overall, the aim of both justification and advice literature—which were
often written by the same authors—was to defend the feasibility and improve the functioning of that institution which they deemed the "Best,
Most Ancient and Legal Form of Government."[36]

RUSSIAN ADAPTATIONS

Prior to the eighteenth century, Russians thought about monarchy in
conventional—indeed superficial and impressionistic—ways that reflected
the regnant traditions and rarely addressed the niceties of political theory
over which some of the greatest minds in the Western tradition had pored.
As Georges Florovsky noted, they were rather "silent."[37] Nonetheless, some
writers and occasionally rulers themselves grasped the essence of the discourse of justification and, like their intellectual forebears, acclaimed
monarchy as the most practical, natural, legally based, and divinely ordained form of government known to humankind and its leaders as legitimate and virtuous. At the same time, authors also appropriated the genre
of advice literature and warned rulers not to stray from a righteous path.

The pragmatic justification dominated Russian writing about monarchy
from the very first and can be found in the *Russian Primary Chronicle* and
The Lay of Igor's Campaign, the two most important cultural monuments of
the Kievan era, which embraced the late ninth through the early thirteenth
century. The monks and unknown bard who authored these works were living through the general turmoil that befell Kievan Rus' at the end of this
period and hoped that a strong monarch could assure the political survival
of the state. The chroniclers told a simple and pointed story. Before the creation of Rus' in 862, the multiethnic core area that ran from the Baltic to
the Black Sea consisted of a loose federation of tribes; the inhabitants "govern[ed] themselves," but this form of government brought only "discord"
and a "war of one against the other." Consequently, the people "selected"
Riurik and his retinue of Varangians or Normans to restore order. The
Chronicle described this political moment in one of the most famous, perhaps notorious, passages in Russian history and literature.

> They said to themselves: "Let us seek a prince who may rule over us, and judge
> us according to the law." They accordingly went overseas to the Varangian Rus
> . . . and said . . . "Our whole land is great and rich, but there is no order in it.
> Come to rule and reign over us."

Soon, "Riurik assumed the sole authority" among his kin and thus founded
Russian monarchy as well as the dynasty that bore his name.[38] Kievan Rus'

was a mixed polity; the ruler, or grand prince, was elected and shared power with aristocrats or boyars and with democratic town assemblies, called *veches*. Nonetheless, the *Chronicle* relentlessly conveyed the conventional lesson that single rule enabled the state to thrive, but divided authority led to civil war, fratricidal strife, and disintegration.[39]

The thesis of the *Lay* was similar. The poet averred that the lack of unity among Riurik's descendants was a "misfortune" since their "feuding . . . brought the infidels into the Russian land."[40] Beginning in 1220, the Mongols conquered Rus' and began their two-century domination; the country lost its sovereignty, and the khan of the Golden Horde appointed the grand prince. The invading Tatar force was probably invincible. Nonetheless, the notion that without a single, strong leader the state was doomed to anarchy and/or conquest emerged as a fundamental political principle, and "tsarlessness" *(bestsarstvie)* became inconceivable.[41] As the centuries progressed, the historical evidence could easily be amassed to support the pragmatic justification. The grand princes and then the absolutist tsars of Muscovy reassembled the state in the fourteenth and fifteenth centuries, and the aptly named Time of Troubles began when the Riurikid line died out in 1598, bringing in its train anarchy and near disintegration at the hands of Sweden and Poland. The establishment of the Romanov dynasty in 1613 restored luster and stability. Thus, when Russians began conceptualizing about monarchy, they utilized evidence from their own history to reiterate the most basic and venerable argument in its favor.

Russians legitimized their rulers, as did other states, through dynastic inheritance and election. Whatever the truth of the famous invitation to the Varangians, Omelian Pritsak averred that later rulers "took great pains to establish their legitimacy by tracing their descent to Riurik."[42] The celebrated eleventh-century rhetorician Metropolitan Ilarion in his "Sermon on Law and Grace" apotheosized Grand Prince Vladimir—who oversaw Russians' conversion to Orthodoxy in 988—primarily because he was "born the glorious son of these glorious fathers, the noble scion of the noble." Part of the attraction of hereditary monarchy is that the heir serves as the carrier and emblem of tradition, and chroniclers praised Vladimir for ruling "according to the prescriptions of his father and grandfather." Ilarion in turn praised the son, Iaroslav, who "strengthens . . . , embellishes . . . , repairs . . . , finishes . . . the unfinished works" of his father, a set of verbs that often accompanied praise of a Russian monarch.[43]

Less conventionally, Russians added a unique twist to the dynastic sanction by absorbing the Inner Asian concept of a sacred clan, which meant that any of Riurik's descendants could claim the mandate to rule, contrary to what happened in England or France, where the eldest son automatically succeeded. Charles Halperin has demonstrated the translation of the nomadic-pagan cult of clan into Muscovite times, and shown that even later it maintained influence.[44] Primogeniture lends a monarchy stability, whereas the over-populous Riurikid clan caused a political mess with the cyclical outbreak of civil wars and accession crises.[45] In the 1400s, the Muscovite tsars began designating their eldest sons as heirs in testaments in order to redress this problem, but succession was still not normalized. In 1499, Ivan III would claim: "To whomsoever I please will I grant the right to rule."[46] Through it all, dynasty remained important; no one in Kievan or Muscovite Russia dared attempt to assume the princely or royal title unless he was a Riurikid.

Besides the dynastic justification, early Russian political culture also incorporated the legitimizing usage of election. Arguably, the invitation to Riurik represented a form of election, and some eighteenth-century writers would later treat it as such. More concretely, in the mixed polity that was the Kievan government, justification by popular election formed an overt ingredient in political life; the *veche* acclaimed a successor, and the prince "kissed the cross" as a sign of a pact forged with the urban democratic forces. In the Muscovite era, from the fifteenth century, new monarchs read a speech to the assembled throng justifying their right to rule and seeking approbation from the "people."[47]

Throughout Russian history, the juridical conception of the ruler was the weakest and least developed justification. Politics tended to operate more in the moral than the juridical realm, and the patrimonial stress on personal loyalty and relationships retarded the development of rule by law and individual rights in the state. Still, the *Chronicle* described a contract between the Riurikids and the people in 862; in Muscovite Russia, both grand princes and tsars occupied positions as legislators and judges, and the monarch was expected to behave according to time-honored rules and regulations, including consultation with the boyars, or aristocrats of the realm. For instance, when Metropolitan Makarii orchestrated Ivan IV's coronation in 1547, to display the fullness of the sovereign's power, he still emphasized the need to obey the laws of God.[48]

The centuries-old fixation—the dilemma of a human prone to error holding an office that nearly all agreed was divine in origin and dignity—became a familiar concern in Russia as did the legal and moral problem of how to react to tyrannous behavior. Ihor Ševčenko has proved the popularity in Rus' and Muscovy of the *Hortatory Chapters* of the sixth-century Deacon Agapetus of Constantinople, who emphasized the twofold nature of an absolute monarch:

> Though an emperor in body be like all other, yet in power of his office he is like God, master of all men. For on earth, he has no peer. . . . For though he be like God in face, yet for all that he is but dust and equal to every man.[49]

Russian writers, like most others who grappled with this problem, constantly restated it without finding a solution. A twelfth-century lament on the death of a prince intoned: "For the Tsar, in his earthly nature is similar to any earthly man, but, because of his power, he is of great dignity—like unto God."[50] Five centuries later, a cleric quoted Agapetus and commented that the office of tsar remained "sinless" even if its holder transgressed.[51]

In Kievan Rus', the attitude toward malfeasance on the part of a ruler was quite straightforward. A common instance occurred in 1068: when Grand Prince Iziaslav could not mount a defense against the Polovtsy, the people simply revolted and elected another.[52] Once that forthright era passed, the problem of resistance posed its age-old dilemma. Some writers quoted the usual passages from Scripture or the Church Fathers: "The Apostle Paul writes: 'Every soul should be subject to the powers, because the powers are instituted by God.' . . . The great Chrysostom says: 'He who opposes the powers, opposes the law of God.'"[53] Iosif of Volokolamsk emphatically concluded that "a tsar-tormentor is not God's servant but a devil . . . and should not be obeyed," but he nonetheless balked at overthrowing a legitimate ruler.[54]

Following the ubiquitous practice, Russians gave their rulers a religious patina and expected them to reinforce their role as God's representative on earth by acting like model Christians. The monk-chroniclers elevated Vladimir to an equal rank with the Apostles for his role in bringing the "miracle" of Orthodoxy to Rus', while the twelfth-century Vladimir Monomakh in his *Testament* portrayed himself as a hard-working man of God. He took "no rest" and "did whatever was necessary" both to defend the Russian land and to shepherd his flock: "I did not allow the mighty to distress the common peasant or the poverty-stricken widow and interested myself in the church administration and service."[55] In the Kievan and Mongol eras, as throughout medieval Europe, the ruler was circumscribed in actual power but acquired a compensating religious position as a martyr or a Christ-figure who suffered for the sake of his subjects.[56] Russia, though, was unique in the number of what Michael Cherniavsky called "saintly princes and princely saints." By 1700, over one hundred princes and princesses counted among the eight hundred people canonized by the Orthodox Church; in the Mongol era, the proportion was highest since death on the battlefield counted as both martyrdom and a patriotic act in defense of Holy Rus'.[57] In Muscovy, according to Viktor Zhivov and Boris Uspenskii, writers "sacralized" the tsars by endowing them with innate virtues.[58]

Rulers themselves engaged in a conscious effort to elevate further their religious stature by drawing upon a fantastic blend of Roman, Byzantine, and Mongol imperial ideas. They combined the notion of a steppe empire ruled by a sacral clan with the Byzantine claims of heading a universal Christian realm, while at the same time instituting imperial ceremony and asserting descent from Augustus, Prus, and Constantine the Great.[59] Two facts lent these claims from a formerly Mongol-dominated satellite state of the Byzantine Empire some slight credibility. First, in reality in 1380 and officially in 1480, the Mongol yoke ended, and the ruler could adopt the title of "Sovereign of All Russia and Autocrat," which signified, in Marc Szeftel's phrase, that the monarch held "his power directly from God, and not by delegation of any other ruler."[60] Second, in 1453, the Greek Empire had fallen to the Ottomans, and Muscovy remained the sole independent Orthodox realm. By 1510, Philotheus of Pskov was ready to assert:

> All Christian realms will come to an end and will unite into the one single realm of our sovereign, that is, into the Russian realm, according to the prophetic books. Both Romes fell, the third endures, and a fourth there will never be.

Fifty years later, an official document hailed Ivan IV as the "Tsar and Sovereign of Orthodox Christians of all the universe from east to west and to the ocean."[61] This doctrine of the Third Rome was essentially a statement of religious imperialism, which, whatever its political significance, lent an uncommon liturgical quality to the state and its rulers.[62]

Much more than his European counterparts, the Muscovite tsar was strapped by religious ritual, trapped in the Kremlin, and wrapped in a "nightmarish religiosity" that symbolized the symbiosis of church and state.[63] As Daniel Rowland has noted, the tsar had a great public responsibility to maintain his own piety so that he could remain privy to the will of God and protect Orthodoxy.[64] Political theorists, such as the fifteenth-century "bold innovator," Iosif of Volokolamsk, elevated the ruler into the supreme arbiter in both secular and religious matters and awarded the tsar such ecclesiastical functions as the punishing of heretics and the "legitimation of the faith."[65] Histories, beginning with the *Book of Degrees (Stepennaia kniga,* c. 1563), depicted the saintliness of the Riurikids as the core of Russian history and thereby replaced the earlier focus on the saga of the development of the Russian land; the text claimed, typically, that of all the rulers "even until now . . . there was not one who was not pious."[66] In the late sixteenth century, Tsar Fedor I became universally revered because "externally he was a tsar, but internally a monk."[67] Paul Bushkovitch has concluded that "the political realm was inseparable from the religious-moral realm," and the underlying ideal was that of static harmony among all the elements of secular and religious life in the state.[68]

Along with the tradition of justification, Russians absorbed the tenets of advice literature. The *Chronicle* and the *Lay* qualify as prime examples. At the same time that they argued monarchy's superiority, they also served as an "admonition to the princes of Rus'." The writers exhorted the princes to strive for unity, found churches, establish laws, promote book learning, build towns, consult with boyars and elders, and not "drink wine amid music and in the company of young counselors." The pacifist theme that would remain prominent into the imperial period began early: the monks praised the tenth-century Grand Princess Olga for her wise domestic policy but chided her son Sviatoslav, a classic warrior-prince, for "visiting and frequenting foreign lands" while "neglecting [his] own country."[69] In the sixteenth century, Ivan Peresvetov and Maksim Grek concentrated on the moral dimension of the office; they repeated the usual list of required virtues that acted as limitations on power and erected contrasts between good and bad rulers. A major requirement included, once again, consulting with boyars. In addition, thinkers enjoined monarchs to act *po starine* (according to tradition), which translated into a duty to maintain the divinely ordained status quo, "the old laws of our fathers," and the Orthodox codes of behavior as summarized in the *Domostroi,* published during the reign of Ivan IV the Terrible.[70]

A real challenge to justification and advice literature occurred with Ivan's long sixteenth-century reign. He was the legitimate holder of a divinely blessed office and a classic tyrant.[71] During most of his reign, his policies made a mockery of every justification of absolute power. Instead of the practical benefits that monarchy promotes by serving the common good, he fomented a domestic war against the boyars and, through prosecuting the lengthy and disastrous Northern War, brought impoverishment to both rural and urban classes of the population. Instead of preserving his dynasty, in a fit of rage he murdered his son and ensured the end of the Riurikid line.[72] Instead of maintaining virtuous behavior and the religious dignity of his office, he twisted the doctrine of the dual nature of a monarch, claiming he could do anything he chose because of his connection to the divine and excusing his legendary transgressions as the "small sins" of a mere mortal. At times, he deified himself and abused his authority by asserting that his whims were God's whims, for instance, torturing victims in churches while clad in a monk's robe.[73]

Both religious and secular figures condemned Ivan's actions. Metropolitan Filipp's sermon to Ivan, a perfect example of advice literature, censured him for spilling blood and reminded him of his mortality and responsibility before God; in not respecting the limitations on his power, he ceased being a true tsar. Other notables, most famously Prince Andrei Kurbskii, attacked the tsar-tormentor's lapse from Christian and moral rulership and lamented the perilous loss of legitimacy.[74] Writers, in the classic pattern, hesitated at resistance and offered the usual excuses: Ivan's rule was aberrant; his sins were the punishment of Providence; he demonstrated statesmanlike behavior in the earlier part of his reign, which should offset the latter part; his ability to inspire awe *(groza)* was a sign of a true tsar; he expanded the realm; anything was better than the anarchy of oligarchy or mob rule. After Ivan's death, when the results of his reign became evident, writers ascribed his evil deeds to his moral decline, identified his atrocities, and condemned him for violating the traditional standards of tsarlike behavior.[75] Nonetheless, as could be expected, the actual appearance of a tyrant on the historical stage failed to shake the traditional faith in monarchy.

CONCEPTUALIZING MONARCHY IN THE SEVENTEENTH CENTURY

Advice literature had always predicted that tragedy would flow from the tyrannous behavior of a monarch, and Ivan IV's policies proved the point;

they provoked the Time of Troubles. From 1598 to 1613, the country experienced class struggle, civil war, foreign invasion, and natural disaster.[76] A central aspect of this upheaval was a dynastic crisis that brought forward most of the arguments previously used to legitimize and justify monarchy and that also inspired a spate of advice literature.

The Riurikid line ended in 1598, when Ivan's younger son, Fedor I, died without an heir; another son, Dmitrii of Uglich, had earlier died under mysterious circumstances. In this crisis, Patriarch Iov turned to the practice of election to legitimize the selection of a new ruler; he hoped to elevate Boris Godunov, Fedor's brother-in-law and a boyar who had earned a reputation as a good and just administrator in the previous reign. Boris suggested calling a *zemskii sobor*, or land assembly. Ivan IV had founded the institution in the reforming part of his reign as a representative body of the free and propertied classes; usually compared to the contemporaneous Estates-General of France, it was summoned in moments of crisis to approve tax or policy measures.[77] The delegates, carefully orchestrated, unanimously chose Boris to become the first elected tsar. The patriarch, repeating the commonplace in Western tradition that God acted through intermediaries, provided divine endorsement by intoning: "The voice of the people is the voice of God."[78] Nonetheless, Boris lacked legitimacy: he had manipulated his "election," he was not of ancient house, and he was not particularly pious. Uncertain in his office, the new tsar began to terrorize real and imagined opponents, thereby ignoring the limits on his power. Soon, rumors spread among the population that he had ordered the death of the boy Dmitrii, or that Dmitrii had escaped death and was waiting to secure his rightful throne. A devastating famine and plague began in 1601 and were regarded as punishments by God for not having a "true" tsar, but a murderer, on the throne.[79] As Polish forces approached Moscow under the leadership of the First False Dmitrii, Boris died in 1605, his children were killed by a mob, and the Godunov line abruptly ended.

The remaining upheavals of the Time of Troubles reinforced the pragmatic argument that the Russian land was destined to perdition without a single, unifying leader. In fact, Poland and Sweden threatened to annex vast portions of the country. A boyar-tsar, Vasilii Shuiskii, for a time seized the throne at the head of seven other aristocratic families, and they predictably divided the spoils. Ivan Bolotnikov, a runaway slave, led a bloody revolt in the name of the masses. Adding to the disasters of oligarchy and anarchy, a host of ludicrous pretenders tried to prove they were the "true" tsar by claiming divine will, Riurikid blood, or election.[80] Narratives condemned them all as bad tsars, whose lack of piety, virtue, and good advice doomed the state; indeed, the First False Dmitrii flirted with conversion to Catholicism, and this in part caused his overthrow. For all these reasons, Muscovy, "which previously was so brilliant, like the morning star, fell from highest heaven."[81]

In the end, a national rally turned back the Polish and Swedish invading forces, and Russians had to organize a new government. Writers made clear that "without a sovereign" the Russian state would be "completely destroyed" and that a monarch should be chosen "by consulting . . . all the people, both humble and great." Roughly five hundred delegates were selected from among prelates, nobility, and urban residents to sit in a *zemskii sobor* and elect the new ruler and dynasty. They convened in January 1613 and deliberated and intrigued for six weeks before deciding on a candidate who could be justified and win wide support. Mikhail Romanov emerged as "the choice of the people."[82] The *zemskii sobor* in reality participated in drawing up the usually fictive contract between ruler and ruled so beloved by political theorists, and the transfer of power provided the required legitimacy for rule.

The documents and descriptions surrounding the accession culled every argument in the Western and Russian traditions to justify the ascent and legitimize the candidate.[83] While election conferred fundamental legitimacy, bloodline remained a central concern. As could be expected, writers rushed to point out the links between the old and new dynasties: Fedor's mother was Mikhail's great aunt, and hence the last Riurikid and first Romanov were first cousins once removed. Already a respected, powerful clan, the Romanovs' luster was enhanced by a clerk, who wrote a history that manufactured, yet again, descent from Prus and Augustus.[84] Fortifying the idea of dynastic intersection, a Pskov chronicle popularized the myth that Tsar Fedor on his deathbed had actually handed the scepter to Metropolitan Filaret, Mikhail's father and a respected leader in the Orthodox Church; his son's election thus also operated within the Muscovite tradition of designation.[85]

Having claimed Mikhail's Orthodox and dynastic qualifications, documents emphasized that the new ruler lived up to other normative signs of a "true" tsar. First, his election was divinely ordained. Similar to the interpretation of the election of Boris, writers asserted that God miraculously inspired the delegates throughout the proceedings of the *zemskii sobor* so that His will was revealed in their choice. Avraamii Palitsyn, a chronicler of the events, introduced a Christological element that featured preordination: Mikhail had been "chosen by God before his birth and anointed since the time he was in the womb of his mother."[86] Adding to this, the myth arose that traitors and/or Poles had nearly murdered him and his mother, but God had intervened and spared him "to rule the realm." Second, Mikhail's virtue was of major concern because of the usual causal connection between the ruler's character and a country's fate. A childlike sixteen years of age, the new tsar projected the timid saintly quality so valued in Russian tradition. Finally, at his coronation, Mikhail recognized the limitations on royal power; he promised to be merciful and just and "think about all things" governmental as had the "true" tsars of the past in performing their duties. In addition, he vowed to seek constant counsel from experienced advisors and rule in coordination with the *zemskii sobor*.[87]

After Mikhail's coronation, at a time when other European monarchs were becoming ever more absolute, the power of the Russian monarch was institutionally limited since the polity that arose out of the ashes of the Time of Troubles encompassed aristocratic and democratic elements. In the course of the seventeenth century, the Boyar Duma grew from roughly 30 to 170 members and came to include not only the aristocracy but also the more recently ennobled servitor gentry. The Duma, a long-standing royal council, met daily and legislation bore the traditional formula, "the tsar has decreed and the boyars have concurred" *(tsar' ukazal i boiare prigovorili)*. In a centralizing state, the group also provided the bureaucratic element. At the same time, its awesome reputation for intrigue and corruption confirmed hostility to purely aristocratic rule and gave rise to the folk adage, "The tsar desires [the good of the people], but the boyars oppose" *(tsar' khochet, a boiare soprotivliaiut)*.[88]

After electing Mikhail, the *zemskii sobor* continued to meet on an ad hoc basis and figured prominently in all major decision making during the reign. When his son, Aleksei, came to the throne in 1645, the approval of the *zemskii sobor* was requested; in the seventeenth century only Fedor II, who succeeded his father Aleksei in 1676, did not receive some recognition from the "voice of the land."[89] At midcentury, Aleksei sought support from the provincial gentry and the urban elite for compiling a new law code and called together a gathering of "worthy and prudent men" so that these "great decisions" could be made in conjunction "with all the delegates."[90] Even though the Ulozhenie, or Law Code of 1649, legally established serfdom and perfected the partnership between the tsar and the upper and middle echelons of society, the bonded peasants still continued to maintain belief and hope in their "true" tsar, who oversaw their interests and worked to redress their grievances.

Writers confirmed the seventeenth-century image of a monarch limited in power, but also emphasized the earlier Muscovite idea of a tsar absorbed in pious duties. Valerie Kivelson has examined the gentry petitions of the 1630s and 1640s, and they iterated the gentry's idea of monarchy as combining "divine selection and direction of the tsar with election and advice 'from all the land.'"[91] The widely distributed didactic poetry of Simon Polotskii, the tutor of Aleksei's heir, conceived the ideal tsar as one "chosen" by the people, advised by wise counselors, and guided by his piety and vigilance over church affairs. Polotskii also portrayed a good tsar as radiating the usual virtues: humility, mercy, wisdom, diligence, kindness, and love of learning, while the tsar-tyrant exacts heavy taxes and burdens the people with his mindless brutality.[92] The Old Believers—perhaps one-third of the population since their break with the official Orthodox Church in the 1660s—defined monarchs as "the gift of God among us," but only if rulers kept the "Orthodox faith pure and undefiled," as defined by the sect; otherwise, they were branded as antichrists. Their great leader, Avvakum, however, in contrast to Polotskii, denied the monarch's power over spiritual matters and, disappointed with Aleksei's pretensions, plunged into criticism of his policy.[93]

Alongside these older concepts of rulership, in the seventeenth century, more modern images of the monarch were stealing into the Kremlin and spreading among members of the elite. The scholars of the Kievan Academy played a central role in this transmission after the annexation of Left Bank Ukraine in 1667, and the ideas they propounded were very much at variance with the Muscovite frame of reference. At this time in the rest of Europe, a radical rethinking of the notion of kingship was taking place, caused by Europe's own troublous times. Civil wars, frondist activity, and religious controversy had produced near anarchy in the sixteenth and early seventeenth centuries, and rulers seemed ill-equipped to handle the chaos. England emerged from her turmoil and opted for a monarchy with de jure limitations to provide national stability, but this direction proved unique.

In order to handle the types of disorder that marred the landscape in the sixteenth century, writers in continental European countries favored a single strong authority. French theorists rushed to justify the monarch's need to possess absolute power. In *The Six Books of the Commonwealth* (1576), Jean Bodin forcefully argued that the essence of sovereignty is its supreme and unrestrained nature, and he idealized the activist monarch, whose possession of executive, legislative, and judicial power could best bind a nation together. Still, unless they accepted the limits set by natural and divine law, monarchs became guilty of "treason and rebellion against God."[94] Cardinal Richelieu in the first half of the next century advised removing any perceived obstacles to a monarch's power to ensure domestic stability; he also advocated striving for *gloire* in foreign affairs to enhance the ruler's image.[95]

For even greater enhancement of a monarch's authority, theorists cynically began utilizing the forceful doctrine of justification by divine right. At first the doctrine had been used to counteract papal claims to sovereign power as well as popular claims to sovereignty and the right to resist: monarchs who aspired to absolute power tried to eliminate competition from above and below through seating themselves ever more closely to the godhead. In the seventeenth century, Bishop Bossuet replicated the pagan practice of deifying the ruler; he announced that "the royal throne is not the throne of a man, but the throne of God Himself," just as earlier, James I of England had written that monarchs "even by God are called Gods."[96] Politically, the doctrine had great advantages: a belief that monarchical power came directly from God provided clear and irrefutable legitimacy; the contention that God manifested his choice of monarch at the birth of the heir supported the indefeasiblity of hereditary right and militated against changing dynasties; the idea that the monarch was accountable to God alone worked against potentially disruptive criticisms of policy; and the injunction of passive obedience no matter what the circumstances gainsaid any right to resist.[97] In other words, the monarch no longer held his power from God through the people, but straight from the hand of God, and this disbarred revolt or even criticism. Louis XIV, during his long reign from 1643 to 1714, embraced with panache the doctrines of absolute power, *raison d'état,* expansionism, and divine right and became the widely imitated model for the modern monarch.[98] These doctrines, though, made ethics subordinate to politics and made of the monarch a supra-moral person, which contradicted millennia of thinking about monarchy.[99]

At about the same time, Hugo Grotius and Samuel Pufendorf were offering an alternative justification for absolute monarchy in their Dutch and German contexts that more closely evolved from tradition. The pandemic wars of religion had also instilled in them the necessity for a single strong authority, and they, like the French theorists, trusted in the laws of God and nature to provide sufficient assurance against the misuse of power. The Dutch school put fresh sparkle into the old contract theory of government by lending the monarch a legitimacy based on popular consent, not divine right, and an honor-bound central duty, based on paternal concern and not *raison d'état,* to care for the common good in preference over external affairs.[100] The cameralists fortified the newer justification. These proponents of the "well-ordered police state" taught that the general welfare demanded the forceful development of all a state's potential under the leadership of an absolute monarch; in this way, power legitimated itself by serving a high moral and social purpose.[101] Overall, in the seventeenth century, a mix of rational need, divine right, secular benefit, contractual obligation, and benevolent paternalism competed in defining a "modern" monarch.

Russian conceptions slowly began echoing these trends, but the idea of monarchy retained its medieval flavor.[102] Nonetheless, like his European counterparts, Aleksei leaned toward more absolute power. He continued to consult regularly with the Boyar Duma, but the *zemskii sobor* ceased functioning after 1653; similarly, the French Estates-General last met in 1614.[103] In the 1660s, Aleksei also effectively quashed the papal-like pretensions of Patriarch Nikon to supremacy in both religious and secular spheres. The tsar, a sincerely pious man, was attracted by the movement in the direction of divine right to solidify power over both state and church. Like Louis XIV and James I, he described himself as a deity, equating "divine command and Our sovereign order" and his person with "Christ Himself."[104]

In another reflection of European trends, paternal concern took a central place, with tsars officially claiming to rule their subjects "as a father and mother love their children."[105] Although security of person and property remained unprotected, the election at the end of the Time of Troubles defeated the medieval patrimonial conception of rule since the Russian land could no longer be considered the *votchina* or property of the tsar. The newer parental model served to reinforce the culture of supplication surrounding the tsar, who acted as fount of all blessings to subjects interceding with him personally to obtain favors, in the faith that he would be responsive to their needs. On a more modern level, the concept of father-tsar easily translated into a ruler's contractual obligation to serve the general welfare or common good, the political byword in the seventeenth century.[106] Fedor II became the first tsar officially to use the phrase "the common good" in his edicts.[107] Under the influence of political tourists such as the Croat Iurii Krizhanich, officials in Aleksei's administration began justifying monarchical power in more rational and secular terms, as an institution that could "more quickly and more easily" disseminate practical knowledge, "expand commerce," or overall improve the lot of the population.[108] But, as in the rest of Europe, the lines were not clearly drawn; some proponents of Western ideas supported Avvakum as well.

Aleksei, while open to innovation and reform, nonetheless felt more comfortable continuing the traditional ambience around his throne and justifying his power principally in terms of dynastic descent, divine right, and devotion to *starina* (tradition or the old way of life). At religious ceremonies, the tsar stood as the most important member of the laity, and at official functions he appeared "as a senior colleague, representing his people with the help of his leading courtiers."[109] This meek, Most Pious Russian Tsar considered the salvation of his subjects his principal duty. He lived a monastic life, participating in a five-hour daily marathon of liturgical ceremonies. A seventeenth-century biography addressed Aleksei:

> O, possessor and most zealous guardian of the fatherland's piety and most merciful and gentle ruler . . . , the preserver of true dogma, and of the traditions of the fatherland . . . , and a savior, who cares for the dignity and honor of the living and also for their immortal lives . . . and blessed peace.[110]

The Muscovite conception of a monarch idealized a "negative" ruler, one who avoided change since it might bring confusion or disturbance, ataxia, to use the Byzantine term.[111] When Aleksei died in 1676, a political consensus based on traditional practices seemed firmly in place. A simple announcement noted the passage of the throne to his eldest son Fedor II, and the populace dutifully swore allegiance.[112] However, when Fedor died without issue six years later, festering religious, social, and economic conflicts began to unravel the political culture and "threatened the legitimacy of tsarist rule."[113]

The turmoil surrounding the choice of a successor to Fedor II signaled a crisis in ruling circles. Without primogeniture or gender restrictions as fundamental laws, any one of Aleksei's remaining fifteen children by two wives was theoretically eligible. The Naryshkin clan at first succeeded in placing their candidate on the throne—the ten-year-old, clever, and robust Peter—despite the presence of an older boy, Ivan Miloslavskii, who was sixteen but dull and sickly. Patriarch Ioakim, confirming the fundamental law in operation since 1589, determined that only election could resolve the issue. He first consulted with the upper ranks and then stood on a Kremlin balcony asking the lower ranks, "Who shall be the successor?" When, by "unanimous consent," they all called for Peter, he recognized this as "the will of God": "Let it be, by election of all ranks of people of the Muscovite State." In the three-page official document describing the event, the word election (*izbranie*) occurred four times as the chief sign of legitimacy.[114]

Less than one month later, Sofiia, twenty-four years old and the eldest of the Miloslavskii children, led a bloody revolt that resulted in Peter I and Ivan V becoming co-tsars, with her the regent and effective ruler. In the short announcement of this unique compromise, Sofiia repeated nine times the lengthy list of those who had been consulted so that the coup d'état could be conceived as having carried out the will of the "people," fickle though they might seem.[115] Adherence to the Orthodox faith and *starina* provided the remaining signifiers of legitimacy. Ioakim addressed the young tsars as "pious, Orthodox, divinely crowned, divinely bestowed, and Christ-loving." He then advised them to keep the country "in as pure and unspoiled condition as it now is" and maintain it "gently and calmly, in peace, quiet, and prosperity."[116] Although Sofiia and her advisors ruled "wisely" and moved in the direction of modernization, the state retained its medieval atmosphere and remained in disarray. In 1689, Sofiia attempted to seize the crown for herself but failed, and Peter's mother replaced her as regent.[117] After the death of his mother in 1694 and Ivan's in 1696, Peter I acquired sole power.

In the next three decades, Peter would use his power to escape the confines of traditional Muscovy and to introduce a new, dynamic style of leadership. He would blend the French model of kingship with the Central European ideas of the cameralists and, in the process, revolutionize Russian thinking and writing about monarchy.

The Reforming Tsar

s the first step in his monumental program to modernize the Russian state, Peter I revolutionized the centuries-old style and substance of rulership. In his justification of absolute power, secularism and a program of rational reform replaced divine right and commitment to the status quo; emphasis on undivided sovereignty undermined election and consultation; the figure of the European emperor supplanted the picture of an eremitic tsar; and fitness for office challenged heredity as the basis for succession. Peter's transvaluation of monarchy, his call for a reversal in the criteria by which to judge legitimacy, met with a mixed reception that ranged from outright rejection to enthusiastic cooperation. Responses tended to fall into a generational pattern: those born prior to 1660 illustrated various degrees of antagonism, while most of those born after 1680 became "fledglings of Peter's nest"; those whose birth dates fell in the middle usually faced Janus-like toward both Muscovy and Imperial Russia.[1] Peter's methods of conversion were dual: he wielded his absolute power to force acceptance, but he also tried to attract the assistance of the ablest minds he could find to help him propagate his modernizing mission. He worked to expand the ranks of the educated elite and directed much of his legendary energy at winning its approval for his views by means of a political dialogue that he usually encouraged. The process of transformation was long and challenging, but by the end of Peter's reign his own edicts and the writings of those he recruited had demonstrably changed the discourse about monarchy.

FROM DIVINE RIGHT TO DIVINE DUTY

The most intense source of opposition emerged among those whose concept of a "true" tsar was one who upheld the world of their Muscovite fathers. Peter shocked adherents of tradition by erasing the Orthodox signature of his office. For any absolute monarch to abandon the religious underpinnings of his power was a startling step, since throne and altar had worked in tandem for millennia. But especially in Russia—where the monarch's legitimacy rested on piety, Orthodox decorum, liturgical function, and maintenance of a static harmony between church and state—secularization was tantamount to a revolution.

Feeling rather humble before God, Peter had no use for theories resembling divine right. As soon as he achieved full power in 1696, he enjoined officials from writing "theology," as he put it, when referring to his titles in state documents; by the end of his reign, a fully secular formula was adopted, "We, Peter the First, Emperor and Autocrat of All the Russias." Similarly, he abhorred the Muscovite custom of kowtowing before the ruler; a memoirist recorded Peter's ordering people to stop kneeling before him because they should learn the "difference between God and tsar."[2]

Peter's religion was one of simple piety: he believed in God and Orthodox teaching, knew his Bible, liked singing in church, and passed decrees fining people for talking during services.[3] He blended belief in a God who intervened in princely affairs with a voluntarist conviction that God will only help those rulers who help themselves. At the happiest moment in his reign, when the Russians finally achieved victory over Sweden in the Great Northern War that was fought from 1700 to 1721, he wrote:

> 1. I very much wish that our entire people would clearly recognize that the Lord God gave us both this past war and the conclusion of this peace. 2. It is meet to thank God for every strength; however, while desiring peace, it is not meet to become militarily weak, so that what happened to the Greeks [in 1453] with the Greek monarch would not happen to us.[4]

Peter's rather uncomplicated attitude to God and religion shocked believers because of its disregard for the traditional liturgical function of the tsarist office. Perhaps after witnessing the brutal murder of dozens of his family and entourage during Sofiia's coup of 1682, Peter abhorred the Kremlin and medieval Muscovite ways. He seemed determined to distance himself from the ideal of a saintly prince; he refused to justify his power as an Orthodox, Eastern, eremitic tsar, and he openly ridiculed religious ritual and traditional behavior. His shaving of beards, ending the seclusion of women, use of tobacco, introduction of a new calendar, trips abroad, decreeing foreign dress and entertainment, drunken cavorting with foreign friends, divorce from a proper Kremlin wife and marriage to a Livonian servant girl, and his preference for the bawdy, the sacrilegious, and the informal horrified the Orthodox faithful.

Peter's dagger thrust at the heart of medieval tsarist legitimacy led to "an anguished opposition."[5] Despite the notorious practice of punishing any word or deed against the sovereign *(slovo i delo gosudarevo)*, the new ruler

The young Peter I, as a traditional Muscovite tsar. *Rossiiskii tsarstvennyi dom . . .*

St. Petersburg, 1896

was met with neither acquiescence, nor even dialogue, but attack.[6] Because he disregarded *starina*, the Old Believers denied Peter's legitimacy in a stream of pamphlets that railed against the "Heretic Tsar," "wild beast," and "bloodsucker" who "carries out Satan's will" and assaults "Holy Rus'." While the Old Believers could never become reconciled with the new Russia, others, like the scribe Grigorii Talitskii, wrote that Peter proved himself to be the antichrist because of his blasphemous "way of life"; and, because Talitskii concluded that the whole Romanov clan was "a bad branch," he plotted to change the dynasty. Similarly, a nobleman, Ivan Tsikler, was executed in 1697 for planning to assassinate Peter and have another, rightful tsar elected.[7] Widespread rumors depicted Peter as an imposter or a foreigner (German, Swede, or Muslim), since he was patently not a "true" tsar in the Muscovite mold. In 1698, the *strel'tsy*—the armed guards permanently residing in the capital and the nucleus of the regular army—revolted for many of these same reasons.

Peter's rejection of the idea of a tsar overseeing a harmony between church and state, the hallmark of both the Byzantine Empire and the Russian polity, appeared just as blasphemous as his "way of life." He believed in a principle of toleration that was anathema to church authorities. The future emperor's conquests resulted in a multiconfessional empire and led him to abandon the Muscovite premise of a homogeneous Orthodox realm; instead, he thought that "each Christian should work for salvation in the way he chooses."[8] In addition, Peter bristled at Orthodox prelates challenging his power. Early in his reign, Patriarch Adrian claimed superiority over the young monarch; Adrian described himself as the "Supreme Pastor, the father and head of everyone, . . . since everyone is our spiritual child: tsars, princes . . . simple men and women. . . . Who does not obey my pastoral voice is not one of my sheep, but is a goat or wolf."[9] Peter stood his ground; when Adrian died in 1700, the tsar refused to appoint a new patriarch and then secularized church land and insisted on the subordination of church to state.

The Russian clergy rose in opposition, and the educated among them constituted a prominent sector of the writing public and played an influential role in the formation of public opinion. Recognizing their influence, Peter appointed, as a countermeasure, a Ukrainian man of learning and oratorical skill from the Kievan Academy to be the acting patriarch. Stefan Iavorskii, a proponent of secular reform, derided the tsar's opponents as "creeping snakes" or "seducing serpents," and he refuted the widespread contention that Peter was the antichrist by demonstrating the absence of the omens that should precede the Apocalypse.[10] However, to Peter's chagrin, the prelate, born in 1658, upheld traditional Muscovite values concerning the issue of a tsar's relation to the church.[11] Stefan's sermon of March 1712 stands as a major piece of advice literature. Challenging the legitimacy of Peter's position, Stefan "cried out to the people" to stop the tsar and his "Lutheran friends" from putting church matters in the hands of state officials.[12] Attempts to "destroy the law of God," he warned, brought dire political and social evils, and he alluded to rebellions in Astrakhan (1705) and among the Don Cossacks (1707) and Bashkirs (1705–1711): "Thus do not be astonished that bloody uprisings harass this Russia of a thousand rebellions" as "from the head of the fish, from the leaders, societies often decay, rot, and perish." Peter reacted furiously, and Stefan re-

Peter the Great, as a modern secular emperor. *Rossiiskii tsarstvennyi dom . . .*

St. Petersburg, 1896

canted.[13] Nonetheless, he continued to write advice literature and steadfastly uphold Muscovite values. The prelate's homilies offered only praise of Peter, but in a baroque, metaphorical, hyperbolic fashion that stressed a medieval type of religious legitimacy. For instance, he eulogized the tsar as "an eagle in his unattainable heights of sacred lineage, of divine birth, tracing his descent from God himself." Iavorskii also used the time-honored technique of criticizing the tsar by praising him for virtues he did not possess.[14] These sermons were not to Peter's liking for he "wanted political propaganda, not artistic panegyrics with an ecclesiastical content."[15]

Peter eventually won the war between church and state, which lasted as long as the one with Sweden. In 1721, he issued the *Spiritual Regulation,* making the church subordinate to the state. The new rules replaced the patriarchate with a Holy Governing Synod headed by a layman; Iavorskii, more interested in position than principle, accepted a seat on the council.[16] Peter personally worked on the *Regulation* with the assistance of his next apologist, Feofan Prokopovich, another professor of theology from the Kievan Academy, born in 1681 and possessing the keenest mind in Russia.

The decree, Peter understood, needed careful justification, since it dictated a profound break with centuries of tradition. The tsar and his advisors justified the new arrangement between church and state, first and foremost, by a ruler's need for undivided sovereignty. With two centers of authority, a monarch and a patriarch, the "Supreme Pastor . . . seems like a second sovereign, equal in strength to the autocrat or even greater than he," and then "revolts and confusion reign," especially when a quarrel erupts between "sovereign and pastor," and "power-hungry clerics throw dry brushwood onto the fire." Second, the monarch needed to protect the general welfare. Instead of upholding the Muscovite idea that a tsar protect the interests of the church, Peter averred that he had the obligation to protect the "simple people" from the clerics; no longer would they "constitute some kind of faction, a secret group working for its own interest, but would work for the common good under the command of the Autocrat."[17] Dmytro Tuptalo, a cleric, rued the new type of ruler: "There are no Constantines among them, no Vladimirs, no other God-fearing lovers of the splendor of the house of the Lord."[18] Whatever the nostalgia, Peter had broken the conception of a Russian monarch as a pious Orthodox ruler whose primary duty involved overseeing a harmonious balance between church and state.

Peter's abasement of the patriarchate also indicated his refusal to justify his power by claiming its limited nature. Instead, he argued in favor of the policies of concentration and centralization that characterized European absolutist monarchs, all of whom worked to disencumber themselves of ecclesiastical, aristocratic, and other "constitutional" reins on royal office. The *Military Statute* of 1716 stated firmly: "His Majesty is a Sovereign Monarch, who is not answerable to anyone in the world in His affairs, but holds the power and authority to rule His realms and His lands as a Christian Monarch by His own will and good opinion."[19] Peter ceased consulting with the Boyar Duma and never imagined calling a *zemskii sobor.* The teachings of Hugo Grotius and Samuel Pufendorf, whose works he ordered translated, inspired him to celebrate the fullness of power, based on natural law rather than theology, a power that earned legitimacy by an unhindered ability to serve the high moral purpose of effecting beneficial change.[20]

Peter aimed to replace the static partnership of church and state with a dynamic symbiosis of monarchy and progress, and the duties of a "Most Pious" ruler with those of a secular reformer.[21] In the process, he demystified the monarchy by making it less a divine calling than a normal job. Nonetheless, the sovereign remained a God-fearing believer, whose primary attribute was devotion to duty before God and man: "It is meet to work for the general welfare and benefit, both within and without, [a task] which God puts before our eyes and which will help the people." In another decree, Peter added that like "other Christian rulers" his "single purpose is diligently to care for the welfare, education, and prosperity of our faithful subjects."[22] In 1700 at Narva, Peter accepted the ignominious defeat at the hands of Charles XII of Sweden as a "divine demonstration" that his duty lay in modernizing Russia.[23] In sermons, Feofan flung aside the Muscovite emphasis on ritual and asserted that a tsar's "deeds" held a higher priority than his prayers; for if a tsar prayed but neglected his duties, "how can this prayer be anything other than sinful!"[24] The primacy of "deeds" in justifying power squarely contradicted divine right theory, which held that the legitimacy of monarchs rested on their inherited characteristics and not on being accountable for one's actions. Like other absolute rulers, Peter believed himself answerable to God alone but translated this into a further reason to work for the general welfare: "Thus, when He the Judge, without pretension, asks Us for an accounting of what We have done with the responsibility given Us by Him, We will not be dumbfounded."[25] Peter's was a doctrine of divine duty with justification through good works, not divine right with its justification through faith.

The Transvaluation of Monarchy

The most towering figure of the Age of Enlightenment, Voltaire, recognized that Peter pioneered a new model of rulership not only for Russia but for all eighteenth-century Europe. His reign fell midway, both conceptually and chronologically, between the glorious absolutism of the latter half of the seventeenth century and the enlightened absolutism that followed fifty years later. Peter wrote with admiration that Louis XIV's policies of administrative centralization and military absorption led him "to achieve glorious deeds . . . not only in warfare but . . . in everything in his realm."[26] Peter, however, had no use for the divine aura and aloof royal luster cultivated by the Sun King. Also in contrast to Louis, who is credited with the aphorism "l'état, c'est moi," Peter cast himself as subordinate to the state an entire generation before Frederick II of Prussia more famously promoted himself as the "first servant of the state."[27] From the beginning of his reign, Peter boldly incorporated into statecraft innovative doctrines that had made only timid appearances in Russia before: those of the cameralists, of Pufendorf and Grotius, and of their disciple Christian von Wolff, a favorite philosopher of both Peter and Frederick.[28] Working within a seventeenth-century framework, Peter constructed a model for the eighteenth-century ruler by splicing together French, Dutch, and German concepts of kingship and thereby fashioned an original creation: the reforming tsar.[29]

If the concept of the "reforming tsar" were merely an artificial sobriquet attached in hindsight to the aggregate of Peter's policies, it would still be useful and descriptive. However, it possesses historical importance because it was Peter's self-image and informed his justification of monarchical rule from the moment he assumed personal power.[30] Peter was not a theoretician of power but one who exulted in its pragmatic application. He became a reformer in part by attempting to imitate western and central European models of development and in part by reacting to the necessities that emerged in fighting the two-decade-long war against Sweden. Even earlier, his extensive contact with foreigners and then his own eighteen-month trip to Europe in 1697–1698 led him to the conclusion that Russia lagged behind and that his mission would be to transform it. The Genevan Franz Lefort, before he died in 1699, suggested the policies that would make his friend Peter an "authentically Great Sovereign": maximize productive capacity; discipline and westernize society; foster the arts, sciences, and technology; and reach for great power status militarily by replacing the current "crowd of unruly Asians."[31] In agreement, Peter aimed to justify his power by rapidly raising Russia out of its proverbial backwardness. As Vasilii Kliuchevskii has pointed out, he conceived his power not as an end in itself, but as "the means for achieving his ends."[32]

Peter introduced a new category into the genre of justification literature, becoming the first European ruler to bind monarchy together with the Enlightenment notion of progress. Rather than devotion to *starina*, he would vindicate his absolute power with a breathtaking program of reform. This idea soared beyond pallid notions of the contract and ruling for the common good—which can just as easily safeguard the status quo as effect change—and raised them to the new qualitative level enshrined in the doctrine of enlightened absolutism.[33] To be sure, serious programs of reform characterized many rulers throughout Europe, seventeenth-century Muscovite tsars included, since adaptation to change is the normal preoccupation of any decent leader. In the third century B.C.E., Antigonus II Gonatas of Macedonia referred to himself as a "service king" and called his office "noble servitude."[34]

Peter captured the spirit of the century with his new discourse of justification and provided Russian monarchy with a vitality that had seeped away in the waning years of the Muscovite era. His invigorating activism filled the edicts, memoirs, and projects of his reign with a recognition that reform from above had become the central driving duty of the monarch and the prime justification of absolute power. In working toward his goals, he emerged as "a primary political hero of the Enlightenment."[35] Peter epitomized the modern model of monarch: the secular, hardworking, reforming ruler capable of creating through force and fiat. Voltaire marveled at Peter's audacious example: "He coerced nature in every respect, in his subjects, in himself, on land and on sea . . . and Russia was created," or, more precisely, a Europeanized Russia.[36]

Peter justified his power specifically because of Russia's glaring need for reform in two areas: the strengthening of the military and westernization of economic and cultural life. Throughout his reign, he contended that the latter objective would be threatened unless a strong army and navy provided the tranquility in which it could prosper; and he stressed that it was the "duty and obligation of all Christian rulers" to train and equip as good an army as possible, since it is "one of the greatest mainstays of every state." However, Peter stubbornly insisted that his military pursuits represented a secondary aim. He even claimed, not very convincingly, that the Great Northern War was purely defensive, and only Sweden's threat led him reluctantly to the "timely recognition" that his principal attention should turn to "the maintenance and defense of our borders from all hostile attacks." Despite the protestation that he was a reluctant warrior, Peter's love of soldiering remained central all his life: he organized "toy-soldier" *(poteshnye)* regiments as a teenager, and his reign knew only two years of peace. Richard Wortman has fully illustrated that the emperor cultivated the image of conqueror, as did his forebears and successors. Peter assuredly displayed his military might and prowess, but he did not justify his power principally on military grounds or on the imperial designs of which he was so proud, even though he sponsored what has developed into an indelible identification of "Russia" with "Empire."[37]

Besides thinking of himself as a soldier, Peter nourished a self-image of domestic reformer, and he adopted the age-old justification from nature that analogized the monarch as the father of a family. Buttressing this conception, Peter subscribed to the classic belief that a monarch molds the character of his subjects: "Everyone looks to the ruler to follow his inclinations . . . in what he takes interest, all take interest, and what he spurns, all spurn."[38] In Russia, though, the paternal image necessitated making a final break with the Muscovite *votchina* concept of the realm as the private property of the tsar. Peter insisted that the populace take two separate oaths, one to the ruler and one to the state, and on the eve of the momentous Battle of Poltava in 1709, he chose to inspire his soldiers by telling them that they were fighting "not for Peter but for the state entrusted to him."[39] And, in the role of overseer, Lefort had early inspired Peter to act like a "Father of the Fatherland," a title he officially adopted in 1721.[40]

As a paterfamilias, Peter justified his stern measures and fast pace of change with the need to modernize rapidly "the behavior of our subjects" so that soon they "could become people in customs similar to all other Christians." This self-proclaimed "enlightener" hoped to establish Russia's first school system since "the introduction of learning is the very first duty of a monarch," who should "educate his people in every possible military and civic science." Peter viewed himself as a linchpin in this process, because in his opinion all European peoples had languished in barbarity until "the constant work of their leaders opened their eyes" to arts, sciences, civic virtue, and a work ethic.[41] The tsar would have agreed with the eighteenth-century English traveler, Arthur Young, who declared: "There is but one all-powerful cause that instigates mankind and that is GOVERNMENT!"[42] The vision was grand, if idiosyncratic. Peter somewhere absorbed the idea of *translatio imperii,* the notion that at each period in history one state would enjoy political and cultural dominance. He explained that human knowledge "circulated much like blood in the human body": its center had gone from Greece to Italy and the Austrian lands and made its current home in England, France, and Germany; soon, he prophesied, the seat of knowledge, before eventually returning to Greece, would settle in Russia and "remain with us for several centuries."[43] To prepare his subjects for that happy moment of maturity, Peter would argue that he needed to use every power at his disposal.

The cameralists, whom the tsar admired, encouraged the cultivation of a parental image and justified the absolute power of a monarch/father by his responsibility to carry out duties that covered every aspect of state/family life. In particular, these theorists emphasized the need of a backward population for paternal guidance in creating the eighteenth-century idyll of the "well-ordered police state." Feofan's primer of 1720 explained that the Fifth Commandment meant not only obeying one's parents but all persons "who exercise paternal authority over us."

> The first order of such persons are the supreme authorities instituted by God to rule the people, of whom the highest authority is the tsar. It is the duty of kings to protect their subjects and to seek what is best for them, whether in religious matters or in the things of this world; and therefore they must watch over all the ecclesiastical, military, and civil authorities subject to them and conscientiously see that they discharge their respective duties. That is, under God, the highest paternal dignity; and subjects, like good sons, must honor the tsar.[44]

Laws, manifestoes, and regulations gushed forth in a steady stream throughout Peter's reign and were part of his dialogue with those he wanted to involve in the work of reform. These imperial pronouncements were designed to order the economy, maintain public peace, train people in Western ways, and develop a moral sense.[45] To activate a country's potential, a ruler taught subjects to become "regulated" *(reguliarnyi):* to operate according to state-defined rules and regulations and to cease being the antonymous "barbaric." The historical preface to Peter's *Military Statute* of 1716 rued that formerly Russians suffered defeat "at the hands not only of regulated people but even barbarians," but rejoiced that Peter's policies had redressed the situation.

Now, such great progress has been made with God's help, that we have been victorious over famous and regulated people. And thus everyone can surmise that this resulted from good regulation alone; for the completely disrespectable barbarian custom is worthy only of laughter and nothing good can possibly come of it.[46]

According to Peter's and most theorists' discourse of justification, the monarch/father of a state reaching for "regulation" required absolute power, since his responsibilities applied not only to the military but to all manner of organizations and areas of life, whether villages, cities, the court, the monasteries, schools, architecture, or medicine.[47] A well-ordered state also assumed what later would be called welfare responsibilities and earlier were considered the classic duties of a traditional ruler. "Regulations" would heed "the cries of the poor," care for "widows and orphans, the voiceless and the helpless," and "put the lazy and the poor to work."[48] Moving beyond these responsibilities, a decree on magistrates listed the duties of officials that indicated a vast sweep of parental powers and concerns. They were obliged to

assist in rights and justice; further good order and moral instruction; provide every security against brigands, thieves, assailants, swindlers, and other similar types; drive out dishonor and incompetence from life and force everyone into work and into an honest trade; provide good inspectors and careful and good subordinates; maintain cities and their streets regularly; keep prices down and let prosper everything needed for human life; take all precautions against disease; ensure cleanliness on the streets and in homes; forbid extravagance and all clear transgressions in household expenditures; look after beggars, the poor, the sick, the crippled, and other have-nots; protect widows, orphans, and foreigners; instruct the young in the commandments of God on chaste purity and honest study; in short, the police is, in every area, the moving spirit of citizenship and of all good customs and the fundamental support of individual security and comfort.[49]

Marc Raeff has summarized the thrust of this legislation: "The effect of all these regulations was to . . . enhance the role of the government as the planner and guide of society's productive activities, a role that legitimated and justified the exercise of sovereign power."[50]

Using a parental conception to justify monarchy can also camouflage a ruler's despotic tendencies. Thus, Peter relied on the image of paternal reformer duty-bound to work for the common good in order to excuse his use of compulsion and his regarding of subjects as children who required prodding and punishment. He explained the need to invite foreign "masters" to run Russian factories in a type of joint venture on the basis of the recalcitrance of the population and consequent need for force:

There are few [Russian] volunteers, and it is true that our people are like children who, because of lack of training, will never even learn the alphabet, will never apply themselves unless they happen to be forced into it by a master; at first they are annoyed but, once they learn, they are grateful.[51]

A decree on increasing foreign trade reiterated: "Everyone knows that our people do not start anything themselves, unless they be compelled," and so the government must "act like a mother standing over her children until they learn how to do things properly."[52] On the one hand, decrees aimed at the rational exploitation of Russia's natural resources so that "God's blessings underground not go untapped," and privileges were awarded to those who engaged in mining.

In contrast, those who hide ores that are discovered and do not inform about them, or forbid or hinder others in their search or in the construction and expansion of such factories . . . will witness our cruel wrath, certain physical punishment, the death penalty, and deprivation of all property, as disobedient and disdainful of our will and enemies of the general welfare.[53]

Similarly, in the absence of a law code, government officials who failed to keep abreast of recent legislation were punished by fines that ranged from one year's salary to loss of title and rank. Generally, lack of cooperation on the part of an individual led to the "immediate loss of all possessions and property."[54] Peter believed that these draconian measures were justified by his success in refashioning his brood. Toward the end of his reign, he credulously explained to a group of foreigners that "formerly, Russians were given to idleness," and his first and most frightening task as ruler had been to acquaint them "with knowledge and with courage and with loyalty and with honor."[55]

Roughly fifteen years after the reforming father-tsar had justified his absolute power because of the need to modernize, Russia had indeed made progress; it was on the brink of winning the Great Northern War and had become part of the European family of nations. In the process, the country had undergone the massive changes Peter had projected: he modernized the army, founded a navy, revitalized trade and industry, built a new westernized capital, and reorganized the administration. His originality lay in proclaiming and then proving that the *dirigiste* force of an absolute monarch could not only win *gloire* but could also unleash the potential of a backward society and thus provide the best assurance for progress in the eighteenth century.[56] Peter realized that he had created something new and spectacular: "We have emerged from darkness into light and from being unknown to being respected."[57]

The dark cloud hovering over Peter's achievements was the perception among many, both at home and abroad, that he acted like a tyrant, the most heinous accusation that can be leveled against a monarch and which nothing can justify. He even had to defend himself against the hated characterization of "barbarism." In a late evening conversation with some members of his entourage, Peter became rueful since he knew that he was accused of being an "Asian despot," who ruled over slaves not citizens, unlike a true "European monarch." He rejected the reproach and called it "slander that this monarch rules more by force or on his own whim than by justice and truth."[58] Peter understood the age-old definition of a tyrant as one who eschews advice and ignores the common good. He countered that he had "advisers better to search for the truth" and that Russia had become a "regulated state": "I rule subjects who obey my decrees; these decrees are beneficial, not harmful to the state." Nonetheless, he sullenly agreed that force had been necessary, because "ignorance and stubbornness have always taken up arms against me from the moment I decided to introduce useful change and improve crude customs." Thus, Europeans "don't know the circumstances": "English-style freedom is out of place here, like being up against a brick wall." He concluded that he was not "hardhearted": "I dressed my subjects in new clothes, regulated military and civilian affairs, and schooled people in service; it is not tyranny when the law sentences a criminal to death." He said with finality: "My conscience is clear. God will be my judge!"[59]

Peter probably had less to fear from God than from historians. Most scholars have not found his justifications of power convincing enough to enroll him among the "enlightened" monarchs of the later eighteenth century. Kliuchevskii best stated the complex case against Peter:

> [He] hoped by the threat of supreme authority to stimulate spontaneous activity in an enslaved society and through the slave-owning nobility to establish in Russia European science, public enlightenment as an essential condition of public spontaneous activity; he wanted the slave, while remaining a slave, to act spontaneously and freely. The simultaneous operation of despotism and freedom, enlightenment and slavery—this is the political squaring of the circle, the dilemma that we have been trying to resolve for two centuries since Peter's time and which has not yet been resolved.[60]

Kliuchevskii wrote at the turn of the twentieth century, but Evgenii Anisimov continued this trend of thought in the 1980s and 1990s. While a case of reading history backward, Anisimov, among others, sees in Peter's ruthlessness the antecedent of Soviet-style rule. He admits that dedication to the common good was an "indispensable element" in Peter's thought, but was offset by "progress through coercion."

> Peter I himself personified fully the unlimited monarch who disposed of the property and even the lives of his subjects without limitations, appointing or dismissing at will officials of all ranks, holding in his hands each line of executive, legislative, and judicial authority, resolving without anyone's knowledge or consideration every item of domestic and foreign policy.[61]

Anisimov and Kliuchevskii have ample reason to criticize Peter's methods, especially with respect to the peasantry, which remained in a seventeenth-century frame of reference and outside the circle of discussion, achievement, and modernizing ways inhabited by the monarch and those who supported him.[62] The illiterate majority suffered from constant warfare and the resulting high taxes, heavy recruitment, and poverty, while an expanding bureaucratic apparatus disrupted local customs and privileges. Indeed, opposition was "constant and pervasive" throughout Peter's time in power, and the archives of the Secret Chancellery bulged with evidence of seditious behavior that ran the gamut from drunken imprecations (the great majority) to treasonable activity.[63] Even those members of the educated elite who supported the reforming tsar often found themselves caught in the web of arbitrariness that marks a state based on personalization of power rather than rule of law.

THE CALL FOR PARTNERS IN REFORM

Peter certainly possessed the "absolutist personality" that Leonard Krieger has described as typical of eighteenth-century monarchs, and political "dialogue" tended to be one-sided. But, at the same time and despite the contradictions, Peter pioneered an "enlightened" style of statecraft.[64] His stream of justification literature, besides formulating the concept of the reforming tsar and working to create a symbiosis of monarchy and progress, made a further innovation in seeking partners for bringing his plans to fruition by asking for the support of the educated elite. Despite the classical definition of an absolute monarch as "unrestrained by . . . public opinion," Peter came forth as one of the first European rulers to utilize its force.[65] However, the process that he initiated took many twists and turns. The dialogue Peter tried to encourage required some freedom of expression and a spirit of criticism, but his style of government found these difficult to tolerate.

Peter regarded the educated elite as a service nobility and the appropriate partner for a new service monarchy in modernizing Russia. He understood that his "superhuman effort" required like-minded people to "support me in all these important endeavors" so that "in this century [Russia] could put other developed nations to shame."[66] In addition, the new justification for power could claim success only if subjects accepted it as a sign of legitimacy in a "true" tsar, and Peter's near obsession with communicating his idea of monarchy ranked among his most startling revolutions in Russian royal behavior.[67] This new style of tsar treated the reading public as an informal electorate, with whom he wanted to engage in dialogue and before whom he felt compelled to vindicate his policies in writing.[68] Rather than alluding to tradition, religion, dynasty, or virtue, the prefaces of Peter's many decrees barraged his audience with the rational principles upon which he based his actions.[69]

The historian M. S. Anderson concluded that any eighteenth-century monarch who broke with the feudal past "could rely on the support of many of the leading intellectuals of the age, however despotic his power."[70] And, certainly, Peter's reign possessed despotic characteristics, but quite unlike a sultan with kowtowing slaves, the tsar demonstrated a charismatic ability to articulate a mission, stimulate discussion, and invite participation in a new "secular religion of statehood."[71] He energized, reeducated, coopted, and rewarded not only intellectuals but also old boyars, new service elites, and commoners and thereby effected a partnership between ruler and ruled that formed the basis for a cohesive political culture and signaled a major step toward a modern state. While not lessening absolute power, eighteenth-century reforming monarchs tried to avoid dissatisfaction and revolution by cultivating an enlightened and progressive cluster of supporters and creating a consensual community. Seeking advice from and dialogue with the elite countered the stain of arbitrariness while still maintaining the existing political framework. Enlightened absolutism thus represented a transition in and modernization of monarchy. Absolutist rulers usually regard themselves as the sole public person, but rulers like Peter took the lead in recognizing and enlisting public support through a dialogue with their subjects.

As early as 1701, Peter claimed that he hoped to get his subjects to imitate his own dedication to duty and reform, and to instill in them the idea that "devotion to duty is the homage appropriate to a tsar."[72] Peter's invitation to cooperate in his reforming activities struck a responsive chord from the beginning to the end of his reign. Even members of the older generation, although decrying Peter's "way of life," recognized the many problems in their state. Testifying to the general ferment in Muscovy, these pious men became "daring reformers" in response to the tsar's new justification of monarchical power.[73] The old custom of offering the monarch unsolicited advice in a petition dovetailed with Peter's courting of the elite and inviting its members to participate in his grand plans. The combination spawned a group of "projectors," or designers of reform projects, among the literate public and initiated a novel type of advice literature that formed a major ingredient of political dialogue in Petrine Russia.

The prototype of the Muscovite "projector" was Avraamii, born in 1644 and father superior of the Andreevskii Monastery.[74] Working within the tradition that prelates have the right and duty to advise "Orthodox tsars on all secular matters" and that tsars manifest their legitimacy by seeking advice, Avraamii presented his "Notebooks" as a lengthy petition to Peter in 1696.[75] He was also stepping forward as a representative of the educated public since he conversed with people from all classes and held regular meetings with a half dozen civil servants, all of whom reported rampant dissatisfaction: "At present many grieve and are sick, and indeed there is much about which to grieve and become sick." The "Notebooks," written in high biblical language, catalogued a range of problems from Peter's "way of life" to corrupt judges, faulty taxation, and inadequate staffing in civil service.[76] Well before Peter and Feofan articulated the new vision of monarchy, Avraamii intoned that Russia needed a tsar "to reform all these things for the better" and that such "deeds" justified a ruler, not "long prayers, nor constant bowing, nor vigils, nor giving alms to the poor, nor building churches and monasteries, nor prolonged fasts." A tsar "suffered damnation" if he neglected his duty to the common good. Although Avraamii's circle consisted of exactly the type of servitor Peter said he wanted to attract, in paranoid fashion the authorities exiled the prelate to a Kolomna monastery, and the others were given the knout and sent as clerks to Azov.[77] Dialogue clearly came at a risk. Nonetheless, Avraamii's type of advice literature continued to surface and indicated an eagerness among the educated public for participation in state affairs.

Ivan Pososhkov, born in 1652, was an unlikely candidate to respond favorably to Peter's new conception of absolute monarchy.[78] Deeply pious and devoted to Muscovite ways, Pososhkov wrote a moral guide for his son based on the sixteenth-century guide to traditional deportment, the *Domostroi,* and condemned foreign innovations in dress and behavior as "diabolical." But the entrepreneurial activities of this autodidact marked him as a modernizer working to realize Russia's industrial and commercial potential.[79] Neither a nobleman nor a cleric—the usual social profile of the educated elite in this era—Pososhkov's store of practical experience enabled him to pen an important tract on political economy, *The Book of Poverty and Wealth,* which also stands as a splendid example of advice literature.[80]

Pososhkov's conception of rulership in *Poverty and Wealth* would mark him as Europe's first proponent of enlightened absolutism, if it were not for his religious frame of reference. He blended the medieval and the modern by justifying absolute monarchy as the most pragmatic and natural form of government, and also as the institution most capable of effecting reform. Pososhkov dismissed aristocratic government in Russia since the boyars had discredited their ability to rule for the common good, and he found it unthinkable for people to "exercise rule over their own rulers!" He boasted that "our Monarch is absolute and all-powerful, and no aristocrat or democrat." The old Muscovite analogized Peter's power as "god-like": "our Sovereign can, like God, always do what he desires by the exercise of his power . . . [for] just as God rules the whole world so our Sovereign exercises power in his realm."[81] But, like Avraamii and Prokopovich, the entrepreneur believed that a program of reform was "more necessary in a Sovereign than fasting and prayer." Similar to the philosophes who came after him, Pososhkov marveled at absolute power's potential to transform the state, and he articulated a detailed agenda to guide "the one and only majestic white eagle."

> Should it become His Majesty's will that all the proposals which I have herein rehearsed be put into effect, to wit, those affecting the Clergy, Military Affairs, Justice, the Merchants, the Craftsmen, the stamping out of Brigandage and ap-

prehension of runaways, the Land, the Peasantry, and easy ways of increasing His Majesty's revenue—then, with God's help, I can say with confidence that our great land of Russia will be much improved both in its spiritual and its civil order, and not only will His Majesty's coffers be filled but also all the inhabitants of Russia will grow in riches and esteem. And if the art of war is also brought to perfection among us, Russians will not only gain great glory but become the terror of all neighbouring states. Amen.

Peter's potential ability to install this moral and economic utopia, where "righteousness shall be firmly established" and "each and every man is rich," justified his awesome power.

However, like a legion of thinkers before him, Pososhkov betrayed a wariness of absolute power, and he went beyond Peter's prescriptions to advocate some type of institutionalized advisory body. Still thinking in Muscovite terms, he rejected the Boyar Duma as merely self-interested but advocated some type of *zemskii sobor* with representatives from all sections of the population. This "taking counsel of all and allowing a free voice to the people" seemed essential to Pososhkov, "since God has not given any one man perfect understanding in all matters." Indeed, the whole quest for a Russian utopia was hampered by the fact that Peter's "counsellors are crooked" and leave him ignorant. For instance, the soldiers were destitute, but "His Majesty . . . is led to believe that they are all well fed and contented." Similarly, among the state servants, Peter had the duty of "extirpating oppressors, malefactors, brigands, and robbers of every sort, both overt and covert."[82] In *Poverty and Wealth,* Pososhkov never criticized Peter but he did name several corrupt officials. In another travesty of the emperor's campaign to involve his subjects in schemes for reform, Pososhkov was arrested for reasons never quite defined and died in jail.[83]

Whatever the dangers, a score of other "projectors" emerged during Peter's reign; in her doctoral dissertation, Margaret Olswang Blamberg has identified seventeen whose writings are extant. Their class origins ranged from nobleman to serf, and with the exceptions of Avraamii and Pososhkov, they all counted among the newer generation born after 1680, who comfortably shed the Muscovite mentality and unconditionally accepted the new course of reform and imitation of the West. None of the projects—which offered unsolicited suggestions on everything from shipbuilding to primary education—mentioned monarchy as an institution, but all were imbued with the spirit of confident optimism in absolute power that Pososhkov expressed so well in religious terms. The signed efforts of the "projectors" were seconded by a "flurry" of "anonymous letters" that likewise offered constructive criticism and that the tsar was able to utilize in drawing up his reform projects.[84] Thus, Peter's sowing the notion of a tsar who reforms in league and in dialogue with his subjects had found fertile ground.

Ironically, the majority of those who subscribed to and worked for Peter's program of reform proved notoriously guilty of malfeasance and attended to their own enrichment. Nearly all "projectors," Russia's best citizens, were found guilty of some form of extortion or embezzlement of state funds. Although Peter ordered "a spate of investigations and trials for corruption," his failure to curb the evil marked a very real limitation of his power, especially over his own favorites and courtiers. As one of the tsar's closest collaborators, Procurator-General Pavel Iaguzhinskii, famously put it: "We all steal, only some do it on a bigger scale, and in a more conspicuous way, than others."[85] Nonetheless, official brigandage did not weaken the popularity of monarchy in eighteenth-century Russia, since the blame for failings was placed, typically, on the tsar's entourage.

The dialogue that Peter had instigated demonstrated that his new conception of ruler as reformer had breathed vigor and dynamism into an arthritic monarchy. As the major reforms reached completion, and victory in the Great Northern War was assured, writers began a celebration of Peter that would continue throughout the imperial period.[86] Aleksei Mankiev, a diplomat and Russia's first secular historian, whiling away his time in a Swedish prison, wrote *The Kernel of Russian History* in order to bear witness to the accomplishments of the Petrine era and place them in the context of Russia's past.[87] Mankiev followed his hero's lead in abandoning the equation of the history of Russia with the history of Orthodoxy in Russia that had characterized the earlier ecclesiastical histories and instead concentrated upon material progress and secular events.[88] Lengthy lists of Peter's "deeds" in civic and military endeavors were used to demonstrate his legitimacy and to provide evidence of how he caused Russia to "flourish" *(tsvesti),* that verb so commonly used over the ages to describe the reigns of good rulers. Ivan Kirilov was likewise motivated to write *The Flourishing Condition of the All-Russian State* specifically to catalogue Peter's achievements in the domestic sphere, while Prokopovich chronicled the military exploits.[89]

Similarly, sermons by the younger generation among the clergy legitimated the Petrine model of rulership, and the homiletic genre was one of the most popular in the era; Peter, too, was very fond of sermons.[90] Prelates had a captive audience since new laws were always read in church, and the government demanded attendance at Sunday services. The more polished sermons were published and enjoyed wide circulation throughout the century. Prokopovich considered sermons his avenue of communication with the educated elite and personally oversaw their publication and distribution. Although Dmitrii Likhachev considers the Petrine era "an unliterary period in Russian history," Feofan's carefully crafted homilies constitute significant examples of literary prose.[91] The prelate had "no equal in knowledge" of classical and contemporary European arts and sciences and articulated the most intelligent analysis of Peter's version of absolute monarchy.[92] Feofan had early broken ranks with his fellow clerics on the issue of reform; when Peter visited St. Sofiia Cathedral in 1706, his closest advisor, Aleksandr Menshikov, informed him that "in all Kiev, I have found only one man, namely the prefect of a monastery, who is tolerant to us."[93] Even Feofan's first publication, the "school drama" *Vladimir* (1705), attacked obscurantism and stagnation and promoted the importance of monarchical leadership in setting a new course for the future. His next work, *De Arte Rhetorica* (1706), listed first among the ten uses for rhetoric the praise of wise rulers so that their deeds would be emulated and memorialized.[94]

Once Peter summoned Prokopovich to St. Petersburg in 1716 as an apologist, Feofan's sermons created the Petrine legend, which became an essential part of the discourse of justification for the rest of the century and beyond. True monarchs were legitimated not by the age-old formulaic list of virtues or by a Muscovite "way of life," but by "tectonic skill," "foresight," "breadth," and "a willingness to embark on new and difficult projects." Peter was raised to the ranks of saintly princes "because of his deeds"; he had wrought the "miracle of miracles" with "a truly unheard-of thing. . . . At one and the same time he both armed and adorned Russia, and by himself."[95] Peter equaled the feats of the greatest Roman and biblical leaders: serving the "common welfare" through his "military strength" and "political skill," he achieved the heights of "Romulus and Numa and David and Solomon at one and the same time." Feofan was the first to enunciate forcefully the most dramatic part of the myth, the contrast between pre- and post-Petrine Russia, and the theme became ubiquitous. Before Peter, foreigners profaned Russians and held them in contempt as superstitious barbarians and ignoramuses, "a willing fish for a bird of prey."[96] After Peter, Russia possessed "imperial grandeur, imperial magnificence": "With one foot on land and the other in the sea, wondrous to all, awesome to all, and glorious."[97] Prokopovich sang a litany of Peter's accomplishments that served as the criteria against which all future monarchs would be judged: the country had become powerful and feared but also civilized; new buildings, palaces, and gardens had been built as well as canals, factories, and pharmacies; public officials possessed a new ethos of service; Petrine statutes had created a new sense of jurisprudence; the basis had been laid for learning in the liberal arts; strides forward had been taken in architecture, geometry, philosophy, and politics; and because of "everyday courtesy and suitable rules of customs and behavior," even the "external aspect is transformed."[98] However exaggerated the picture, Feofan's depiction became an indelible part of monarchical lore.

The celebration of Peter became prominent in the performing arts as well. The monarch wanted plays to popularize his labors for the common good and his "battles and victories." The Moscow Academy leaned on the Jesuits' experience in presenting political allegories in the German states and Poland; in imitation, authors staged Peter as Moses, David, Samson, Mars, and Hercules. These panegyrical plays were presented at the academy before a "select audience that could understand and appreciate all the hieroglyphics" or at least read explanatory programs before the production.

But then they attracted a wide national audience "not just in the capitals, but in distant out-of-the-way places, not excluding Siberia" and spread the "right of citizenship" as well as the Petrine idea of monarchy throughout the country.[99]

While Peter may not have seduced everyone into adopting a new conception of monarchy, by the end of his reign most of the educated elite had accepted reform as a fundamental justification for absolute power and a prime legitimizing sign of a Russian ruler. In addition, older conceptions were given invigorating color through being interwoven into a more modern pattern. While Russia required a reforming tsar to accomplish the new goal of westernization, the traditional idea of a ruler/parent underscored the need for paternal or maternal guidance to achieve that aim. The notion of divine duty indicated the monarch's understanding that his power ultimately came from God, but his turning to the educated elite as partners indicated a recognition of the popular origin of power. The ancient desire for a ruler's demonstrable virtue became a more achievable goal since its sign was the deeds that were carried out as part of a contractual obligation to foster the common good. Utilizing elements both old and new, Peter determinedly refashioned the idea of monarchy in Russia.

The Problem of Dynastic Justification

Peter's new justification of power proved to be a great creative achievement. However, he committed an error of judgment that was just as great by thinking reform could replace the most universal legitimization of rule, dynastic succession. The reforming tsar shared a belief that "royal powers were dynamic, not static, and were not acquired automatically."[100] A successor had to earn the right to rule by demonstrating that he or she was "worthy" or "fit" *(dostoinyi)*, which, in Peter's view, meant continuing his program of reform. Fénelon's *Télémaque,* a depiction of the ideal eighteenth-century ruler and the most popular novel of the day throughout Europe, contained the passage: "Minos decreed his sons should never reign, / Unless they chose his maxims to retain."[101] Peter's intention to change the rules for succession involved two issues: the fitness of the heir, and who should take the crown if the heir were deemed unworthy to rule.

The tsar's determination that his heir exhibit the new signs of legitimacy produced a tragedy that ended in the "Father of the Fatherland" sacrificing his son to the cause of justification by progress. Born in 1690, Aleksei was the product of Peter's short-lived marriage to Evdokiia Lopukhina, a woman with a Muscovite mentality whom he forced to take the veil in 1698. Aleksei proved to be his mother's son and the opposite of his giant father: short, dull, lackluster, lazy, passive, and certainly not the soldier Peter tried to make of him. In the normal pattern of generational conflict, Aleksei evinced a preference for the old Muscovite ways—against which his father had rebelled—and thus threatened all the new justifications for power. The heir admired the apocalyptical writings of Talitskii, was devoted to tradition, and became the "only hope" of the Muscovite "old beards," including Iavorskii.[102] As early as 1705, Peter used the rhetoric of service to warn his heir apparent: "unless you serve the well-being and honor of the fatherland and spare no effort to work for the common good . . . I will not recognize you as my son."[103] Ten years later, Aleksei had still not changed, but Peter had a choice of male heirs since both his second wife, Catherine, and his daughter-in-law gave birth to sons. Adding to a sense of urgency, the tsar himself was in poor health at that time, and he resolved to settle the problem of succession.

Peter wrote a scolding letter, in which he articulated the theory of rule that had informed his reign, and demanded that his son conform to the expected behavior.[104] The monarch lectured that, unless Aleksei developed an interest in military affairs, his reign would threaten the state internally and externally, because "order and defense are two necessary tasks of ruling." Once again, Peter noted that lack of military preparedness had led to the fall of Constantinople in 1453 and that external threat prevented, as he had argued in 1702, the introduction of needed domestic reform. Hence, continued ignorance of military matters would prove that "the heir is completely unfit for governing." In domestic matters, an "autocratic monarch" required "will and good judgment," while Aleksei's timidity caused him to look to others for guidance and to "be fed gaping like a young bird . . . even not knowing how to reward good and punish negligence." Peter unequivocally recognized the good of the state as the highest moral value and harshly warned his son of the consequences of not acquiring appropriate monarchical interests and traits:

> I will cut you off from succession like a gangrened limb even though you are my only son . . . since I have never spared and never will spare my life for my fatherland and my people, then how can I spare you, who are unfit? It is better that it be someone unrelated but good, than your own, but unfit.[105]

This letter provided the first indication that Peter might negate the dynastic basis of monarchical power in Russia, a despotic move since it was a customary and hence fundamental law of the realm.

Peter would make no compromises on this issue; he wanted assurance that his successor would continue both his domestic and foreign policies and justify power in "modern" terms; unfortunately, the son could not live up to his father's expectations. A fearful Aleksei admitted his sins "both as a son and a subject," renounced the throne, and fled abroad. Peter, clearly tortured, issued a manifesto of explanation in February 1718. It informed the public how he had tried everything—education, mercy, punishment, marriage—to turn his son into a "worthy" heir but had to conclude that he was not "fit" for the throne.[106] The affair dragged on to a dreadful conclusion: Peter made false promises of safety and forgiveness and cajoled Aleksei into returning; once back in Russia, he was placed on trial and found guilty by 128 dignitaries; during incarceration and torture, he died in June of 1718.[107]

Opposition in a monarchy usually gathers around a crown prince. During Aleksei's trial, Peter found no evidence of a farflung conspiracy to unseat him, which he had expected. The institution of monarchy went unquestioned, and hostility to Peter centered around his erring ways as an individual. Kondratii Bulavin, the leader of the Don Cossacks, exhibited another common attitude when he blamed Peter's advisors; the rebel claimed to act in the name of "our sovereign, our tsar," who remained ignorant of the suffering of his people.[108] During his son's trial, however, Peter did unearth "widespread loathing of his methods" and style of rule.[109] Predictably, the old boyars and some clergy, while accepting secular changes and foreign influences, objected to the pace of reform and the militarism of the reign that demanded superhuman sacrifice from the entire population. Many in this group still interpreted Peter's rejection of *starina*—especially his divorce, remarriage, and diminution of the role of the church—as a rejection of Orthodoxy.

In the midst of the criticism, Feofan delivered his most famous homily, "A Sermon on the Power and Honor of the Tsar," which represented a direct effort to reverse the flow of public opinion.[110] The polemicist "spat upon . . . those dregs of the nation . . . the assorted ne'er-do-wells surrounding Aleksei." He included in this ilk "worm-like" prelates who considered themselves a "separate state," who "like the pope, while exempting himself and his clergy from a sovereign's power, dreams of giving himself the power to confer and remove the scepter of kings." After condemning this "papal spirit"—one of the worst epithets in Orthodox Russia—Feofan next derided those "Pharisees" who yearned for a pious tsar draped in liturgy: "Christ freed us . . . from man-made laws concerning rituals, seemingly necessary for salvation but only arbitrary." These same critics misinterpret Scripture to conclude that "wisdom, power, glory, and every human activity are loathsome in the eyes of God." They cannot understand that Peter pleased God by doing his duty in effecting secular improvement; his deeds had "renewed Russia in everything . . . given her a new birth." In a semiotic reverse, Feofan visualized Peter, not as an Orthodox ruler with the duty of eliminating heresy in the realm, but as a Christian monarch who had the duty of eliminating opponents of his reforms.[111] With a withering shot, the orator declaimed: "The monarch is worthy of such a state, but the state is not worthy of such a monarch."

Whatever the effect of Feofan's diatribe, Russians remained quiescent, even though, once Peter's actions resulted in his son's death, questions arose of the monarch's own "fitness" to rule. The issue of succession remained unresolved. Finally, four years after Aleksei's death, Peter published his solution. An official decree reinstituted, ironically, the old Muscovite system of a sitting ruler designating his successor. The edict denounced Aleksei for his "Absalom-like malice," derided the system of primogeniture as a "bad custom," and contained no stipulation that an heir be either Orthodox or a Romanov. Peter argued that the new system offered the assurance that he would choose a "worthy successor," who would not "squander Our inheritance," as "We ought to keep intact the entirety of Our realm which with God's help is now so extensive." The populace was ordered to take an oath to respect whoever was chosen—or suffer the death penalty.[112] Anisimov considers this act the "apotheosis" of despotic rule as Peter took upon himself "the right to designate an heir at will without considering anybody's opinion of the country's traditions."[113]

Indeed, the decree of 1722 raised a score of sensitive issues. Abolishing primogeniture and dynastic succession contravened both the universal principle that a monarch cannot abrogate a fundamental law of the realm and the Russian custom of convocating a type of *zemskii sobor* before altering the rules for inheritance of the throne. Given the emperor's justification of his power on the basis of progress, the edict at least had the merit of logic: if a program of reform legitimizes a monarch and if the heir proves incapable of similar deeds, the claim to the throne is lost. Nonetheless, while most educated Russians could accept the transvaluation of the monarchy, few were willing to abandon the tradition of primogeniture, let alone dynastic succession. Peter might have remembered that in 1682 his family had claimed the throne on the basis that he was more "fit" than his elder half-brother, but Ivan's family won a reprieve by appealing to primogeniture. Montesquieu would later opine that, concerning succession, "that which most sensibly strikes them [the people] is a certain order of birth."[114]

However bad Peter's judgment on this issue, he appears to have understood that his decree could warrant the charge of tyranny and that causing the death of a son represented a contravention of moral law; in other words, Peter was guilty of having disregarded the monarch's prescription to abide by "the laws of God and nature." Six months after the 1722 decree was published, his advisors, under his and Feofan's direction, issued a forty-one-page defense, *The Right of the Monarch's Will to Designate an Heir to His Throne (Pravda voli monarshei, vo opredelenii naslednika derzhavy svoei).*[115] The authorities ordered the wide dissemination of the document and printed twelve hundred copies, five times the norm.[116]

Pravda represented a real effort at communicating with the public and stands as a monumental example of justification literature. It was addressed to the "Simple-hearted Reader," who was informed that Peter, "the Author, the Emperor of All the Russias, has not simply issued an edict but is giving strong reasons or arguments" why he had the right to do so.[117] This statement contains a profound lesson on the definition of "absolute" power in eighteenth-century Russia: the monarch was issuing a public document to vindicate his right to change a law when, paradoxically, the same document defined his power as "unrestrained by law and not subject to human judgment." Clearly, whatever the contradiction, Peter and his entourage attached enormous importance to public opinion and treated it as a limitation in exercising his authority. The fact of publication admitted the existence of widespread doubts about policy and a challenging, independent, and critical spirit among the educated elite. Because the decree in question related to the monarch's right to choose an heir, the apologia attested to the continuing belief that popular participation remained an essential component of the succession process.

The pedagogical measures of a "regulated" state, of course, are in part intended to generate an educated public, but the result always discomfits its originators, who themselves might prefer the traditional comforts and stabilizing force of blind obedience. The tone of *Pravda* was noticeably defensive. It attributed the questioning of Peter's policies to the "ignorance" or lack of "skill" in analyzing political issues on the part of the public, or to the "contradictions" of "hotheads" with "evil hearts" who challenged monarchical authority, or to foreigners who denigrated Russians as "barbaric" slaves ruled by a despot.[118] Whatever the origins of dissatisfaction, Peter felt called upon to respond; he had, after all, initiated the idea of dialogue.

The repetitiveness of arguments in favor of absolute monarchy is an extraordinary feature of intellectual history, and Feofan's rhetoric represented a classic case of an apologist supplementing in theory what a ruler had already done in practice and using all the weapons in the traditional arsenal. Celebrated as an "encyclopedia" of Russian political thought in the era and the *"pièce justificative"* for Peter's policy of reform, *Pravda* blended the older religious and paternal analogies with natural law and the contract and wove them all into the new justification through progress.[119] A tour de force of argumentation, the document contained rational, traditional, and charismatic legitimizations of authority.[120] Like a legal brief, *Pravda* offered sixteen proofs and forty-seven historical precedents, drawn from the ancients and from the "laws and customs of various people," to defend the proposition that Peter had every right to issue new criteria for succession. In a parallel theme, the emperor was repeatedly cast as a father and a sovereign who had full rights over his son and subject. The fourteen reasons given in the Justinian Code for dispossessing children were listed, and Peter was granted every right to punish his son, "even with a death penalty."

Pravda utilized arguments hallowed over the centuries to quell discontent and justified absolute power on the basis of its origins in God and in the people, with both aspects demanding unquestioning obedience to civil authority. The usual quotations from the Old and New Testaments were trotted out, including St. Paul's epistle to the Romans (13.1): "Let everyone be subject to the higher authorities, for there exists no authority except from God, and those who exist have been appointed by God." And the usual conclusion followed: a ruler, as the "highest power on earth under God" and an embodiment of God's will, must be obeyed out of both fear and conscience. The treatise reminded the reader of the argument put forth most famously by Hobbes; man's "corrupt nature" needed to be curbed by "state authority," otherwise would follow "innumerable woes . . . bloody civil wars . . . wailing, weeping, affliction . . . plunder, and murder." *Pravda* made the additional observation—a sticky point throughout the reign—that Peter had the right to change even time-honored practices; his absolute power extended over "all civic and church rituals; changes in customs; directions for using dress, homes, buildings, offices; ceremonies at feasts, weddings, funerals, etc., etc., etc." While the ruler in Russia was an autocratic "majesty" possessing supreme power, significant restraints existed to prevent the ever feared devolution into tyranny: "[He is] subject to God's authority and must answer to the law written by God on the hearts of men and given in the ten commandments . . . and all this is given sufficient witness by natural reason, Holy Writ and the teachers of antiquity."

The absolute monarch was not only empowered by God but contractually by the people: "Wherever there is monarchy, there is also the will of the people as in the beginning the people decided to hand power over to the Monarch." In a hereditary monarchy, the people grant the right to rule forever by saying: "We have all agreed that we want you to rule over us eternally and for our common welfare." In an elective monarchy, in contrast, power is returned to the people after the death of each monarch. *Pravda* stressed that hereditary rather than elective monarchy worked best in most states including Russia. Its advantages, besides avoiding the problem of competition for the throne, centered around the heir, who could be brought up to learn his craft, profit from the mistakes of his parents, easily grasp the identity of the general welfare with family interest, and rule with a long time horizon, since policies would become part of the patrimony he passed to his successor. Cutting to the heart of the issue, the treatise admitted the one problem with hereditary monarchy was genetic. If an incompetent heir legally acceded to power, nothing could be done, since disobedience, revolution, or assassination were not permissible. The political theory in the treatise followed Grotius's concept of the contract as obligating unconditional obedience rather than Locke's idea of the right to revolt. Interpreted in this light, Peter's decree on succession eliminated the only negative aspect of hereditary monarchy and would incorporate the only positive feature of elective monarchy, namely improving the chances of having a capable and popular ruler succeed.[121]

The iron structure of the argumentation in *Pravda* skillfully led the "simple-hearted reader" to the inexorable conclusion that if Peter had not acted to dispossess his son, he himself would not be worthy of his office. Since "the *raison d'être* of supreme power is nothing other than the benefit of all the people," Peter was obligated to protect them from an incompetent ruler against whom they would be powerless once he took office. Aleksei had demonstrated he was not equal to the awesome tasks, both traditional and modern, facing a ruler, who ought "to protect, to defend, to keep from harm in every way, to edify, and, yes, to reform his subjects."

The duty of the Tsar is to keep his subjects from harm and to exhort them to do better in everything from piety to an honest living . . . the Tsar ought to see to it that there will be true justice to protect the aggrieved against the aggrievors; also that there should be a strong and well-trained army for the defense of the fatherland against its enemies; and so that there would be better instruction in everything the Tsar ought to see to it that there are a sufficient number of skilled teachers, both clerical and secular.

Aleksei's incompetence in these areas threatened to undo what Peter had achieved. While Peter was unable to reform his own son, the document extolled him as a "true Father of the Fatherland, [who] with his own deeds not only preserved it whole but expanded it widely; by means of innumerable laws and decrees, he instituted both civic and military reforms that better provided for its defense and raised it to new heights of glory."[122]

Peter survived the crisis over the succession law, but its destabilizing effects would plague every reign for the rest of the century. The activist image of monarchical rule would also haunt his immediate successors, who struggled to keep up, but Catherine the Great confirmed and enhanced the new tradition, which continued well into the nineteenth century. Whatever the positive and negative aspects of Peter's long time in power, he doubtlessly revolutionized the Russian conception of rule. He changed the language, obligations, myths, and theories surrounding monarchy, and after a stormy public dialogue, they became part of the new intellectual framework within which writers commented, criticized, and raised expectations of their form of government. At the same time, the older views of a Saint-Prince or Orthodox Tsar persisted or, better said, coexisted among the populace, so that Peter's new justification strengthened the Russian monarchy by adding yet another source of legitimacy.

CHAPTER THREE

The Elected Monarch

*T*he discussion of monarchy shifted ground dramatically in post-Petrine Russia. In his justification literature, the emperor had articulated an aggressive and teleological validation of absolute power that lent new life and a modern style to the institution. His engaging in public dialogue invited the expanding ranks of the educated elite into a partnership where, however, he set the terms of cooperation. In contrast, Peter's less than charismatic successors in the first half of the eighteenth century concentrated on justifying their own individual claim to the throne, with the "people" sitting in judgment over them. The determination of the legitimacy of each successor, in fact, emerged as the central issue of the era, since Peter's misguided decree of 1722 muddled the criteria for establishing the qualifications to rule and destabilized the entire process of succession. In addition, the despotic element in the tsar's wielding of power, coupled with the weakness of the next occupants of the throne, led to an attempt in 1730 to replace absolute monarchy with a limited form. The endeavor failed, but the problems connected with succession continued. Each transfer of power provoked a crisis, and an intricate etiquette of accession developed that furthered the political role of the elite because the choice of a new ruler came to include an elective element that involved them and even the broader populace. Each succession was problematic in its own way, but once in power, the dialogue that Peter had initiated continued: monarchs with constancy justified their reigns as those of reforming tsars, while writers among the educated elite demonstrated an expectation of that type of behavior.

THE ETIQUETTE OF ACCESSION

Peter's succession decree of 1722 destroyed one of the main attractions of absolute monarchy, the smooth transfer of power. Centuries of political theory and practice demonstrated the destructive force of regular competition for royal office and confirmed the popularity of dynastic succession and primogeniture.[1] The simple announcement, "The king is dead, long live the king," celebrated the seamless passage from one reign to another. In contrast, the Petrine edict stipulated that appointment by the previous monarch of a "worthy" heir provided the sole de jure qualification for rule. Montesquieu decried the measure in his *Spirit of the Laws:* "By the constitution of Russia, the Czar may choose whom he has in mind for his successor, whether of his own or of a strange family. Such a settlement produces a thousand revolutions and renders the throne as tottering as the succession is arbitrary."[2] The statistics plainly confirm this judgment. From 1725 to 1801, eight monarchs occupied the Russian throne, at a time when there were only two kings of France, three of Great Britain, and four of Poland, Prussia, and Spain. The accident of natural death played its role just twice, while six full-scale accession crises erupted, four of which constituted coups d'état and two included assassinations.

The decree caused havoc because it erased longstanding signs of legitimacy and replaced them with poorly functioning or unpopular substitutes. Designation by a sitting monarch remained the sole legal qualification for the throne, but three rulers, Peter included, neglected to appoint a successor before they died. Even when a designation had occurred, the decree's criterion of "fitness," which found a receptive audience, was linked to the Lockean notion of a revocable contract and operated as an excuse for overthrowing a perfectly legal but undesirable ruler or entourage. Adding to the disarray, Russians never accepted designation as the exclusive sign of the right to rule and demanded additional traits in a monarch. The dynastic idea retained its strength, and no one dared claim the throne unless related to the Romanov clan, if only by marriage. However, since Peter had abolished primogeniture, the line of succession zigzagged; not once in the eighteenth century did a Romanov come to the throne the first time he or she was next in dynastic order. Russians also expected that their rulers be Orthodox communicants, although they conceived of their duties as secular in nature. Indeed, once in power, monarchs demonstrated their "fitness" by pursuing the policies of a reforming tsar, which had become the sign of legitimacy replacing the liturgical conception of Muscovite times.

The unpopularity of designation, coupled with the uncertainties and malfunctions of Peter's law, made a return to the concept and practice of election inevitable. Precedent, expedience, and legal theory warranted some form of election nearly every time the throne changed hands in the eighteenth century.[3] When monarchs failed to name an heir, their demise caused an interregnum. According to Russian custom since 1589, resolving a hiatus in the line of succession demanded consultation with the "people." When a coup d'état occurred, leaders, not wanting to depend on brute force, could only appeal to the public to support and ratify their insurgency through some sign of election. Furthermore, Byzantine theory, which Russia adapted, stipulated that the "people" were to be consulted in moments of crisis or doubt, and every accession proved irregular.

Openly recognizing the central role of the elite, new monarchs in this century issued yet another novel form of justification literature: detailed manifestoes, proclamations, and supplementary decrees, which carefully argued the case for their right to the throne. As one nineteenth-century scholar has noted, this appeal was wise.

> It is a big mistake to think that there is no public opinion in Russia. Because there are no regular forms for the expression of public opinion in Russia, it is manifested in irregular ways, by leaps and bounds, in fits and starts, solely at crucial historical junctures, with a force that is all the greater and in forms that are all the more peculiar.[4]

The "peculiar" forms involved in eighteenth-century successions led to the strong conception of a monarch as "elected" or "chosen by all the Russian people." Translated and original works of literature reflected and reinforced this idea. They repeatedly described rulers as "elected" and suggested that "changing tsars who rule unjustly" should occur by "common consensus," while choosing the "best person" to succeed should be done "by everyone."[5] The poet and dramatist, Aleksandr Sumarokov, claimed that willing obedience resulted from the fact that the people "picked" their rulers.[6] Prince Mikhail Shcherbatov, the historian and political thinker, wrote that in Russia "the Sovereign is raised to the throne either by election or by right of birth."[7] Political texts agreed that when a ruler dies without instruction and there is no clear successor, the matter "reverts to the entire people" who have "the natural freedom to choose whom they want to rule over them."[8]

In the eighteenth century, the word election *(izbranie)*, in a political context, always referred to choosing heads of state, and it was this word that was used in accession documents. Election, though, should be understood in the traditional, informal sense, meaning a process by which consensus was reached, with "consensual" *(sobornoe)* government posited as the ideal.[9] The elections were nonetheless real, even if sometimes contrived, and the term was not just a rhetorical device. The electors were actual individuals and not merely members of an abstract body politic as in some medieval uses of the term. In Russia, after the disappearance of the *zemskii sobor*, election by the people or "by the common will of all" or by "all the Russian people" meant primarily by agreement with the magnates of the realm.[10] Shcherbatov, for instance, considered the terms nobility and the people synonymous.[11]

Russia's ex officio electorate was drawn from the political elite, those directly involved in the affairs of church, state, army, and court; normally in premodern or early modern states, this group was equated with "the people" since it was expected to represent the interests of the rest of the population, although it rarely did. In Russia, this elite included the dozen members of the Governing Senate, the central administrative and judicial organ of the state, created by Peter the Great; the twelve members of the Holy Synod; and the *generalitet,* the roughly two hundred military and civil service officers of highest rank who normally came from aristocratic families.[12] As in Byzantium, these magnates debated and took the initiative in selecting a new ruler, and other parts of the population were called in to ratify the choice. Widening this rather narrow circle of power brokers, other members of the nobility, if present at the time of the succession, also became numbered among the "people." As John Le Donne has pointed out, the nobility as a whole constituted a ruling class "coterminous" with civil society and including most of the educated public.[13]

When the throne was contested, the successful faction usually required the allegiance of the roughly six thousand guards of the Preobrazhenskii or Semenovskii regiments, who had replaced the *strel'tsy* as the elite nucleus of the regular army. Their status and personal interest in monarchical selection resulted from their duty to protect the person of the ruler and from being subject to his or her direct command. Ninety percent of their officers belonged to middle-level noble families, as opposed to aristocrats, and thus expanded the ranks of the electorate. While the guards relished demonstrating their growing political awareness and their influence over the political elite, they were not mere praetorians. After the creation of a school for cadets in 1731, which rapidly became an important center of learning, the men of the regiments qualified as informed members of the educated elite.[14]

When post-Petrine accession documents used the term election, then, it meant that the available members of the ruling class had crafted a consensus about the new ruler. How did they reach this consensus? During the previous reign or at the outset of the crisis, contending factions lobbied for their candidates, and issues of self-interest and kinship politics predominated. Intrigue and highhanded repression predictably plagued every reign, and adding to the machinations, foreign powers intervened with money and influence hoping to affect foreign policy. Competition was fierce, and stakes were high. Victors would become the new ruler's "favorites," the reviled *vremenshchiki* (those temporarily in power), and they stood to rake in the spoils, presiding over a court clique and patronage network at the center of power and positioned to receive gifts of money, land, jewels, and high offices. Losers, along with their family and entourage, suffered any combination of arrest, torture, confiscation of property, exile, or execution. As Brenda Meehan-Waters has pointed out, everything "rested ultimately on the personal favor of the autocrat" once he or she was installed in power, and the Russians "devised no face-saving way of letting the new 'ins' come in without demolishing the 'outs.'"[15]

The succession, though, was not decided solely by intrigue, force, or patronage politics. Accession documents warrant a conclusion that issues of legitimacy figured just as prominently, and successful candidates needed to demonstrate their better credibility and greater ability to achieve the backing of the electorate in comparison with other contenders.[16] This literature, central to the discourse of justification, demonstrates that in post-Petrine Russia, four signs conferred legitimacy: designation, dynastic inheritance, worthiness, and election. No eighteenth-century monarch possessed all four signs at accession, but each could claim at least two. This may have been an "era of palace revolutions," but it was not anarchic power grabbing; there were rules. A new, informal political process, an etiquette of accession, had come to govern the selection of a ruler.[17]

Weighing all the arguments (and bribes, threats, and promises), the political elite reached a consensus and made their choice. They then sought endorsement of the election through the acclamation of the guards and other members of the nobility who happened to be on hand during the crisis. This was a crucial moment; in the complicated election of Anna Ioannovna, for instance, approval was delayed nearly a month. Endorsement was next sought from the rest of the population. The accession manifesto became the most significant document at the onset of a reign because it served as the preface to the traditional oath of loyalty, which was printed and disseminated among the entire population. The manifesto not only announced but also justified the election of a new monarch; it narrated the circumstances of coming to the throne, defended the legitimacy of the imperial person, sometimes elaborately, and conveyed the direction of future policy, which normally entailed a promise to rule as a reforming tsar. The document thus represented a conscious effort to win the approval and support of those who had not participated in the election and became a pivotal publication in the continuing public dialogue over the meaning of monarchy in eighteenth-century Russia.

A convincing justification for the new monarch's ascent was considered an essential part of the oath, as failure to prove legitimacy might lead to the appearance of pretenders or other forms of unrest. Neither automatic nor a rote exercise, the administration of the oath developed during the course of the century into a serious, far-flung, and time-consuming exercise that was the equivalent of seeking national ratification of the choice. Churchmen reminded the faithful that "taking an oath is a serious matter, and eternal damnation awaits anyone who swears to anything contrary to his conscience or against what he wishes or believes." With this caveat, all Russian subjects (eventually, except serfs) and resident foreigners were asked to swear to uphold the new monarch.[18] Printed in thousands of copies, the manifestoes and blank oath forms were sent by express messengers to all the provinces, every regiment and fleet, the Cossacks, and all foreign embassies.[19] Officials, who faced imprisonment if records were incomplete, exchanged nervous correspondence about whether there would be trouble during these ceremonies held both at home and abroad. The signatures and any unused forms were then returned to the capital.[20] Afterward, elaborate coronation rituals and celebrations, so well described by Richard Wortman, were orchestrated to reinforce the notion of "a consensus in favor of the new monarch."[21] In the coming reign, the process of election and the political discourse it entailed served to reconfirm what Le Donne has described as "the consensus without which the ruler's will could not be translated into effective policy."[22]

Election conferred moral and political authority on the new ruler and provided at least a partial antidote to a bad law that ushered in "mutiny and disorder," coups, pretenders, and rule by those favorites who had won the throne for their candidate.[23] The Russian response to this challenge appears quite civilized when one considers that half of all eighteenth-century wars were connected with successions, among them the War of the Spanish Succession (1700–1714), the War of the Polish Succession (1733–1735), and the War of the Austrian Succession (1740–1748).

In an age that held women inferior, female monarchs especially needed to engage in dialogue and reach out to a larger constituency in order to obtain and maintain their grip on power.[24] Of the eight monarchs in Russia from 1725 to 1801, four were women, and they reigned for sixty-eight of the seventy-five years; during this time, the only other female monarch in Europe was Maria Theresa of Austria. Tsarevna Sofiia's coup in 1682 provided an instructive example of the classic female accession crisis. She took advantage of the confusion as to who should succeed (the "fit" Peter or the older, but simple, Ivan) to install herself as regent; she courted the guards; she held elections; she offered public justifications; she made dramatic rewards and punishments. She herself had much at stake since the practice for female members of the royal family—on the grounds that no one was worthy to marry a tsarevna—was sequestration in the *terem* and a life of prayer, fasting, boredom, and spinsterhood. An official explanation followed Sofiia's bloody coup to make it palatable to the public; Sil'vestr Medvedev, a cultured and prominent member of her inner circle, heralded her as a "savior," which became the usual appellation in the eighteenth century for a new ruler after a forced change in power. When eventually ousted after trying to win the throne for herself, Sofiia was forced into a convent and then had to take the veil, the fate that awaited unsuccessful female power players.[25] In hindsight, it might seem that Sofiia's mistake was to be satisfied with the title of regent and not to press immediately for power in her own right.

Perhaps with this example, Catherine I, Anna Ioannovna, Elizabeth, and Catherine II all claimed election, all sought the support of the guards, none served merely as a regent, and all held the throne until their natural deaths. The four male monarchs were designated and felt more secure; neither they nor their entourage sought electoral endorsement or strove to build a consensus when in power. Three of them lost the throne (the fourth died of smallpox after a two-year reign). Clearly, the new importance awarded to electoral or consensual politics and public dialogue represented innovations that new monarchs could only disregard at their peril.

AN ALTERNATIVE TO ABSOLUTE MONARCHY

After Peter died in 1725, oligarchs assumed control of the Russian government but maintained the fiction of an absolute monarch elected "by all the people." The erosion of absolute power occurred primarily because the remaining members of the Romanov clan seemed capable of reigning but not ruling, even though the emperor had left behind a gaggle of possible heirs from both the Miloslavskii and Naryshkin families, including one nine-year-old male and eight females. In the scramble for the throne, four of Peter's family members would rule, but not in any logical dynastic order, which was ignored whenever someone died. Because so few males were available and Russia had no Salic law barring women, the fight over the throne centered around the female branches of the Romanov family, including the dubious dynastic claims of wives. While in the rest of Europe no wives had actually succeeded their husbands as monarchs, ample and recent precedent existed in Spain, France, England, and Sweden for inheriting a crown via the female line.

Catherine I's claim to the throne was weak since the emperor had not designated her; this former servant girl lacked the ability to rule; and she was not of Romanov blood. Nonetheless, she won election on the strength of her role as Peter's helpmeet and beloved wife.[26] Another faction favored the sole male, Peter's grandson, but Aleksandr Menshikov manipulated the events. Menshikov, now titled the Most Serene Prince of the Holy Roman Empire, was a former pie vendor, who had become Peter's closest associate and had introduced him to Catherine. Feofan Prokopovich participated in the debate and described "the most distinguished nobility" gathering "in one room" in the palace, deliberating, and deciding on Catherine. The guards surrounding the chamber, out of loyalty to Peter, also vociferated in favor of his wife "on the strength of her recent coronation" as empress, in which they had played a prominent role (Menshikov had also given them sixteen months' back pay).[27]

The accession manifesto, a masterpiece of what late-twentieth-century American pundits call "spin," stretched to prove that Catherine possessed all four signs of legitimacy. Election was most prominent, with the announcement issued in the name of the senate, synod, and *generalitet*. Even though Catherine had no substantial dynastic claim, her "marital kinship" was stressed. Since she had not been designated, Peter's coronation of Catherine six months before was offered as proof that she was the "worthy" successor Peter had in mind to carry on his policies.[28] In addition, he had often publicly recognized her "manly services to the Russian

Catherine I, surrounded by rulers of both the Riurikid and Romanov dynasties in an attempt to establish her dynastic legitimacy. D. A. Rovinskii, *Materialy dlia russkoi . . .* St. Petersburg, 1884–90, vol. 1, no. 28 left

state." After this manifesto, all new monarchs promised the continuation of the Petrine legacy, and the attribution of manliness became a staple compliment for female rulers.[29]

With such contrived legitimacy, the senate expected dissension among the common people, and the oath did not ask them to recognize Catherine's own claim to power but, oddly, to confirm the promise of loyalty taken to her and Peter as an imperial couple after the coronation.[30] In another move designed to dispel the Russian preference for primogeniture and for elevating Peter's grandson, Menshikov and Prokopovich ordered an unprecedented print run of 22,000 copies of *Pravda voli monarshei,* the document from the previous reign arguing Peter's right to abolish primogeniture. Orders were given to read the treatise in every church and monastery on Sundays and holy days in order to buttress Catherine's claim to the throne.[31] All to no avail: a multitude of "anonymous letters" were posted by "villains in various cities and districts," raising doubts about Catherine's right to rule and the propriety of the 1722 succession law.[32] Even aristocrats contended that "by blood, by birth, and by sex . . . the lawful heir to the throne of Russia" was Peter's young grandson, Peter Alekseevich.[33]

Whatever her right to the throne, Catherine's absolute power was wrested from her early in the reign, and the conception of a timid figurehead replaced that of a mighty imperial ruler. In 1726, a Supreme Privy Council *(Verkhovnyi tainyi sovet)* was formed; tellingly, its six members took an oath to Catherine as sovereign *(gosudarynia)* but not autocrat *(samoderzhitsa).* The council aimed first to dilute the influence of the empress's favorite, Menshikov. Then, it usurped the power of the more broadly based senate, which was trying to remain faithful to Peter's program of reform. The council bypassed monarchical authority by issuing decrees in its own name; in the next year, of 222 edicts, all but two dozen carried the signatures of the oligarchs, not the empress or senate.[34] With the advice of Menshikov and of the Duke of Holstein, the husband of her elder daughter Anna, Catherine tried to outmaneuver the council by donning the mantle of a reforming tsar, and she supported the Bering Expedition, the founding of the Academy of Sciences, and renovations in taxation, justice, and the mint.[35] But her death on May 6, 1727, cut short any attempts to regain authority.

When the empress died, the election of Peter II was a foregone conclusion; the "distinguished nobility" gathered, this time in Menshikov's apartment, and all agreed that Peter's grandson, as the sole surviving male Romanov, was rightful heir to the throne; the prince had by now connived to arrange for his son and daughter to marry Peter and his sister.[36] The young boy appeared on the balcony to the sound of cannon, drums, and music, and the guards three times hailed him with the cry of "Vivat!"[37] However, primogeniture carried no legal weight, and so a designation was concocted. The accession manifesto claimed that, in keeping with "our Grandfather's" law of 1722, "our beloved Grandmother" (actually, step-grandmother) had appointed him heir in a "Testament" that was "signed by Her Majesty's

Peter II, as a dashing adolescent. *Tsarstvuiushchii dom Romanovykh . . .*

1913, pg. opp. 152

own hand"; as proof, the will was appended to the oath of loyalty. The document, created while Catherine was on her deathbed, was never actually signed by her, but its authenticity was not really an issue; Russians rallied around Peter's grandson.[38] Even though the Duke of Holstein was commander of the Preobrazhenskii Guards, and a member of his entourage was in charge of the Semenovskii regiment, the duke could not marshal their support to have him or his wife accede to the throne, and they both left the country.[39] In other words, the guards alone could not put a monarch on the throne, as historians have often implied; they frequently supported, but never led, a coup.

The Supreme Privy Council retained its position of power; indeed, in the oath to the twelve-year-old heir, its members were listed ahead of the synod, senate, and *generalitet*.[40] Within four months, Menshikov's high-handedness led to his exile to Berezov, Siberia, and two aristocratic families, the Dolgorukiis and Golitsyns, became the new favorites. While not against westernization, they worked to undo other aspects of the Petrine system: the capital was moved back to Moscow; Stefan Iavorskii's work, *Rock of Faith (Kamen' very)*, which attacked Prokopovich and the subjugation of church to state, was ordered published; and all 22,000 copies of *Pravda* were ordered seized in order to rehabilitate Peter II's father Aleksei and return to a policy of primogeniture. An atmosphere of recidivism hung over young Peter's pronouncements and the planning for his coronation. The documents returned to a Muscovite biblical tone and a legitimacy based solely on dynastic and religious considerations and the traditional duties of earlier centuries. Once again reverting to the tsarist title that Peter I had abandoned, this "true Sovereign and one by birth" understood that "Tsars . . . [as] earthly Monarchs possess their most sovereign and supreme power only from the glory of the Heavenly Tsar alone." Prokopovich's coronation message remained isolated in its references to the Petrine doctrine that a ruler is judged "not by words but by deeds."[41]

The Supreme Privy Council, under the sway of the Dolgorukiis and Golitsyns, who held six of the eight seats, jealously guarded its power and "distanced the Sovereign from everyone else." The council planned to cement its influence over Peter II by having him marry the young Princess Ekaterina Dolgorukaia, whom he adored, and thus to fulfill the dream of every aristocratic family to control the throne.[42] But, as often happens with the best-laid plans, the day before the wedding, at one in the morning on January 19, 1730, Peter unexpectedly died of smallpox, and the male Romanov line came to an end. No one harbored any thought of searching outside the dynasty, so the new ruler clearly would be a woman, but which one?

In camera the Supreme Privy Council debated the possible successors, without consulting the senate, synod, or *generalitet*. Aleksei Dolgorukii made the most ridiculous bid of the century by suggesting his daughter be declared empress on the strength of her official title as Sovereign Fiancée.[43] Because of a hostility to Peter the Great and a conviction that Catherine had never been legitimate as a monarch and her children had been born out of wedlock, the imperial couple's offspring were dismissed out of hand.[44] The field narrowed to the daughters of Ivan V, the eldest of whom, Ekaterina of Mecklenburg, was separated from her lout of a husband, who—the councilors worried—would return to Russia for the throne. The middle daughter, Anna, was a widow in her thirties rusticating in the Duchy of Courland and possessing a reputation as a person of imperial bearing but weak will: in short, an ideal candidate.

Docility in a future empress held prime importance since the council was planning a revolution that would divest her of absolute power. Unwilling to relinquish their hold on the throne, the Dolgorukis and Golitsyns devised a bold plan to change Russia's form of government from an absolute to a constitutional monarchy, with the ruler's prerogatives severely curtailed by the council. The moving force behind the new order was Prince Dmitrii Golitsyn, whose knowledge of politics was nonpareil among the educated elite: he was first cousin to Vasilii Golitsyn, Sofiia's favorite, who structured a far-reaching plan of reform during her regency; he spent eighteen months in Italy and was familiar with Venice's aristocratic Council of Ten; like all educated Russians, he was acquainted with Poland's elective monarchy; he was also well versed in the natural law and contract theories of Locke, Pufendorf, and Grotius; he had studied England's Glorious Revolution of 1688, whereby James II was expelled and his daughter Mary offered the throne on condition of signing the Bill of Rights; and he was well aware of Ulrica Eleonora being elected queen of Sweden in 1718 at the death of the last male Vasa and accepting limitations on monarchy from the aristocracy.[45] This was a broad political menu. However, Golitsyn and his colleagues were caught by surprise when young Peter died; they ended up choosing eclectically from among the options and proposing a political order that resembled old-fashioned frondism more than modern constitutionalism.

The council improvised a new monarchical form of government for Russia that included limiting the power of the ruler and institutionalizing a narrower variant of the informal elective process that had developed since Peter I's death. Working in secret, the councilors devised a set of "Conditions," which Anna would have to sign before accepting the crown. These provisions transferred final authority from the monarch to the council on fundamental issues: waging war, making peace, imposing taxes, fixing a budget, and adjudicating the nobility. The Conditions would also prevent the empress from creating a coterie of her own favorites: she was denied the right to appoint anyone to high office; she lost control of the guards and court; and she could not reward servitors with gifts. In a subsequent codicil, the councilors arrogated legislative powers.

An equally drastic innovation gave the Supreme Privy Council the right to decide on succession. The Russian monarchy was to become elective with the councilors serving as electors, but since they constituted such a small coterie, the provision made a mockery of any notion of election. In forbidding Anna to marry or appoint an heir, the Conditions highhandedly abrogated the decree of 1722. To guarantee the new order, the councilors framed the usually theoretical idea of the contract as iron reality: Anna was to agree that "if I do not carry out or keep any of these promises, I shall be deprived of the Russian crown." The tiny number of duties left in the empress's domain were Muscovite and reduced her to a figurehead: to take "good advice," presumably from the councilors; to "glorify the name of God"; to "not only preserve but propagate as much as possible our Greek Orthodox faith"; and to ensure "the welfare of the entire state and of all our loyal subjects."[46]

The Conditions proposed a defiantly new conception of Russian monarchy, and these ideas might have won a warm reception among the educated elite, many of whom recognized the negative aspects of absolutism. The problems intimated by the councilors tapped an undercurrent of hostility toward the severity of Peter's form of rule and the lack of security of person and property; for instance, 25 percent of the wealthiest members of the *generalitet* had suffered some form of confiscation.[47] As early as 1718, Feofan observed that "some have thought of decreasing the sovereign power," and indeed, once the Conditions finally became public, support for limitations on monarchy seemed general.[48] In addition, the available Romanovs presented a practical problem; the successors for the foreseeable future would be young children or women, who presumably would require assistance in ruling.

The Supreme Privy Council never acquired the necessary legitimacy to carry through its program. The loss of potential support occurred for three reasons: in trying to implement change, it acted illegally; its conception of constitutional monarchy was too narrowly circumscribed; and it failed to engage in serious dialogue with the rest of the elite. These half dozen individuals proceeded unilaterally to choose a successor and change the form of government, when the country's unwritten laws viewed the former as the province of the senate, synod, and *generalitet* and the latter as requiring some form of representative assembly.[49] The councilors understood the illegality of their actions; they worked in secret and when they sent emissaries to Anna asking her to sign the Conditions, they lied that the idea had been approved by the "entire Russian people." While some scholars believe that Golitsyn planned a new order with broad political participation, others discredit the effort to make him a protoliberal.[50] As events unfolded, it became clear, at least to contemporaries, that the councilors had little intention of sharing their power with other members of the nobility.[51]

After the death of young Peter, the Supreme Privy Council also violated the rules governing the etiquette of accession. The manifesto was published eighteen days after Peter's death, rather than immediately, and it was issued in the name of the council, rather than the senate, synod, and *generalitet*. The document referred to Anna as imperial highness, rather than autocrat, and defended her right to rule based on "her tsarist blood line," the "will of God Almighty," and, falsely, on election with the "general desire and agreement of the entire Russian people." The manifesto did not mention the Conditions, although rumors spoke of their existence.[52] For all these reasons, the electorate would not endorse the proclamation.

The council's attempt to act like a self-styled constituent assembly inaugurated what might be called the February Days, nearly a month of intense political debate among the educated public about Russia's future form of government. Hundreds of members of the nobility had gathered in Moscow for Peter's wedding and were now awaiting his funeral. They became politically charged, when on February 2, they received news of the Conditions. The council called a meeting with roughly eighty members of the *generalitet* to read the restrictions on rule, and the council pretended that they originated with Anna, but no one believed that she "could have gotten it into her head" to dream them up.[53] The presence of armed guards and rumors of arrests created an intimidating atmosphere at the gathering, but Prince Aleksei Cherkasskii broke the silence by wondering aloud, "In the future what form would this government have?" Golitsyn, prepared for the question, called for suggestions, and so it seemed that the council was inaugurating a public discussion.[54] Since the presentation of projects had become a part of the elite's political culture, the nobility eagerly set to work writing proposals and counterproposals for altering the legal and institutional bases of the Russian government. In the first week of February, members of the nobility "met every day" forming salons at various homes, and a dozen projects appeared.[55] An English envoy reported that "they have gone too far to go back" and assuredly "will make some considerable alterations." A French envoy likewise expected "a new form of government" either on the English or Swedish model.[56]

In the course of the February Days, hundreds of signatures—scholars count anywhere from 416 to 1,117—were affixed to various projects attesting to the high degree of political consciousness and public spirit among the Russian elite. None questioned the choice of Anna as the best of Ivan V's descendants; at the moment, those of Peter I were unacceptable: his grandson, two-year-old Karl Peter of Holstein, was burdened with an irascible father, and Peter's twenty-year-old daughter, Elizabeth, preferred dancing, riding, and falling in love to the responsibilities of rule. Many members of the elite, including Feofan, also applauded Anna's signing of the Conditions.[57] From the beginning, a concern emerged that the empress, as a woman, would need assistance in ruling; in fact, no one paid Anna much heed at all during the discussions. The main theme in the projects was how best to fill the expected vacuum in monarchical ability.

Despite the historical tensions between aristocrats and rank-and-file nobility, during the February Days they mostly agreed. First, they demonstrated unity of purpose in wanting to break the power of the Dolgorukiis and Golitsyns.[58] Most proposals called for outright abolition of the council, a restored senate of anywhere from eleven to one hundred members to handle executive matters, and a "large assembly" of nobility to participate in legislation and consider "important affairs . . . such as war [or] the death of a sovereign." Other projects suggested enlarging the council, but always with the stipulation that "no more than two persons from any one family" should sit in the major governing institutions.[59] All ranks of nobility also tried to guarantee "the reform and welfare of the state"; the various suggestions included tax relief for the peasants; abolition of quartering troops for the merchants and clergy; additional schooling for clergy and a cadet corps for the nobility; the abolition of single inheritance in noble families; and improvements in the nobility's pay, promotion, and length of service in the military.[60]

The discourse on monarchy, however, revealed a basic difference about what the concept meant for aristocrats, on the one hand, and run-of-the-mill nobility, on the other. Some projects, mostly of aristocrats, assumed that limited monarchy would become the Russian form of government and envisioned the sovereign co-ruling principally with representatives from the ranks of the upper nobility in some way yet to be decided. In contrast, an important grouping of the rank-and-file nobility, along with some aristocrats, gathered around Cherkasskii, and they retained a fidelity to absolute monarchy, conceiving the proposed political arrangements as temporary. Vasilii Tatishchev, one of the principal "fledglings of Peter's nest" and a close collaborator of Feofan, wrote a "Discourse" based on "three days" of discussions among the Cherkasskii group and signed by 288 members of the nobility.[61] They envisioned a unique form of regency based on the recognition that the new empress was "a female person . . . [and] her knowledge of the laws is inadequate. And so for a time, until the Almighty gives us a male person on the throne, it is necessary to arrange something for the help of Her Highness." A senate, including the councilors, would "be with Her Majesty" to run the executive branch while an assembly would assist with legislative matters if "it does not please Her Majesty to draft laws herself."[62] Of course, if the monarchs of the "weaker sex" had agreed to this helpful arrangement, the temporary government would have become permanent, for women ruled nearly the entire century.

In response to these outpourings of suggestions, the Supreme Privy Council seemed intent on proving that government by aristocrats inevitably descends into the tyranny of oligarchy: they arrogantly declined any need for advice from the rest of the nobility; they ordered the arrests of thirty of their presumed enemies; and although they tinkered with plans of compromise, they decided not to pursue them.[63] Because of these "mistakes," and Feofan listed sixteen others, the prelate asked: "What kind of government beneficial to society could one expect from them?"[64] Hatred and fear of the councilors overrode the desire for a limited monarchy, and those who had once opined that "now is the time that autocracy should no longer be," changed their minds.[65] As Meehan-Waters concluded: "The expectations of the elite varied according to their hope of sharing in the political action; when all such hopes were crushed by an obstinate council, they readily supported the restoration of autocracy."[66] One of the oldest justifications of absolute monarchy came into play: it was better than the alternative. Anonymous pamphlets made the rounds in Moscow defending absolute monarchy as preferable to the alternative of limited monarchy dominated by aristocrats:

> God forbid that instead of one autocratic ruler there should be ten despotic and powerful families; and so we, the nobility, will be completely ruined and compelled more than ever to go worshipping idols and seeking everyone's favor. And this will not be easy to obtain; for however much agreement there may be among the most important people (i.e., aristocrats), they will of course not be without disagreements in the future. Hence, one of them may show favor, while the other, because of that will react with anger and cause harm and ruin.

The pamphlet offered yet another classic justification: an absolute monarch acted rapidly for the "common good," but with aristocrats, things that should take "a week will take six months or a year to complete."[67]

As events unfolded during the February Days, fear of oligarchy assured the victory of absolute monarchy. Confirming every apprehension, when Anna arrived from Mitau on February 18, the councilors, as they had done with Peter II, tried to keep her incommunicado on the outskirts of Moscow until her coronation. However, exhibiting more willfulness and wiliness than anyone expected, Anna kept in contact with the various factions of nobility through her sister, Ekaterina of Mecklenburg, and the wives of supporters.[68] All sides had underestimated distaff intelligence. For a week, nothing definitive occurred. On the morning of February 25, the Cherkasskii group tried to end the impasse by petitioning the sovereign empress (not autocrat) to resolve the government crisis. Anna should neither go along with the councilors' Conditions nor return to the past, but agree "to convene the entire *generalitet* . . . and the rank-and-file nobility, one or two from each family . . . who on the basis of the majority opinion would write up a form of government for the state and submit it to Your Majesty for approval." Earlier, aristocrats proposed that about fifty of their rank be empowered to draft a new form of government and to "request her confirmation." Neither group intended to call in representatives of the other classes as had occurred in the convening of a *zemskii sobor.*[69]

This "female person," however, was not interested in a new form of government; she was holding out for full power. Anna demonstrated surprise and annoyance at the Cherkasskii suggestion of a constituent assembly and retired for lunch with the councilors. This gesture caused consternation, and the elite probably felt that promise of a middle way had dissipated and that they were confronted with a choice between absolute monarchy or Anna co-ruling with the council. A concern also surfaced that if the confusion continued, "the majority of people stand in fear of future unrest," maybe of civil war or foreign invasion.[70] While disappointment may have been setting in, Prokopovich held out the lingering hope that Anna might still summon a "grand assembly" after her coronation. At any rate, the tide had turned.[71]

After lunch, a second petition, signed by three times more people (262) than the first, addressed Anna in full complement as "Most illustrious, Most powerful, Great Sovereign Empress Anna Ioannovna, Autocrat of All Russia!" These members of the nobility and guards, acting as an electoral body, asked her "to accept AUTOCRACY just as Your glorious and worthy ancestors did and to annul the Conditions sent to Your Imperial Majesty from the Supreme Council and signed by Your Majesty's hand." The document, they pointed out, was illegal since it did not represent the desires of "all the Russian people." The petition then requested abrogating the council, restoring the Petrine Governing Senate, and enacting a variety of needed reforms.[72] With a flair for staging that never left her, Anna had the Conditions brought to her and graciously tore them to shreds.[73] Thus ended the February Days.

A long-honored interpretation of the February Days is to describe them as "lost liberty" or a "tragedy."[74] Scholars with a proleptic bent have assumed that a constituent assembly would have established limited monarchy in Russia, but as in 1613 the greater probability would have been for the delegates to "choose" absolute rule. Such a choice would not have demonstrated "the absence of political theories and principles" among the elite or that they had come to a "standstill."[75] As in France, "the popularity of strong monarchy was beyond doubt," and protests against the despotic abuse of power by a small group rarely indicated a "constitutional" attempt to dismantle "absolutism."[76] European political theorists contended that vast imperial domains required absolute monarchy as a form of government for the maintenance of order and prestige. Russia officially declared itself the defender of Sweden's aristocratic Constitution of 1720 and of "Polish liberties," understanding that both were a prescription for political chaos, which would lessen the threat of one state and make the other susceptible to conquest. Overall in the eighteenth century, whether in the Netherlands, the Ottoman Empire, or Denmark, nonabsolutist states were marked as "declining powers."

> The particular path of descent taken by the declining powers varied with the local conditions, but their terminus was remarkably uniform: a long era glorified as "liberty" but actually signifying a return to government by a traditional oligarchy which stifled and limited the central authority of the state in favor of aristocratic privileges and exemptions.[77]

Thus, in the eighteenth-century context, the elite could conclude that restoring absolute power was in the national interest. In addition, in most of continental Europe at this time, frondist activity was considered reactionary, and aristocratic "liberals" supported absolutist rule.[78] The domestic tragedy was that the Russian government, unlike those in the rest of Europe, did not eventually institute "clearly defined private and public rights" and remained a state where "laws rule by means of men and not men by means of laws."[79]

Official coronation portrait of **Anna Ioannovna.** *Opisanie koronatsii . . .*

Moscow, 1730, Frontispiece

Whether another outcome of the February Days would have one day resulted in rule by law will never be known, but the actual outcome indicated a new consensus on the conception of monarchy.[80] The Russian elite had demonstrated that they wanted an absolute monarch, who was a Romanov; who ruled in partnership with them as signified by an electoral process; and who, although Orthodox, would be dedicated to the common good as signified by a program of secular reform. In accordance with these conceptions, the new monarch justified her power on the basis of popular consent, royal lineage, and adherence to the Petrine tradition of reform. The accession manifesto of February 28 noted the disarray of the past weeks and announced the resolute conclusion: "And since all our loyal subjects unanimously asked that We deign to accept Autocracy for Our Russian Empire, as had our forefathers from the earliest times, We have so deigned." Although her Romanov ancestry was mentioned, for the rest of the century it was recognized that Anna came to the throne "by election, not by blood."[81] The empress dissolved the Supreme Privy Council, and its members were all eventually exiled or executed. She quickly restored the Petrine senate, returned the capital to St. Petersburg, reaffirmed the 1722 succession decree, described herself as a "Christian Autocrat" rather than as an Orthodox tsar, and passed a flurry of reforms that responded to the problems raised by the nobility during the February Days.[82] Two years after her accession, Anna claimed to have reestablished a "regulated" state in Russia, and scholars have concluded that her reign "on balance . . . was one of good management and positive achievement" in both domestic and foreign policy.[83]

Once the maelstrom had subsided, leading members of Russia's educated elite, with no official encouragement, justified the outcome of the February Days in their sermons, odes, and memoirs. As Wortman noted, "the compact between throne and nobility was sealed" in 1730, and writers rushed to celebrate the unity of purpose, praising Anna as "Mother of all the nobility."[84] Feofan, whom Anna greatly admired, stood at the center of a "Scholarly Guard" hailing Anna as an elected monarch and defending absolute monarchy in Petrine terms.[85] He recognized that "sovereign power" was transferred to her "from the entire people," and the rhetoric of other orators repeated that her rule "was established by popular choice."[86]

Prokopovich used his coronation festival speeches as advice literature to remind Anna and his audience of the normative standards governing absolute rulers: "It was not enough for her to repair what had been damaged, she conceived ways to bring new benefits to the fatherland." Russia's advances in arts, crafts, and sciences; the building of cities, roads, and border fortifications; the strengthening of the military; the expansion of the empire; care for the old and the orphaned; the revitalization of trade and the merchantry; the country's prestige: "All these benefits and gains come to us from our autocrats."[87] Tatishchev, who also worked to identify absolute power with progress and other forms of government with backwardness, opined that "one can see how our monarchical form of government is more beneficial than other forms since with it our wealth, strength, and glory increase, while with others they dwindle and perish."[88] Prince Antiokh Kantemir, another member of the guards and Russia's first satirist, used his literary gifts to establish an equation between opponents of reform and ignorant clergy, fops, old beards, and other unattractive sorts. His "Petrida," written between March and August of 1730, was offered to Anna as a guide for imitating her uncle's reforms.[89] Russia's first native member of the Academy of Sciences, Vasilii Trediakovskii, also encouraged his ruler: "What Peter began, Anna will perfect, adorn, and multiply. . . . She will summon back the exiled arts and sciences."[90]

However, a dark side overshadowed the reign. The leading reason for limiting monarchical power is to prevent tyrannical behavior, and Anna, ironically, proved the need for restrictions on absolutist rulers. Brutal collection of taxes, persecution of the old aristocracy, and the reinstitution of a secret chancellery—which tortured, exiled, and executed even suspected political enemies—led to the identification of the 1730s with a reign of terror.[91] Police reports recorded that Anna was being reviled as an "extortionist," a "dog" surrounded by "foreign scoundrels," who caused a "great weeping" by taking recruits and horses from her people, giving nothing in return, and leaving them in "ruin."[92] A dozen pretenders arose claiming to be Peter's son or grandson.[93] Among the elite, the empress's favorite, Bühren (later changed to Biron for a touch of French panache), the Duke of Courland, became feared as the architect of the *Bironovshchina* and hated because of his disdain of all things Russian.[94] Although he held no official post, he wielded the major influence in court and cabinet, which became heavily populated with fellow Germans.[95]

In response to these developments, the membership of the "Scholarly Guard" widened to about thirty and included many people educated abroad, officers of the guards, archbishops, and Elizabeth's personal physician. They discussed their dissatisfaction with German "dogs" running the government, the atmosphere of fear in the capital, the lack of policies that would benefit the common good, and the need for a native assembly of noblemen to help Anna formulate a program of wide reform. Artemii Volynskii, a member of the circle and of the old nobility as well as a stalwart "fledgling of Peter's nest," rose to the office of cabinet minister and decided to approach the empress. In the tradition of the petition, he presented her with a "Project for the Reform of State Affairs" that his confidants thought "will be better than *Télémaque*" as a normative guide to monarchical behavior.[96] He and two other members of the circle were arrested, interrogated, and underwent a hideous public execution. The hangings and mutilations shocked the population of St. Petersburg, both high and low, especially since the men were all respected Russian officials, and Volynskii was the perceived leader of the "Russian party" at court.[97] A popular song began circulating at the time, with the verse:

The tsar no longer rules us
And it is not a Russian prince who issues orders,
Instead, it is the evil tyrant from Germania
Who commands, who amuses himself.[98]

The perception that Russia was being run by foreign despots challenged the legitimacy of the government.

THE CONCEPT OF LEGITIMACY AT MIDCENTURY

Anna's designation of an heir exacerbated the notion of a German captivity of the Russian throne and rendered justification of her successor's power problematic.[99] Just before her death in October 1740, the empress named as heir Ivan Antonovich, the two-month-old son of her niece Princess Anna of Mecklenburg and Prince Anton Ulrich of Braunschweig-Lüneburg; the infant was three-quarters German, and his parents were baptized Lutherans.[100] Mikhail Lomonosov, usually a facile odist, could only bring himself to recognize Ivan as a "branch of a tsarist breed" and, reaching, recalled Riurik's Prussian ancestry.[101] In another unpopular move, Empress Anna appointed Biron to manage the government until the infant came of age. Although the duke tried to reinvent himself as a reforming regent, he lasted in office for only twenty-two days, and then he made the usual trek to Siberia.

Ivan VI's mother announced her assumption of the duties of regent in a manifesto that tried to conform to the etiquette of accession by explaining the change "as a result of the humble and sincere wish and request of all Our loyal subjects," but the election was fictional, and widespread trouble arose during the administration of the oath.[102] Her regency lasted a bit over a year. Certainly not meeting the criterion of "fitness," the regent was poorly educated and indolent, "spending most of her time lying on a couch or at the card table."[103] Her husband, Prince Anton, intrigued to obtain the title of regent for himself, jealous as he was of Anna's position and of her intimate relations with both Count Karl Lynar and Fräulein Julia Mengden (reaching for a curious ménage à trois, Anna planned for her lovers to marry). Anna and Anton quarreled constantly while ministers, both Russian and German, took sides with one or the other. In the circumstances, the government became dysfunctional, reform projects were ignored, and the impression became ever stronger that Germans were fighting over the spoils of the Russian throne; even the Swedes offered to send an army to get rid of the carpetbaggers.[104]

Although barely noted in the historical literature, a major reason for public dissatisfaction with the Germans focused on their intent to effect a change of dynasty.[105] Archival documents demonstrate an intense preoccupation over the issue of succession, and for good reason: infant mortality rates throughout Europe averaged 50 percent. Secret protocols of about a

Depiction of the infant **Ivan VI**, with German shields above his crib and a
German translation of the Latin inscription. D. A. Rovinskii, *Materialy dlia russkoi . . .*
St. Petersburg, 1884–90, vol. 7, no. 241

dozen meetings—most conducted in German with the minutes translated into Russian—reveal bitter infighting, but all sides agreed that no solution would be valid without the imprimatur of Russia's electorate. Anna's faction wanted to declare her empress and to restrict her successors to Ivan's future brothers and sisters if he died without issue. Denying the rights of Peter the Great's daughter, Elizabeth, and his grandson, Karl Peter of Holstein, signified that the House of Braunschweig would replace the House of Romanov as the ruling dynasty. Anna maneuvered to unite the clans, but Elizabeth refused to marry Anton's brother.[106] After negotiating among the factions for about a year, Anna lost patience and decided to issue a manifesto, dispensing with any demonstration of the will of "the people." Archbishop Amvrosii of Novgorod insisted that she had to honor the "custom" of election as it had become "a fundamental law of the Empire," but she ignored the prelate's warnings.[107]

Elizabeth was waiting in the wings and walked on stage as an elected monarch. Peter the Great's daughter was now thirty-three years old, desirous of the throne, and worried that Regent Anna might force her to take the veil. Recognizing that she had wide support, early in the morning of November 25, 1741, Elizabeth knelt before an icon vowing there would be no shedding of blood, roused the guards, proceeded to the palace, and easily toppled this "government of foreigners."[108] Demonstrating a forceful transition and a sure grasp of the new etiquette of accession, Elizabeth readied the mandatory manifesto within hours of the coup.[109] She also understood the seriousness of the oath. Within twenty-four hours, two officials and a secretary were stationed in every church in the capital with copies of the oath and manifesto ready to sign, with the orders that "no one was to be overlooked." The oath was published in all the provinces and military units and translated into German in the appropriate districts; the ritual proceeded smoothly.[110] However, Elizabeth disenfranchised the serfs and continued the Romanovs' dismissive treatment of Russia's bonded labor force.

In the accession manifesto, the new empress admitted that Ivan held legal appointment to the throne, but overriding that consideration, she justified the seizure through claiming election. She was the choice of the people, she claimed, to save them from the grim rule of the regents, who had brought "such unrest and disorder that the country was threatened with ruin": "All Our loyal subjects, both clerical and lay, and especially Her Majesty's Own Guard, beseeched Us." For the rest of the century, it was commonplace to praise Elizabeth's accession as the "wish of the people."[111]

Elizabeth in truth had supporters galore, both for dynastic and nationalistic reasons; one memoirist recalled that backing for her was "certainly general in Russia."[112] It was reported that when her carriage rode through the streets of Petersburg, "people shouted to her to ascend the throne of her ancestors."[113] Her manifesto was the first to use the adjective *otecheskii* (paternal or of the fatherland), which emphasized her "legal right [to rule] by dint of the closest blood tie" as Peter I's and Catherine I's daughter, while Ivan was only a grandnephew of Peter the Great via a half brother and was three-quarters German. Throughout her reign, she relentlessly depicted herself as The Daughter *(Dshcher')*, who signified the return of "Russian blood" to the throne (Livonian mother notwithstanding).[114] Actually, Karl Peter of Holstein should have succeeded, according to Catherine's "Testament," but he was thirteen years old and would have presented the prospect of another regency, presumably of Germans. In addition, as Elizabeth pointed out, the "Testament" stipulated that the successor be Orthodox and not in possession of another crown; Karl Peter was a baptized Lutheran who was heir to the Swedish throne.

Soon after her seizure of power, Elizabeth issued two more manifestoes justifying her legitimacy in more detail before the tribunal of the educated elite.[115] She accused the major participants in the regency of treason for not honoring the electoral process; as evidence, she pointed to their plot to change the dynasty without consulting the senate, synod, and *generalitet*.[116] Yet another sign of legitimacy was lacking; the regents, "godless criminals all," were "spoiling the work that Peter the Great had accomplished for the common good." Elizabeth promised to undo these "violations" and restore the senate so that the administration would operate "the way it did when Our Father . . . and Our Mother" were monarchs; she conveniently forgot that Mother was dominated by the Supreme Privy Council.

To make her case even stronger, the new empress exaggerated that the very legitimate Ivan never had "any claim, lineage, or right" to the throne, which "invidious" ministers had twice "stolen" from her, the "legal heir." She attempted to obliterate his reign by ordering the public burning of all edicts, manifestoes, coins, documents, etc., that bore his name or likeness, and she ordered the alteration of the official collection of laws so that his name never appeared, rendering him a "non-monarch."[117] In another Stalinesque move, she supposedly attended the trial of the regent's government and listened secretly from behind a curtain. Any ex-monarch while alive always represents a threat, and the infant was inhumanly incarcerated in the Schlüsselburg Fortress, where he would spend the rest of his miserable life.[118] In the final episodes of the drama, those connected with the regency, including Mengden and the entire Braunschweig family, were subjected to confiscation of property and exile, and the new "outs" passed the former exiles streaming back into the capital after Elizabeth had granted them political amnesty. Also in keeping with the etiquette of accession, the guards who had participated in the coup received estates, promotions, and money.[119] Five months later, Elizabeth staged a splendid coronation that enacted a "scenario of rejoicing" at The Daughter's saving Russia from ruin and introducing a golden age.[120] In November, to escape the mistakes of the past, she named her nephew, who was now an orphan, as heir; Karl Peter of Holstein was brought to the court, gave up the right to the Swedish crown, and accepted Orthodoxy.[121]

Elizabeth clothed herself in layers of legitimacy. She justified her coming

(above) **Elizabeth I.** *Russkii graver Chemesov.* St. Petersburg, 1878, no. 4

(right) Detail from a map of St. Petersburg in which the words being engraved celebrate **Elizabeth I** as the daughter *(Dsher')* of Peter the Great. M. Makhaev, *Novoi Plan stolichnago goroda,* 1776.

to the throne principally on elective grounds, and once in power, she projected the interlocking images of Peter's direct offspring and of a Petrine-model reforming tsar. In Weberian terms, she acquired two additional types of legitimate authority besides being the choice of the people: the traditional, through heredity; and the charismatic, through routinization of the duty to reform.[122] In addition, Elizabeth had always been a sincere believer, and she wore the traditional mantle of Orthodox ruler well.[123] Writers accepted and celebrated all these signs of legitimacy.

For the next twenty years, the empress was mythologized as Peter's branch *(otrasl')*, his fruit *(plod)*, or simply The Daughter *(Dshcher')*, a word with biblical overtones that she proudly wore as an additional title. Russians displayed a strong preference for legitimacy based on heredity, and Elizabeth was extolled in all her reflected glory in a constant stream of poetry and prose publications, which often devoted half their length to The Father's deeds.[124]

By the time Elizabeth assumed power, writers had also accepted the idea of the reforming tsar who oversees the country's progress as an abstract and generalized criterion for judging "fitness" and justifying absolute power. Nearly every ode, manifesto, or sermon that defined the duty of a monarch made Peter's program its central theme; from 1725 to 1760, in 125 of 129 odes and speeches on the topic of royal responsibility, no other member of the Riurikid or Romanov dynasty is named as a model. In complete contrast to conceptions of monarchy at the beginning of the century, the former antichrist now figured as a legendary hero, and those branded "heretics" were the opponents of reform.[125] During Elizabeth's first years in power, writers concentrated on her having saved the Petrine legacy and Russia itself from "alien hands." Evgenii Anisimov counted an unprecedented 120 sermons on political themes in the first three years of her reign that congratulated her resolution "to cast out those night owls and bats seated in the nest of the Russian eagle, to capture and defeat the perfidious despoilers of the fatherland, to tear from alien hands the legacy of Peter the Great." Other prelates rued that in the previous decade a person was arrested "simply because he was . . . a student of Peter the Great," and Russians "slept while the foreign brood undermined" Peter's deeds. Pamphlets, newspaper articles, plays, and odes repeatedly hailed Elizabeth as the "Atlas," who had ousted the "monstrous tyrant."[126]

As a ruler, the empress fostered enough reform to make her image as Peter's political heir credible.[127] Viktor Naumov credits Elizabeth with being a "subtle politician," who was qualified to rule and played a personal role in both major and trivial decisions, at least in the beginning of her reign.[128] Later, she reverted to her lifelong taste for amusement and finery, as attested by the fifteen thousand dresses left in her wardrobe when she died. In the spirit of advice literature, on the sixth anniversary of her accession, Lomonosov preached that she should be a servant of the state, a working tsaritsa, a "queen bee," and reminded her in vain of Peter's simplicity in dress.[129] Her popularity continued, though, since she had the talent to pick as her favorites able men who oversaw programs of useful change; Aleksei Razumovskii dominated the court in the 1740s and the Shuvalov brothers in the next decade. Naumov concludes that her reign was pivotal: "It was she who brought Russia into the channel of unhurried and measured development after the vast upheavals of Peter's epoch, the short-sighted experiments of the members of the Supreme Privy Council, and the terror of the 'Biron era.'"[130] In fact, Elizabeth provided a more palatable version of a reforming tsar: she offered progress but without the trauma and force that had been the hallmarks of her father's reign. Her abolition of the death penalty symbolized the more humane conception.[131]

In the spirit of dialogue, prominent writers responded to Elizabeth's discourse of justification with advice literature. During her reign, a remarkable cultural flowering took place, and the increased size and sophistication of the educated elite provided the opportunity for wider discussions of monarchy. Men returning from their education abroad and students graduating from institutions such as the Cadet Corps consciously worked to build a new secular and civic culture; they translated French and German works, set up circles, sponsored theatres, and submitted projects of reform.[132] Foreigners working in Russia were no longer drawn from the ranks of technicians, as in Peter's reign, but now included writers, painters, sculptors, architects, actors, and professors. The leading lights of this generation—Kantemir, Trediakovskii, Lomonosov, and Sumarokov—were fully literate in contemporary Western thinking and oversaw a coterie of native writers enthusiastic about their potential to help modernize their country.[133] Authors believed that they reflected and often formed the opinions of their audience, and they regarded their literary works as active participation in political life. Their influence was augmented because powerful patrons often supported the leading literati; for instance, Razumovskii sponsored Sumarokov, and Ivan Shuvalov collaborated with Lomonosov on founding Moscow University and editing a journal, *Monthly Essays (Ezhemesiachnyia sochineniia)*.

When writing advice literature, authors at midcentury preferred the genres of odes, tragedies, and journal articles for communicating with their monarch and their readers. With Lomonosov's example, the solemn ode became the most highly regarded literary form of the century and established the poet's role as civic spokesman.[134] On the surface, odes idealized their monarchs in the tradition of the justification from virtue; Lomonosov, for instance, described Elizabeth as "virtue resplendent on the Russian throne," and Stephen Baehr has analyzed the splendid artistry and artifice involved in such praise.[135] But, as in other European states, the panegyric also served as a tactful form of instruction, describing the ruler not "as he was but as one hoped he might be."[136] Through their odes, writers updated the agenda for a reforming tsar in a way that reflected a new wave of Enlightenment influence; as Raeff has noted: "The Russian nobleman of Elizabeth's time, less than one generation after the death of Peter the Great, bore no resemblance to his grandfather, or even father."[137] While the older generation of supporters of reform—for instance Prokopovich and Tatishchev who were born in the 1680s—focused their energy on secularization and criticizing traditional practices, the next generation, born in the early decades of the century, isolated the promotion of education as the "core" of all other progress and a prime legitimizing activity for monarchs. "Peter our father founded schools," Prince Kantemir proclaimed and then warned rulers to fear "the judgment of an all-powerful Providence . . . if all measures are not employed for the propagation of knowledge in the fatherland, of what is most precious of all in its life." Sumarokov tersely phrased the new priority: "Trade enriches, the military defends, but learning enlightens a state"; he likewise threatened that Russia would perish without the dissemination of knowledge and meet the fate of Rome. A younger poet, Nikolai Popovskii, repeated both aspects of the theme: "Through your augmenting knowledge / Appears the Petrine vision and spirit."[138]

Lomonosov, the most brilliant man of the epoch, made even more central the conception of ruler as educator. A bold practitioner of advice literature, this son of a peasant believed it was his duty to teach monarchs theirs. In over twenty odes and essays, his most characteristic verb was *obnovit'* (reform or renew), and his tone, while laudatory, was didactic.[139] The Daughter deserved praise only if she imitated her father and specifically in the area of enlightenment. While Peter "wanted to enlighten Russia" and "sowed the seeds," much work remained: "The wise monarch has the foresight to see as her necessary task the dissemination of every type of knowledge in the fatherland." Elizabeth should "open wide the door to learning across Russia, and know . . . that, having disseminated it, Russia will acquire new expanse, new adornment, new enlightenment . . . and she will leave the night of barbarism far behind." Also a scientist, Lomonosov the polymath—whom Pushkin called Russia's first university—promoted the value of studying ship and canal building, metallurgy, chemistry, astronomy, geography, and exploring the riches of Siberia, in fact any subject that would harness the "force of nature," the leading concern of the Middle Enlightenment among deists like Lomonosov. Sometimes, monarchs follow advice. In 1755, Elizabeth ordered the founding of Moscow University, and in 1756 the Academy of Fine Arts in St. Petersburg, claiming that she was "rushing to propagate all useful knowledge . . . for the common good, in imitation of Peter, the *obnovitel'* of our country."[140]

A second didactic theme in odes concerned issues of war and peace. Peter, once again, served as the ideal because he did not neglect domestic reform, whether in the tool industry or in matters of justice, despite the long and costly war with Sweden. Similarly, Elizabeth received praise in the midst of war for promoting commerce and manufacturing, establishing banks for nobility and merchantry, patronizing the Academy of Sciences, and in general for "placing higher than the sounds of the war, / The beauty of the sciences."[141] When wars were in progress, writers were equivocal. They spoke of armed conflicts as necessary evils and justifiable only when defensive. While constantly counseling peace, they occasionally applauded some military entanglements because, for instance, they were waged against "barbaric Turks."[142] Sumarokov rejoiced when the war with Sweden ended in 1743: "We leave the battles and the victories, / The bloody sword is set aside."[143] On the eve of the Seven Years' War, the poet advised against entangling alliances: "Do not look for bloody wars / That sacrifice your subjects." Once the conflict was in progress, however, he hailed Elizabeth as an Alexander the Great and welcomed Russia's new proud standing: "All Europe needs your sword, O Russia."[144] Lomonosov warned Elizabeth about becoming embroiled in the War of the Austrian Succession: "Be still the fiery sounds"; and during the Seven Years' War, he regularly called upon Elizabeth to be "an angel of peace," end the conflict, and "banish wars from the earth," but at the same time he applauded the victories over Prussia.[145]

Toward the end of Elizabeth's reign, the first nongovernmental journals were launched, and their initial forays in the genre of advice literature also included objections to the Seven Years' War. In one "dream" with a pacifist theme, a student at Moscow University is escorted up a mountain path trod by monarchs who succumbed to their passions and fell victim to pride, vanity, and vainglory. He meets Alexander the Great, with whom Elizabeth had often been compared in odes, but Alexander is condemned for having failed to realize that true glory comes with improving the general welfare, not with military conquest and its "bloodletting" and "laying waste." On another mountain path, the path of true glory, the guide meets Augustus, Marcus Aurelius, and Peter the Great as those whose policies embodied reason, virtue, and concern for their subjects rather than the fighting of unnecessary wars.[146] Other articles repeated similar definitions about true glory and the need for monarchs to imitate Marcus Aurelius rather than Alexander the Great; but they added further advice: the age-old warnings to rely on good and virtuous counselors and to avoid flattery and luxury.[147]

During Elizabeth's reign, the novel emerged as another popular vehicle for discussing political issues. In 1749, Trediakovskii translated one of the best-known examples of advice literature in Europe; John Barclay had introduced *Argenis* as a novel that intended to show "how a sovereign should act and how to run a state." Published originally in 1621, it defended absolute monarchy against aristocratic pretensions and hence, in Russia, could be read as a political allegory of recent events. A "true" king staves off a powerful aristocratic revolt, which he understands would bring ruin upon the country (1730). A sage Nikopomp (Prokopovich) passionately defends the monarchical principle, which alone can provide for the common good. In another scene, the good but aging King of Sicily, Meleander (Peter), decides to entrust his kingdom to his young and virtuous daughter, Argenis (Elizabeth). As during the February Days or in Prokopovich's *Pravda*, the political digressions of the mentor Nikopomp follow traditional arguments: the potential malfunctioning of democracies and aristocracies are more to be dreaded than absolute monarchies; the hereditary principle has the disadvantage that sometimes an infant (Ivan VI) comes to the throne, but it provides stability and continuity. Throughout the novel, the sage delivered severe lectures concerning the danger of flatterers and favorites who entrap the monarch and ruin the state with their factionalism. But the strongest and most constant advice, predictably, was to avoid tyranny: "How pernicious this evil! O! . . . The powers of tsars like god's; / Such madness blinds all peoples! / They do not see how a tyrant weighs them down!"[148]

Tragedies in this century provided yet another popular vehicle for engaging in political discussion. For instance, during the reign of Ivan VI, Elizabeth, a lover of theatre, enjoyed seeing plays that depicted princesses, who, after much adversity, reclaimed their rightful thrones.[149] Once she had fulfilled her fantasy, political themes became a staple in drama and were one reason for the theatre's extraordinary popularity. A succession of plays qualified as advice literature. Whether their moralizing was mild or pointed, they established norms of behavior and a standard of conduct to which a monarch should conform and by which the public judged performance in office. Lomonosov's historical tragedies supplemented his odes in depicting the monarch as a figure of "utopian stature and symbol of timeless political virtues" like wisdom and generosity.[150] In addition, Lomonosov wrote plays that indicated his definition of monarchical legitimacy. *Tamira and Selim*, set in the fourteenth century, tells of a despot forcing the heroine into marriage, the usual signifier in fiction of overall tyranny; the tyrant, Khan Mamai, meets his just fate by suffering defeat in battle and dying at the hands of the righteous Selim.[151] In *Demofont*, which Lomonosov wrote for Elizabeth because she was bored, the hero is deemed unworthy to rule because he lacks constancy and virtue.[152]

Sumarokov was the midcentury master of advice literature. He believed that drama should depict civic virtue rather than private passion and showed his audience what they should demand of their monarchs and what they should fear in them. His concepts would flower into a central theme of political discourse during the reign of Catherine II, whom he supported for the throne from the late 1750s.[153] In his political attitudes, the playwright was motivated by his hatred of despotism. He searched both in Western thinking and in conversations with Russian statesmen, for instance Nikita Panin, for ways to prevent any recurrence of tyranny in Russia, which had only recently experienced the *Bironovshchina*.[154]

Sumarokov characterized a legitimate monarch as one who ruled on the basis of laws, not whim or "passion," and he offered this legal justification as the only real answer to the age-old problem that absolute monarchy can so easily degenerate into tyranny. His *Khorev* was first staged in 1750 at the new Imperial Theatre in St. Petersburg at Elizabeth's request. Kii, the Prince of Kiev, sighs: "O heavy the burden of the purple and the crown! / Everywhere under the sun roars the royal passion, / For turning great power into tyranny." The solution was for the monarch to rule not through force of arms, but according to the unwritten "laws of nature."[155] In Sumarokov's very loose adaptation of *Hamlet,* the eponymous hero saves his people from tyranny. In the first act, the conflict is established: Polonius claims that a tsar "is a God, not a man" and "above the law, possessing all authority," but Gertrude retorts that a "wise tsar" is a father who avoids flattering advisors and rules according to "laws."[156] In *Aristona* as well as in *Sinav and Truvor,* Sumarokov's heroines languish because they are forced to marry rulers against their will. These monarchs are duly branded tyrants, who exhibit no "control over passions," who listen to the "flattering words" of favorites rather than wise counselors, and who rule in arbitrary fashion rather than according to the laws.[157]

Sumarokov continued this legal justification of monarchy in his prose, but moved from a reliance on unwritten to codified law. He became dissatisfied with the government, starting in 1756, when Elizabeth's health began to fail, and her favorites took control of policy. In 1759, culminating a series of journal articles suggesting various needed reforms, he published an alternative view of beneficent rule in his newly founded independent journal, the *Industrious Bee.*[158] His "Dream of a Happy Society" criticizes Elizabeth, indirectly of course, for her indolence in office, aloofness from her subjects, dreams of military glory, and inattention to needed reform projects, such as educating the clergy or codifying the laws."[159] His ideal society is run by "a great man whose unflagging care . . . results in the prosperity of the people subject to him." His chosen assistants "are honest, intelligent, and skillful in their work." This good ruler listens patiently to everyone and never thinks about his own glory. Learning and freedom of conscience characterize his realm and the clergy resemble enlightened Stoics.[160] Although Sumarokov came from an old Muscovite family, his utopian state was based on equality of opportunity: "The son of a peasant has as much a right to become a great lord as does the son of a magnate."

Of greatest significance, Sumarokov's "Happy Society" revived the idea—expressed by the nobility in 1730 and never forgotten—of sharing power with the monarch and thus preventing despotism. In the utopia, a state council is the highest political body and oversees all governmental matters either at the behest of the monarch or on its own initiative. The council appoints judges, who dispense justice swiftly and honestly. These civilians supervise military affairs and condone only defensive wars. The council had also codified the laws in a brief, masterful document, based on the Golden Rule and natural law. Sumarokov's dream described a diligent monarch coruling with the state's most talented citizens on the basis of fundamental laws to the benefit of society as a whole. This vision would hold the greatest appeal in the next reigns.

At midcentury, writers continued to respect traditional signs of legitimacy and expected their rulers to be Orthodox and members of the Romanov clan. But more modern measurements had taken root as well. Literary works, and even peasant lore, reflected a demand that only reforming tsars occupy the Russian throne and project a progressive image that matched contemporary perceptions of needed policy in domestic and foreign affairs.[161] In addition, the February Days, the *Bironovshchina*, and Sumarokov's plays had, each in its own way, raised the age-old specter of tyranny. In the second half of the eighteenth century, the public dialogue spelled out another ingredient in the Russian conception of rulership: to offset the possibility of despotism, a monarch was to operate on the basis of the rule of law.

CHAPTER FOUR

The Legal Sovereign

*R*ulers, royal subjects, and political theorists had long worried that absolute monarchy all too easily crossed the line into despotism. The Russian case was especially acute. Like many political tourists over the centuries, Adam Olearius, an emissary to Muscovy, regarded despotism as the country's habitual form of government and opined that the subjects "remain tranquil in slavery and terror."[1] During her long reign from 1762 to 1796, Catherine II the Great aimed to break the identification of Russian monarchy with despotism—in the minds of her own citizens and in the minds of other Europeans. The educated elite embraced this objective. The political ideals of the Enlightenment and the moderate rule of Elizabeth had engendered an impatience with heavy-handedness; indeed, Peter III's display of despotic tendencies during his brief tenure became so resented that his ouster was welcomed. When Catherine seized the throne late in June of 1762, she claimed to embody a new and improved version of the Russian monarchy, a polity to be based on the rule of law and on institutionalized procedures rather than on royal whim or caprice. Ironically, while vowing to cloak herself in the mantle of legality, Catherine came into power by unseating her husband, who had clear legal right to the throne. Nonetheless, Peter's actions had weakened his claim to legitimacy, while Catherine's first several years in office witnessed a honeymoon period with the educated elite, whom she engaged in dialogue and with whom she purposefully forged a partnership in building a state that conformed to the latest criteria laid down by the philosophes of the European Enlightenment. In her justification literature, she promised rule of law, equality before the law, division of power, and security of person and property, and she fulfilled much of her program.

PETER III AND THE PROBLEM OF LEGITIMACY

Peter III retained his imperial position for only six months, and historians entertain diverse opinions about the reasons for the brevity of his reign. Two facts, though, remain uncontested. First, Peter had every legal right to the throne. Twenty years before her death on Christmas Day of 1761, Empress Elizabeth sought the now customary approval of the senate, synod, and *generalitet* to appoint her nephew heir, and the populace took an oath vowing to support her choice; a stable succession seemed assured.[2] And yet, despite having a seemingly unassailable mandate to rule, the second fact remains that Peter's wife, who had no legal claim to power, had little trouble cutting short his reign on June 28, 1762.

By the mid-eighteenth century, Russian monarchs were expected to justify their power and thereby establish their legitimacy in some form of public dialogue with the elite. The evidence demonstrates that a major reason Peter lost the throne involved his losing the legitimacy he originally possessed because of a propensity to "command," rather than rule through consensus.[3] Welcoming his overthrow, those disaffected brought into play an underlying belief in a revocable contract between ruler and ruled. Catherine, in contrast, won her backing and mandate through a deft understanding of the process of justification and worked to muster support for herself and her policies in communication with the elite. She quickly established the full legitimacy that had eluded her husband. The drama that revolved around Peter's failure and Catherine's success brought into bold relief the Russian conception and demands of monarchy as they had developed from the beginning of the century until the 1760s.

Peter III only partially understood the subtleties of the new process of justification. For him, the issue seemed indisputably resolved on three grounds. His aunt had appointed him, the only objective legal basis for the right to rule; as the son of Peter the Great's daughter Anna, he could possess no more sterling or popular bloodline; and, upon ascending the throne, he played the role of reforming tsar to perfection thereby displaying his "fitness" for the throne. In addition, he was male; Iakov Shtelin, an academician and Peter's tutor, recalled that the guards greeted Peter's ascent with a strong sexist note: "Thank God! Finally, after so many women ruling Russia, we now once more have a male emperor!"[4]

Peter III's accession manifesto laconically affirmed that he had the sanction to rule "by right, by privilege, and by law." In tribute to the popularity of his aunt and grandfather, he promised to imitate Elizabeth's "generosity and mercy" and "in every way to follow in the footsteps of the wise Sovereign, Our Grandfather Emperor Peter the Great, and thus to restore prosperity to Our loyal Russian sons."[5] Even though acknowledging the importance of appointment, bloodline, and reform in earning legitimacy, Peter erred in underestimating the need at least to make a feint at establishing a partnership with the elite and a kinship with the broader population. The young emperor felt so secure in his power that he neglected the administration of the oath, and "many did not take it."[6] In the same confident spirit, he delayed his coronation and the public legitimacy it conferred; in the words of the memoirist Andrei Bolotov, he thus lost the opportunity "to attest his fidelity and devotion to his subjects."[7] More fatally, while his ascent required no election, he failed to seek the acquiescence and support of the senate, synod, and *generalitet;* instead, he alienated their members, who formed an essential prop of a monarch's power.

The political elite translated Peter's highhandedness as his belief—so dangerous and feared in a monarch—that he actually possessed unlimited power and could rule through royal dictate rather than consensus. By ignoring the elective or contractual aspect of governance, Peter raised the specter of despotism. The last instance had occurred not long before, during the *Bironovshchina* of the 1730s, and was associated with rule by Germans. Peter compounded his error of estranging the elite by showing preference for his paternal German roots and creating the impression that he would rule with advisors imported from his native Holstein, favoring the duchy's interests and Lutheranism over those of Russia and Orthodoxy.

Peter's errors in judgment played into the hands of his worried wife, whom he had also alienated and who feared being packed off to a convent.[8] Catherine, the former Sophie of Anhalt-Zerbst, in her nearly twenty years at Elizabeth's court, had become thoroughly russified, a devout Orthodox, an avid student of politics, and not averse to power. Catherine, along with her and Peter's eight-year-old son Paul, provided an appealing alternative to the seemingly dangerous proclivities of the husband and father.

Peter's short six months have been, predictably, dismissed in Hobbesian fashion as "brutish, stupid, and generally hopelessly inadequate," especially in contrast to the spectacular thirty-four-year reign of Catherine, soon to be called "the Great."[9] Her splendid, but spiteful, memoirs inaugurated the portrayal of Peter as a driveling idiot and herself as a spirited woman of intelligence; while she read Plato, he played with toy soldiers. Josef von Sternberg's *The Scarlet Empress* (1934) provides a vivid example of the traditional, and rather warped, image.[10] From this point of view, the overthrow appears to be a foregone conclusion.[11] On the other hand, historians who view Peter's reign favorably—notably Carol S. Leonard, Aleksandr Myl'nikov, and Sigurd Shmidt—provide so much evidence of a capable individual and enlightened rule that the overthrow might seem incomprehensible.[12] Indeed, the sensible direction of most of Peter's domestic and foreign policy is attested by the fact that Catherine continued his major initiatives.[13] The tragedy of this thirty-four-year-old monarch unfolded in his intelligent striving for legitimacy as a reforming tsar and then his loss of credibility through political actions that bespoke a despot.

At first, writers greeted Peter III with a burst of high hopes. The last years of his aunt's reign had brought disillusion because of a lackluster domestic policy and a costly involvement in the Seven Years' War. The new monarch, in contrast, seemed a harbinger of reforms and peace. The two leading midcentury littérateurs, Mikhail Lomonosov and Aleksandr Sumarokov, exulted that "the country of Russia once again meets Peter the Great," and in the now established tradition of advice literature, they offered a stream of suggested improvements from religious toleration to peace with Prussia. Other poets published odes in the newly founded journals with the same message of hope, advice, and weariness with the war effort; they admonished Peter to admire the many "trophies" won by Elizabeth but seek "renewed peace."[14]

Peter accepted the counsel of advice literature, and his domestic policies seemed destined to assure him wide popularity and a high place in the ranks of Europe's enlightened absolutist monarchs. The new emperor became actively involved in the political process and gathered together a stellar group of advisors so that reforms "might be put into action as quickly and as effectively as possible" and thus perfect the work of his grandfather and aunt.[15] Belying Catherine's depiction of her husband as indolent, during Peter's 186 days in office, he issued 192 decrees, 44 more than she passed during her first six months in power.[16]

In the spirit of enlightened absolutism and armed with the theories of the well-ordered police state, this reforming tsar reduced the hated salt tax, secularized church land, abolished the Secret Chancellery and its torture chambers along with the tradition of denunciation or *slovo i delo gosu-darevo,* while at the same time introducing the right of habeas corpus to prevent the "unfounded arrests and even torture" perpetrated in previous decades.[17] Thousands of political exiles were pardoned. Old Believers were invited to return from Poland under promise of toleration, a policy then extended to people of all faiths. Plans were drawn up for new asylums to house orphans, widows, and invalids and for urban improvements that included better policing and fire-fighting methods, sanitation, and street lighting. Merchants benefited from the abolition of government monopolies in cloth, cattle, and rhubarb and the loosening of restrictions on trade. Roughly one-seventh of the peasants were shifted into a category that exacted less taxation and led to rumors that Peter, as a humane, reforming tsar, intended to emancipate the serfs.[18]

Most famously, Peter III freed the nobility from obligatory service to the state—a hated burden for many since the time of Peter the Great—and aimed to release their energy for agricultural development and participation in provincial government and cultural life. In addition, the government offered the nobility loans at low interest rates and allowed the freedom to travel abroad or serve in the armies of Russia's allies. These and other long-sought benefits won the new monarch popularity and prompted poets to exclaim that each nobleman should "erect an altar in his heart" to the emperor.[19] Overall, as Marc Raeff concluded, the domestic policies of Peter III's government promoted Russia's "evolution toward 'modernity,'

Peter III. *Tsartvuiushchii dom Romanovybh . . .* 1913, pg. opp. 182

secularization, and increased economic activity, as well as 'bureaucratization.'"[20] Peter's chief minister, Dmitrii Volkov, in his memoirs, remembered that at the beginning of Peter's reign "it was easy to serve both the Fatherland" and the emperor because their "interests" so clearly coincided.[21]

Peter's subsequent attacks on the political elite and the German direction of his policies and tastes created a conviction that those "interests" no longer meshed. The emperor, by all counts, alienated the senate, synod, and *generalitet,* thereby losing essential support for rule. Raeff sees as crucial Peter's circumventing the senate in making policy.[22] Orthodox clergy were appalled by the new monarch's displaying a preference for the religion of his youth and building a Lutheran chapel at Oranienbaum, where he attended services and distributed hymn books. In further provocation, he ordered priests to shave their beards, to remove most icons from churches, and to dress in Protestant garb. In addition, his toleration of Old Believers, Catholics, and Freemasons may have been enlightened but was heretical to the clergy, and they concluded that it might not be amiss if Peter were cast aside even if they did not care to participate in any plots.[23] The members of the *generalitet* were not spared. David Ransel noted Peter's "head-on attack against the most powerful interests in the court and high administration."[24] Similarly, Isabel de Madariaga focused on his alienation of "all the powerful parties at court," while Myl'nikov recognized Peter's overall infringement on "the political and material interests of the ruling elite."[25]

Peter III replaced reliance on the senate, synod, and *generalitet* by deciding policy in camera with an inner circle of favorites, a practice that excluded the usual members of the ruling elite from power. A system of personalized power represented a dreaded regression to the time of the Supreme Privy Council or the ascendancy of the favorite, Biron, over Anna Ioannovna. Instead, the cherished desire of the ruling elite was to move forward toward sharing power with the monarch through regularized institutions and routinized legal procedures.[26] As Raeff summarized the situation, Peter's policy "clearly aimed at replacing the administrative chain of command that traditionally culminated in the senate with the personal authority of the monarch's new men."[27]

The universal loathing of a ruling elite for royal favorites was exacerbated by the perception that Peter III was germanizing his court. One memoirist, in fact, reported that the emperor remained popular "until the arrival of his Uncle Georg" from Holstein. With an unfailing knack for sending the wrong message, Peter planned to have him head Courland, Biron's old duchy.[28] The Russian ruler's love for his native Holstein and things German was so well known that Lomonosov's New Year's Day ode warned the new monarch to forget his German ancestry; he should prove himself "the fruit of Peter and Anna" and remember that Elizabeth came to the throne to "save the people from the danger" of German rule.[29] This flaw is not necessarily fatal; George I of England evinced more interest in his native Hanover than in his royal realm and kept the throne.[30] Peter, however, overplayed wearing his Holstein heart on his sleeve and displayed a "marked hatred and disdain for Russians."[31] He replaced the Life Company of the Guards—which had been responsible for putting his aunt on the throne and now consisted of the "flower of the nobility"—with Holsteiners and dressed other regiments in Prussian uniforms. Overall, as the scholar Nikolai Firsov concluded, the emperor made mistake after mistake, blinded by "German patriotism and miscomprehension of Russia."[32]

Of greatest importance, Peter's foreign policy reflected German interests that seemed deleterious to Russia.[33] An irrational reverence for Frederick II of Prussia led Peter to withdraw victorious Russian troops from the Seven Years' War in order to save his idol from sure defeat.[34] Perhaps overall a far-sighted decision, many contemporaries viewed pulling out of the war as ignominious.[35] Exacerbating the situation, while the emperor could have capitalized on the desire for peace, instead he embarked on a new campaign. He failed to see the folly, if not treason, of planning to use Russian troops to retrieve Schleswig for Holstein, which had lost the province to Denmark in 1721.[36] The war he would have provoked would have brought no advantage to the state over which he ruled but would have satisfied a personal hatred for the Danes that he had inherited from his father.

Charges of despotism and lack of "fitness" to rule could not but help circulate among the political elite. Demonstrating little common sense and political judgment, Peter became inaccessible, decided policy on the basis of personal whim, acted against advice in religious and foreign policy matters, and began the demotion and arrests of those who were not part of his "party." Contemporaries claimed that the people began to hate this "bad tsar."[37] His irritating personal traits, which ranged from rudeness to an obsession with soldiery, confirmed the picture of a budding tyrant.[38] Peter III appeared to possess all of his grandfather's negative, and unpopular, qualities —hyperactivity, lack of refinement, love of barracks life and horseplay, hatred of regal formality, disdain for clergy, love of things foreign, consorting with the lowborn—but without the redeeming political acumen, ability to command, or understanding of the tenor of the times. As Frederick II put it: "The poor Emperor wanted to imitate Peter I, but he didn't have his genius."[39] Of greatest consequence, Peter III failed to grasp that his grandfather's severe and willful, often despotic, style of rule was out of place in mid-eighteenth century Russia.

Peter III's myopia led him to believe that, as an autocrat, he actually possessed unlimited power and could do as he pleased; he thus committed the capital offense of despotism in the minds of the public. A Georgian bishop summarized the fear the monarch engendered: "Peter III, after the death of Empress Elizabeth, became an unlimited autocrat [*bezpredel'nyi samoderzhets*] and gave free reign to his whims and caprices."[40] Catherine had reached the same conclusion: "In the entire Empire he had no more savage enemy than himself."[41] As she explained: "He became conceited about his monarchical power . . . as though it by chance had fallen into his hands for his own satisfaction, and because of this he let his absolute power become forged with a despotic tendency in all matters of state."[42] A nineteenth-century historian, Vasilii Bil'basov, concurred and attributed Peter's failure as a monarch to a "sad combination of personal traits coupled with unlimited power."[43]

Catherine, like Elizabeth twenty years earlier, was waiting in the wings. Unlike her husband, she possessed enormous political talent and ambition and had worked to gain public favor, both in general and in particular among the "electorate," namely governmental figures, the clergy, and the guards. She was aware of her appeal and popularity as an alternative to Peter in progressive circles; for instance, already in 1759 Sumarokov publicly extolled the "enlightened" Catherine as similar to Peter the Great, a compliment usually reserved only for monarchs.[44] In an unpublished memorandum, Catherine claimed that Elizabeth, toward the end of her life, grew concerned that Peter was not "fit" to rule since "he did not like Russians." Ministers suggested that he return to his beloved Holstein, and Catherine succeed as regent for the young Paul.[45] Once Peter III mounted the throne, the intrigues continued, but as a legitimate heir he refused to believe that plots were being hatched against him.

Strangely, Peter did not fight Catherine's coup d'état when it took him by surprise on his name day, June 28, 1762. Despite his advisors' urging him to "show himself before the people and the guards and point out his ancestry and right," he was fatalistic, as though he knew he could never win against his formidable wife.[46] His whole demeanor was pathetic. Frederick II aptly summarized the moment: "He allowed himself to be put aside like a child trundled off to bed."[47] His letters begged for his mistress, poodle, violin, African servant, and passage abroad. His abdication announcement was meekness itself and agreed that he was unfit to govern.

> In the short time that I ruled the Russian state as an autocrat, I recognized that the burden and weight of rule was incompatible with my strength, that I was not capable of ruling the Russian state not only autocratically but under any other form of government. For this reason, I recognized an internal change in [the state], a veering toward the collapse of its integrity and, through me, to its becoming subject to eternal infamy. Because of this, impartially and freely, I hereby formally announce not only to the Russian state but to the whole world that I renounce the governance of the Russian state for all my life, not wishing to rule the Russian state either autocratically or as any other form of government.[48]

The twice-repeated phrase, "any other form of government," is curious, but perhaps tied in with rumors that Peter "conceived a design either to overturn the laws given to him by his aunt or to hand over the country to outsiders."[49] In other words, fears existed that the monarch might have thought of establishing some sort of Privy Council, presumably dominated by Holsteiners, or that being Frederick II's disciple might lead him to sacrifice Russian interests and/or territory to Prussia.[50]

Political theorists for centuries had waffled over the problem of a ruler who proved tyrannical through abuse of authority and thus illegitimate or "unfit"; they normally advised obedience since no agent could judge the monarch's behavior except public opinion and that was considered unreliable.[51] In the instance of Peter III, the political elite, led by Catherine, claimed to embody the wishes of "all the people" as they had when Elizabeth came to the throne and thus proved a surprisingly consequential force in the midst of an absolutist state.

CATHERINE II AND THE PROBLEM OF JUSTIFICATION

In addressing an ode to Catherine on the day of her accession, Lomonosov provided a historical justification by recognizing her seizure of power as part of a distaff tradition: "Thus also did Elizabeth come to the throne."[52] Indeed, except for the blood tie, Catherine repeated Elizabeth's coup in every detail; clearly, she had made a careful study of the precedent. The two women were almost exactly the same age, and both feared being cast into a convent; they promised bloodless revolutions and relied on seeking immediate support from the guards; they quickly and artfully sought the support of the rest of the population through a series of accession manifestoes and by paying careful attention to the administration of the oath; they both also claimed their essential legitimacy from popular election.

In the important first few hours after the seizure of power, Catherine, like Elizabeth, sought to cement her partnership with those members of the elite who had actually participated in the overthrow and to win the allegiance of those who learned of it after the fact. They both realized that their predecessors had failed to acknowledge the new importance of—and the need to open dialogue with—what had developed into an "electorate." They immediately issued accession manifestoes that condemned the overthrown monarch and justified the seizure of power; detailed explanations followed soon after. Catherine's second manifesto, dated July 19, 1762, was issued both by the ecclesiastical and civic presses. The apologia was rendered more complex because Peter had met with a violent end on the fifth of July.[53] While it is doubtful that Catherine ordered his death, she nonetheless needed to paint Peter in the blackest of colors so that capital punishment might seem warranted.

In both her accession manifestoes, Catherine's justification for seizing power provided a stunning practical application of Lockean contract theory.[54] The argument was straightforward. Peter, while legally appointed, had betrayed his office by pursuing despotic policies that placed the Russian state and tradition in jeopardy. Recognizing this, the elite had agreed to transfer loyalty to Catherine in the expectation she would better fulfill the conditions of the contract between ruler and ruled.

The manifestoes, perfect examples of justification literature, equated Peter's transgressions with treasonable offenses, which, in most societies, carry the death penalty. His reign had presented a "danger" to Russia on three counts: to its Orthodoxy, since Peter had begun a "destruction of its traditions" by threatening "to adopt another faith" and thus break a fundamental law of the empire; to "Russian glory," since Peter had concluded a peace treaty with the Prussian enemy that represented "virtual enslavement" and dishonored the soldiers who had shed their blood in the hostilities; to "internal order" and "unity" in general, since Peter "had little spirit for running such a great empire" and no regard for the "law of God . . . and the laws of nature and civic law." Catherine also accused Peter of outright villainy for his "disdain" of Elizabeth, his "hatred of the father-land," and his "persecution of . . . Our Son" in not naming him heir, as Russian tradition demanded. The breathless indictment continued. His other accursed sins included the "corruption" of the work of Peter the Great, a lack of interest in judicial affairs, the squandering of state revenues on a war "completely useless to the Russian state," and the prussianization of the army, which subverted the notion of fighting for "the Faith and the Fatherland."

The manifestoes accused Peter of the worst sin a monarch could commit, degenerating into a despot: "Absolute power, unrestrained by good and humane qualities, in a state that is ruled autocratically becomes the kind of evil that directly results in many disasters." Indeed, the entire population "began to tremble seeing over it a sovereign and wielder of power who was a slave to his passions" and who ignored the basic political principle of serving the "good of the state entrusted to him." No sterner indictment of a "bad tsar" could have been rendered, and the charges contained enough truth to make them convincing. The manifesto, of course, ignored Peter's beneficent policies, many of which Catherine would continue. Once enthroned, she met with the senate and rendered a more balanced verdict: "Notice how often it is not sufficient to be enlightened, having the best intentions and the power to execute them, but nonetheless often succumb to rash judgments when pursuing a wise course of action."[55]

Once having established Peter's guilt, the narrative then described the ineluctable results of such reprehensible monarchical behavior. Through these actions, Peter fomented a "national dissatisfaction," "an aversion to being subject to him," and lost the "allegiance of Russians." All this time, Catherine was suffering from a "broken heart" seeing the fatherland in such a sad state for which Peter was "the sole cause." While "many were ready to shed his blood," the Russian people were patient and trusted that "God's hand itself would intervene and alleviate the suffering of his people by causing [Peter's] fall." This idea had been propagated, for parallel reasons, during Elizabeth's reign; the speech of a Moscow University professor noted that tyrants were sent as punishment by God, but if the people prayed long and hard enough, God would hear their lament and change the ruler.[56] The hero and patriot attested that she had "neither the inclination nor the desire" to seize the throne, but the "hand of God" or "inscrutable providence" forced this upon her and lent her assistance "to save the country from the revolt and bloodshed" that tyrants foster. God's will and her own sense of obligation prompted Catherine to act. Once she took the lead, Russians rushed to her support.

More than any other theme, the manifestoes celebrated the new monarch's election at the hands of the people. She had decided, for Russia's salvation, to take power, and her decision was immediately seconded by the people. The manifesto equated endorsement with election: "Therefore, having armed Ourselves with sovereign power, no sooner had We an-

nounced our willingness [to rule] to the loyal subjects who had been selected and sent to Us by the people than we saw the general desire to declare allegiance to Us by people of the ecclesiastical, military, and civic
ranks." Catherine concluded, "We acquired the throne without any shedding of blood, but the one God and our beloved fatherland through its representatives assisted Us." One English commentator, startled by the elective
basis of Catherine's power, marveled that "the most absolute power on
earth is now held by an elective monarch."[57] In an elective monarchy, however, power is returned to the people only after the death of the sovereign.
This episode provided better evidence of the contract theory, wherein, to
quote Christian Wolff, a political theorist popular in Russia, "[s]upreme
sovereignty is originally with the people, and it remains the property of the
people." The monarch had betrayed his subjects and paid the price.[58] The
people decided to choose another, with Catherine the embodiment of their
will. For these reasons, Bolotov and others could hail this episode as the
Russian version of a "glorious revolution."[59] Later, Catherine would admit
that Russia had experienced many "revolutions" because "we never yet
could be patient under poor reigns." Continuing her identification with her
aunt by marriage, Catherine later wrote that the only reason for Elizabeth's
accession was that she was "the choice of the people" and described her
own reign as "based on the voice of the people."[60]

Election—the "love" of the people for her and their "clear desire" that
she rule—provided Catherine the only basis for claiming to be a "true sovereign." Like Catherine I, however, she tried to suggest appointment by
speaking of the "extraordinary love" Elizabeth showed her.[61] In the manifesto, she claimed to act "for the faith, for the fatherland, for Us, and Our
Heir." Paul clearly had the more legitimate claim to the throne, and many
expected and might have preferred that she act as regent for her eight-
year-old son. Perhaps remembering the fate of both Sofiia and Anna
Leopol'dovna, Catherine demanded power in her own right. This was also
part of the distaff tradition; all the female monarchs in the eighteenth
century took power even though a male Romanov was available. The new
monarch recognized popular preference for a rightful male heir, however,
and Paul figured prominently in the official oath, which was taken by
Russian subjects both to the mother and the son. At her coronation, a
Moscow University professor dutifully praised Catherine for her "extraordinary manliness" but concluded his speech by claiming that "Grand
Prince Paul Petrovich is our single hope for the restoration in Russia of
the family and seed of our Enlightener and Restorer, the Sovereign Emperor Peter the Great."[62] While the usual epithet of "true and born" ruler
was never used to describe Catherine's right to the throne, she nonetheless used her marital and maternal ties to perch herself on the Romanov
tree.[63] Not everyone among the populace accepted the official version of
events. A score of pretenders, Emilian Pugachev most prominently,
claimed to be the "rightful" tsar, Peter III.

The events of 1762 indicate that for the elite the electoral and contractual elements of power and Peter the Great's criterion of "fitness" had become paramount in determining legitimacy. In the peroration to her manifesto, Catherine promised policies and behavior that would make her "worthy of the love of Our people, for whom We recognize we were elevated to the throne." She promised to protect Orthodoxy, strengthen and defend the fatherland, preserve justice, extirpate evil, abjure despotic acts, imitate Peter the Great, and overall rule for the common good. These were the time-honored duties of a good tsar, and odes and sermons underlined their importance.[64] Catherine, however, was attuned to the demands of her times. With a modern sense of statecraft, she "gave her Imperial word" to rule by law:

> To enact the type of statutes by which the government of our beloved fatherland would maintain its rightful borders in strength and that even in the future each government position would have its limits and laws for the maintenance of good order in everything and thus we hope to preserve the integrity of the Empire and of Our Autocratic power.

She thus brought a new conception of monarchy to the fore, one based on legal precepts.[65] And well she might; a political maxim of the day suggested that "usurpers of states become their just princes when they give just laws."[66]

THE IDEA OF LEGAL MONARCHY

Catherine's promise to establish a "legal monarchy"—a central motif of political dialogue during her reign—attempted to remove the threat of despotism by establishing laws that would "tie a monarch's hands from doing evil."[67] In the 1750s, the ruling elite had realized that this newer conception of the relationship between them and monarchical power was the logical next step in the modernization of the Russian state. Despite the recurrence of unfit rulers, another form of government remained .out of the question. Sumarokov summarized the enduring preference for monarchy and its attendant dilemma when he remarked that "there is nothing better on earth than absolute power, when it is good, and nothing more disastrous to humankind than when wielded by one not worthy of the diadem."[68] Russians and most Europeans continued to maintain that democracy in a large country always proved "harmful" and inevitably caused the "revolts and discord" that led to anarchy.[69] The workings of an aristocracy resulted in equally dismal consequences. Prince Mikhail Shcherbatov, even though a public proponent of aristocratic privilege, rued the fact that his fellow magnates had proved time and again that they were unable to rule: "They prefer the interests of their own clans over the interests of the state and try to secure for all time positions and wealth for their own houses to the exclusion of others and oppress the common people, who are never so unhappy as under an aristocratic government."[70] Thus, political wisdom stipulated that large states had to make do with absolute monarchy, but at midcentury a new determination had emerged to install mechanisms designed to prevent the recurrent degeneration into despotism, or what Russians often called "unlimited autocracy" *(bezpredel'noe samoderzhavie).*[71] In his *Spirit of the Laws* (1749), Montesquieu reflected contemporary concern about abuse of power and intimated its frequency by adding despotism to monarchy, aristocracy, and democracy as a fourth category of government.

The Russian elite possessed a heightened awareness of the problem. Because of growing political sophistication and recent experience, a revulsion had developed against any repetition of Peter the Great's oppressive style of rule, although Russians continued to value his connection between absolutism and progress. In fact, the elite had deposed two regents and one emperor between 1740 and 1762, paradoxically, for both despotic behavior and not living up to the Petrine ideal. Grand Duchess Catherine had studied these concerns and demands during her political apprenticeship at Elizabeth's court, "long before acceding to the throne."[72] Writers constantly brought up the need for legal reform, and in the last eight years of the empress's reign a legislative commission had met intermittently, thus raising expectations.[73] Upon becoming empress, Catherine knew she must confirm her legitimacy both by equaling Peter the Great's record of progressive reform and by surpassing him through rule by law rather than by coercion.[74]

Throughout Europe, monarchs, Catherine included, adopted the policies that came to comprise enlightened absolutism and thus distanced themselves from the dreaded label of tyrant[75] Rulers no longer found their legitimacy in prescription, custom, or divine right but in a contractual political obligation to do good, and they justified their absolute power as an attribute needed to achieve the common welfare efficiently and quickly. In effect, this new doctrine spread Peter's identification between ruler and innovator across all Europe, and Catherine first earned the praise of philosophes through her nonpareil record as a reforming tsar. In the beginning of her reign, she responded to the perception that Russia needed a new cycle of invigorating change by announcing quite simply: "[S]tate your grievances; say where the shoe pinches you. We will try to reform it. I have no particular system. All I want is the common good."[76] Her administrative style incorporated this aim; when she appointed Iakov Sivers governor of Novgorod in 1764, for instance, she held twenty audiences with him the month before he left, to discuss reforms that ranged from village clergy to forest preservation.[77] Her early "reforming zeal" proved wide in its embrace: the reorganization of the senate, the procuracy, the armed forces, and the Baltic provinces; the continued secularization of church land; improvements in town planning, medical care, and public health; the abolition of most state monopolies; and a review of commercial policy.[78] While a new emphasis on foreign policy and the Pugachev Revolt in the early 1770s stemmed the tide of innovations, it never stopped entirely, and the later years of her reign witnessed such seminal accomplishments as the reorganization of local administration, a regularization of state finances, the issuance of a cameralist police ordinance, the definition of the rights of the nobility and townspeople, and proposals for an educational system.[79]

Besides the idea of the reforming ruler, the doctrine of enlightened absolutism also diffused throughout Europe Louis XIV's images as conqueror and Renaissance patron of culture. Respected eighteenth-century rulers displayed a foreign policy just as ambitious as their domestic program. During Catherine's reign, Russia expanded south, west, and east through conquest and colonization and achieved a greater place in the family of Europe than ever before in the state's history. Like the era of the Sun King, the Age of Catherine witnessed a flourishing of the arts and sciences because of the empress's conscious patronage.[80] Her ambitious agenda established a picture both at home and abroad of a hardworking, visionary monarch. By the 1770s, Voltaire enthusiastically identified Catherine with the cause of the Enlightenment in eastern Europe: "We are the lay missionaries who preach the cult of Saint Catherine, and we can boast that our church is quite universal."[81]

Reform, conquest, and cultural patronage did not obviate the problem of despotism. During the early Enlightenment, philosophes failed to be explicit about any limitations on the power of monarchs and instead flattered them for their unbounded ability to issue beneficial edicts. However, in roughly the last third of the century, a consciousness developed throughout Europe that rulers needed to add another item to their reforming agenda and accept a legal definition of their power. On Catherine's first day in power, Lomonosov lectured her: "Listen, earthly judges / And all you heads of state / Restrain yourselves from breaking rules / From breaking holy laws."[82] Responding to such demands, Catherine—along with the other enlightened absolutist rulers—attempted to take monarchy to an even more enlightened level and establish rule by law. These monarchs reached for "immortality" by setting themselves up as legal sovereigns, and saw themselves as leaders in the battle against despotism.[83]

Prior to the late eighteenth century, political thinkers relied on the "laws of God and nature" and man-made fundamental laws to prevent tyranny; neither proved very effective. Natural laws are fuzzy because of their general injunction to follow the Ten Commandments, the Golden Rule, and the bidding of a civilized conscience; in effect populations were left with the simple hope that the monarch would practice self-limitation in accordance with universal norms of behavior. Natural law nonetheless remained a vigorous concept since it encompassed the long-held view of government as patriarchal. Political texts ubiquitously visualized the "best and most natural form of government" as resembling a family with a father at its head and offering the "best hope for peace, liberty, and prosperity."[84] Fundamental laws usually referred to the handful of traditional rules and procedures that remained inviolate, for example the French Salic law that forbade a female monarch. In Russia, even the few such injunctions did not prove sacrosanct, because Peter I changed the succession law, which most European monarchies placed under the rubric of fundamental laws.

To rectify the inadequacies of natural and fundamental laws as bulwarks against despotism, political thinkers and enlightened absolutist rulers propounded a concept of an absolute monarchy based on rule by law, a combination of *Rechtsstaat* and *Ständestaat*. Monarch and citizens alike would be subject to a single code of laws; the rights and responsibilities of all estates would be spelled out with precision; clear statutes would define authority and establish regular channels for legislative and executive functions; the courts would comprise a separate entity, have the power of judicial review, and be accountable to the public. These principles guided Catherine, and she emphasized her image as a legal sovereign by making the overhaul of Russia's code of laws and "rendering justice to the people" her "primary concern."[85] Her second accession manifesto promised that "each government position would have its limits and laws." Two years later, her *Directions* to Prince Aleksandr Viazemskii, upon his assumption of the office of procurator-general, specifically pointed out the need to replace the outmoded Law Code (Ulozhenie) of 1649 and to differentiate between fundamental and positive laws: "Our laws demand correction, firstly, so that all might be arranged in one system which is to be maintained; secondly, so that those which contradict it are got rid of; thirdly, to separate the temporary and the personal from the permanent and indispensable."[86] In her dissertation, Karen Rasmussen has demonstrated that the empress pursued legal reform with great diligence, no hypocrisy, and some success throughout her reign, and not merely during her "liberal" years.[87]

The only sure way to prevent despotism involved de jure limitations on the ruler's power, but the conviction that large states required absolutist monarchs lent little support to that idea with Catherine or among Russian writers. While the discourse surrounding the struggle for legal norms sought solutions within the framework of absolutist rule, the sources demonstrate contrasting conceptions of what kind of monarchy conformed to the Enlightenment ideals that most shared. Catherine and many authors and statesmen envisioned a legal sovereign as a wise legislator who regularized all aspects of state life and assured security of person, property, and honor, but was self-limited in the exercise of power. Others among the political elite, while agreeing with the vision of a legal sovereign as an active lawgiver, wanted the ruler's exercise of power institutionalized and confined to set procedures.

Russian writers expressed their fear of capricious or arbitrary behavior on the part of monarchs but, perhaps even more, on the part of "accidental favorites."[88] Some noted that favorites, historically the most hated men in Russia, represented the antithesis of rule by law because they operated outside any legal framework, considered themselves "not subject to the judgment of the public or responsible to it," and thus oversaw a state that was "absolutely despotic." They created an administration more dominated "by the influence of individual personalities than by the power of state institutions." In such a situation, "although there are written laws, they are inferior . . . to the beck and call of a malicious magnate," for instance the "spiteful" Biron. Their "capricious" practices seemed even more repugnant than a monarch's since they lacked any right—whether of "work, rank, or blood" or "talent and merit"—to exercise power except for their personal liaison with the ruler. Even then, they often, in effect, imprisoned the ruler, and "cut the Monarch off from the business of state and . . . knowledge of their activities." Moreover, the elite resented favorites' placing a barrier between the monarch and the general nobility's constant quest for favors and promotion. In a word, "notwithstanding laws . . . the Russian citizen" is thrown into a position where "neither his life, honor, nor property is secure, like a feeble boat without a rudder in the midst of a storm-tossed sea."[89]

In order to curb arbitrariness and favoritism, monarchs' actions had to become bound by law and their power institutionalized. But, as Richard Wortman has noted, absolutist rulers reacted ambivalently to anything hinting at a de jure restriction on power since they wanted to reserve the right to exercise authority either personally or via the very favorites others wanted excluded from the corridors of power. While codification was attempted nine times in the century, "the tsar's attachment to his personal power made him chary of all legal definition of authority."[90] In addition, enlightened monarchs, Catherine included, imagined themselves as modern, law-abiding rulers but also as patriarchs or matriarchs who wanted the leeway to exercise reform or largesse. The ruler reluctant to relinquish or even limit existing authority became commonplace, and one sees in hindsight that no European monarch in the modern era abjured absolute power without a revolution forcing the issue.[91]

During her first months of rule, Catherine appeared willing to have her exercise of power regulated. The empress requested a leading statesman, Nikita Panin, to present her with a plan for rationalizing imperial decision making, in the light of her predecessors' capricious behavior and reliance on favorites.[92] While a power struggle among patronage networks inspired Panin's project for an imperial council, it nonetheless proposed a mechanism for preventing arbitrariness on the part of a monarch. According to Panin's biographer David Ransel, Panin's political program reflected the general desire for a *Rechtsstaat*, which "would place the autocratic power within an immutable legal framework guaranteed by the participation of leading families in the policymaking and administrative institutions."[93] Panin acted as a spokesman for the "aristocratic party" in Russia, but his group did not constitute *frondeurs*, as Soviet scholars long insisted. In the spirit especially pronounced in the German Enlightenment, Panin and his cohorts intended to regularize the existing absolutist government, not argue for another form.[94]

Briefly, the projected imperial council consisted of the four state secretaries of the army, navy, and internal and external affairs plus two or four more individuals, who were to discuss every item of business brought before the monarch and assist in drawing up legislation. The ruler could sign no law unless it had been discussed in the council; this represented a gentle brake on the sovereign's actions and also meant that "a law would become explicitly something more than the arbitrary will of the monarch."[95] Nonetheless, there was no overt "restriction of autocratic authority," since the monarch reached the final decision on matters and appointed and dismissed the council members.[96] The project also maintained the stature of the senate by giving it the power to remonstrate about actions the monarch and council approved, but which the senate deemed contrary to the good of the people or to the vague notion of fundamental laws.

Catherine signed a manifesto establishing the council late in December of 1762, an indication that she saw no threat in the proposal, but then she shelved it. The empress had requested opinions on the project, and she may have come to agree with the critics. One advisor worried about "making public" passages that hinted at "some kind of contraction of Your Majesty's autocratic power," presumably because of hostility to any step in the direction of oligarchic rule.[97] Another advisor, General A. N. Vil'boa cringed at the latter possibility:

> Although [the author] wishes to appear to be defending the monarchy, he is much more inclined in his own way toward an aristocratic government. A binding and legally established Imperial Council with members of importance (especially if they possessed as well sufficient arrogance, ambition, and wit) would be able in time to grow very conveniently into co-rulers. At least if there is a design for such an edifice, then this Imperial Council is certainly the first step toward it; and such an outcome would bring unmistakable ruin to the power and greatness of the Russian Empire.[98]

As in 1730, some members of the elite preferred absolute monarchy, "legal" or not, to any threat of oligarchic rule. While Panin's specific plan died, the idea of a council or a new form of senate empowered to assist in the lawmaking process recurred in the literature throughout Catherine's reign.[99] Nonetheless, legislative power remained concentrated in the empress's hands, and the senate retained its traditional administrative and judicial functions. Thus, while rulers like Catherine applauded the theory and relished the image of legal monarchy, they faltered at putting many of its tenets into practice.

THE PROMOTION OF A LEGAL MENTALITY

Rather than altering the formal arrangements of power, Catherine turned her attention to revising Russia's code of laws and working to create a legal consciousness among the educated elite.[100] According to standard eighteenth-century theory, new legislation worked effectively only if the citizens' legal awareness was raised commensurately. To assist in this process, Catherine funded translations of political thinkers such as Montesquieu and Blackstone.[101] The publication of the *Encyclopédie,* which she patronized, became a principal agent for propagating Enlightenment concepts of civil society, freedom, and the contractual obligations between ruler and ruled to a wide audience among the reading public.[102] In an absolute monarchy, the elite tend to imitate the interests of the ruler. In 1764, bowing to popular demand, the first compendium of natural law, drawn from a variety of unnamed authors, was published for the benefit of the Russian reader. It made the point that knowledge of legal norms of behavior was accessible to all literate people, who thus had the wherewithal to judge both their fellow citizens and their monarchs. The text also extolled a monarch as providing the best "ruler of a citizenry" *(grazhdanstvo),* especially when governing with "openness" *(glasnost')* and "with the agreement of all subjects."[103] In the next year, fifteen members of the nobility founded the Free Economic Society that fostered public discussion of peasant property rights. Similarly, readers began demanding the publication of major laws and provided a market for books of jurisprudence for the first time in Russian history.[104]

Catherine's stature as a legal sovereign reached its climax with her calling of the Legislative Commission of 1767, arguably the most significant moment of her reign and certainly the most direct invitation in the century to public dialogue between ruler and ruled.[105] The manifesto announcing the convocation reminded Russians that, upon receiving the scepter "from the beloved fatherland through its elite," she had promised to focus upon enacting laws so "that each department of government would have its rules for the maintenance of good order in all areas." However, having recognized the inadequacies of the existing code of laws and the enormity of the task at hand, she was calling for the help of deputies "from every place" to advise her on specific needs throughout the empire.[106] Her stated model was the *zemskii sobor* of 1648–1649, at which Tsar Aleksei had gathered representatives of "all the people" to assist in preparing a new law code.[107] In 1767, elections were held throughout the country to choose 557 delegates; they were drawn from among nobility (160), merchantry (200), bureaucracy (27), Cossacks (70), state peasants and small independent farmers or *odnovortsy* (50), and non-Russian sectors of the population (50). The delegates were asked to bring cahiers—to use the apt term made famous during a similar convocation of the French Estates-General in 1788–1789—and each of the "notebooks" would describe conditions in the deputies' towns, districts, or estates. In a gesture to the tradition-minded, the commission would meet in Moscow, where all previous *zemskie sobory* had gathered, and members would articulate their concerns before their cohorts.[108]

In one brilliant stroke, the calling of the Legislative Commission announced that Catherine intended to rule by law and through consensus. Codification constituted Russia's most pressing legal need, and it would be met through discussions in a public forum so that she could "test the temper of public reaction and solicit the stamp of public approval with regard to reform projects."[109] While neither private serfs nor clergy were asked to serve as delegates, the composition of the commission indicated the empress's intent to support the development of a middle class and generally expand the notion of open discourse about the central issues of the day. No absolute monarch in Europe had proved so daring and so ambitious in advancing the politics of consensus and opening up avenues for the expression of public opinion.

The very calling of the commission would have gained Catherine the "immortality" and "eternal praise" so prized among Enlightenment figures who curried favor with the *philosophes*, but she went one step further.[110] True to her inaugural promises in the first year of her reign, she began work on a document that was to serve three functions: it offered a set of ideals to which any legal monarchy should aspire; it proposed a preliminary set of fundamental laws for the empire; and it outlined the legal principles upon which any future code of laws would be based. In 1767, the guide was published in Moscow under the title *Instructions to the Commission for the Composition of a Plan of a New Code of Laws,* or *Nakaz.* The document's 526 articles provided the first systematic treatment of Russian law in the eighteenth century and an encyclopedia of political thought in the era.[111] The *Nakaz* displayed a glittering array of sources. Some 290 articles were drawn from Montesquieu's *Spirit of the Laws* and 108 from Cesare Beccaria's recently published *On Crimes and Punishments* (1764). Catherine's treatise lauded not only the uniform administration and maximization of resources favored by proponents of the well-ordered police state but also the idea of the *Rechtsstaat,* wherein everyone including the monarch was subject to the rule of law, and the *Ständestaat,* wherein social groups were defined and given rights and responsibilities. A reliance on natural law, as described by the German philosopher Christian Wolff, was invoked to establish norms of behavior and to elevate notions of civic responsibility, and the physiocrat François Quesnay provided approval "of an absolutism complemented by a public sphere."[112] The sovereign had clearly done her homework and proceeded to use the then respected methodology of culling sources nearly verbatim to meld them in an original way and apply them to the Russian scene. As Gary Marker noted, "Catherine's intellectual ambition in those years was virtually boundless."[113]

Not only Catherine but also the educated elite got their ideas from the Enlightenment, and, when she published her *Nakaz,* they discovered they all spoke the same language, "that the desires from below and the appeal from above coincided." Franco Venturi beautifully described this moment:

> The great convergence of those who were ahead of the times, and those who were behind, of those who had shown the way, and those who had tried to follow, took place in the sixties, at a time when the men of the Enlightenment seemed to work in unison, a decisive time for the whole of Europe . . . , [and] the *philosophes* became the soul of eighteenth-century Russia.[114]

Never before or again would a Russian monarch and the elite be so in ac-
cord. This legal sovereign was suggesting juridical principles based on the
French and German Enlightenments and a code of laws arrived at by a consensus of elected delegates. The British literary scholar, W. Gareth Jones,
applauded Catherine's acumen: "With her eighteenth-century *Nakaz* and
her seventeeth-century staging of the Commission, Catherine appealed to
both progressives and conservatives and kept them in superb political balance."[115] Critical opinion on the commission and *Nakaz* runs the gamut
from awed respect for Catherine's political vision to her depiction as a hyp-
ocrite who "threw dust into the eyes of Europe."[116] Whatever the interpretation, the cahiers and publications of the commission certainly provide a
glimpse of the delegates' attitude toward monarchy in Russia, and the *Nakaz*
offers a fully focused statement of Catherine's conception of her office.

The sea of documents that poured into and out of the commission devoted little space to the topic of absolute monarchy since delegates viewed
it as Russia's accepted form of government. Nonetheless, conceptions varied from the medieval to the modern. Some deputies spoke of the immea-
surable distance between a "most autocratic power" and "most humble
slaves"; another delegate clung firmly to the Muscovite model: "I, for my
part, cannot agree freely to render homage to any but a single absolute
monarch, because the sovereign ought not be responsible for his actions to
anyone on earth . . . and to whom one and all most loyal slaves must
obey."[117] Others echoed the time-honored concept of patriarchal government, with adjustments for gender: Catherine's "humble slaves prostrate
themselves before the most maternal will" or "throw themselves at the feet
of Her Most August Imperial Majesty in all Her autocratic power, a true
mother of the Fatherland," under whom "the numerous peoples of the vast
empire will live in prosperity and peace, just as the children of a fond father live peacefully in one home."

Most delegates blended old and new attitudes. Because many cahiers
took the traditional form of the petition, they greeted the ruler with fulsome praise and rapturous rhetoric. They expressed enormous gratitude to
Catherine for her "magnanimity, wisdom, and love of mankind" in "giving
a small sign of her monarchical trust to her faithful subjects" by allowing
them to participate in a legislative assembly. Indeed, the delegates attempted to award her the sexually confused title of "Catherine the Great,
Wise Mother of the Fatherland," an honor she graciously demurred.[118] In
blessing the empress as "the sole source of good and prosperity," delegates
betrayed the traditional presumption that government emanated from the
will of the ruler.

Moving in a more modern direction, the majority of delegates enthusiastically greeted the idea of basing the monarchical will on the rule of law.
The Moscow nobility looked forward to "a new legal order," and those from
Mikhailov welcomed the creation of "a clear and unshakeable code of law
that would forever preserve, defend, and restore the honor, life, and property of sons of the Fatherland." Artisans expected "autocratic power . . . to

lay down a foundation for the peace and prosperity of all fellow citizens . . . through permanent laws." Peasants welcomed "the New Code . . . which will care for the needs of all civil society": "We deputies were convoked . . . to care about the legalization of everyone in general and of each in particular . . . and not to leave anything without legalization . . . even the beggars, the poor, the aggrieved." To accomplish this "salutary aim," a deputy pointed out the need for "the freedom safely to speak and think about the needs of society."[119] Clearly, some delegates had begun operating as though they moved in the milieu of an "enlightened state with subjects participating in central and local affairs, with some estate rights, and, furthermore, as they supposed, with a certain measure of civic freedom."[120]

Catherine's *Nakaz* had prompted this new political self-image in Russia. While overtly a set of premises on which to codify rules governing nearly every facet of Russian life and development, the *Nakaz* contains a strong subtext that reads like a brief filed before a court of enlightened public opinion. The underlying theme argued against the long-held opinion that Russia's form of government was despotic and in favor of its being ranked among the "true" monarchies, those compatible with legality, equality, and liberty. Catherine presented her evidence persuasively, and the French government deemed her depiction of rulership so incendiary that it banned its publication. She won her case for the time being, until faults in the disquisition appeared: the problem of serfdom; the observation that only the good will of the monarch guaranteed the vaunted rights of citizens; and the fact that much of the evidence for a legal monarchy resided merely on the recently published and untested *Nakaz*. At any rate, Russians began conceiving of their monarchical institution in new terms and with new hopes.

The *Nakaz* presented a rather systematic philosophy of monarchy. But strangely, Catherine ignored the question of the origin of power. When ascending the throne, she had utilized the contract theory and projected an image of an elected monarch; both postures acknowledged popular sovereignty, a doctrine about which the *Nakaz* remained silent.[121] Never mentioning the stock phrases about all power being of divine origin, Catherine projected a totally secular view of monarchy with the exception of one article in an appendix that referred to a monarch's "God-given title."[122] She called *The Spirit of the Laws* her "prayer book," and it provided the framework for her political discourse. The empress agreed with Montesquieu that only "absolute Powers vested in one Person can be suitable to the Extent of so vast an Empire."[123] From the beginning of her reign, she remained convinced of the conventional political wisdom that other forms of government held only disaster for Russia.

> [W]hile I live, we will remain as duty commands. The Russian Empire is so large, that apart from the Autocratic Sovereign every other form of government is harmful to it, because all others are slower in their execution and contain a great multitude of various horrors, which lead to the disintegration of power and strength.[124]

Circumstances demanded an absolute monarchy, but luckily, Catherine explained, it also best achieved the "Glory of the Citizens, of the State, and of the Sovereign." Absolute monarchs like herself, unlike democratic or aristocratic leaders, tended to the needs of all groups in society and could do so with quick efficiency. She claimed that her greatest glory rested in saying "We are created for our People" and making those "People the most happy possible of Mankind" by supplying "all the Citizens with sure Maintenance, Food, proper Clothing, and a Way of Life not detrimental to the Health of Man."[125] Catherine clearly continued to relish the patriarchal image of the absolute monarch, "of a Father anxiously concerned for his Children and Servants."[126]

While absolute power was used to benefit the people, its potential for harm was curbed because, in Catherine's description, the Russian ruler acted within limits. Self-limitation remained a valid ideal and essential attribute of a virtuous ruler as it had for millennia, although by the next century it would seem ironical. Even in the eighteenth century, the idea warranted skepticism, since only a thin and often-crossed line separated unlimited and self-limiting power. Catherine's *Nakaz* provided a perfect example of hedging: "The greatest Art of Government is to distinguish exactly what degree of Power should be exerted in different Circumstances," since "there are Cases in which Power may and ought to be exerted in its full Sway, without any risk to the State, but . . . there are also others in which it must be exerted under Limits fixed to, and by, itself."[127] In reality, the only assurance against despotism still remained the good will and intentions of the ruler.

To offset the vagueness of the principle, the *Nakaz* stipulated specific ways in which the sovereign practiced self-limitation. Although the absolute monarch was the "Source of all Power," such power was exercised through the laws. These laws stood as the "firm and immovable" foundation of the state, by which even the ruler abided, because "in any State however extensive there should be no place independent of the Laws."[128] According to eighteenth-century standards, once fundamental laws were decided upon and the code of laws devised, Russians would enjoy equality, which was equated with "all being subject to the same Laws."[129]

The *Nakaz* also repeated the formula that self-limited monarchs ruled, not directly, but through "smaller Channels" and extolled the idea that "the intermediate Powers subject to and dependent upon the Supreme Power form the Substance of Government."[130] While Catherine judged the full application of Montesquieu's separation of powers impractical in Russia, she agreed that the judiciary should function apart, with the senate acting as the depository of the laws and the monarch appointing "other Persons to judge according to the Laws."[131] In another modification of Montesquieu's theories, Catherine substituted bureaucrats for nobility under the rubric of "intermediary powers" who would limit the power of a monarch, even though functionaries of the crown had no independent base; later in her reign, however, she tried to create estates with defined rights in order better to conform to Montesquieu's dicta.[132] But throughout her reign, Catherine, like any good administrator, did operate through "channels"; she set the direction of policy and let her ministers work out the details.[133] Fulfilling another sign of a "true" monarch, she also had the reputation of appointing able officials to run what was sometimes called a "bureaucratic monarchy," a political system that indeed acted as a brake on arbitrariness, because a ruler was forced by logistics to delegate spheres of authority.[134] Arbitrary rule on the part of subordinates presented a separate and perhaps even more thorny problem.

In addition to equality before the law and the division of administrative functions, the *Nakaz* outlined several rights that served as preventives against abuse of power. The purpose of limitations on the power of an absolute monarch, of course, was to guarantee security of life and property.[135] Article 3 of the *Nakaz* declared that the aim of the state was to ensure each citizen's being "protected by Laws, which . . . will shield him from every Attempt against his Welfare."[136] The document championed religious toleration: "In so vast an Empire which extends its Dominion over such a Variety of People, the prohibiting, or not tolerating their respective Religions would be an Evil very detrimental to the Peace and Security of its Subjects." Albeit cautiously, freedom of the press was avowed a good idea since censorship might "only produce Ignorance, destroy the Gifts of the human Mind, and damp the inclination to write." Of equal importance, the *Nakaz* flatly stated that the only political crimes consisted of "overt Acts" against the person of the ruler or the state and certainly not of thoughts and intentions. Other articles defined the right of habeas corpus, reiterated the abolition of torture and the death penalty, and called for punishments commensurate with the crime. Improvements in the courts and judicial procedures, including the publication of judicial decisions, were promised to implement the newly defined rights.[137]

The *Nakaz* thus confidently asserted the compatibility of absolute monarchy with the Enlightenment desiderata of a law-based state, equality before the law, and civil rights. Liberty provided another byword of the era. The classic eighteenth-century definition equated liberty with freedom of person and property and the right to do whatever is not prohibited by the law.[138] Full freedom was impossible since people required the paternal authority of a monarch and firm laws to keep in check the evil propensities of human nature.[139] Catherine echoed these precepts with precision.[140] She signaled the difference between unrestrained "natural" freedom *(svobod-nost')*, a bestial trait, and liberty *(vol'nost')*, the basis of "civil society" in an absolutist state. The monarch passed laws that emerged from the "People at large" and reflected the "Genius of the People" and their inclinations, so that it was "natural" to obey the edicts.[141] These laws played a transformative function as well. They curbed the "headstrong Desires and stubborn Inclinations" of natural man and produced a citizen: "Civil Liberty consists not in doing every one as he pleases," but in doing what one "ought to desire" and being forbidden from doing "what should not be desired" along with "doing whatever is permitted by the Laws." Such a "Civil Society," best guaranteed in an absolutist state, resulted in a "Tranquility of Mind" that arose from having every individual enjoy personal security, with the only fear that of transgressing the laws.[142]

The *Nakaz* had presented its readers with a new image of the Russian sovereign that complemented the earlier representations of a father, a reformer, and a ruler elevated through election. Catherine drew a portrait of an absolute monarch with self-limited and defined powers, who ruled not alone but delegated authority to experienced statesmen; an autocrat who bowed before the laws of the state; a legislator whose edicts benefited every social group; and a propagator of civil liberty, civil rights, and equality before the law. With this evidence, the empress claimed that despotism had been "destroyed" in Russia. "Caprice" no longer guided the monarch, but "his good Intentions from which all Laws have flowed, and still do flow," and he rules by suasion not force.[143]

The Legislative Commission broke up in 1768 because of the hostilities with Turkey, and it officially disbanded in 1774. In the end, it failed to write a new code of law or agree to a set of fundamental laws for Russia. Nonetheless, the commission's work laid the basis for reforms for the rest of Catherine's lengthy reign. For example, the Charter of 1785 defined the status and privileges of the nobility and awarded them security of person and property against the arbitrary will of monarchs and their administrations.[144] The idea of public participation in the issues of the day also continued, as John T. Alexander's forceful statistic demonstrates: "One estimate counted 15,000 new officials after 1775 (out of a total of 27,000 in 1796), with 10,608 of them elected—4,053 nobles, 3,851 townsmen, and 2,704 peasants."[145] Overall, the Legislative Commission and *Nakaz* sponsored among the elite a new legal mentality and new expectations of the legal sovereign.

The concept of a legal sovereign certainly received wide publicity.[146] Besides delegates, hundreds of members of the elite worked in the plenary sessions and in the nineteen subcommittees of the Legislative Commission, and as the scholar Nikolai Chechulin pointed out:

> During the reign of Catherine II the *Nakaz* was published eight times; in the sessions of the Commission for the composition of a new law code it was read out in its entirety once a month—that is, it was heard several times by hundreds of people; in 1767, fifty-four copies of the *Nakaz* were sent out to various offices; one copy was sent to each provincial chancellory in like manner; in 1768 the Senate directed that in each office the *Nakaz* should be read out at least three times a year.[147]

During the reign, the document went through twenty-five editions in nine languages, and Catherine often reiterated its principles both for foreign and domestic consumption.[148]

Because of this wide dissemination, the ideas took root and spread. Soviet scholars lamented that the *Nakaz* awakened "illusions" among both the nobility and the peasantry and strengthened support for the monarchy.[149] The Russian philosophe Iakov Kozel'skii in 1768 published the first Russian book on philosophy, and his *Propositions* reinforced the idea of a sovereign who ruled "not by force but by the superiority and goodness of the laws and through equality before the law to level the rights and privileges of peoples."[150] Semen Desnitskii, a jurist trained at Glasgow Univeristy and a pupil of Adam Smith, in a dialogic response to Catherine's *Nakaz,* presented the empress with a proposal to make the Legislative Commission permanent by enlarging the senate to roughly six hundred members elected every five years from all groups (save peasants) so that "complaints would always be made public." The new body would assist the monarch in legislation as well as matters of taxation, war and peace, and budget, but with no diminution of the ruler's power.[151]

Literature reflected the new image. Poets linked their ruler to Astraea, "the virgin goddess of justice who left the earth when mankind became corrupt and whose return would signal a new golden age," and writers projected Catherine's policies to represent "the principle of law as a path to the good life."[152] Publications praised her for exceeding Peter's great deeds by understanding that "the first duty of a Monarch, the one that maintains a nation's happiness is justice, which preserves the divine deposit of laws . . . and maintains security of person and property."[153] An odist proclaimed: "Law, reason, and liberty. . . . These are monarchical deeds," and a journalist from Iaroslavl wrote in reverence that "the laws, traced by the finger of her Majesty's right hand . . . have become a radiant light."[154] Children's books, a novelty in Russia, defined monarchs as ruling "in conformity with some type of laws," unlike a despot whose will is the only law.[155] In the next generation, Aleksandr Turgenev would credit the *Nakaz* for fostering "a sincere respect for the freedom of the citizen, elevated feelings about his honor and defense, with the inviolable right of person and property."[156] Catherine's *Nakaz* and her convocation of the Legislative Commission, her continuing efforts at reform, her consensual style of rule, and the overall respect for civil rights that marked her reign until the last years earned the empress her aura as a legal sovereign.

Catherine enjoyed less success in breaking the identification of Russia's form of government with despotism. In the *Nakaz*, whether consciously or unconsciously, she crafted the description of the Russian polity so that it mostly met the criteria laid down by Montesquieu for a "true monarchy" rather than a despotism. But even the great theorist went back and forth on the issue, for Russia was a complex land.[157] Montesquieu noted despotic features in Russia's government, but marveled at its "endeavors to temper its arbitrary power" and congratulated the elite "for its marks of impatience and discontent" with oppressive rule.[158] The relativism shared by political thinkers of the eighteenth century also militated against outright condemnation of any nation's peculiar forms. The influential

Desnitskii, Russia's first theoretical jurist, taught his students at Moscow University that they must focus on the historic development of institutions and not rush to impose new forms or neglect the efforts made by Aleksei, Peter, and Catherine.[159]

Despite the rationalizations, some basic signs of a "true monarchy" were lacking in Russia: a separation of powers, which Desnitskii among others championed; an independent nobility acting as an "intermediary power"; and an independent supreme court with a right of remonstrance. And, of course, there was the problem of serfdom. Montesquieu and other philosophes found a necessary connection between despotic governments and enslaved populations.

> In despotic countries, where they are already in a state of political servitude, civil slavery is more tolerable than in other governments. . . . But in a monarchical government, where it is of the utmost importance that human nature should not be debased or dispirited, there ought to be no slavery.[160]

Catherine perhaps planned a means for ending serfdom in Russia, and Count Sivers, a statesman of great common sense, warned her that "slavery will be the undoing of the state."[161] The Pugachev Revolt of 1773–1774 provided ample substantiation for this fear.

Russia, on the other hand, projected an image of a relatively backward country rapidly developing under the leadership of a progressive sovereign, whose reforms continued to be in the forefront of Enlightenment trends.[162] The commonplace belief in gradual change and organic development encouraged optimism. Denis Fonvizin, the dramatist and political thinker, believed in a young Russia that would experience "inevitable evolution," since "society is a type of organism with a certain natural life cycle from infancy to old age."[163] The dramatist Mikhail Kheraskov promised "new peoples, new kingdoms," and the educator Ivan Betskoi summarized the recent progress toward maturity: *"Peter the Great created people in Russia: Your Majesty has invested them with souls."*[164] Catherine shared the historical thesis that Russia "had approximately the same customs, went along the same path, and ended up on nearly the same level as all the other European countries."[165]

More pessimistic observers found Russia still mired in a medieval past. Jean Chappe d'Auteroche published a piece of travel literature, *Voyage en Sibérie,* that pinned "the hated appellation of despot" on Catherine and claimed the country's untarnished inferiority:

> The love of fame . . . is unknown in Russia; despotism debases the mind, damps the genius, and stifles every kind of sentiment. In Russia no person ventures to think; the soul is so much debased that its faculties are destroyed. Fear is almost the only passion by which the whole nation is actuated.[166]

Catherine became irate and penned a line-by-line rebuttal that she published anonymously (neither work won any acclaim). While ostensibly defending her country against dishonor, she was actually defending her own reign. The majority of her arguments highlighted examples of her enlightened reforms and pretended that the *Nakaz*, which had no legal validity, had "become the law among us, a form of government," and had thus ended despotism in Russia.[167]

The crux of the problem was that the ideal of an absolute monarch governing on the basis of unshakeable fundamental laws and a single, universally applicable code of laws had taken root, and yet the ideal was not forthcoming, despite a dialogue over the issues that continued unabated. As the reign moved along, the honeymoon gave way to disappointment; Russian political thinkers reminded the empress of her promises and made recommendations that merely repeated the suggestions that Catherine herself had proposed. The Panin brothers and Fonvizin grew weary of arguing for a set of "immutable fundamental laws" that would bring "stability" and "durability" and turned their hopes to Catherine's son and heir.[168] Shcherbatov, the most erudite Russian in the last third of the eighteenth century, likewise grew irritated; Russia needed a new code and fundamental laws "not to hamper the monarch's power to do everything beneficial for the state, but to curb his sometimes immoderate desires" and to "protect the life, honor, property, and security of citizens."[169] In his unpublished writings, which he hoped Catherine would read upon his death, the prince mocked the empress for defining Russia as a monarchy in her *Nakaz*, when in reality it remained a despotism (*samovlastie* or *despotichestvo*).[170] Poignantly, his conception of an ideal monarch proved identical to Catherine's:

> And thus I deem the greatest and most successful monarch one who thinks of himself as a father to his people, never attempting to repudiate the laws and rule despotically; he does not differentiate between his interests and the interests of the state; he knows the great art of choosing as advisors those people who conjoin a zeal for their Sovereign with love for their fatherland and the laws.

But, he lamented, "such monarchs are few." Most who have supreme power give in to "their ambitions, passions"; worse, "women are more inclined to despotism than men," since they are more prone to flattery.[171] Shcherbatov was a sexist curmudgeon and angry that he was not included in the inner circles of power, but his other indictments accurately recorded abuse of power, greed, thievery, cupidity, immorality, and supposed reliance on a series of favorites. While the latter problem proved the most notorious aspect of her reign, until her last years, the empress held the reins of power firmly in her hands.[172]

The picture Catherine so carefully painted or commissioned at the beginning of her reign had faded by its end.[173] Nonetheless, what Shcherbatov had written of Peter I applied even more to Catherine II, that he "gave his subjects enough enlightenment to be able to criticize despotism."[174] A new generation raised the cry to transform the self-limiting monarch who was ruling by law—but above it—into a monarch subject to the law, who, to repeat the political cliché of the century, "would do good, but have his hands tied against evil." The program crystallized around an urgent need for legal guarantees to provide security of person and property, to check against arbitrary actions on the part of a ruler or favorites, and eventually to divest the ruler of unlimited personalized power. This is, of course, the logical and ironic consequence of enlightened absolutism: monarchs so enlighten their people that they no longer need or want their absolute rule.

CHAPTER FIVE

The Agent of History

ussians who wrote histories of Russia figured among the leading articulators of the varying ways in which monarchy was being reconceived in the eighteenth century. These historians were nearly all amateurs, coming from the variety of milieus that the educated elite inhabited. And, since monarchs read their works, they became major participants in the century's political dialogue. Their writings as a matter of course dealt with conceptions of monarchy, because the writing of history throughout Europe in the eighteenth century centered on interpretations of rulership. In addition, histories in this epoch were unabashedly subjective. For all these reasons, they offer ideal gauges for charting the reconception of monarchy that occurred in this century.

The first secular histories of Russia were written beginning in the 1710s, but they only started appearing in 1755 during the publication explosion of the last half of the century and were usually published in editions of 600, 1,200, or 2,400 copies. Each generation reflected the idea of monarchy current in the era.[1] Catherine II, herself an amateur historian, encouraged the trend. During her reign, histories bombarded the reading public with all the conceptions of monarchy that writers had developed in the course of the century: the reforming tsar leading his state forward in every sphere of human endeavor; the elected ruler united with the populace in contractual obligation; and the sovereign dedicated to rule by law. They thus wrapped Catherine in a multilayered cloak of legitimacy. The historians as a group added their own legitimation by celebrating the great monarchs of their country's past (and present) as the primary cause for Russia's greatness and the guardians of its destiny. In keeping with the rational and critical spirit of the Enlightenment, writers condemned or dismissed rulers who failed to meet measure and thus reconfirmed the criteria for good and bad rule that became embedded in Russian conceptions about monarchy during the second half of the eighteenth century.

WRITING HISTORY DURING THE ENLIGHTENMENT

Writing history during the Enlightenment involved didactic purpose and figured among the most prominent and popular varieties of advice literature. Histories plainly aimed to instruct rulers and readers about the art of governance. Historians of this era certainly understood the importance of Baconian methodology in the search, compilation, analysis, and publication of major historical documents.[2] However, they prized interpretive history even more and viewed it as a branch of literature or as a practical extension of philosophy—philosophy teaching by example.[3]

Because of their amateur status, the writers who delivered lessons drawn from history seemed more typical of the educated elite than did the monastic annalists who were their forebears or the trained academics who were their successors.[4] Sources reveal that forty-seven Russian historians penned major interpretations of their country's past. A various group, they emerged from the ranks of many different professions and spanned the century. Aleksei Mankiev (d.1723) was a diplomat who wrote *The Kernel of Russian History* while imprisoned by the Swedes during the Great Northern War.[5] Vasilii Tatishchev (1686–1750), an expert administrator in the areas of mining, manufacturing, and minting, spent thirty years writing his multivolume *Russian History* "at night" and between assignments.[6] The fame of Mikhail Lomonosov (1711–1765) rests on his position as the father of modern Russian literature and modern Russian science, but he also found time to author *Ancient Russian History*.[7] And Catherine II (1729–1796) was interested enough to publish "Notes Concerning Russian History."[8] Mikhail Shcherbatov (1733–1790), the court historiographer, confessed that he wrote the many volumes of *Russian History from Ancient Times* "more for my own personal pleasure," while he spent a lifetime in state service.[9] Ivan Boltin (1735–1792) published historical critiques while serving as an army officer and administrator.[10] Timofei Mal'gin (1752–1819) wrote *A Mirror for Russian Sovereigns,* alongside his duties as a translator with the eighth rank in civil service, collegiate assessor.[11] Six literary figures wrote less ambitious works about Russia's past; Vasilii Trediakovskii, Aleksandr Sumarokov, Ivan Elagin, Ivan Barkov, Fedor Emin, and Nikolai Novikov complete the list of fifteen published amateur historians.[12] The works of thirty-two anonymous writers remained in the archives, but their interpretations offered no departures from those that reached print.[13]

Russian historians thus formed a rather representative group of the educated elite and also of Enlightenment figures. In the spirit of the age, they wrote lexicons, collected libraries, and translated Western works that interested them.[14] In their own works, they consciously imitated contemporary histories in the rest of Europe, which were being assiduously translated for interested readers, and these books centered on the conceptions and justification of monarchy.[15] Iurii Lotman and Boris Uspenskii pointed out that the emergence of people who could "think historically . . . was one of the basic innovations of post-Petrine culture" and an example of "real, not mythological Europeanization."[16] As full-fledged participants in their century's trends, Russians wrote history *en philosophe:* they formulated an idea of progress, demonstrated secular causation, and displayed interpretive sweep and didactic intent. Enlightenment histories intertwined each of those features with royal activity—understandably, as nearly all European countries were monarchies—and Russians likewise placed their own rulers at center stage. The current wisdom dictated that "the object of the history of a Kingdom or Nation is the Prince . . . there lies the center, as it were, around which everything else must revolve."[17]

Another reason why European eighteenth-century histories were bound to center on monarchs was that the majority were written at their behest. Fedor Emin noted that "all over Europe, Christian monarchs are trying to assemble accurate histories that document reigns, actions, attitudes, morals, various changes."[18] In Russia, the writing of history turned into an exercise in national self-consciousness since monarchs wanted historians "to do battle" with foreign detractors.[19] Peter the Great appealed for a national history to counteract "Polish lies" and the "jealousy and hatred of the Swedes."[20] Empress Elizabeth summoned historians to refute German scholars whose Normanist version of Russia's origins described the early Slavs as "barbarians, resembling beasts."[21] Catherine urged denunciation of the "falsehood . . . slander . . . and insolence" of the "frivolous Frenchmen" who wrote histories of Russia, for instance, Jean Chappe d'Auteroche. Offended to the point of fury at the "black colors" in which foreigners painted the country, Catherine wrote her own version of early history that unabashedly strove to "present a most glorious Russia."[22] A sensitivity to writing history was not confined to Russians; a historian, Fréret, was sent to the Bastille for maintaining that the Franks were not of the Gallic race.[23]

Aside from the need to please a sponsor, philosophes genuinely regarded monarchs as high priests of the new secular morality. Eighteenth-century thinkers were not interested in stabilizing society but in improving it, and the linchpin in these plans for making progress toward secular salvation was the enlightened ruler.[24] The secular philosophy of history, propounded by Voltaire, to a degree replaced the reliance on theology for explanations.[25] The Sage of Ferney, who dominated historical thinking in the century, replaced providential with royal causality and trumpeted the flattering thesis that it was "the great actions of kings which have changed the face of the earth." He enshrined monarchs as those rare examples of human genius who brighten a historical landscape otherwise filled with struggle, folly, and crime. His fame and influence reached the world over; for instance, in 1756, his *Essai sur les moeurs et l'esprit des na-tions* went on sale in St. Petersburg and sold an unprecedented three thou-sand copies the first day.[26]

Led by Voltaire, Enlightenment history, in announcing a new secular-ism, was reacting against religious interpretations of monarchical rule that had reached their climax in France with the writings of Jacques Bossuet. Although a strict theory of divine right was not a prominent fea-ture in Russian political cultue, there did exist the tradition of ecclesiasti-cal histories, really chronicles, that originated in medieval Kiev.[27] They stressed the monarchy's biblical origins and its ties with the House of Palaeologus, but especially its role in the expansion of the Orthodox Church.[28] About a dozen eighteenth-century historians continued the tra-dition, but only one was published; most, often lengthy and laboriously copied, remained in the archives.[29]

Since neither history nor its writing can be neatly compartmentalized, the old religious aura surrounding the institution of monarchy continued to attract authors and readers and existed alongside the secular image.[30] The seventeenth-century *Synopsis* by Innokentii Gizel', a monk of the Kievan Academy and a representative of the traditionalism of the pre-Petrine genera-tion, retained an audience; published twenty times, it was one of the most popular books in the eighteenth century.[31] This short work possessed an ap-pealing triumphal quality with its emphasis on religious feats: the glorious conversion of Rus' to Orthodoxy under Vladimir I (980–1015) and the equally glorious victory of the Orthodox over the Mongol horde under Ivan III (1462–1505). The rest of the book consisted of brief descriptions of princes and tsars whose quiescence was their paramount feature; they seemingly did little more than come to the throne, build a church or monastery, and then go to their heavenly reward. Eighteenth-century Russian historians aban-doned the *Synopsis* conception of a tsar as a passive ruler and also moved away from a religious teleology; instead they began to write what the Russian philosopher Tatiana Artem'eva has called "historiosophy" *(istoriosofiia),* which emphasized a secular, activist ruler.[32]

In Peter the Great, the Russian secular histories could find a vivid exam-ple of Voltaire's necessary connection between progress and the royal per-son. The tsar's full-scale program of reform made him the prototype of en-lightened monarchs in Europe and prompted Russian historians to advance the dynamic interpretation of absolute monarchy that became a hallmark of the century. The 1770s and 1780s witnessed a demand for works about the great tsar. As the writer of one preface declared, reading about Peter's deeds "lifted the heart of every Russian citizen," and printing houses rushed to "republish everything."[33] These publications imposed the Petrine validation on past sovereigns, and *rois fainéants* were given deprecating epi-thets since "they made no important changes." Mal'gin, for one, slurred over Rostislav the Prayerful, Vsevolod I the Quiet, and Fedor III the Sickly, despite their formerly revered reputations as monk-rulers.[34]

The new secular histories emerged as one of the most important components of the genre of advice literature and presented images of monarchs far more activist than any in the genre's long tradition. Writers lectured that the activity expected of a dynamic tsar went beyond the customary functions of warrior and judge and superseded the old primary role of defender of Orthodoxy. According to Lomonosov's typical list, the new duties included increasing the population, eradicating idleness, fostering prosperity, raising the cultural level, battling superstition, encouraging geographical exploration, and, more traditionally, expanding borders.[35] Absolute monarchs were also to provide moral leadership in a secular society breaking away from religious norms: Catherine II claimed that a ruler needed to save people "from envy," interestingly the vice most prominently mentioned by eighteenth-century Russian historians; Mankiev lauded monarchs who tried to eliminate drunkenness; Mal'gin looked to them to banish anti-Semitism from the realm.[36] Tatishchev portrayed Peter as an ideal monarch because he enabled his country to thrive in everything from manufacturing to the reorganization of the state—despite a long and costly war.[37]

As the century wore on, not only the traditional image of Orthodox tsar but even that of warrior-king receded in the wake of the perceived need for reform. Sumarokov deemed "domestic improvements . . . the greatest tasks of monarchs." Mal'gin agreed that "domestic accomplishments are infinitely more precious than all victories and conquests"; his entry on Peter the Great, for instance, devoted 50 percent to domestic deeds, while Lomonosov devoted 95 percent to military exploits; 95 percent of Mal'gin's entry on Catherine related to internal reform, while Peter III was condemned because of his "enthusiasm for military affairs."[38] Foreign histories of Russia, however, continued to stress military feats.

With monarchs considered the ultimate causal factor in the state, historians felt the need not only to hail personal virtues or triumphs but also to condemn vices or failures. Shcherbatov announced in the foreword to his first volume of *Russian History:*

> History alone, directed by truth itself, has the right with equal daring to praise the illustrious deeds and virtues of earthly Tsars and to condemn their vices in order to let posterity remember what it must imitate and avoid; to insure to good Tsars, worthy and glorious immortality, and to those evil, punishment.[39]

This didactic purpose moved the art away from its medieval moorings wherein "the purpose of all who have written history is to extol the famous deeds of valiant men."[40] For instance, in Tatishchev's work, warnings took the place of mere eulogies: "With the good judgment and proper behavior of a sovereign, a state is enhanced, enriched and flourishing, but laziness, love of luxury, and cruelty [in a sovereign] are ruinous, and our history is filled enough with such examples."[41] Similarly, Boltin quoted Abbé Guillaume Raynal that a populace tends to "remain on its sovereign's [moral and cultural] level," and thus it was a civic responsibility to raise the monarch's standard.[42] In this way, Enlightenment historians became zealous practitioners of advice literature as they felt duty-bound to instruct monarchs on their tasks and to provide them with textbooks of political morality.

Histories served a political function in the eighteenth century. They explored the mutual interests of tsar and people, the place of war and conquest in the royal agenda, the role of great people in a country's development, and the broader questions of the meaning and direction of history. The very first statement about writing secular history in Russia offered the hope that it would demonstrate to sovereigns the "results of good and evil acts."[43] Lomonosov expected his history to "give sovereigns examples of governing," while Tatishchev claimed that history's "use" was providing rulers with "a knowledge of the past" so that they may "wisely discuss the present and future."[44] Nikolai Novikov suggested that a "Philosopher-King . . . could inculcate, spread, implant . . . support, encourage, and patronize knowledge," thereby using the entire litany of hortatory verbs typical of eighteenth-century writers in spurring or motivating their monarchs into enlightened action.[45] Histories were envisioned as providing a guide for all of society.

> All readers are aware that the reading of history brings people much benefit. It teaches the lower ranks of people to be content with their station. It admonishes magnates to work hard and be diligent in fulfilling their duties toward those subject to them and to provide their monarch with useful and salutary advice. It reminds monarchs of their responsibilities, it shows them the meaning of justice, it holds them back from excess and setting bad examples.[46]

When Catherine herself wrote a history of early Russia, a project into which she put much work, her didactic purpose involved demonstrating to her readers that all good things come from the throne and had since the days of Rus'. Her descriptions of the great rulers of Kiev tended to allude to herself.

> Grand Prince Vladimir was by nature a wise, thoughtful, kind, and just man. His court was splendid. He built cities and many edifices for the people and populated the wilderness. He attracted learned people to Russia as well as the arts and sciences. Courageous knights came from everywhere, and he rewarded his servitors generously. The Chronicles say that Vladimir was fond of the opposite sex, but so was Solomon.[47]

The Russian historians all wrote within the framework of absolute monarchy, but in reflecting the specific concerns of their generation they elaborated three distinct patterns for interpreting their form of government, patterns that can be referred to as "schools" even though they remain the historian's construct. The dynastic approach found its inspiration in the Petrine reforms; the empirical emphasis reacted to the February Days of 1730; while the nondespotic school responded to Catherine's battle to break the identification of the Russian monarchy with despotism. The interpretations differed according to what authors understood as the basis for the legitimacy and feasibility of absolutism in Russia, and each paradigm offered its own version of historical events, often contradicting the others.

The differences in these three interpretations is underscored when each fixes on an antithetical moment in history, one that undermines absolute monarchy as legitimized, justified, or defined by the "school," and thus threatens its thesis of Russian development. When describing this antithetical event, the historians wrote at greater length and used emotional and hyperbolic language in contrast to their usual dry and factual presentation, which more often than not consisted in a ponderous rephrasing of old chronicles. During the narration of the antithetical event, history became transformed into a morality play or cautionary tale, and the authors confirmed their dedication to the Enlightenment's stress on didactic purpose. These various interpretations did not constitute neat categories and did not replace or argue against each other but instead accumulated, overlapped, and offered complementary assessments of the merits and problems of the Russian monarchy. In the end, all three coexisted and thus helped produce a rich and nuanced intellectual context for the political dialogue that characterized the century.

THE DYNAMIC DYNASTY

Peter the Great's radical moves to modernize Russia and secularize the state coincided with the early Enlightenment's movement away from medieval structures of knowledge and value systems based on tradition and religious authority. This atmosphere gave rise to a secular and dynamic interpretation of Russian monarchy by emphasizing a dynastic reading of Russian history. Mankiev made the first break with the Orthodox interpretation of Gizel's *Synopsis*. The novelty of the dynastic interpretation lay in its emphasis on secular events and material progress, and its replacement of religious with dynastic sanction. For instance, while dynastic histories concentrated on the political struggle between absolute monarchy and republicanism in fifteenth-century Novgorod, the ecclesiastical histories were concerned with the Novgorodians' flirting with foreign faiths. Again, in striking contrast to the *Synopsis*, Lomonosov's enormously popular *Short Russian Chronicle* devoted only six lines to the Christianization of Russia.[48] In a word, previous works equated the history of Russia with the history of Orthodoxy in Russia; the new histories equated it with the fortunes of Russia's two dynasties.

Mankiev charted a teleological approach; his motivation for writing history arose from his desire to bear witness to the accomplishments of the reforming tsar and to trace the origins of this phenomenon in Russia's past.

Given the lackluster character of post-Petrine rulers, this emphasis remained strong until Catherine II ascended the throne. Lomonosov, Trediakovskii, Barkov, a dozen unpublished historians, and most children's histories imitated Mankiev's dynastic approach, since the authors shared his dynamic interpretation of Russian development.[49] Of course, these men knew, but never mentioned, that Peter had abrogated hereditary succession and primogeniture in Russia. Given the popularity of keeping rulers within the Romanov clan, these works may have also been inspired by a desire to buttress the cause of dynastic legitimacy.

This group of historians sought the roots of Russia's contemporary achievement in the long line of Riurikid and Romanov rulers, whose secular leadership, they argued, resulted in the country's past strength and greatness and guided it toward an even more glorious future. In a way, dynastic causality remained old-fashioned, for it stayed within the premise of the chronicle tradition that "the genealogy of monarchs forms the basis of Russian history," and that archives contain dozens of lengthy genealogical studies that examined every rivulet of the Riurikid clan.[50] These historians also betrayed a polite attitude—not valued among critically thinking Enlightenment figures—that any legally born monarch "deserves praise," even an Ivan the Terrible.[51]

Dynastic historians presented Russian readers with a monarchy that could boast of a ruling house the equal to any in the rest of Europe, an important desideratum when the country was still often regarded as a barbaric backwater. In this version of events, the legitimacy of a Russian monarch rested on resplendent lineage and constant efficacy, traits the historians accentuated even when describing the dawn of Russian history. The eighteenth-century public generally accepted the idea that "Russia" originated in the ninth century when discordant Slavic tribes called Riurik and his kin from some distant land to rule over them. The dynasts, however, wanted to downplay the foreign origin of Russia's first dynasty, heighten its grandeur, and challenge the Normanist theories of the German historians, Gottlieb Bayer and Gerhard Müller, who denigrated the Slavs as being primitive before the coming of the Varangians, often called Normans.[52]

Embellishing a then dubious and now discredited chronicle, the dynastic historians upgraded Gostomysl'—the legendary last leader of ancient Novgorod—into an internationally renowned prince whose advice was sought by rulers from "distant countries." They then claimed that his daughter, Queen Umila of Finland, was Riurik's mother; this genealogy resulted in a happy intersection *(peresechenie)* of bloodline—the same term used to connect the Riurikids and Romanovs—that linked the founding dynasty with the family of the last Slavic "prince." In Lomonosov's histories, Riurik came from a Slavic tribe, the Roksolani.[53] By the end of the century, Riurik began to "speak Slavic," and Catherine included all these embellishments in her history and play about Kievan Rus'.[54] To underscore further that Riurik was "of the highest blood and lineage," these historians resurrected the old myth that he descended from a long imperial line that stretched from Assyrian and Egyptian monarchs to David and Solomon, Alexander the Great, Julius Caesar, Augustus, and Prus.[55]

For the dynastic school, the invitation to Riurik demonstrated that, like any proper people, the Russians recognized the need for an illustrious ruling clan, which "by dint of a single blood and for the common good" could "unite the Slavic peoples into a single tribe under single rule." Once Riurik "established autocratic power," simultaneously Russia came into being and immediately "flourished," to use the most common verb *(tsvesti)* associated with dynastic leadership.[56] It was important for all the historians to interpret Russia's origins, since there existed a significant body of thinkers in eighteenth-century Europe who considered that "only the practices that existed at the founding of the monarchy were . . . legitimate," and thus the attitude toward Riruik provided the keystone of a historian's historical thesis.[57]

For these authors, the reign of Peter the Great proved the benefits of nearly a millennium of dynastic leadership. He was not just the "culmination" of the Romanov dynasty, but of all dynasties; one history allowed half of its nearly seven hundred pages for recounting Peter's day-to-day activities and recognized him as the best issue of an ancestral line traced back to Noah. One anonymous author began in the style of an ecclesiastical history but then, as if unable to suppress himself, spent the rest of the manuscript recounting Peter's deeds.[58] Mankiev saw in Peter's reign a demonstration of the intimate connection between monarchy and progress: "He enlightened all Rus' . . . , and it was as though reborn."[59]

Lomonosov, likewise awed by Peter's dynamism, pioneered a progressive but cyclical view of Russian history, whose fortunes rose and fell depending on the strength of dynastic leadership. Each stage arose from the ashes of the previous, more glorious than before: "Far-sighted sovereigns" ensured that "each misfortune was followed by a prosperity greater than before, each fall by a greater renewal."[60] The dynastic historians possessed little sophistication in their political views, but, inspired by Peter's achievements, they happily celebrated his long line of Riurikid and Romanov ancestors. By no longer anchoring legitimacy in divine prescription or merely in bloodline, they announced a dynamic and secular definition of absolute monarchy, pronouncing it the one form of government with proven historical capacity to assure Russia's stability, grandeur, and progress.[61]

The dynastic historians were rooted in classical learning, and their works also served to counteract the frequently idealized democratic republics of the ancients. Mankiev noted that Russians lived under such a democratic form of government before Riurik arrived, and he portrayed a Hobbesian state of "envy, feuding, discord, and enmity"; another historian found it laughable that any Slavs might want their former "freedom" back.[62] Lomonosov rued that medieval Novgorod's "free charters resulted in a not small cause for the division of Russia"; he claimed delight when finally Ivan III "abolished the republic . . . and brought it under his own autocracy."[63]

In the first half of the eighteenth century, it seemed good form to recognize a similarity between Roman and Russian history.[64] Although Lomonosov felt forced to admit that Rome thrived when a republic, he concluded: "On the contrary, with difference of opinion and freedom Russia nearly fell into total ruin; autocracy from the beginning strengthened her and, after the unfortunate times, restored, fortified, and made her illustrious." An anonymous historian elaborated that under monarchic leadership Russia's history had become "greater than even that of Greece or Rome." The dynastic interpretation cast republicanism in a negative light and associated it with a bestial type of freedom *(svobodnost')* that in Russia had led only to anarchy, civil war, and bloodletting. However, this did not imply that Russians had settled for slavery or despotism, for their monarchs were not tyrants but legitimate and dynamic monarch-legislators in whom breathed "the spirit of Numa, the ancient Roman law giver."[65]

The antithetical event, the very historical episode that threatens the thesis of Russian development, occurred for the dynastic historians when "illegitimate" monarchs tried to interrupt normal dynastic succession and brought the state close to ruin. Mankiev's *History* reads like a calm, rather dull, genealogical tale. The author treated the legitimate Ivan the Terrible with gentle courtesy. He recognized Vasilii Shuiskii as a legal monarch because he could trace his lineage back to Riurikid grand princes, and the boyar-tsar's problems were attributed to "the envy and lack of unity among Russians themselves." The tone dramatically altered when the "illegitimate" Boris Godunov ascended the throne. The dynastic historians maintained that Fedor, the last of the Riurikid rulers, wanted the throne to go to his cousin, a Romanov; there would then have been yet another "intersection," this time "with Riurikid blood," since Anastasia Romanovna had been married to Ivan IV during the "good" part of his reign. This handing over of the sceptre, with "Godunov looking on with envious eyes," is one of the great "moments in Russian history," which Lomonosov thought should be depicted in painting.[66]

In this version of events, Boris, Fedor's brother-in-law, conspired to seize the throne, and the "illegitimacy" of his reign caused the Time of Troubles. Mankiev described Boris as odious and personally responsible for flood, famine, inflation, widespread crime, smoking, and drunkenness; in addition, Boris stood accused of arresting and robbing boyar clans; supposedly, his policies in Astrakhan resulted in such poverty that parents were forced to sell their children into slavery; and of course he had Dmitrii of Uglich, the last of the Riurikids, killed. With nearly audible relief, Mankiev welcomed the end of the drama: "And thus, although Boris Godunov, having wanted to rule himself, killed the Tsarevich Dmitrii and sought to kill others, nonetheless, he could not kill the legitimate successor to the Muscovite throne," Mikhail Romanov.

As a proper tsar, the first Romanov was able to undo Boris's damage and "save Russia from the Swedish and Polish wolves." In dynastic histories, tirades against Godunov for "alienating the whole people," as Barkov put it, often filled more pages than the deeds of good rulers and occupied as much as one third of the narrative. Boris, of course, had been elected—but this carried no weight with dynastic historians—and his wife was a Riurikid, so she could have provided the "intersection" of bloodline; hence, one suspects a scapegoat was needed on whom to blame the Time of Troubles, once the power of providence no longer sufficed as a causal factor.[67] The reader, of course, might remember and feel doubly certain that Elizabeth had every right to wrest the throne from the regent, Anna Leopol'dovna, who planned a change of dynasty to the Braunschweig line.

Other dynastic historians found their antithetical event in Sofiia Alekseevna's attempt to seize the throne from two legitimate sovereigns, the boys Ivan V and Peter I. Lomonosov's *Chronicle*, while popular, could not have been duller in presentation; it consisted of columned tables with the names and dates of rulers, their degrees of removal from Riurik, and pithy descriptions of their years in power. But when confronting the usurper Sofiia, Lomonosov wrote a separate essay that depicted confiscation, terror, pillage, heresy, and ill-gotten gains that resulted from her illegitimate rule and her "lust for autocratic power." Although "the boyars, the nobility, and the people loved their sovereigns and ardently desired that they take the reins of government into their own hands," they were filled with "fear," the mark of a despot. Lomonosov even condoned Peter's personally taking on the role of executioner in order to undo the power of Sofiia's supporters, the *strel'tsy*: "He made silent his mercy in order to render the justice due."[68] Dynastic historians thus offered clear warnings of the tragedies that could befall Russia when an illegitimate monarch attempted to rule, and they forecast untold progress under rightful dynasts.

THE EMPIRICAL NECESSITY OF ABSOLUTE POWER

While the dynastic model became a standard way of viewing monarchy among the educated elite, Tatishchev originated a second more theoretical interpretation in the 1730s and 1740s, a view later repeated in the works of Emin and three unpublished historians.[69] Whereas Peter's reforms inspired the thrust of the dynastic historians, Tatishchev's impetus came from post-Petrine events and possessed a defensive tone absent in the earlier pattern. Tatishchev had been an ardent "fledgling of Peter's nest" and shared Feofan Prokopovich's views on strong rulership.[70] He thus rued the succession of weak rulers in the second quarter of the eighteenth century and witnessed their lessening of the prestige and political control of absolute monarchs in Russia. He also participated in the February Days of 1730 and the threat of some members of the aristocracy and nobility to place the famous Conditions on the monarch's power.[71] Arguing within the intellectual context of the Enlightenment and focusing on its two most cherished traits, Tatishchev's *History* set out to prove empirically that absolute monarchy remained the most "rational" and "natural" form of government for Russia. Of course, these arguments originated with Greek and Roman thinkers but were reinvented within the context of the Age of Reason. Interestingly, in the 1780s in France, royalist historians followed nearly identical argumentation in their attempts to buttress the Bourbon monarchy.[72]

In the empirical model, history became a laboratory for those abstract principles and natural laws of politics "which we comprehend . . . through our senses and our reason" and which could be "scientifically" observed and tested.[73] Tatishchev had developed the natural law defense of absolutism along with his intellectual companions, Prokopovich and Prince Antiokh Kantemir. Kantemir wrote that Peter "knew by heart all the natural laws," and other writers compared him to "the glorious Bacon."[74] This empirical emphasis was strengthened by the influence of Christian Wolff and Christian Thomasius.[75] These two leaders of the German Enlightenment promoted basing political observations on reason and experience. With such tools, they arrived at the usual conclusion that democracies are appropriate only in small states, aristocracies only where there are protected borders and an educated population, and limited monarchy of the British variety only where people are both enlightened and well acquainted with notions of individualism.

None of these characteristics applied to Russia. Without such conditions, these thinkers insisted that the only possible polity was a state headed by a willful ruler who would wield unlimited powers and work through a bureaucracy to effect the common good. Logically, Tatishchev denied the feasibility of any form of government except absolute monarchy in a country of Russia's size, location, and cultural level: "Large regions, open borders— in particular where the people are not enlightened by learning and reason and perform their duties from fear rather than an internalized sense of right and wrong—must be an [unlimited] monarchy." Anything less than absolute power would invite anarchy and invasion. Hence, Tatishchev reasoned, Peter's unlimited power even gave him the right to choose his own successor without regard to bloodline; on this issue, the empiricists stood alone since the other historians respected the overwhelming sentiment in favor of hereditary monarchy.[76]

After asserting that absolute monarchy figured as Russia's sole rational or pragmatic choice, Tatishchev then followed the age-old tradition of describing this form of government as most natural or innately correct, because it functioned like society's most natural institution, the family. The justification of absolute power flowed from the proposition that "the monarch is like a father," with the state a family writ large; thus, the child's or subject's lack of freedom was natural and just—until the father or monarch could guide his charges to maturity. This paternal structure also implied an ethical foundation for absolutism, which had been missing with the retreat of the previously dominant religious sanction. Tatishchev believed that there existed natural prohibitions against arbitrary or despotic behavior since fathers and monarchs had no reason and "no power to harm or ruin" their children or subjects, only to promote their "welfare, happiness, [and] security"; as assurance, "natural law will always dictate what is useful or harmful." Thus, Tatishchev embraced the optimistic early Enlightenment belief in the necessary functioning of natural laws that accorded with man's innate sense of morality; he could then conclude that unlimited power was not only necessary, but by nature benevolent. The argument put a modern patina on the centuries-old paternal view of monarchical stewardship and gave it double resonance.

Switching similes, Tatishchev and Emin also based the legitimacy of absolute monarchy upon its contractual origin, an argument that was considered empirical in the eighteenth century and that was made popular in Russia with the repeated translation of the writings of Samuel Pufendorf.[77] These thinkers imagined the individual *(poddannyi)* as being a child of the ruler and the people as a whole *(narod)* as being his or her spouse. Tatishchev equated the contract between ruler and ruled with a marriage contract, since it is entered into "fully and rationally" and is "freely made."[78] While the dynastic historians wrote that Riurik had simply "established autocratic power" to bring order to the tribes, Tatishchev and Emin emphasized that a contract had been forged between him and the people. It was the people who recognized the disaster of "freedom," of "each living according to his own will," and it was the people who concluded "that autocratic rule was preferable to anarchy."[79] Next, it was the people who besought "Riurik to take all the power alone" and "firmly establish absolutism"; they "deemed it best to submit to a single rule and, after unanimous agreement, they called Riurik."[80] Thereafter, his descendants signed themselves "tsar and grand prince and autocrat of Russia," again in keeping with popular consent since the people reasoned that without an unlimited monarch "there existed neither order nor justice."[81] Catherine, whose historical views wandered from school to school, agreed on this issue. In her *Antidote,* she made it a central point that "a sovereign without limits" was the choice of the people—in this instance after the Time of Troubles—in order to stop the strife in the Russian lands: "the peoples' voice upon that occasion was, '*We will have one sovereign and not twenty masters.*'" Later, Anna responded to the "voice of the nation" when she ripped up the Conditions."[82] Locke and his followers excepted, most thinkers in the first half of the eighteenth century, including Tatishchev, believed that the original contract, formulated in the state of nature, "can be destroyed by no one."[83]

Tatishchev was so convinced of the continuing necessity for unlimited monarchy in Russia that, throughout his *History,* he judged tsars almost solely on their maintenance and increase of absolute power. For instance, he had no trouble applauding Ivan IV's supposed strengthening of monarchical prerogative, even through a policy of terror; he recognized that Godunov was a "despoiler of the throne," but at least he ruled with a firm hand. Like the dynastic school, the empirical historians extolled Peter; however, they praised him not as the culmination of the dynasty but of unlimited power; by ending the patriarchate and denying the need for boyar assent to legislation, Peter more firmly confirmed uncontested absolute power.[84]

The empirical school thus presented to the Russian educated public a monarchy whose unlimited power was empirically necessitated by dint of physical and cultural circumstances, conformity to natural law, and force of contract. Nonetheless, although Tatishchev believed that absolute monarchy alone was suitable in Russia for the foreseeable future, he also believed in forward movement. He defined progress as the gradual accumulation of knowledge—under the leadership of a firm monarch/father—with each generation building on the achievements of the previous until a fully enlightened population developed. Then, and only then, could he envision a lessening of the Russian monarch's unlimited power and, presumably, only when both tsar and people agreed to renegotiate their contract.[85]

Tatishchev and Emin predictably recognized antithetical events each time absolute monarchy was replaced by aristocracy. Darkness and disgust clouded their otherwise arid prose until joy emerged at the return of unlimited power. For instance, monarchy disintegrated in the eleventh and twelfth centuries and that in part paved the way for the Mongol yoke of the thirteenth and fourteenth centuries. Tatishchev's sympathies were clear:

> Thus arose aristocracy, but it was without decency . . . and there was a great bloodletting; and all this gave free rein to the Tatar invader to destroy everything and subjugate everyone to its power and, because of this, autocracy, the strength and honor of Russian sovereigns, was extinguished . . . as was church learning, and the people were plunged into superstition. . . . And thus it continued for 130 years . . . until the restoration of the ancient monarchy.[86]

In marked contrast to the dynastic school's interpretation of the Time of Troubles, Boris did not upset the empirical historians—for he ruled with absolute power—but they accused Shuiskii, elected tsar by his fellow boyars, of overseeing "a pure aristocracy" of seven families and that, "because of this wayward government, soon the state fell into such extreme ruin and collapse that it barely escaped partition or Polish overlordship." In Tatishchev's circles, open comparisons noted that the same seven families attempted to substitute aristocratic rule in 1730: "A great many of those vindictive grandees," wrote Tatishchev, "were power-hungry, others money-hungry, and others filled with uncontrollable spite against their opponents," and none had any concept of working for the common good or the enlightenment of the people, "the true aims of government."[87] With the fierce denunciation he drew from these two historical events, Tatishchev hoped to discredit forever proponents of aristocracy in Russia.

THE DANGERS OF DESPOTISM

The dynasts presumed absolute power on the part of the monarch, and the empiricists regarded it as a necessity; indeed, throughout Europe, philosophes uncritically applauded monarchs for their capacity quickly to enact enlightened reforms. At the same time, of course, they assumed that natural laws and self-limitation provided sufficient insurance against power being wielded in an oppressive, unjust, cruel, and arbitrary manner, and despoiling the common welfare and security of person and property. However, beginning in the 1760s, the focus shifted from the benefits of unlimited power and an examination of its origins to the dangers of despotism. In Russia, the *Bironovshchina* during the reign of Anna Ioannovna, the alleged tyranny practiced by Peter III, and Catherine II's assiduous contrast between her own "rule of law" and the "despotism" of her husband also encouraged discussion of the nature of absolute power and prevention of its dangers. In this atmosphere, historians gave birth to a new model for interpreting absolute monarchy; this "school" includes seven published authors and a half dozen unpublished ones whose histories were written in roughly the last third of the century. The nondespotic school strove to validate Russia's form of government as a "true" monarchy and to fight its equation with despotism, even eschewing the title of "autocrat" to make their point.[88]

These historians absorbed the established image of a dynamic and secular tsar of glorious clan, proven competence, and empirical necessity. However, the dynasts and empiricists applauded unlimited power. In contrast, the nondespotic group lectured monarchs and readers that all power, save despotic, is circumscribed. For the nondespotic school, history would demonstrate that the legitimacy and feasibility of absolute monarchy lay in the fact that its authority had always been de facto limited. From studying the past, this school would also draw the assumption that de jure limitations were close at hand.[89] Shaping the past to suit the political needs of the present also proved common in France and Britain, as historians constructed a "stereotyped model or contesting models" and used past examples to legitimate current practices or aspirations.[90]

The authors in this school of historians took a defensive posture vis-à-vis Europe in describing Russia's monarchy. Probably, this stemmed from their feeling that they were full-fledged participants in the Enlightenment but that many Europeans did not yet recognize Russia as having come of age. Certainly, they were angry that some Europeans regarded the Russian monarchy not as a variant of absolutism but as a separate form of "primitive despotism." Boltin, for instance, was incensed by the statement of a French historian that "from ancient times they [the Russians] lived in slavery and always recognized bondage as their natural condition." Boltin penned two volumes of uninterrupted spleen trying to refute this conception, all the while insisting, "We are Europeans."[91] Catherine II had begun the attack in 1767 by starting her *Nakaz* with the flat statement, "Russia is a European state." In her "History" of 1783, she reminded Enlightenment thinkers of their precept that "humankind everywhere and forever has the same passions, desires, and inclinations and for achieving them not rarely uses the same means." Boltin agreed: "Read through the past centuries of all kingdoms and of all republics and you will find the same behavior, conduct, and actions . . . virtue and vice belong to all ages and to all nations," and to both sexes, he added, when someone tried to claim that female monarchs are more kindly and moderate than male ones: "Women are simply people and have the same virtues and the same vices."[92]

In keeping with this spirit, Boltin was willing to admit that Ivan IV was a tyrant but only while insisting that he was little different from other rulers of the era—such as Louis XI of France—and the empress, in one of her more defensive moods, contended that Biron was similar to Cardinal Richelieu.[93] Catherine's optimistic thesis was that Russia "had approximately the same customs, went along the same path, and ended up on nearly the same level as all the other European countries"; although this happy progress had been interrupted by the Time of Troubles, the country was rapidly making up for its backwardness. Russia's evolution had thus led her to the stage of true monarchy—under Catherine's leadership of course.[94] These historians also followed Catherine's lead in the *Nakaz* by postulating a firm connection between their form of government and civic freedom, that is, security of person and property, and by contending that monarchy was grounded on rule by law. They thereby "reinvented" Russian monarchy—sincerely one can believe—and their description made it more in step with Enlightenment ideals and Russian aspirations.

Prince Shcherbatov, himself a member of one of Russia's oldest aristocratic families, was unique among this group in arguing that the aristocracy had always limited monarchy and prevented its slip into despotism. His depiction of absolutism centered on its necessity in Russia and on how an absolute monarch needed to cooperate with the magnates; both aspects resulted from the weakness of human nature. Shcherbatov greatly admired David Hume, especially his emphasis on the psychology of both rulers and ruled as causal factors in history. Similarly, Shcherbatov believed that people in general lack moderation; they act either like "wild beasts after blood" or "like lambs" and eternally engage in a contest between passion and reason and virtue and vice.[95] While Tatishchev marshaled cool abstractions to prove a natural need for absolute monarchy, Shcherbatov stressed that mankind's natural bestiality required the guidance of an authoritarian ruler.

The prince believed, like most Enlightenment thinkers, that monarchs were the primary causal factors in state and society, but he deviated by viewing the people as inert or passive under a ruler's dominance. A more enlightened population would make more freedom possible, he agreed, but until then, the people were tabulae rasae upon whom the monarch impressed his mark. The ruler's psychological makeup, intelligence, and character informed the level of laws and these in turn informed the level of morals and manners among the people. In Russia, Shcherbatov warned, whenever the people prematurely tried to control the government, for instance in the Republic of Novgorod, freedom "turned into an evil and one of the causes for Russia's ruin."[96]

While arguing the necessity for absolute monarchy in Russia, Shcherbatov recognized that such a realm also had an inherent weakness: rulers themselves were human and hence tempted by such vices as "ambition and despotism." In a theory reminiscent both of premodern Russian conceptions of a "good tsar" and of Montesquieu's *thèse nobiliaire*, he averred that Russian monarchs had avoided these weaknesses by acting in harmony with a council of wise aristocratic elders or boyars; from the time of Riurik, only this "holy union" had provided Russia's defense against despotism. In other words, for Shcherbatov there were two collective actors on the historical stage, rulers and aristocrats. He alone of all the historians made the causal connection that "the state flourishes and its prosperity increases where there is fidelity, honor, unity, and strength in the hearts of the aristocracy," not just of the monarchs. For instance, Shcherbatov directly blamed the dim and childless Tsar Fedor for the rise of despotism during the Time of Troubles since he relied on the upstart Boris Godunov for advice rather than on "the most worthy, most farsighted true servants of the fatherland," the old boyars, a criticism the dynasts never mentioned. The problem was compounded by Boris's psychological makeup; he demonstrated a capability for ruling, but his fatal vice, "lust for the throne," led to his hostility to the boyars and thus to his "becoming despotic." The causal flow led, in turn, to the collapse of the economy and autocracy and near extinction at the hands of Sweden and Poland.[97]

Shcherbatov's treatment of Peter the Great was more equivocal. The emperor committed Shcherbatov's trio of mortal sins: he was a man of passion, he failed to consult with boyars, and he used despotic measures. However, Shcherbatov forthrightly admired Peter and forgave his sins as normal in the era, and because backward Russia needed a forcible thrust into the modern age. Shcherbatov continued the thesis first expressed by Feofan Prokopovich, namely, that Russia before Peter was a dark and isolated land plunged in ignorance and lacking any concept of human dignity. While Shcherbatov agreed that Peter "raised despotism to a new extreme," at the same time he brought "Russia out of weakness into strength, out of disorder into order, and out of ignorance into enlightenment."[98]

Shcherbatov's sponsorship of his own small group's ability to curb despotism had limited appeal among the broader ranks of the educated elite. In addition, the fact that the boyars were powerless to prevent Ivan IV's despotism weakened Shcherbatov's own confidence in the aristocratic limitation. By the last volume of his *History*, which extends to the year 1610, he seemed to concede that formal guarantees offered more certainty, a solution that grew ever more popular as the century wore on. Shuiskii, the "unlucky" boyar-tsar who ruled during the Time of Troubles, was adjudged "glorious among all earthly rulers," because he wanted to take an oath "in keeping with the institution of monarchical power" but with guaranteed legal protection of at least boyar life and property. Shcherbatov, in the dedication of his history to Catherine, prodded her to follow suit: "Since the people have been oppressed for so many centuries already, they await from Your hand their happiness and freedom . . . , the most precious gift of mankind."[99]

Other writers reexamined the historical evidence for curbs on despotism and discovered a Russian political tradition rooted in the elective principle that the recurrent succession crises had brought to the fore. This interpretation completely contradicted the dynasts' picture in which Riurik imposed absolute monarchy and Tatishchev's empirical concept of a contract in which the people once and forever gave Riurik and his descendants unlimited power. Elagin emphasized that, among the early Russians, "we do not find the slightest sign of autocracy, and even less of despotism, and neither an hereditary throne," but rather "examples of the free election of Leaders or Princes." Other historians of this epoch claimed that Riurik was "never given unlimited power," and that is why his descendants never took a kingly title or crown.[100] Russian rulers, they contended, were never "considered the image of God or earthly gods," and hence "princes, boyars, and the people took part in government and the power of the Grand Princes was not autocratic"; in fact, from the beginning, "the Russian people were free." Boltin cited the people of the city of Vladimir saying: "We are a free people. We chose the princes ourselves, and they kissed the cross before us." Professor Khariton Chebotarev of Moscow University, Catherine's mentor on history, confirmed that "autocratic government in Russia . . . was founded on free and voluntary election" but added that over the centuries people had constantly renewed the election because the rule of an absolute monarch was consonant with the common good.[101] The motif of the monarch being "chosen" became a constant theme in histories written in the last third of the century, reflecting the circumstances surrounding Catherine's version of her own ascent.

While agreeing with the dynastic school and the empiricists that monarchy was the only suitable form of government for Russia, the nondespotic school did so on different grounds. Their point was to demonstrate that throughout Russian history absolute monarchy better guarded freedom, or security of person and property, than did the other two forms of government. Medieval Novgorod, according to Chebotarev, demonstrated "the natural and ruinous results of a democracy": "It is not strong enough to uphold and defend the freedom and rights of its citizens." Boltin concurred: "Experience demonstrates that a democratic government cannot preserve the security and tranquility of individual people" as "freedom turns into willfulness or lack of restraint." For this reason, he explained, Russians long ago understood that "the rule of a single person is incomparably better, more profitable, and more useful both for society and especially for the individual than the rule of many," where "envy, squabbling, and hatred reign." In addition, "monarchy in a large state is preferable to aristocracy, which normally wastes time in argumentation and is not given to daring views; only a Monarch can launch and carry actions of great import." Boltin concluded: "Monarchical government occupies the middle ground between despotism and republics and is the most reliable safeguard of freedom."[102]

In their association of freedom and absolute monarchy, the nondespotic school tended to be critical of Peter the Great for his use of force in promulgating legislation. Boltin, unlike Shcherbatov, believed that the people, not the tsars, should ultimately make the laws because "laws conform to behavior rather than behavior to laws." He thus preferred Catherine the Great as a "model of wise and great sovereigns" since, in her "golden age," Peter's use of force was abandoned. Russians wrote forcefully on this issue. Iakov Kozel'skii, the philosopher, translated a work of Danish history and wrote in an annotation that the eleventh-century King Canute, despite his fame, must be considered an "unlawful" ruler; his use of force made him "a great tyrant, a great thief, and an inhumane spiller of blood, but not a great monarch."[103]

In Russia, serfdom remained a problem, since force was being used to ensure servitude. After agreeing with Rousseau that slavery is "the primary sin against nature," Boltin temporized and took the position that became standard among moderate and enlightened Russians until the eve of emancipation: only after the soul is freed through education could the body be freed and, then, only "by degrees and gradually." He depicted Catherine the Great as pushing the process forward because she understood how "to teach each subject to use freedom for the benefit of himself as well as of his neighbor and the fatherland." The owner of nine hundred male "souls," Boltin hoped that soon legislation would be passed "to limit the powers of landowners over their serfs" and trusted that full freedom, even for the serfs, would be harvested as the "fruit of Catherine's labors."[104] Elagin was equally optimistic. Although he was nearly alone among the Russian historians in ruing the "beating down of Novgorod's freedom," that "indubitable beginning of Russian history," he was confident that under Catherine, Novgorod's form of government would be resumed in Russia.[105] Another instance of history being written backward, Elagin's ideal government not so mysteriously resembled the balance of power and rule of law attained by the eighteenth-century British monarchy. Ippolit Bogdanovich's *Historical Depiction of Russia,* which carried only to 1015, viewed Vladimir the Wise as the culminating ruler of Kievan Rus' because Vladimir established a council—similar to Panin's imperial council—and ruled with the advice of elder statesmen, a next step he was suggesting to Catherine in this conscious example of advice literature.[106]

Thus, this pattern defined absolute monarchy as inherently nondespotic because its power had always been limited de facto by aristocratic counsel, rule by law, and an elective principle that offered continuous validation.

Furthermore, these historians nurtured a hope that the problem of despotism would finally be resolved when—under the guidance of the "ever wise legislator," as Catherine the Great liked to be called—de jure limitations on power would be put into effect.[107]

Instances of perceived despotism, as expected, provided the material for antithetical events for this school of historians. Sumarokov, like Lomonosov, decried the rule of Sofiia, but with revealing contrasts. Sumarokov anchored the true legitimacy of a monarch in both "inheritance and laws," but he considered the regent and hopeful monarch a usurper not because of bloodline (she herself was a Romanov) but because "the public had elected" Peter tsar. With the support Sofiia received from those "most vile and venomous" armed guards, the government became the tyranny that the nondespotic school was warning against. Indeed, Sumarokov rendered an exceptional portrait of a good monarchy's antithesis, one similar to the rule of a Caligula or Nero: "the love and warm feeling between monarchs and subjects" disappeared; subjects were turned into "slaves who trembled day and night"; "weapons and willfulness" replaced regularity of rule; there was a disregard of law, "the foundation on which the prosperity of all the Russian people is based." Sumarokov ended with the didactic peroration that the *strel'tsy* episode was "our disgrace!" and Russians should "know the truth and learn."[108] Catherine, on the other hand, correctly and in a spirit of sisterhood, claimed that history had not treated Sofiia "fairly," since she "ruled quite ably."[109]

Shcherbatov defined a good monarch as one who took boyar advice, and thus his antithetical event was the reign of Ivan IV, against whom he directed 1,223 pages of diatribe. When Ivan first began to reign, Shcherbatov asserted, "the conduct of the ruler was completely praiseworthy, as he did nothing of importance without the advice of his relatives and boyars."[110] It should be noted that most other historians, regardless of "school," attributed Ivan's problems to the "envy, bribery, and hypocrisy" he witnessed while under boyar care as a youth.[111] At any rate, for Shcherbatov, when the union between tsar and boyar was broken, "good spirit, love for the fatherland, and fidelity to the ruler were extinguished with fire and sword and, in their places, were put fear and trembling." The publicist concluded that the inevitable result was "unbridled power," or despotism, "which autocrats so desire" and can obtain unless restrained by their best and brightest boyars. Another historian who shared Shcherbatov's views devoted 312 pages of a 675-page narrative to the "Tsar-Tormentor."[112]

In the nondespotic school, Boltin and Mal'gin considered Ivan an aberration and recognized that Boris Godunov had been elected to the throne by a legal assembly. Their antithetical event occurred during the reign of Anna Ioannovna, herself not a despot, but rather a ruler who was dominated by her German favorite, Biron, "an ignoble tyrant" who "robbed the people blind." (This left Ivan as the "only" despot.) To heighten their accusation, Boltin and Mal'gin contrasted the era of Biron with the golden age of Catherine, when "everyone expresses his opinion freely." But, in the 1730s, "a wife was afraid to speak with her husband, a father with his son, a mother with her daughter about their disastrous condition for fear they would be overheard by servants and denounced." Boltin treated Biron's control of the government and subsequent weakening of monarchical power as a de facto aristocracy: "There you have the fruits of aristocratic power. . . . The evil will incessantly multiply, and its politics will turn into intrigues, into conspiracies, into confrontations, into discord . . . while ambition and cupidity profit from its disorder." Mal'gin quotes Boltin's condemnation word for word but adds that Biron was just as bad as Ivan the Terrible.[113]

FOR ALL THESE SCHOOLS OF HISTORIANS, inflation of prose, character, and incident occurred whenever arguments in favor of the legitimacy and feasibility of absolute monarchy were refuted by actual events that displayed the flaws of that form of government: rule by favorites; the chaos that ensued when the line died out; the incapacity or youth of a monarch that left the opportunity for usurpers; the tragic results of despotiism. Nonetheless, the historians rejected the alternatives. After all, aristocracies and democratic republics were held in low repute or deemed unworkable throughout most of Europe, especially in a large state, and it would seem wisest to take a chance with absolute monarchy. As a member of the dynastic camp, Lomonosov feebly claimed that "the insolence" of a tyrant would be "cut short by death." Tatishchev, the empiricist, considered Ivan IV the single despot and judged that "it would not be sensible to change the former order for such an extraordinary situation." After intense analysis, Boltin concluded: "The ills of a monarchy are ephemeral and light," but "weaknesses in republics are never rectified and remain heavy and lasting"; indeed, "all things considered, it is better to leave things the way they are."[114] Such conclusions were neither reactionary nor even defensive of the status quo. The hope gleamed among these historians that, once Russia had achieved an enlightened population, an enlightened monarch would establish institutionalized limits on absolute power so that, in the words of an often-quoted political aphorism, the ruler would "have all the power to do good and none to do evil." Such a government was the "last, best hope" of most eighteenth-century Europeans, not just Russians, as they moved from adulation of absolutism to a desire for its constitutional limitation.

Overall, the more the critical spirit of the Enlightenment induced eighteenth-century Russian historians to analyze absolute monarchy, the more they became persuaded that it best suited the country's interests, and they became natural partners in a dialogue with their monarchs. Peter inspired Lomonosov and Tatishchev with his modernizing, westernizing vision, and they, both as historians and in their other positions, in turn tried to communicate the idea of progress to his successors. Historians writing during Catherine's era were as anxious as she to cooperate in making Russia as "civilized" and up-to-date as the rest of Europe. Throughout the century, the historians' negative pictures of antithetical tsars and positive pictures of ideal rulers fulfilled the didactic purpose of Enlightenment history, and their monuments of advice literature invited monarchs to apply current Enlightenment standards to their own reigns. Especially during Catherine's era, writers of belles-lettres in general joined historians in reminding their empress of the criteria by which monarchical conduct was being judged.

The Good Tsar

*R*ussian historians tried to inspire monarchs to heroic deeds by emphasizing their role as the principal motive force in their state's development. The men and women who wrote in other branches of literature, especially during Catherine's reign, engaged in dialogue with their ruler most often through utilizing the conceit of the "good tsar" in their works of advice literature. Since the days of Muscovy, the epithet has acted as shorthand for the type of leader the Russian people needed or wanted at any particular historical moment. In pre-Petrine times, the phrase usually referred to an Orthodox ruler who would relieve his subjects of their burdens in dire times. In the chaos of the late Soviet era, Mikhail Gorbachev was irked when his fellow citizens seemed to yearn for a "good tsar . . . someone at the top [who] will impose order and organize change."[1]

For the writers in Catherine's day, the concept of a good tsar incorporated the conceptions of monarchy that had emerged in the course of the century: the patriarchal head of the grand Russian family; the reforming tsar as the captain of a forward-moving ship of state; the elected monarch responsible to his subjects; the legal sovereign whose power rested on the firm foundation of law; and the tsar as the agent of history. In addition, the generation that came of age during Catherine's reign defined a proper monarch as one who avoided despotism because he or she possessed a moral, ethical, or virtuous character. These themes were evident in a steady stream of advice literature that ran throughout the realm of print culture.

ADVICE LITERATURE AS POLITICAL DIALOGUE

Political literature brought to center stage a public discussion of the advantages and dangers of absolute monarchy. This supragenre consisted in passages of significant length in any work that discussed monarchy as a form of government or the monarch as a head of state. Writers did not necessarily present their works as studies of monarchy, although a few texts, particularly among the plays, could qualify as political treatises. Much of the literature dealt with the topic peripherally, for instance as episodes in the plot of a tale of adventure. The political passages in works of literature worked in a more subtle and complex way than would forthright analyses of monarchy. The sections provided a method for communicating to the ruler the expectations of loyal, but discriminating, writers and functioned as an avenue on which to structure and exchange opinion about the Russian form of government, thus engaging in dialogue with the empress. Historians, as already discussed, were notable for their participation in this discourse. In addition, poets, playwrights, novelists, biographers, journalists, memoirists—really anyone who published—eagerly took part in the interchange, so that political themes permeated late-eighteenth-century writings and encompassed a rich panorama of publications and authors that included the empress herself. During Catherine's reign, the subject of monarchy was prominent in roughly 500 of the 2,500 works of belles-lettres examined for this work; and this chapter alone will cite 204 publications and 112 authors.[2]

The writers of this political literature emerged between 1755 and 1775 and constituted a new and more sophisticated generation, according to the compelling analysis of Gary Marker. They had studied in the institutions of the cadet corps, in the military garrison schools, at Moscow University and its boarding affiliates, at Smolnyi Institute, and many at European universities; upon graduation, their intellectual, political, and cultural interests were reflected in print. Through their involvement, littérateurs wrested control of publishing away from the government, whose "guiding and nurturing authority" they had "outgrown."[3] This new generation thus provided both authors and audience for a rather frank discourse on monarchy, with writers and publishers making the conscious decision to address political topics.

The idea of a good tsar figured prominently in this dialogue between ruler and ruled. Historians were seeking to replace theology with the philosophy of history as a way of understanding the course of human affairs. In similar fashion, others among the Russian educated elite—with the Masons at the forefront—much like their European brethren, sought to replace religion with morality as a guide for discovering the norms of and spurs to personal, and monarchical, moral conduct outside the established churches.[4] Their quest involved a variety of excursions: among the ideals of enlightened absolutism; in the *Aufklärung*'s emphasis on the responsibility of the individual to and within the community; and to the neo-Stoic, Pietist, and Masonic stress on the drive for moral self-perfection in the service of mankind.[5] All these influences figured prominently in late-eighteenth-century discourse and were called upon to define standards of behavior for the individual and monarch alike.

Not surprisingly, then, much political discourse falls into the category of advice literature. Russians had a healthy tradition in place, but the number of works exploded during Catherine's reign, when over three times more books were published than during the previous two centuries combined, and the new field of journalism burst forth.[6] By writing advice literature, authors once again demonstrated their participation in the cultural trends on the continent. Advising monarchs was modish, indeed obsessive, throughout Europe in the eighteenth century, and a critical and didactic spirit suffused every literary genre. An Enlightenment sensibility and regnant doctrines dictated the urgency of establishing moral guidelines for both private and public life and of educating men and women to abide by them. Monarchs were no exception. Philosophes confidently explained their special insights on proper governance to rulers whom they sought to enlighten and from whom they sought employment as advisors.[7]

As in the rest of Europe, Russian writers found it *"fashionable* to instruct tsars, to give them advice, to show the path."[8] At first glance, it might be easy to dismiss this literature for its "naïveté and boring didacticism."[9] But in the eighteenth century, audiences loved and lived by books of moral maxims, tales, and fables; literature with a didactic quality was the one area of publication that sold consistently well.[10] The freshness of the Russian utilization of this old genre lay in two aspects: first, the advice literature expanded outside the confines of "mirrors" and into other branches of literature; and, second, the writers successfully used advice literature consciously to establish a dialogue or an avenue of communication with the empress. Realizing that the empress, too, read (and wrote) in nearly all the literary genres, littérateurs freely extended her their counsel from the pulpit of the printed word.

Catherine recognized these works as advice literature; she noted that they intended "to point out the defects of the present form of government and its vices."[11] Writing thus became a form of participation in political life, and the writer identified with the hero of many tales, especially the Wise Counselor, to whom a monarch might listen and who would foil the influence of the villainous Corrupt Courtier. Biographies of good rulers contained unsubtle admonitions: "We hope that *our* rulers will follow his example."[12] Morality tales apostrophized: "Monarchs! Try to rectify your vices for the well-being of your subjects."[13] Name day, birthday, and accession odes were almost always hortatory and directly addressed Catherine and her presumptive heirs, the grand dukes Paul and Alexander.

Literature also sought to act as a mediator between the ruler and the ruled. Authors regarded themselves as the conscience and mouthpiece of the Russian educated elite who were their audience and with whom they "found themselves in a close relationship"; they regularly addressed their works "to all educated society."[14] Writers considered it their Enlightenment duty to use their art to influence the politics of the day. They wanted to mold public opinion, to instruct their readership in systematic political thought, to guide their expectations of government, and to set the standards of what people should approve or disapprove; they tried, in Rousseau's words, to *"dominer les opinions."*[15]

Strong didacticism was coupled with the utopian hope to build a new society based on the professed norms. Mikhail Kheraskov—a prolific author, Mason, and the chief voice of a group of authors centered around Moscow University—in his novel, *Numa Pompilius,* presented readers with a well-run polity, an ideal for which they should strive: "If successful societies do not yet exist on earth, then let us find them in books and console our thoughts that we, in time, can end up happy." He claimed Catherine was heading in the desired direction and that "truth, virtue, and justice . . . are now beginning to triumph in Russia."[16] In order to hasten the process, many of the littérateurs held positions in civil service and regarded both of these activities as "complementary" or "part of a single moral endeavor."[17] Catherine, a self-proclaimed enlightened monarch and a prolific author, found this development congenial, since she wanted Russian writers "to help in developing the ambiance of the *philosophes"* in her own realm.[18]

In eighteenth-century Russia, as throughout Europe, didactic literature became ennobled as an exercise in citizenship, and both traditional and new genres reflected the emphasis. In Catherine's reign, roughly three hundred sermons were published and could have been expected to emphasize religious morality, but surprisingly, in keeping with the times, their message came "very close to a secular ethics."[19] Over three hundred odes were also published. Mikhail Lomonosov, believing in the poet's role as civic spokesman, composed seventeen addressed to five monarchs. His masterful example ensured that the didactic ode would remain a staple of Russian literature into the nineteenth century.[20] Plays, under the influence of Corneille and then Voltaire, remained "traditionally didactic."[21] Littérateurs viewed theater as an "excellent instructional tool" for both monarchs and subjects, and critics urged playwrights to write dramas revolving around episodes in the lives of Russian rulers.[22]

Newer genres demonstrated the same inclination. Novels were suffused with didacticism, following the model of the ever popular *Adventures of Telemachus, Son of Ulysses* (1699), which was published nine times in five translations in Russia and was considered essential reading for every educated Russian child; Andrei Bolotov in his memoirs recalled that it was the first book he read as a child. Fénelon, reputedly the best-educated man of his era, wrote the tale as a guide to the dauphin on how to be an enlightened ruler; Mentor, the voice of wisdom in the novel, provides the young Télémaque with an encyclopedia of knowledge on the practices of good government. Russians not only translated Fénelon's "political" novel, they imitated it, and the genre became an integral part of eighteenth-century literature.[23] The didactic tale set in the East, introduced by the prolific writer Fedor Emin, also emerged as a staple; as in other parts of Europe, it "was often used to discuss philosophical and ethical problems."[24]

Nearly forty journals opened in this era and offered another avenue of discourse since many operated independently of the government and imitated the didactic thrust of Addison and Steele's *Spectator,* "the most fashionable literary invention of the eighteenth century in Europe."[25] The variant of the moral weekly featured depictions of virtuous monarchs and nobility with the hope of improving both and hence the polity. Even government-sponsored journals contained articles of a hortatory nature, often masked as satire.[26]

Genres centering on individual achievement or development also won an audience in the century. Besides the 28 editions depicting the life and deeds of Peter the Great, 77 Russian biographies appeared; of those, 20 limned monarchs and promulgated the notion of the enlightened sovereign. Catherine admitted she read portrayals of monarchs to find inspirational models of behavior. Among foreign works translated into Russian, she preferred Plutarch's *Lives* (published three times in eighteenth-century Russia), and she and her public avidly read the biographies of Marcus Aurelius (6 editions) and of Alexander the Great (5 editions).[27] About 100 memoirs and diaries recount Catherine's reign, and she stood at their center; for instance in Sergei Glinka's recollections, she is mentioned on 110 of its 372 pages and on nearly every leaf of Denis Fonvizin's life of the statesman Nikita Panin.[28]

All these varieties of advice literature might seem timid in comparison with the juicy *libelles* that circulated in France before the revolution or with the fierce attacks on the French monarchy in the 1790s; nonetheless, the genre was not benign. Louis XIV ordered Fénelon's *Télémaque* burned when it appeared, because the author dared to set up norms of behavior for a divine right monarch, and in 1767 the Sorbonne censured Jean François Marmontel's *Bélisaire*—a *Télémaque,* "but without the style"—for giving a "false and odious characterization of sovereign authority, the destruction of the principle of obedience."[29] Catherine found advice literature less threatening. She shocked Marmontel by engaging her courtiers to help translate *Bélisaire* into Russian on a trip down the Volga, so that her public could read his cry for religious tolerance and enlightened rule. Marmontel "refused to believe that the empress herself had translated a whole chapter, above all one in which autocracy is subjected to merciless criticism."[30] But the empress was secure in her goodness and power in 1767. Later, advice literature would pose an inherent danger to her golden image as ruler. Once the sphere of morality sets itself above and in judgment over the sphere of politics, a ruler's actions that are seen as contravening moral laws become acts of violence with the ruler labeled a despot.

The relationship between Catherine and the writing public went through three phases during her reign, running from harmony to counterpoint to dissonance. In the 1760s, there occurred a "great convergence" in what the new ruler and her articulate subjects wanted.[31] Catherine's concern with the general principles of good government stimulated a desire to speak about political issues, and writers rushed to join this energetic administration headed by a model monarch in order to work for peace, legislative reform, and the ending of cronyism or corruption. The empress facilitated the explosion of political literature in yet another way. She held the conviction that she embodied the characteristics of a good tsar and had nothing to fear from writers' commentaries. Thus, as Marker has demonstrated, the empress instituted no "formal mechanism for reviewing books prior to their publication," and "political censorship of Russian books, in fact, almost disappeared in the 1760s." While Catherine still had the right to ban a book, express distaste, or levy indirect sanctions, "none of this activity really amounted to a systematic policy of censorship, indirect or otherwise."[32] Another scholar has suggested that Catherine, in the many publications that appeared in her reign, including the translation of the *Encyclopédie*, wanted to show that "the government no longer regarded the utterance of views critical of absolute monarchy as treasonable or even dangerous."[33]

In the 1770s and 1780s, a certain disappointment set in; while continuing an enlightened program of reform, the empress opted for war with Poland and Turkey and relied more on her favorites, while the Pugachev Revolt stained the picture of enlightened rule. Abundant praise gave way to criticism, and writers—placing their barbs in a way no intelligent reader could miss—described ideal kingdoms in contrast with, rather than as identical to, Catherine's Russia. In this phase, after the disbanding of the Legislative Commission, public discourse took place almost solely in the arena of print. Since the empress kept failing to deliver a new code of law, advice literature began putting more emphasis on encouraging correct policy and avoiding despotism through the ethical individual rather than legal reform.[34] In the usual pattern of monarchical politics, some writers placed their hopes in the heir, the Grand Duke Paul. Others practiced self-censorship when publishing, or privately penned splenetic attacks on her regime; the latter authors made the same criticisms as those who published but heightened the intensity and specificity of the attack. In the 1790s, while still not setting up an organized system of censorship, the empress, alarmed by the French Revolution and the assassination of Gustavus III of Sweden, began her notorious assaults on leading writers that would turn the model monarch of the early reign into the "bad tsar" of the last years.

Advice literature took several approaches during Catherine's reign. Writers at times underscored the monarch's frailty as a mere mortal and counseled a struggle for moral rectitude, since the character of the ruler determined the well-being of the state. In addition, authors used the technique of praise to commend and encourage policies of which they approved. In another variant, writers employed outright criticism to lecture on misdirected policy and behavior.

THE NEED FOR A MORAL MONARCH

Most writers prior to the modern era believed that the morality of a ruler determined the fate of the state; thus, nurturing royal rectitude figured as the central task of a concerned citizenry. Russian writers began goading and criticizing their monarchs once newer theories of kingship agreed that rulers were human beings and not gods immune from judgment. Although Peter the Great demonstrably secularized his office in the beginning of the century, some scholars argue that "sacralization" in its Muscovite form persisted among the elite, and formal odes certainly continued to attribute poetic divine qualities to the tsars.[35] However, the overwhelming majority of belletristic sources displayed a secular attitude that emphasized the ruler's humanity.[36] A children's tale tells of King Canute of England who grew weary of his courtiers' equating him with God. While walking with his attendants along the shore, he ordered the sea to stop lapping at his feet, and when it did not obey, he told his entourage: "Learn from this that the power of a king should not be likened to that of God."[37] A journal article likewise chastises advisors who tell monarchs "they are divinity itself and distract them from the duty of ruling, filling their hearts with the poison of pride."[38] Gavriil Derzhavin, arguably the best poet of the era, reworked a psalm that reminded tsars of their mortality:

> Yet passions rule you, as they do me,
> And you, as I, are mortal too;
> And you shall fall, in no way different
> Than withered leaves shall fall from trees;
> And you shall die, in no way different
> Than your most humble slave shall die![39]

The very popular *Bélisaire* (it went through two translations and seven editions in Russia) similarly displayed no hint of divine right and described a monarch as "a weak individual, a feeble mortal like ourselves, subject to the same infirmities, open to imposition, liable to self-delusion, and prone to errors, which in a moment may prove destructive to millions!"[40] Early in Catherine's reign, Emin's novel *Themistocles*—written for the edification both of "the public" and of the heir—made the point "that rulers are great people, nonetheless *they are people;* consequently, they are susceptible to many passions" and "delusions."[41] An anonymous tale revolved around the contention that "a monarch, just like a citizen, and a citizen, just like a peasant, have weaknesses."[42] Derzhavin reminded Catherine: "The rulers of this world are people all the same, / Crowns they wear, but passions they must tame."[43] The playwright Iakov Kniazhnin put the problem bluntly: "Their power is the power of gods, but their weakness is that of men."[44]

For over two millennia, writers had recognized that the human tendency to err presented no small problem in a monarch. Russians shared the belief that the fate of the country depended "on a great man whose unflagging care . . . results in the prosperity of the people subject to him."[45] Kheraskov addressed Catherine at the height of her popularity and reminded her: "It is not from golden ores, nor from the huge expanse of the borders, not from the large number of people, nor from strength and manliness that the prosperity of a society is recognized; all these depend on the care of a sagacious and humane Monarch."[46] Bolotov, in his memoirs, called Catherine "a great ruler of many millions of people, all of whose fate and happiness depend on her person."[47] Nikolai Novikov, the founder of the book trade in Russia, reminded the empress that a "sovereign or ruler of the people, gifted by nature with the proper qualities for ruling and having supreme power brings happiness and prosperity to both himself and the entire people."[48] Ivan Krylov, the renowned writer of fables, constructed a story about Caliph Kaib with the happy ending that once the Asian ruler had found inner peace, so too followed "the prosperity of the entire kingdom."[49] A public document culled another example of royal causation from recent history, when Catherine replaced Peter III on the throne.

> Wondrous changes suddenly followed. Joy drove out the shadows of grief. Despair gave place to the sweetest hope. . . . From the day of the ascent of her Imperial Majesty to the All-Russian throne, every day we can count Her good deeds: dangers and disorders have been tended to and stopped. Our Orthodox faith celebrates and praises the Monarch, who gives an example to her subjects of piety. Justice reigns with Her Majesty on the throne. The love of humankind dwells in her soul but without weakening the strength of the laws. Vices have disappeared and their root ripped out; while manners have been gently corrected, minds enlightened, and good deeds made to flourish under the holy canopy of the throne. The arts most needed by humankind— agriculture and household management—are encouraged by the monarch's care; trade increases, and with it the abundance of goods multiplies.

In addition, the document noted that the empress had won renewed respect for Russia, since all Europe witnessed these wonders "with astonishment."[50]

The ruler influenced not just the overall prosperity of the realm but the behavior of the populace. Some writers tried to inspire monarchs to achieve a "revolution in the manners" of their people by setting the pace, since any civilizing process "depends entirely upon the will and example of the sovereign." Prince Mikhail Shcherbatov, in his unpublished utopian novel *Ophir,* concurred: "When a tsar is of good behavior, so too will be his subjects, as they love to imitate him."[51] Princess Ekaterina Dashkova, the empress's sometime advisor and the president of the Russian Academy and director of the Academy of Sciences, adjured Catherine that it was important for the state that she possess "wit, taste, good sense, and propriety." In the eighteenth century, Nature often replaced God in poetry, and Dashkova concluded, "Nature, gracing you so well, as well endowed your realm."[52] Nikolai Karamzin's *Letters of a Russian Traveler* contains a passage in which the young writer—eventually the most influential of all eighteenth-century authors—exudes patriotic pride as he quotes an English poet who said of Peter:

> What cannot active government perform. . . .
> *Sloth* flies the land, and *Ignorance*, and *Vice* . . . .
> Taught by the Royal Hand that rous'd the whole,
> Once scene of arts, of arms, of rising trade:
> For what his wisdom plann'd, and power enforc'd,
> More potent still, his great *example* shew'd.[53]

The morality of the ruler, in other words, provided the key to the well-being of the state. But rulers are fallible individuals.

Russian writers, Catherine included, recognized that monarchies, headed by all-too-human beings, were risky forms of government. Nonetheless, Russians and most other Europeans continued to regard the alternatives as even more perilous. Passages, whether in sermons, university speeches, or children's books, repeated the same maxims. Along with a legion of historical and political studies, these passages postulated that Russia's historical "experience has demonstrated that Monarchy is preferable" and "the *best*, most characteristic, and most successful form of government for a vast state" and that Russians "have always had the wisdom to recognize this truth." At the same time, writers held as axiomatic that democracy and aristocracy, especially in a large territory, invariably led to "moral bankruptcy," or "dissension, envy, and enmity" or "executions, plots, confrontations, and discord."[54] Using the convention in didactic literature of having women embody truth and redemption, Petr Plavil'shchikov in his play, *Riurik*, has Palmira act as the voice of wisdom; she contends that only monarchy can prevent "Anarchy, where citizens are blind / And divided in welfare, heart, and mind."[55] In Sumarokov's *Dmitrii the Pretender*, Ksenia and her love, Prince Georgii, agree that aristocracy is a lesser form of government: "Unhappy the country, where there are many magnates: / Truth there is silent, and the lie holds sway."[56] The biography of Marcus Aurelius repeated the maxim that democracy would prove possible only "in those lands where there was no danger at all" of foreign invasion.[57]

From a political point of view, then, monarchy on balance seemed the best alternative. The weakness of human nature also seemed to necessitate the institution. Given the Hobbesian idea that man is a wolf to man, one prelate concluded that the population required the "leadership, protection, supervision" that only a single monarch could offer. A ruler could be impartial and stand above the fray, protecting the common people from the nobility and vested interests and the latter from each other. Palmira unequivocally pointed out that people, when they become impatient with monarchical leadership, will desire some type of "mythical freedom"; sadly, it will simply turn into a tyranny of aristocrats or the mob.[58] The publicist Vasilii Levshin wrote a Masonic fantasy about a flying machine, where the main character, Narsim, flies to the moon and finds an idyllic democracy at work. For earth, though, he concludes that only monarchy is workable: "Once evil entered society and human hearts became corrupt, then a leader and the use of the sword became necessary. If society were not subject to a single ruler and to a wise, well-structured government, then folly and strife" would rule instead.[59] Catherine, in her play on Riurik, commented that Russians easily become "infected with envy; but an intelligent Sovereign, not rendering justice on the basis of passion and talk but more on the quality and merit of the case, easily curbs envy and discord among us."[60]

Ippolit Bogdanovich made a similar case for the necessity of monarchy based on the fall of Adam and Eve. A Mason affiliated with Kheraskov and then the Panin brothers, in 1765 and again in 1773, he dedicated to Paul "The Happiness of Peoples: A Poem."[61] It tells the story of mankind in three "songs": part one describes the state of nature as one of felicity, wherein complete equality reigned and vices "were not known"; people enjoyed an Eden of "innocence, truth, love, and virtue." The second recounts the fall, the degeneration of mankind as a result of innate passions and the breakdown of equality: "Weapons and death devastated the land, / Then vice and sin became the fate of man." The third song tells of regeneration under an enlightened monarch. The people recognized their frightful and anarchic condition and chose "a man to make laws for everyone." Then, "The people submitted and named him Tsar, / And saving the unhappy people from treacheries, / He restored the tranquility of former centuries." The current elected tsar, he implied, went further, for Catherine had restored the "golden era" of mankind's first epoch.[62]

The axioms about the necessity for monarchy and the fears of what might occur in its absence were ingrained in the political discourse during Catherine's reign. Even Russians enthusiastic about and conversant with constitutional monarchies and republics wrote that their application to Russia was at the least premature.[63] Catherine told her courtiers: "I am at heart a republican, and I hate despotism. But absolute power is necessary for the good of the Russian people. You saw from experience what the people did during the Pugachev Revolt." On another occasion, she said: "I do not like autocracy, at heart I am a republican, but the tailor hasn't been born yet who would know how to cut the coat to fit Russia's frame."[64] Criticism operated inside the box of absolutism as well, and the institution as such was never questioned, even in unpublished manuscripts. In the context of the time, voices of consent did not necessarily indicate "immaturity" or illusion.[65] Historical experience and the weakness of human nature led men and women—like Baron Paul-Henri Holbach, one of the most influential philosophes of the Enlightenment and in Russia—to pin their political hopes on "enlightened, just, resolute, virtuous monarchs," whom they credited with reason, conscience, and educability.[66]

If monarchy is necessary and monarchs are prone to human weakness, it follows logically that shaping or improving the character or attitudes of the monarch and heirs to the throne would become the century's prime political challenge. Locke's sensationalist psychology encouraged an optimism about learning ability that promoted confidence in the task. At the same time, the Enlightenment's preoccupation with finding a secular basis for morality provoked an obsessive concern with establishing norms of behavior based on reason and natural law. Ever in the lead, writers hoped to appeal to the ruler's conscience and common sense in order to instill principled behavior in government; thus they injected large doses of didacticism into literature and lectured about the art of statecraft. A further consideration was that an absolute monarch with no de jure restrictions on power required virtue or moral strength in order to practice the self-limitation of power that prevented despotism or despotic features in governance.

Given the strong dualism evident in the thought of the century, writers imagined monarchs fighting a constant battle between the forces of virtue (often, truth or reason) and passion. Derzhavin wrote an ode in which a monarch worried: "Today, I am my own master, / Tomorrow, a slave to my whims."[67] The pages of journals cried out: "O Sovereigns! Control your passions and control yourselves."[68] In a biography of Marcus Aurelius, the paragon is quoted as extolling any ruler "who controlled himself and never gave his will power over himself, but obeyed truth and reason in every instance"[69] Another biography credited Frederick II of Prussia with greatness, not for his many accomplishments, but because he had control over his passions.[70] In a novel of Sergei Glinka in the Fénelon tradition, the hero, Selim of Baghdad, is taken to the "Temple of True Glory" and wonders at the absence of Alexander the Great. His guide, Al'tsima, responds that "he could not restrain even one of his passions"; consequently, "dreaming of becoming a god, he ended up less than a man."[71] In contrast, the Dikany, who inhabit an island in Pavel L'vov's novel, *A Russian Pamela,* have a self-controlled monarch, of whom they boast, "in brief, his virtues were the best laws."[72] Fonvizin, a leading literary light of the epoch, explained to Catherine that it was the monarch's virtue "which assures the happiness of the people and informs the sovereign of his duties to his subjects."[73] In Nikolai Nikolev's play, *Sorena and Zamir,* the heroine lectures that "the politics of tsars is . . . virtue."[74]

Catherine herself, in the spirit of this new preoccupation, wrote a fairy tale for her grandson, Alexander, whose theme echoed the need for moral awareness and development in a monarch. A Kirghiz khan abducts Tsarevich Khlor, a character based on a French tale of 1713, and sets him the quest of finding the "rose without thorns," the symbol of virtue and the secret of ruling firmly and wisely but without undue force. Temptations are placed in his path, and he is surrounded by companions who urge him to pursue a lazy, carefree, lighthearted existence. Nonetheless, the khan's daughter Felitsa (happiness) and her son Rassudok (reason), along with Truth and Honor, help Khlor discover the path of virtue; he then follows the strictures of morality and becomes an exemplary monarch.[75]

This struggle to achieve inner perfection became an even more dominant theme as the century wore on, and the Masonic movement flourished.[76] In every country, Masonic doctrine attracted the political and social elites, and in Russia an astounding one-third of the government
officials in the top eight ranks of service, or roughly 2,500 men, belonged
to lodges in the latter third of the century.[77] While dozens of "systems" of
Masonry sprung up, its members absorbed the current emphasis on morality and natural law and capitalized on the Voltairean hostility to established churches to create a fraternal organization dedicated to personal
moral improvement outside official control. With their avowed goal to enlighten their fellow man, Masons consciously aimed to spread their ideas
among the public through educational, philanthropic, and publishing activities; hence, their "mental attitude" deeply permeated the arts and letters
of their day including the discourse on monarchy.[78]

Kheraskov's epic of 1785, *Vladimir Reborn,* provides a perfect example of
a literary work promulgating the Masonic idea of struggle for virtue as the
noblest activity of the monarch. In his introduction, the poet characterized
the story as that of a remarkable person, who "encounters worldly temptations, is subjected to many trials, falls into the darkness of doubt, struggles
with his own innate passions, finally overcomes himself, finds the path of
truth, and, having attained enlightenment, is reborn."[79] Vladimir's personal conversion gave him the ability to act as the instrument for bringing
Orthodoxy to Russia. The allegory may have represented Kheraskov's hopes
for a lapsed Catherine or for the future of Russia under Paul.[80] In general,
Masons dreamed of an ideal monarchy with a good tsar at its head and
with both inspired by good moral purpose.[81]

The Russian educated elite in Catherine's era, recognizing the advantages
and dangers of absolute monarchy, emphasized the concept of the moral
monarch in order to stave off the hazards that human frailty brought to the
throne. They well recognized that misdeeds on the part of the ruler produced horrific consequences. In L'vov's classic of Masonic advice literature,
The Temple of Truth, Zoroaster warns the deluded Sesostris, an Egyptian king
who thinks his realm is prospering: "Your delusion will not only cause your
own fall, but of millions of men who depend on your Tsarist will. The passions of rulers sow the seeds of vice among the people. His blindness gives
rise to disorder, which will take centuries to set right."[82] To prevent "delusion" and "blindness," writers tried to communicate to Catherine which of
her policies and what type of behavior warranted praise or criticism.

THE USES OF PRAISE

When Russian littérateurs wanted to advise their monarch, they praised
what they approved and offered implied or overt criticism for what they
found objectionable. Eighteenth-century moralists emphasized the constant conflict in the heart of man between passion and reason and searched

for inducements to make the individual act in ways commensurate with the common good; similarly, writers hoped to regulate monarchical policy through commendation or censure. One mechanism was to play upon the love of esteem and fear of bad opinion, the secular alternatives to the promise of heaven or the threat of hell.[83]

Eighteenth-century thinkers believed in the power of praise. In an original article, David Griffiths has explained that love of praise in the early modern era "was not only an important motivating factor, but also a desirable one," especially since it "transmuted egotism into publicly useful actions, thus stimulating virtue instead of vying with it."[84] A story by an anonymous Russian provides an illustration of the belief in the power of praise, which today might seem rather naïve, as a brake on malfeasance in office. Merkant, the hero and subject of a despot, haps upon an Asian island, where the inhabitants have learned to control the actions of their king. When he carries out good deeds, he is allowed to don a gleaming jewel in the middle of his forehead; for instance, the day of Merkant's visit, he had dismissed a favorite and wore the stone proudly. But, when the monarch pursues policies of self-interest, the jewel is taken away to his public shame. Merkant returns home, installs a similar system, and despotism disappears.[85] With more sophistication, Montesquieu praised monarchy because the institution operated on the basis of honor and the desire for distinction and reward, which can substitute for duty or political virtue as a goad to pursuing the common good.[86]

Because of this mentality, littérateurs felt no embarrassment by tirelessly offering public praise of the empress, and their readers recognized the ability as a high art and civic duty. The result, as Stephen Baehr has noted, was that "paradisal praise of the monarchy resounded everywhere."[87] The first issue of a journal of Novikov, *The Old Russian Library*, carried a typical dedication to Catherine signed by her "most humble slave"; on the surface, it resembles only fancy embroidery, but woven into the design is a statement of policies for which monarchs deserve commendation.

> To Her Majesty, Catherine II, the Empress and Autocrat of All the Russias: a true mother of the Fatherland, a wise legislator, the conqueror of the enemies of the Russian Empire on land and on sea, the disseminator of Russian glory, the rejuvenator of the Muses, the protector of the Sciences and Arts, the defender of Justice and Truth, and the architect of Russia's felicity.[88]

However, it should be noted that Prince Shcherbatov harrumphed that "praise always spoils rulers," and berated Catherine in an unpublished work: "[F]ond of glory and ostentation, she loves flattery and servility."[89]

Purposeful praise, however, was sharply distinguished from crass servility or pure flattery.[90] Most writers in the era held Vasilii Petrov, Catherine's "pocket poet," in contempt because his inflated style and smarmy depictions of ideal sovereigns were geared to currying favor rather than carrying a message. His fellow writers thus accused him of trivializing the craft and especially the ode, which was widely revered as the most sublime of the poetic genres.[91] For similar reasons, Derzhavin tried to save his own reputation and defend his "pure heart" by announcing, "I am not to be numbered among the flatterers," when he prospered (a gem-encrusted snuff box, an audience with the empress, and a job) after writing Catherine the brilliant ode, "Felitsa."[92] Tellingly, although he published four poems in the "Felitsa" cycle, after 1790 he dropped the theme, because, as he admitted in his memoirs, he had become disillusioned and could no longer sincerely sing the empress's praises.[93]

Fonvizin, in 1762, wrote "The Fox as Panegyrist" in reaction to the exaggerated laudatory odes heaped upon Empress Elizabeth at her death. Although not published until 1787, the satire was widely circulated among the educated elite. In the fable, the Lion-King has died, and the fox rises to deliver a eulogy:

> O fate! O cruel fate! Of whom is the world bereft!
> Smitten by the demise of your gentle Sovereign,
> Wail and sob, O honored assemblage of beasts!
> This Tsar, wisest of all the beasts of the forest,
> Deserving of eternal tears, deserving of altars,
> Father to his slaves, a danger to his enemies,
> Lies stretched out before us, senseless and voiceless.

The mole, shocked at this hypocrisy, whispers to the dog: "O basest flattery! . . . he was a perfect ass, malicious . . . and with his supreme power, he did nothing but sate his tyrannical passions." The worldly dog laughs at the mole's surprise: "It's clear you have never lived among people."[94] In a word, writers frowned upon empty praise but condoned, and practiced, praise with political purpose.

Even when writing for a private audience, or only for themselves, memoirists often seemed guilty of servility, but many sincerely believed they were experiencing a golden age. The nineteenth-century Russian scholar, Nikolai Chechulin, was convinced that, in the eighteenth century, memoirists "without any doubt, wrote what they thought."[95] They complained about a negligent administration, general ignorance, the low level of judges, the boorishness of nobility, and the treatment of serfs, but once they turned their attention to Catherine, their "Matushka-gosudarynia," the tone changed. As Vasilii Kliuchevskii observed, memoirists never noticed the contradictions, and they spoke more loftily and spouted phrases such as "the world-wide fame of Catherine, the premier status of Russia, national prestige, and popular pride, the general elation of Russian spirits . . . and fell into a triumphal tone about the Catherinian era."[96]

In general in the eighteenth century, writers viewed public praise as a formal method for approving policies, and the practice of commending monarchs as a moral obligation to steer the course of government. First and foremost, writers of sermons, odes, speeches, and journal articles encouraged the empress to take seriously her duty as a "reforming tsar."[97] Nearly every issue and sometimes entire issues of journals would carry rigorous praise for Catherine's lowering taxes, encouraging trade, opening a loan bank, patronizing schools and charities, fighting smallpox, reforming the provincial administration, or "setting the example" for scholarly and literary work through her own publications.[98] University professors, surprisingly as traditional as most prelates, were notable for emphasizing the corruption of human nature and called upon the empress to extirpate vices, preserve order, and establish schools to rid the populace of ignorance and superstition.[99] Inevitably, littérateurs compared Catherine to Peter, the original reforming tsar, and lauded her for "completing His plans."[100]

Novelists set forth whole agendas for reform, much like the "projectors" of the Petrine era. As soon as Catherine ascended the throne, Emin wrote two novels, both classics of advice literature inspired by *Télémaque*. His first, *Miramonde,* reminded the new empress to continue the reforms of her predecessor. The allegory is wonderfully transparent, with Miramonde—after much adventure—arriving in the realm of the daughter (Elizabeth) of Jupiter (Peter the Great). The throne is surrounded by "geniuses" (probably the Shuvalov brothers) who found schools for arts, crafts, and science; set up mining and metal works; and improve military science. A succession crisis brings an evil monarch (Peter III) and "days of gloom," but he is soon replaced by another beneficent ruler (Catherine II), who, surrounded by the Muses, is expected to "delight intellectuals" by imitating the policies of the previous golden age.[101] In Emin's *Themistocles,* the eponymous hero travels with his son Neocles to a variety of countries, each of which has deep problems. The multitude of digressions qualify the novel as a handbook on cameralism. Monarchs are advised to choose ministers well, avoid vile favorites, build new towns, reform the police, increase trade, preserve peace, pay teachers well, introduce sound pedagogical principles, systematize justice, provide homes for veterans, and introduce freedom of the press, because "only books dare to tell the truth."[102]

Writers also gave Catherine acclaim and gratitude for creating an atmosphere (if not laws) that granted security of person and property. Derzhavin's "Felitsa" circulated widely, and it contained praise of Catherine for her hard work fostering a range of policies, for instance, the administrative reforms of 1775: "Out of Chaos making harmonious spheres, / Their integrity strengthened through union."[103] But, he reserved his highest tribute for her having removed the fearsomeness of the Russian monarchy and taking "no glory in being a tyrant."

> Also an unprecedented thing
> Worthy of You alone,
> That You permit people
> Boldly to know and think
> About everything. . . .
> One may talk in whispers,
> And not fear being punished
> For not toasting Tsars at dinners.

Derzhavin extolled the fact that Russians could now travel freely and engage at will in trade and manufacture. The poet shed "rivers of pleasant tears" when he thought of the contrast with previous reigns, for instance, that of Anna Ioannovna, when minor and stupid offenses against the tsarist person, such as "carelessly dropping her portrait on the ground" or not drinking to her health, were punishable.[104]

Catherine appreciated Derzhavin's portrayal, for it matched her own self-image as a nondespotic monarch. In a widely disseminated children's primer that she authored, the empress flatly stated that the central task of the sovereign was to use power "to defend the life, honor, domains, and property of subjects."[105] The chapter she translated of *Bélisaire* encapsulated her ideal.

> There is no absolute power except that of the laws, and he who aims at despotism enslaves himself. For what is law but the will of the whole community, expressed by one man. . . . The prince . . . must make the laws the sole rule of his conduct; for his authority is derived from the laws; it is founded upon the will and the whole force of the community.

Marmontel continued, a "crown will rest firm and unshaken" only when the "citizen . . . is secure in his civil rights," namely, the protection of life and property and the "liberty to complain of grievances . . . a constitutional right."[106]

Agreeing with Catherine's self-assessment, Lev Engel'gardt remembered in his memoirs that, under Catherine—a "tender mother" who had brought an era of "glory and happiness. . . . [E]ach citizen was certain of the security of his person and property." Another memoirist commented near the end of the century:

> I will let the people of the new century censure Catherine's autocracy, but I will die with the thought that her absolutism was infinitely more fair to the people than all the constitutional charters of new legislators; for when we have a good Tsar, everyone sleeps peacefully and is sure of his property, happiness, and freedom. What more can you ask?[107]

Well, many believed that institutions, not just good intentions, were needed to ward off despotism.

The novelist Mikhail Chulkov, in his popular collection of stories and anecdotes *The Mocker*, cut into absolutist pretensions that self-limitation sufficed as a barrier against despotism by having Nravoblag, the good tsar in a Slavic Eden, claim that monarchs were not above the law and "should never transgress the laws."[108] Kheraskov wanted Catherine to imitate Numa and legislate in conjunction with a national council "where all members are equal." Kheraskov's monumental *Rossiada*, Russia's first national epic, repeated the theme; the tsar muses: "My title of Monarch can only be enjoyed / If I share my power with all the people. . . . And await laws from my subjects. . . . There you have the duty of the Tsar." In *Ophir*, Shcherbatov went further; he claimed that monarchs should be denied legislative power altogether because they "are neither artisans, nor merchants, nor workers, and do not feel the many needs felt by their subjects."[109] But Catherine was not prepared to take any of these steps, despite the prompting of praise.

Even when the empress did not fulfill her own or her subjects' aspirations for rule of law, some writers argued it was beyond her control. The biography of Marcus Aurelius contained an often-quoted political aphorism that the public should not judge a monarch too harshly for "the ills which he has let fall, or the good which he has omitted to do."[110] Ivan Khemnitser, an author of over one hundred tales and fables and active in literary circles, treated Catherine with similar kindness in "The Good Tsar."

> A certain tsar upon ascension,
> Devoted very close attention
> To the welfare of his nation
> As his prime consideration.
>> His first act set up a new basis
>> For a better set of laws
>> By amending all the places
>> Where the standing code had flaws.
> So that this new reform might meet with minimal resistance,
> Old judges were replaced by new ones at the tsar's insistence.
> It was a fine reform, deserving of great praise.
> The problem was the judges who new clung to old ways.
>> The tsar no remedy could find
>> To solve a problem of this kind.
>> The only cure for such a situation
>> Was time and proper education.[111]

The organic theory of development that permeated the outlook of most thinkers made it natural to recognize the inevitability of slow movement in a backward Russia.

Belletrists reinforced their praise of Catherine as a reformer by lauding similar policies on the part of her contemporaries. Journals found newsworthy the good works of any monarch: Louis XVI for enacting a new law on guilds; Frederick II of Prussia for his emphasis on rule of law; or the English king for his speech opening parliament.[112] A Russian biography of Maria Theresa hailed her as one of the greatest rulers since ancient history because she reformed the administration and sought the "general welfare" rather than being concerned about feats of arms, a priority Catherine might ponder. (Despite the praise for Maria Theresa's statecraft, the book devotes more energy to her "most successful" rearing of Joseph II, perhaps a sting at Catherine's neglect of Paul.)[113]

Russians took great pride that Catherine, "even though" female, proved a greater reformer than her male counterparts. Admiral Aleksandr Shishkov, in his memoirs, begins his recollections of the empress with the words, "Catherine, superior to her sex, had a manly, firm character." He mentions all the great monarchs of Catherine's era—Gustavus III, Frederick II, Joseph II—and claims she outdid them all: "Among these great heads of autocracies, a woman found the means to better rule."[114] Similarly, Vasilii Maikov, a poet and secretary of the Legislative Commission, rhapsodized that the empress, although "from Adam's rib," could nonetheless so excel as a lawgiver that she should be elevated above all earthly monarchs.[115] Another Novikov journal, *The Painter,* often featured advice literature in the form of praise.[116] In 1772, it reprinted a letter from Frederick II to his ambassador in St. Petersburg concerning the publication of the *Nakaz:*

> History tells us that Semiramis commanded an army, that Queen Elizabeth was considered skillful in politics, that the Empress Queen [Maria Theresa] showed great resolution upon her accession to the throne but not one woman has yet been a lawgiver. This glory has been given to the Russian Empress who is, of course, worthy of it.[117]

A tale by Levshin describes a wanderer, Balamir, as he comes upon the realm of the Duleby, a people ruled by a female. Queen Milosveta is a foreigner, who saved her new country when it was on the brink of collapse, and her rule proves to the doubting and sexist Balamir that those countries that deny women the throne "lose much of their chance for happiness."[118] A translation of a life of Queen Elizabeth of England contained an impassioned plea for having women as monarchs and criticized the teaching of St. Paul that resulted in, for instance, the Salic law, since women have proved their gift for statecraft.[119]

Writers often envisioned monarchs as androgynous figures, and they extolled Catherine for acting like a "fond father" (*chadoliubivyi otets*) or "a wise father caring for the welfare of his brood," who then deserves the love of his subjects.[120] One writer intoned, "good sovereigns alone can call themselves fathers," and anecdotes depicted them doing paternal things; for example, Gustavus Adolphus of Sweden rewards a little girl for caring for her sick mother, or Joseph II of Austria looks after the daughter and widow of an officer.[121] Letter-writing handbooks suggested that petitions to

Catherine should stress her "maternal concern" or her "maternal heart."[122] But another author chided monarchs for trying to present their subjects with an image of "mother and father" in order to "sweeten their slavery"; it was slavery nonetheless.[123]

Besides praising an individual monarch's policies or behavior, eighteenth-century belletrists obsessively portrayed ideal rulers in order to suggest universal criteria by which rulers should be judged. The prototype of these sketches was aptly entitled "A Dream of a Happy Society" by Sumarokov and appeared in *The Industrious Bee*, Russia's first nongovernmental journal and a leading publisher of advice literature.[124] The "Happy Society" and most novels and books of moral admonitions contained chapters with such titles as "A Discussion of the Qualities of a Good Monarch."[125] Ideal monarchs, like Tolstoy's happy families, are very much alike. They are always parental in their concern for their "children," work hard at providing for the general welfare, pass legislation that assures security of person and property, personify virtue in their private and public lives, eschew any hint of tyrannical behavior, and earn the love of their subjects for whom they provide an Edenic existence. In a typical passage, the reader is introduced to Dorod, a model monarch of an eastern kingdom. "Love and prosperity reigned among citizens as though they were the beloved children of one father in one family." He also knew how to establish a balance between "obedience and freedom" without becoming a tyrant. Dorod is praised as an "angel."

> He instituted fundamental laws and based justice on wise and inviolable principles; he rooted out evil cupidity, which had plunged the people into extreme poverty; he ripped out hypocrisy and brought everything that related to the prosperity of his realm into such a flourishing condition that every subject, because of his prudent administration, could pronounce himself completely and thoroughly happy.[126]

Aleksandr Radishchev provides much the same picture of a monarch's duties in his *Journey from St. Petersburg to Moscow:* "I clad you in the purple that you might preserve equality in society, watch over the widow and orphan, save innocence from calamity and be its loving father, but an implacable enemy of vice, the lie, and calumny; that you might reward merit with honor, forestall evil through order, and maintain purity of morals."[127] Sermons, children's stories, and biographies contained similar portrayals.[128]

The depiction of Numa Pompilius best summarized all the features Russians treasured, including the idea of election. Not only was this noble Roman chosen by the people, but his coming to the throne was made to resemble Catherine's. He accepts the crown out of duty, although he understands the burden and difficulty of battling his own human frailty, and his electors rejoice: "Ah, happy that society which, with open eyes and of its own free will, chooses its ruler, a worthy man . . . and wise father."

Numa proved to be a great legislator, a loving father in regard to his subjects, a man of virtue, and inspired by a worthy theory of government: "The Tsar's crown only serves as an adornment when our subjects are adorned with virtues, and only those thrones are peaceful and firm where the people are securely protected by sweet peace and prosperity abides. And I understand all this to be the responsibility of the autocrat."[129] Chulkov underscored the responsibility of an elected monarch. A tale recounts that, after a new ruler is elected on the islands of Mlakon and Niia, the populace fears that the king will succumb to the usual temptations of luxury and vainglory. However, once the monarch realizes that the people regard him as a "father," he responds with love for these "worthy citizens" and comes to understand that "a man elected to make laws ought never transgress them."[130] A biography of Aleksandr Nevskii, written for the edification of the future Alexander I, also portrayed an ideal ruler as one who is "chosen by the people of Novgorod to rule."[131]

Praise of particular policies can increase support for the existing monarch, and depictions of ideal rulers can increase the popularity of monarchy as an institution. In addition, both provide a standard of conduct that poses dangers for a sitting ruler who does not conform. In that instance, praise gives way to criticism.

VENTURES INTO CRITICISM: WAR, FLATTERERS, AND FAVORITES

Nearly everyone associates the reign of Catherine the Great with her series of lovers or favorites and her aggressive military policy, and those are precisely the features that littérateurs criticized. Kheraskov, in his novel *Cadmus and Harmonia*, described as "evil" a reign in which courtiers rouse the indignation of the people with their vices, and wars take workers from their fields, thus summarizing the principal criticisms levied against Catherine.[132] According to the norms of advice literature, a good tsar, a moral monarch, maintains a virtuous court and a peaceful foreign policy.

Churchmen and Masons, in particular, reminded rulers not to pursue a policy of war, but to find "true glory" in "the welfare of society" and "virtue."[133] *Télémaque*, which set the precedents for eighteenth-century advice literature, contained several sections devoted to haranguing militaristic rulers like Louis XIV, whose wars impoverished his nation. Mentor lectures, "While all the nation is with war afire, / Laws, agriculture, arts, nearly expire."[134] A Russian reader for noble youth contained a similar sentiment: "The heroism of war is not the heroism of kings," and Alexander the Great, throughout the literature, was denigrated as "battle-hungry."[135] Biographies of Charles XII of Sweden condemned the territorial ambitions for which he "sacrificed law, virtue, justice, love for his subjects, and his own life": "How dreadful the name of conqueror, and how unfortunate those subjects who have as their ruler only a Hero and not a King."[136] L'vov censured vainglorious warfare and any ruler who "wants to be a great conqueror instead of a father of the fatherland."[137] Even a collection of stories about the Russian knights of old, the *bogatyry,* warned the reader that militaristic groups in general ought not be lauded.[138]

Maikov, a gifted odist, authored a pacifist poem during the Russo-Polish War of 1768–1769. He fiercely condemned military conflicts because they "pour forth their poison upon the earth"; they "afflict all with sorrow unbearable"; they place "on the captives, heavy irons and on the conquerors their blood"; and they are fought by soldiers who are not heroes but "murderers" and "wild beasts."[139] Just after Catherine embarked upon the First Turkish War in 1768, Mikhail Popov, a writer of comic opera and participant in the Legislative Commission, wrote an adventure novel about Prince Bogoslav, who resembled the empress in every way save one: "From the moment he ascended the throne, he never spilled one drop of his subjects' blood."[140] A journal article criticized monarchs who fancy the title "the Great," but whose military exploits "sacrifice millions of men like themselves . . . only to satisfy their vanity."[141] In a fable, Khemnitser likewise chastised monarchs (lions) for engaging in constant and senseless warfare just because "each lion wants to be the grandest lion."[142]

Some authors condoned conquest of distant lands but only if rulers had already conquered their own vices and embarked on great programs of domestic reform.[143] In a "dream," Sergei Domashev, a student at Moscow University, is escorted up a mountain path trod by those who succumbed to their passions and fell victim to pride, vanity, and vainglory. For instance, Alexander the Great failed to realize that improving the general welfare brought true glory, not military conquest with its "bloodletting" and "laying waste." On the path of true glory, one meets Augustus, Marcus Aurelius, and Peter the Great, whose policies embodied reason, virtue, and concern for their subjects rather than the fighting of unnecessary wars.[144] In his unpublished novel, *Ophir,* Shcherbatov would allow only defensive wars, and Catherine is demonized as the Empress Rikhsheia for waging endless military campaigns. Pacifist maxims adorn the palace walls in Ophir: "It is better to make one village prosperous than to conquer an entire state" or "The glory of the conqueror deafens the ears, but the virtues of a just monarch delight people for many centuries."[145]

Most writers regarded war as senseless, although odists, including Maikov, also sang of victory, as was their duty and commission, and other authors continued to celebrate fighting in defense of "Fatherland, Faith, and Monarch."[146] Kheraskov, despite his being a leading Mason, wrote the nine thousand lines of the *Rossiada* to commemorate the taking of Kazan by Ivan IV, who thus laid the foundations for Russia's imperial grandeur; he published a second edition in honor of Catherine's securing the Crimea in 1783.[147] Because of this epic, Baehr postulated that Kheraskov blessed the "quest for empire."[148] However, in *Numa,* the book's first sentence, "True glory is not always acquired through arms," and its last sentence, "And thus we can be assured that it happens that glory is not only acquired through arms," both carry a pacifist message.[149] In a word, authors remained ambivalent, condemning military action in the abstract but reserving the right to glorify individual campaigns.

The pacifist theme nonetheless remained a constant in the literature, because war remained a constant in Catherinian Russia, just as it did throughout eighteenth-century Europe. Littérateurs had no success in wooing the empress away from a militaristic policy. Derzhavin at one point acted as her cabinet secretary, and his memoirs reveal a very hard-working sovereign, but one who had a "soul preoccupied with military glory."[150]

The second constant criticism of Catherine's regime was directed against her court and the flatterers and favorites that inevitably walk the parqueted floors of any palace.[151] The literature of this epoch demonstrates that Russians despised their ilk, and authors used language much more impassioned than when writing of any other topic. L'vov characterized most courtiers as "crafty kowtowers, servile pundits, flattering liars, invidious fawners, and insidious predators."[152] Khemnitser's fables depicted the lion/monarch's favorites as "asses," whose low moral and intellectual level permeated the upper administration.[153] Petr Zakhar'in, a novelist who was born into a peasant family, wrote an adventure novel, *Arfakad*, that took aim at sovereigns who allow themselves to be surrounded with "insatiable, avaricious advisors" and "hypocrites, flatterers, and haters," whose influence guarantees "an unhappy people" forced to live in a state of "savage force, the spirit of hatred, evil, and vengeance."[154] Novikov, who tirelessly attacked grandees, wondered: "Why do those who rise to a degree of celebrity altogether forget humanity; they become proud, unjust, envious, biased."[155]

Writers understood that favorites and flatterers soiled the conceptions of monarchy that had arisen in the course of the century. First, they blinded the ruler to reality and thus prevented her from being a reforming tsar and accomplishing the good she might if she could see clearly, since "court officials betray each other, but especially the Sovereign."[156] Similarly, in France at the end of the old regime, the concern arose that flatterers gave kings a false impression of public opinion.[157] A central aim of advice literature was to restore Catherine's vision. Staple conventions included a hermit, pilgrim, shepherd, or sage providing the monarch of some eastern land with a magic mirror or vision so that he can see the true condition of his kingdom and the true opinions and needs of his people.[158]

Royal blindness became a theme in every genre. For instance, Catherine's famous journeys throughout Russia were ridiculed because she took her court with her and saw the realm through their eyes. In a reference to the Potemkin villages that lined the empress's route as she toured the Crimea, the residents of Ophir are astounded and grateful that their "sovereigns and rulers could never fall for such a gross deception."[159] Khemnitser's fable, "The Blind Lion," describes how easily a ruler is deceived by his courtiers.[160] A journal article reprinted a Chinese philosopher's advice to his sovereign, and it included a lament that so few sovereigns accomplish good for their subjects, since "they are often gullible and surround themselves with flatterers."[161] Even children's stories satirized a monarch relying on favorites. One fairy tale describes a king, who was born with a huge and hideous nose, but everyone tried to keep this truth from him by telling him that all great sovereigns had similar features, and the courtiers surrounded him with big-beaked attendants. He falls in love, but an evil spell prevents him from being united with his beloved. Once he acknowledges his handicap—"I must admit that my nose is very long"—the witch lifts her spell and lectures that kings must use "reason to recognize their deficiencies and realize that it is contrary to one's self-interest not to."[162] In an anonymous tale, King Amelige receives a magic mirror, which enables him to realize that court flatterers have hidden the real problems of his country from him, and he then constructs a program of sweeping reform.[163]

As well as impeding the ruler's will to reform, favorites shattered the idea of an elected monarch and legal sovereign by breaking the bond between the prince and his citizens: "There is nothing more shameful for mankind than when obscene flatteries . . . grip the hearts of young Sovereigns, and they are limited by no kinds of laws, and all obligations fall only on one side" of the contract.[164] A real "misfortune" occurs when a prince is influenced by "artful and designing men . . . to consider his people as an enemy to be dreaded . . . and the prince lives at variance with his subjects."[165] In Kheraskov's *Rossiada*, Ivan IV the Terrible, surrounded by flatterers, fails in his historical role; instead of leading his state forward, he becomes an evil agent of history and causes the national destruction known as the Time of Troubles.[166]

The doctrine of royal causation meant that the virtue of the monarch defined the state of Russia. Therefore, if rulers succumbed to the influence of wicked favorites, they first became "despots, voluptuaries, and slaves to their passions."[167] Next, the poison spreads out from the court to the population at large. Zakhar'in's novel of 1788, *Kleandr*, describes a monarch, once "great" but then given to "proud splendor and fatal luxury," which led, inevitably in this literature, to moral torpor in the country.[168] The only answer was to rid the court of favorites and their "poison of injurious customs."[169] The author of a journal article stated flatly that a "good tsar has no flatterers," and in Ophir they were banished from the court.[170] The corrective was to seek honest advisors from among "honorable men."[171] Marmontel's *Bélisaire* suggested that kings attend to the opinions of farmers and soldiers, "the voice of the public; that voice which is the oracle kings ought to consult, the best, the unerring decider of merit and of virtue!"[172] In a typical Eastern tale, a Persian king, weary of his court and its flatterers, travels incognito among his people and finds a shepherd who is so full of wisdom and common sense that he brings him to court as an advisor.[173] A fable also encouraged the search for good counselors. A tsar is strolling and comes upon two pastures: in one, all is confusion, the shepherd is unsure what to do, and the wolves are threatening, despite the presence of a pack of dogs; in the other, all is in good order, even though the few dogs seem asleep. The tsar asks the second shepherd:

How can this be? The wolves are many and bold,
While you alone protect this giant fold!
Tsar, the shepherd answered, don't be agog:
I just knew to get *good* dogs.[174]

Of course, some writers, for instance Shcherbatov, wished Catherine would consult them, and Zakhar'in's novel *Arfakad* aimed its barbs at rulers who "disdain free and sincere advice."[175]

Nonetheless, the empress retained her penchant for favorites, and her many liaisons could not help but capture notice and stimulate charges that she lacked the virtue necessary in a good tsar.[176] Unflattering portrayals of the "vices" of that "political actress," Elizabeth I of England, pointed in a clear direction, as did an article on Henry VIII's relations with Anne Boleyn, which complained that the English king "serves as an example of how detested ought to be the man who has no other guide than his own passions."[177] In the *Rossiada,* the figure of Sumbeka, the regent/leader of Kazan, neglected her duty to her people because of her love for Shakh-Ali, and this probably was intended to lecture the empress.[178] A memoirist recalled Catherine as a "lawgiver, a heroine, a great woman, the fulfiller of wise designs of Peter the Great" but, at the same time, a "shameful voluptuary" who changed her lovers like "post horses."[179] A fable by Khemnitser observed that, when they are no longer useful, the lion discards her favorites gently but nonetheless like a cad.[180] Count Vorontsov probably spoke for many when he contended: "The influence of favorites was disastrous during the reign of Catherine II and tarnished her reign."[181] Another memoirist, Aleksandr Turgenev, admitted that the empress was constantly accused of being a "woman given to sensual pleasures," but he maintained that she loved and looked after the Russian people.[182] In truth, Catherine, until her last years, kept firmly in control of the government and used, rather than succumbed to, her favorites. In the other courts of Europe, liaisons were considered yet another sign of power for male monarchs; for female monarchs, writers preferred the image of fidelity and maternity that Maria Theresa projected.

All of these criticisms did not prevent Khemnitser, like so many of these literati, from admitting that Catherine was not a bad monarch; one of his fables concludes: "It has to be said that this lion was better than most lions."[183] Overall, writers treated their empress as educable, and she responded with good humor, even self-mockery. In 1786, when Catherine eliminated the word "slave" in petitions, Vasilii Kapnist publicly praised the empress as though she had actually emancipated the serfs, calling freedom "the gift of true God-Tsars!" Catherine is reported to have remarked, "Why, you want [the abolition of slavery] in reality . . . the words are enough!"[184]

In his "Felitsa," Derzhavin created a charming portrait of Catherine as a diligent monarch, whose only leisure is legislation and the life of the mind and who enjoys simple tastes and habits; she eschews card playing, hunting, masquerades, and even Masonic lodges.[185] However, the poet depicts her closest associates as living lives of luxury filled quite literally with wine, women, and song and engaging in the amusements of uncultured boors. Derzhavin openly stated that he was satirizing Grigorii Potemkin, the Orlov brothers, Petr Panin, and Aleksandr Viazemskii; Catherine sent them each a copy of the ode with the pertinent passages marked.[186] She later wondered why, to the many accusations leveled against them, her "courtiers have never made any reply."[187]

Novikov recognized that "writing satires on courtiers, exalted boyars, ladies, distinguished judges" would formerly have earned authors a trip to Siberia, but Catherine will "permit people to boldly know and think about everything."[188] This champion of freedom of the press was offering exaggerated praise in the tradition of advice literature and knew full well that Catherine approved of gentle criticism of vices *(satira na porok)* but usually frowned upon attacks on individuals *(satira na litso)*; the empress's polemics with the journals over this issue were then, and in scholarship since, highly scrutinized.[189] Nonetheless, Catherine's epoch offered more leeway in publishing than any other until 1905. When Nikolai Nikolev's play, *Sorena and Zamir,* opened in 1785 to popular acclaim, the censors banned it because of its heated tirades against tyranny and its talk of regicide. Catherine reversed the decision, claiming that such criticisms had nothing to do with her enlightened reign. She scolded the censor: "The meaning of the verses you pointed out has nothing to do with your Empress. The author challenges the despotism of tyrants, whereas you call Catherine a mother."[190]

The notion that Catherine warranted the sobriquet of good tsar, despite her many shortcomings, persisted until about 1790, as did the cordial communication between the empress and the educated elite. In her last six years in power, however, writers began warning Catherine that she was transmogrifying into that dreaded head of state, a bad tsar.

CHAPTER SEVEN

The Bad Tsar

*I*n eighteenth-century Russia, a "good tsar" connoted a moral being who acted according to accepted criteria in both public and private life. Such monarchs ruled through law, carried out useful reforms, guaranteed security of person and property, eschewed wars of aggrandizement, controlled their passions, curbed the power of individuals at court, worked hard, and showed parental concern for their subjects. Above all else, writers lectured, the moral monarch abhorred despotism and embraced the contractual nature of absolute power. Only sovereigns armed with such characteristics, it was believed, could perform the duties that made them morally necessary in a society composed of sinful creatures, who required protection from themselves, each other, and, coming full circle, from the threat of despotism.

Since eighteenth-century European thinking moved to a Manichaean rhythm, the conception of a bad tsar emerged as the good ruler's antithesis. Analyzing the woes brought by a bad tsar became an idée fixe in advice literature. Writers also recounted the fate of evil sovereigns with meticulous and sanguinary detail in an effort to keep monarchs on the royal straight and narrow. In addition, authors signaled readers on how to react in the eventuality that an immoral sovereign threatened to corrupt the state and cause the decline of Russia. Paul I would provide a case in point as would, to a lesser degree, the last six years of his mother's long reign. These depictions underscore the notion that advice literature, while nonconfrontational, was certainly not ingratiating. Littérateurs deplored bad tsars, but they considered the absence of a single monarch far worse. Hence, while writers might delight in the overthrow of a specific individual, they never advocated the abandonment of the institution of monarchy, especially after witnessing the events of the French Revolution.

THE DESOLATION OF DESPOTISM

Most European eighteenth-century thinkers invariably described despo-tism as a perversion of monarchy and bad rulers as having revoked their le-gitimacy. Sovereigns, it was agreed, were empowered only to carry out poli-cies that promoted the general well-being. In Vasilii Trediakovskii's reworking of *Télémaque,* Mentor defines the boundaries of legitimate action.

> The Tsar has unlimited power over the people; but the laws have unlimited power over him. He has autocratic power to do good, but none to do evil. The laws were given to him by the people, as the most sacred of trusts. They oblige him to be a father to his subjects. Otherwise, he becomes a false tsar.[1]

In a masterpiece of advice literature, the ode to Paul on his name day in 1771, Aleksandr Sumarokov warned of the loss of legitimacy that tyrannical behavior brings.

> Not in this does a tsar distinguish his rank:
> That he can smite and imprison,
> That people stand in fear before him,
> That he can treat people as carrion,
> Or that he can take lives.
> When a Monarch acts through compulsion,
> He is the enemy of the people and not their Sovereign.[2]

Other sources repeated the refrain: "The Sovereign has no rights other than those the Citizens freely granted him to rule over them."[3] A book for chil-dren described the contract among the monarch, grandees, and people that forbade the ruler from pursuing anything other than the common good; Russians rightly "*gave him* [the monarch] *the right* to rule over them, *only* if it were under the law and in justice and never disrupting internal well-being."[4]

Writers regarded outright despots as a rare phenomenon, but when they arose, these authors agreed that despots brought devastation. Russians of Catherine's generation had recently condemned Peter III as a thorough tyrant. In a public declaration at the time of the Legislative Commission, delegates gave a stirring picture of a bad tsar when, still "trembling" from the memory, they described the "deplorable condition" of the country un-der the empress's predecessor.

> We saw our Orthodox faith . . . subjected to disdain and abuse, two clear omens of its extirpation. We saw laws, which establish and preserve our social existence, led into confusion, inconsistency, and non-fulfillment; with the downfall of the laws, justice collapsed, destroying conscience and morality. Not only did the pillars of the government falter, its very foundation was

shaken. State revenues dried up, losing trust and choking off trade. Robbery, bribery, cupidity, violence, and other vices . . . grew and intensified the disasters of our Fatherland; and in the end disorder everywhere triumphed where order should have reigned.[5]

In Mikhail Kheraskov's grand epic, *Rossiada,* a prophetic dream foretells that Ivan the Terrible's tyranny will cause the end of the Riurikid line, that Russia will be invaded by Sweden and Poland, and that the vicissitudes of the Time of Troubles will descend upon the Russian people: "A profound darkness will settle over your entire land."[6] Kheraskov's novel, *Cadmus and Harmonia,* painted a typical portrait of sovereigns who "could not control their passions" and thus invariably chose bad advisors, lived in luxury, became voluptuaries, abused the law, overtaxed their subjects, and caused their "people to be thrown into slavery and poverty."[7] A play by an anonymous Russian author, *Zelul Overthrown,* contains a heavy-handed passage in which the tyrant exclaims: "Why am I Tsar? To listen to the absurd petitions of the people and subject my personal pleasure to their advantage? Never! This is no Tsar, but a lowly slave and prisoner of the people." Zelul's contempt also results in his subjects being "thrown into poverty and slavery."[8]

Nikolai Nikolev provided a classic description of a tyrant in his play, *Sorena and Zamir.* Mstislav, a fictional ruler of Russia, is passionately in love with Sorena, a Polovtsian princess and the apparent widow of Zamir. She detests and resists the man not only out of fidelity to the memory of her late husband, but because Mstislav is a "savage tyrant," who has turned her people from citizens into "slaves" and forces them to live in an evil kingdom of "violence, robbery, fraud."[9] Zamir returns from battle alive and discovers that his land has become an "absolute hell," where the despot has "left his fatherland in miserable poverty to enrich himself, a monarch without glory," motivated only by "vainglory." Mstislav, the antithesis of a moral monarch and legal sovereign, declares that "without passion there is no happiness" and "power is my law."[10]

Authors treated tyrants with as little mercy as the latter treated their subjects. Catherine could hardly complain if advice literature demanded that bad tsars be removed from their thrones, inasmuch as she had overthrown her husband on those grounds, and he had died as a result of the coup.[11] Writers proposed a variety of cruel fates for anti-tsars, and rightful punishment was pronounced inevitable. In the very first scene of Sumarokov's play *Dmitrii the Pretender,* the tyrant is assured:

> You prepare for yourself an unhappy end;
> Your throne will be shaken,
> The crown will fall from your head.[12]

Authors proposed a variety of sentences against despots. In his ode to Paul, Sumarokov compares bad tsars to tigers, lions, snakes, and other creatures and depicts the contempt and damnation awaiting a "vile idol" or "unskilled helmsman."

> His epitaph will read, He was evil.
> The end of His reign
> Brings the end of acclaim.
> The flattery vanishes, and his soul goes to hell.[13]

In a reworked psalm, Gavriil Derzhavin called upon God to "pass sentence on the wicked." Rulers were chastised for ignoring their duties.

> They hear not! Yet they see—but know not!
> Their eyes are veiled by bribery;
> By wickedness the earth is shaken;
> Injustice makes the heavens reel.[14]

Both Sumarokov and Derzhavin, like a legion of thinkers before them, preferred to let God's judgment or posterity render just deserts. In his early works, Kheraskov agreed that an evil tsar will "answer to the heavens for his rule."[15] However, his later novel, *Cadmus and Harmonia,* centered on a ruler who is expelled from his realm and barely escaped with his life because he could "not control his own passions."[16]

A range of writers abandoned the centuries-old passive attitude toward tyranny and portrayed an aggrieved people taking immediate action against a grievous ruler. Aleksandr Radishchev's biography of his deceased friend, Fedor Ushakov, attacked despotism and took comfort in the fact that people's patience eventually runs out, and they overthrow the offending monarch.[17] Mentor opined that, in the face of tyranny, a people often had little choice: "Nought less than revolution's sudden strength / Can bring the o'erflowing power to bounds at length."[18] In Fedor Emin's novel, *Themistocles,* written just after Catherine seized the throne, the eponymous hero explains to his son that "it is a natural law to change tsars when they rule their subjects unjustly, but nonetheless, such a change ought to occur by means of a general consensus . . . all should elect him."[19] Twenty years later, Iakov Kniazhnin's play, *Rosslav,* featured a tyrannous king who is overthrown in a popular uprising—in favor of a female monarch. The people dispose of the tyrant Zelul in expeditious fashion: they overthrow him; he poisons and stabs himself to avoid being murdered; the citizens throw his body outside the city walls to rot; and then they "elect a new Tsar for themselves."[20]

In Mikhail Shcherbatov's utopian novel, *Ophir,* the country had been in existence for over seventeen hundred years and the inhabitants had been faced with only two evil monarchs, both of whom were "dethroned and spent the rest of their lives in prison."[21] In the real world, Prince Shcherbatov applauded the action of a group of one hundred Swedish officers when they laid down their arms during wartime in 1789 as a protest against Gustavus III's despotic actions in abrogating the traditional rights of the nobility vis-à-vis the crown. Shcherbatov considered these men not traitors, but rather to have "demonstrated themselves to be citizens" by upholding the law.[22]

Defying or even assassinating a tyrant was being elevated into a moral imperative in the last years of the eighteenth century. Nikolev's Sorena decides to kill Mstislav since "to assassinate a tyrant is a duty, not an evil act."[23] Catherine herself had written that anytime in history when "all minds are in agreement" that their Fatherland is in danger because of despotic rule, "a revolution is near."[24] A biography of Nero, translated from the French and published by the imperial typography in 1792, depicted the Roman ruler as a slave to his passions, with predictable consequence: "His every step was a step in the direction of his fall." However, the focus in the biography is on the Roman senate, which is criticized for not organizing sooner a "rebellion to free themselves from a tyrant" and "getting back the rights they have lost." The author condemned the legislators for being more concerned with their wealth and position than the honor and good of the nation. Eventually, the best citizens display the moral courage to take action: they win the support of the people and overthrow the tyrant.[25]

In the eighteenth century, Russians had often acted on the premise that it was morally correct to overthrow a despot; Ivan VI and his regents were toppled as was Peter III, and a stream of popular plays, novels, and biographies reinforced this notion. Thus, once Russians had determined that Emperor Paul I was a tyrant, his ouster and even assassination could be expected: it was part of the script. Political antagonism, though, was directed toward the unfit occupant of the throne and not against the institution itself. The solution to monarchy devolving into tyranny was to enthrone a better ruler, not to experiment with another form of government.

The fear of *beztsarstvie,* of being plunged into anarchy without a single ruler, remained an integral part of Russian political culture; no tsar was overthrown before a successor was already in place, and all unsuccessful rebellions from Stenka Razin's in the seventeenth century to the Decembrists' in 1825 had a "legitimate" heir in mind. The anxiety about anarchy informed most Russians' view of the French Revolution. Once Louis XVI was ousted and beheaded, they saw it as inevitable that the Convention of 1792 to 1794, the government which took his place, would be a mere exercise in mob rule; indeed, a tyranny worse than any under absolute monarchy seemed to have ensued. In a poem published in 1793, Princess Ekaterina Dashkova, a sometime protégée of the empress, exhibited a typical horror at the events in "unhappy France." In her mind, the revolution had ushered in "an epoch of rage, discord, indecency, and anarchy" and resulted in a "greater despotism than the French had ever experienced": "A most horrible success . . . built on tyrannical excess." She rejoiced in a monarch who could act as "Father," "Provider," and "Pastor," and the events in France renewed her faith in Russia's one-person rule *(edinonachalie).*

Here, everyone values single power,
Without which our bliss might founder . . .
Blessed are we now! We have a single kingdom,
For us, a single pastor and a single congregation.[26]

Dashkova's sentimental attitude of sorrow for France and praise of *edinonachalie* epitomized the Russian reaction to the revolution.[27]

Radishchev also deplored the chaos of the French Revolution, but he embraced a more modern sensibility and lamented that tsars had yet "to assert the freedom of the individual." But he was an exception. Most Russians also interpreted the French experience with tsarlessness as a loss of freedom.[28] The predominant legal definition of freedom in the eighteenth century encompassed the security of person and property that comes with living under a nondespotic monarch, and this idea prevailed in Russian advice literature. For instance, in *Sorena and Zamir*, the hero contemplates committing suicide rather than enduring the despotism of Mstislav: "The laws of nature are scorned by tyrants: Here a tiger reigns, and the people are oppressed." His soldiers agree: "We shall die with you for freedom."[29] Petr Plavil'shchikov's play of 1791, *Riurik*, presents another shade of this idea, with freedom defined as security from strife or anarchy. Palmira, the heroine, argues with magnates who are trying to overthrow Riurik and install an aristocratic government on the grounds they want to free themselves of one-man rule and "slavery." Palmira points out the delusion of wanting some sort of "mythical freedom"—which will result in civil war or anarchy—rather than the real freedom offered by a monarch: "When under a crown, sweet peace / Rules everywhere: the whole country is blessed."[30]

Writers interpreted the new revolutionary definition of freedom negatively. Petr Zakhar'in's popular novel, *Arfakad*, dismissed the French view as "the right of the strong to dominate the weak" while claiming to give everyone equality.[31] Kheraskov's third novel, *Polydorus*, published in 1794, devises a political epiphany for the eponymous hero. In the country of Terzitian, Polydorus observes that the general welfare has been destroyed through revolution. He witnesses "cities blazing . . . fields stained with blood . . . the people everywhere, like a flock without a shepherd, thronging and crying out with insolence and unruliness—freedom! freedom!" And yet freedom only means self-interest, instead of the general welfare, which is identified with tsarist rule. "These enemies, these thieves" were misguided by a cry for equality that resulted in everyone equally becoming a despot:

Woe to the body whose members have stopped obeying their head, their Tsar; everything has fallen into disorder, madness, frenzy, illness. . . . All human obligations, respected since time immemorial and preserved by laws, the rights of mankind, the customs, the very faith have been smashed . . . in this rule by the mob.

Polydorus decides that he will establish a "true" monarchy, one limited by laws and public opinion, and he would build "one family, one thought, one heart." For Terzitian, he hopes that in the future, as had happened with a female monarch of a "Northern region," a new sovereign would introduce a golden age with a "wise *nakaz*."[32]

The events in France only confirmed Russians' commitment to monarchy and to Catherine. In the preface to a French biography of Louis XVI, the Russian translator treats the king with sympathy but delineates his part in causing the revolution. Unlike the "immortal Catherine," Louis proved lazy, he failed to appoint good ministers, and his lack of interest in finding out about "his land and his people" led him to underestimate such problems as the inefficiency of the grain trade and the plight of the rural poor. His calling of the Estates-General, while laudable, only exacerbated the hardships he and his ministers had neglected to allay. Louis was well intentioned but unfit, and he paid the price.[33]

THE EMPRESS ON EDGE

Despite the prevailing monarchism in Russia, Catherine became jittery after the outbreak of the French Revolution. In 1785, as already seen, she still felt confident enough in her popularity to override a censor who wanted to ban a play because of its depiction of despotism and assassination; understanding the Manichaean opposition in advice literature of the good monarch-parent versus the evil tyrant, Catherine responded that Russians looked upon her as a "mother," not a bad tsar.[34] But after 1789, Kniazhnin's play of 1784, *Rosslav,* could no longer be performed because the dénouement involved a tyrannous king being overthrown in a popular uprising, and in 1793 Catherine ordered Shakespeare's *Julius Caesar* removed from bookstores because of the theme of regicide.[35] Catherine was clearly reacting to the adoption of a constitution by the Poles, the assassination of Gustavus III of Sweden, and the beheading of Louis XVI, among the many episodes in this age of democratic revolutions.[36]

Even before the outbreak of the French Revolution, by the late 1780s, advice literature began warning the empress that her formerly "all-glorious reign" was coming under attack and that references to a bad tsar might no longer refer to Peter III but to herself.[37] A popular tale told of a monarch "born in Europe," whose vices have "caused his entire empire to fall into disrepair so that his people were "despondent and indignant against him."[38] Vasilii Kapnist, a poet and a Ukrainian landlord, wrote an ironical "Ode to Slavery" after Catherine enserfed the peasants of three provinces in his region:

> O, ye Tsars! Why has the Creator
> Given you a power like unto His,
> So that in areas under your power
> You can create, from those once happy, unhappy people
> And evil instead of the common weal?[39]

Catherine the Great in her later years. D. A. Rovinskii, *Materialy dlia russkoi . . .*
St. Petersburg, 1884–90, vol. 7, no. 278

Kapnist made no attempt to publish the ode, but his bitterness was not unique.

Other writers decried the despotic direction in which they feared Catherine's regime was headed. Denis Fonvizin wrote "A Discourse on the Fundamental Laws of the State" (1780s) as a guide for Grand Duke Paul. Although unpublished, the disquisition represents the ideas of a political thinker who had been active in defining issues among the delegates to the Legislative Commission and became a member of the influential Panin party.[40] This significant document of the Russian Enlightenment repeated the need for two reforms: first, for fundamental laws to protect life and property and provide legal guarantees against arbitrary power and the power of favorites; second, to establish an advisory body with deliberative powers to assist the monarch in running the state.[41] The agenda was not unusual. Statesmen like Nikita and Petr Panin, Aleksandr Vorontsov, and Aleksandr Bezborodko agreed that Peter the Great's legacy led inexorably to this type of "constitutional order in Russia" since he had placed it on a Western path of development.[42] Dashkova, a member of the Vorontsov clan, admitted: "I have always considered a limited monarch, where the sovereign is subordinate to the laws, and in some degree amenable to public opinion, to be amongst the wisest of institutions . . . where a king is surrounded by pomp with power to do good, but prevented from doing the least evil."[43]

In the opening paragraphs of his "Discourse," Fonvizin provided an amalgam of the arguments that had been circulating in favor of installing legal bulwarks against despotism rather than relying on a monarch's self-limitation and good intentions.

> Supreme power is entrusted to the Sovereign solely for the common good of His subjects. Tyrants know this truth, but good Monarchs feel it. A Monarch, enlightened with the clarity of this truth and gifted with great qualities of soul, being clothed with unlimited power and striving for perfection as much as is humanly possible, will Himself at once sense . . . that absolute power only achieves its true majesty when it deprives itself of the possibility of doing some kind of evil. And truly the radiance of the Throne is an empty brightness when virtue does not reside there along with the Sovereign: but if one imagines him as someone whose mind and heart were so superior that never would he stray from the common good and to that end He would devote all His intentions and actions, could one think that by this devotion His unrestrained power would be limited? No . . . because only Almighty God is capable of doing nothing but good . . . but even He has established laws of truth for Himself . . . by which He rules the universe and which He Himself cannot transgress without ceasing to be God. The Sovereign . . . can demonstrate neither His might nor His title in any other way than establishing in His own realm unalterable, fundamental laws, founded on the common good, and which He Himself could not violate without ceasing to be a fit Sovereign.

Fonvizin, a passionate patriot, bemoaned the results that inevitably mark an absolute monarchy when power is not limited by law: lack of "stability" or "durability" in legislation and a "Sovereign enslaved to an unworthy *favorite*," whose vices corrupt the state and the concept of service (their motto: "Those who can—grab; those who can't—steal"). In addition, civil society is destroyed because "you will have a state but not a fatherland; you have subjects but not citizens, and there is no political body that would unite its members through a network of rights and responsibilities." In a word, you have a despot, a bad tsar. Memoirists at about the same time recorded deep dissatisfaction when the empress turned over many official responsibilities to her last favorite, the young and greedy Platon Zubov.[44] Admiral Aleksandr Shishkov explained her excessive reliance: "She was a woman advanced in years, she was a woman in love, she was an autocratic woman."[45]

Fonvizin's essay iterated what fiction had described as the normal fate of a despot. He foretold that, with a legally unrestrained ruler, despite his "personal revulsion to tyranny, his rule will become tyrannical"; then, "suddenly all will strive to break the bonds of unbearable slavery," and this "Colossus held up by chains . . . will disintegrate." Summarizing the Russian theory about despotism, Fonvizin held that the people have the right to overthrow a tyrant for three reasons: such a ruler is by definition "illegitimate"; "power originates in the hands of the nation" and can be recalled; and the bonds tying citizens to the sovereign are "voluntary." He concluded that "a tyrant, wherever he may be, is a tyrant, and the right of the people to save their way of life remains steadfast forever and everywhere." But, like other Russians, Fonvizin could imagine neither aristocracy nor democracy as a form of government for the empire, nor he implies, was the country ready for emancipation of the serfs.[46] In his opinion, a good tsar and gradual measures, beginning with the introduction of fundamental laws, could assure Russia's progress, and he was probably correct.

Although they were not part of the same circle, Shcherbatov, another major figure in the Russian Enlightenment, likewise urged the introduction of fundamental laws, but the flaws he criticized in his unpublished lamentations on the sad state of the country under Catherine concentrated more on the general problem of morality. Like Fonvzin's writings, Shcherbaov's essays represented the private thoughts of a man keenly interested in pubic affairs and at the same time a leading member of the educated elite, whose "traits" he reflected.[47] Shcherbatov's lengthy musings on the Russian condition, "On the Corruption of Morals" (1786–1787), point an accusing finger at the flagrant practice at court of the seven cardinal sins, for which he blames the power of favorites and the lack of moral fiber in monarchs. To a degree he excuses Catherine; he suggests that she probably couldn't help herself since women are inclined to despotism, luxury, and flattery. Shcherbatov describes his empress as "clever, affable, magnanimous, and compassionate . . . prudent, enterprising, and well-read," but these positive qualities are offset by vainglory, capriciousness, dissolute behavior, secularism, and her rewarding of favorites. Unlike Fonvizin, however, he foresaw no upheaval: "We must only beg God that this evil may be eradicated by a better reign."[48] Like many, he placed his hopes in Paul.

In 1789, Shcherbatov wrote another essay critical of the existing order, "A Justification of My Ideas." It remained unpublished, but it qualifies as a piece of advice literature since the author hoped that it would be read by the empress after his death. In twenty pages of text, he cries out *okhuliaiu*

(I censure) sixty-four times and condemns everything from the handling of the Turkish wars and the Pugachev Revolt to the running of the procurator-general's office and local administration to laziness among government figures; he even had the temerity to "censure the Monarch Herself." Shcherbatov displayed the pessimism of a man filled with moral certainty and certain about the baseness of human nature: "What purpose do my words serve? They will not help our unfortunate people, despotism will still exist, lovers and grandees will still be carnal, lazy, ignorant, and evil, and governments will still remain filled with robbers ignorant of the laws." But he retained the glimmer of hope that was so prevalent among monarchists: "I place before the monarchical throne the sad condition of our fatherland and to show her the truth hidden from her, and, with our cries, tears, and submissiveness, to touch her heart so that she might work for the good of the fatherland."[49] The old belief persisted: if only the monarch knew. . . .

Aleksandr Herzen, the great nineteenth-century writer, visualized Shcherbatov as the very antithesis of the views of Radishchev, saying that they stood "like two wistful sentries at two different doors."[50] And yet, Radishchev's *Journey from St. Petersburg to Moscow* of 1790 contains an identical lament about "the sad condition of our fatherland" and the same hope to save the monarch from her blindness through a piece of advice literature. These works were not isolated phenomena. In that year, Pavel L'vov published a novel with similar themes. *The Temple of Truth* relates the story of King Sezostris, who "wanted to be a great conqueror instead of a father of the fatherland"; furthermore, he "has given *flatterers* full power over him and at the same time has lost the trust of the people." The king is warned that without the support of the public "not even the strongest ruler can sustain power," since he runs the danger of being "perceived as a contemptible tyrant." In the end, his blinders are removed, he sees how his ministers have lied to him, and he is horrified at the actual condition of his country, which he vows to rectify.[51]

While hundreds of works had preceded Radishchev's piece of advice literature, his *Journey* became the most famous and certainly best written example of the genre. He adopted the themes and conventions already ubiquitous: a pilgrim, Truth, comes to rip the cataracts off the eyes of the well-intentioned but deluded monarch; good and bad rulers are contrasted; the need for rule of law and the condemnation of flatterers and favorites are paramount; the evil monarch will "die a hundred deaths"; only an enlightened sovereign can rectify the miseries of mankind. Radishchev surely did not expect the empress, even though edgy, to condemn him to death for a book that in so many respects was derivative. In addition, the previous year he had safely published a biography that contained a biting indictment of corruption at court.[52] But the timing of the *Journey's* publication was bad, and it hit too close to home. Princess Dashkova had already worried that Radishchev's "thought or expressions were dangerous in the times in which we lived."[53] The *Journey* also took place in Russia, rather than some exotic land, and as a passionate abolitionist tract, it broke the taboo against speaking of the "sufferings of humanity" that serfdom brings. Indeed, the book begins with a quotation from *Télémaque* to describe the institution: "A grim monster, savage, gigantic, hundred-mouthed, and bellowing."[54] Radishchev's call for equality and equality of opportunity likewise challenged Russia's social order.

The principal reason, though, that Radishchev met with such summary hostility from the empress was that the *Journey,* more than any other piece of advice literature, destroyed the innocence of absolute power. A pilgrim at court utters the terrible truth that a monarch can do unspeakable evil: "For know that thou hast it in thy power to be the greatest murderer in the commonweal, the greatest robber, the greatest traitor, the greatest violator of the public peace, a most savage enemy who turns his malice against the lives of the weak."[55] Following in the great tradition of the genre, the pilgrim hopes to open the eyes of the ruler so that he might see the evil that is perpetrated in his name. The sojourner also begs mercy toward all those who speak the truth.

> If from the midst of the people there arise a man who criticizes thy acts, know that he is thy true friend . . . and do not dare to put him to death as a rebel. Call him to thee, be hospitable to him as to a pilgrim. For everyone who criticizes the Sovereign in the fullness of his autocratic power is a pilgrim in the land where all tremble before him.[56]

But Catherine was no longer secure enough or willing to listen to truth-tellers who offered sincere advice. She became incensed by the two sections of the *Journey*—the narrator's dream and the poem, "Liberty, an Ode"—that focus on the abilities and debilities of rulers.

The narrator dreams that he is a tsar in splendid regalia and surrounded by voices of artful praise: "He is greater than all other kings, he gives liberty to all men." In reality, he is a fearsome picture of a tyrant, whose every twitch is warily followed by trembling magnates. The tsar exults in his power to terrify: "When I laugh, all laugh; if I frown threateningly, all are confounded. You live only so long as I permit you to live."[57] Imitating the language of poetic praise, Radishchev has the monarch commended for commanding armies and navies, erecting magnificent buildings, aiding the needy, and bestowing honors, and the ruler glows with "self-satisfaction."[58] But the pilgrim demonstrates that this is all sham and shame: military commanders were "wallowing in luxury and pleasure" while the soldiers lived in misery; the buildings were in poor taste; public funds had been squandered, ending up in the pockets of the rich; and everyone tried to fool the monarch. Truth derides the courtiers to his majesty as "your real enemies, who dim thine eyes" and utter "words of flattery, emitting poisonous vapors."[59]

The monarch sees the light and discovers that his "glittering garments seemed to be stained with blood and drenched with tears. On my fingers I saw fragments of human brains; my feet were standing in slime." He now realizes that good intentions were not enough: "My commands had either been completely violated by being misapplied, or had not had the desired effect because of distorted interpretation and dilatory execution." The monarch, reborn, welcomes "afresh the responsibility of my high office, recognizing the vastness of my duty, and understanding whence proceeds my right and my power."[60] After the dream, the chapters in the *Journey* repeat staple themes in advising the sovereign: the need to be subject to law, the necessity of striving for virtue, the recommendation to build educational facilities, the injunction to avoid war and conquest, and the urgency of distancing oneself from "court idols." Above all, good monarchs must attend to their public; they realize that the strength of the throne "is rooted in the opinion of the citizens," whom they should impress, not with pomp, but with "glittering argument, seeming conviction."[61] Up to this point in her reading, Catherine's notes on the *Journey* indicate irritation with its "malicious" author, who she determines is influenced by "hypochondriacs" like Rousseau and the "vicious example of France."[62]

"Liberty, an Ode," though, horrified the empress, as well it might have. This section of the *Journey* provides the conventional contrast of the good and the bad tsar, but the depiction is brutal. Citing both Catherine's *Nakaz* and Rousseau's doctrine of the general will, Radishchev begins by repeating the maxim that "liberty means all obey the same laws," before which everyone is equal.[63] But these are empty words, Radishchev claims. In reality, "religious and political superstition, each supporting the other, join to oppress society" on a "tarnished throne of slavery" while claiming that the system achieves the "common good." Not fooled, "the avenger comes, proclaiming liberty . . . and the avenging law of nature has brought the king to the block." The people put him on trial and accuse him of violating the trust and power they granted him: "Forgetting that I had chosen you, you came to think that you had been crowned for your own pleasure, and that you were the master, not I."[64] The bad tsar had perverted monarchy: he destroyed laws and rights; he answered to God and gold, not his subjects; he stole the sustenance of the worker, "tearing the rags" off his back; he rewarded sycophants; he fought vainglorious battles. The tsar's sentence: "Die, then, die a hundred deaths." The throne is razed, and the kingdom of liberty brings "security, peace, well-being, greatness. . . ."

The overthrow of a bad tsar, however, does not bring happiness to sinful humans. Radishchev cited the example of Cromwell: he should be praised for executing Charles "by due process of law," but then he "destroyed the citadel of freedom" and set up his own tyranny. The utopia bows to iron laws, which are pessimistic: "This is the law of nature: from tyranny, freedom is born; from freedom, slavery." Radishchev's pessimism about human nature resulted in an extraordinary prescience that enabled him to prophesy the course of the French (and Russian) revolutions. His final message brought hope that rulers will be "dismayed" once knowing that "humanity will roar in its fetters" at the appearance of tyranny.[65] No wonder the empress was shocked at reading this anti-Felitsa.[66] Catherine fulminated that here was "an ode most clearly, manifestly revolutionary, in which tsars are threatened with the block. . . . These pages are of criminal intent, completely revolutionary."[67]

The edgy empress was wrong. Radishchev was pleading with his ruler to initiate reforms and thus avert a dreadful revolution.[68] Like any other writer of advice literature, Radishchev published the volume in the hope that the empress, the First Reader, would see its truth and undergo conversion, like so many fictional heroes in plays and novels. But Catherine saw only malice and treason and condemned him to death, a sentence later commuted to ten years' exile.[69] To the end of his life, Radishchev remained steadfast in his hope for the reforming policies of a benevolent ruler, a belief buttressed by the excesses of the French Revolution.[70] His poem of 1801, "The Eighteenth Century," which Pushkin considered his best work, rued the bloody excesses of the past one hundred years but eulogized Peter and Catherine for having led Russia into the sun and overcoming the "dark shadows" of the past. His hopes lay in monarchs: "Peace, justice, truth, and freedom shall flow from a throne, / Raised on high by Peter and Catherine so that Rus' might prosper."[71]

In 1792, Catherine made a similar mistake with the writer and publisher Nikolai Novikov. Just as she reviled Radishchev as a Martinist, she was hostile toward Novikov because he was an active Mason, a "fanatic" in her words.[72] She resented Masonic philanthropic activity because it was independent of her control, and she grew angry with the group's overtures to Paul to join.[73] In addition, Novikov and his private press represented the independence of public opinion and free social initiative, trends she no longer cared to tolerate. The publisher, a dedicated monarchist, became another victim of her unease and was sentenced to fifteen years in the Schlüsselburg Fortress.[74]

In 1793, a similar episode occurred when Princess Dashkova approved the posthumous publication of Kniazhnin's *Vadim of Novgorod*, arguably the best play of the eighteenth century (the empress's objections seemed to fall only on good literature).[75] When Catherine read the work in the journal *Russian Theatre*, she broke with the princess and claimed that the play put "much too strong and bitter an evil-eye on absolute power" and "deserved to be burned in public by an executioner" because of its depiction of revolt against a duly elected monarch.[76] Dashkova "laughed at the imputed danger," for the author had been a firm monarchist.[77] The princess was correct, and once again the edgy empress was reacting to passages that seemed dangerous or disloyal, rather than to the underlying assumptions of the text.

As with the *Journey*, the topic was conventional; both Plavil'shchikov and Catherine had written plays on the same theme, and dozens of works described attempted or successful overthrows of monarchs.[78] The legend about Riurik and Vadim was based on an entry in the Novgorod Chronicle for 863: the city, torn by dissension, invites the Varangian princes, with Riurik at their head, to rule over them and bring order; Riurik kills Vadim the Courageous when Vadim leads a revolt to unseat the new leader.[79] In Kniazhnin's version, Vadim must choose between the former republicanism of the city of Novgorod and the new absolute monarchy. Kniazhnin views Riurik's power as legitimate since the people had freely chosen him, and when he offers them another chance to choose between him and Vadim, the Novgorodians opt for the wise and virtuous Riurik. In contrast, Kniazhnin depicts Vadim as a fanatic and also as a tyrannical father: he forces his daughter, who loves Riurik, to agree to marry a man whom she loathes, and later Vadim compels the young woman to commit suicide with him. Riurik, then, is the actual hero of the play, and the rabble rouser, who failed to incite the masses, betrayed himself as a despot: how could he be a loving father to his people if he treated his daughter so viciously? Indeed, reviews at the time pointed out that the play could have been livelier if the author had not portrayed Vadim in such a one-dimensional way as an "insane Republican."[80]

Apparently, at this stage in her reign, Catherine took any ambivalence personally. Vadim's lengthy tirades against monarchy in the abstract rested on the age-old maxims that power corrupts (and certainly would have corrupted Vadim), but Catherine, with some justification, took Kniazhnin's traditional formulations as reflections on her behavior, and she was no longer in a frame of mind to tolerate advice literature.

> Every monarch is corrupted by the purple.
> Autocracy, everywhere brings misfortune,
> It ruins even virtue most pure,
> And, opening an unrestricted path to the passions,
> Gives tsars the freedom to be tyrants.
> Look at the examples of all tsars and centuries,
> Their power is the power of gods, but their weakness that of men.[81]

Kniazhnin's *Vadim* and Radishchev's *Journey* appeared at about the same time and used similar sanguinary imagery: "Some compare criminals in crowns with immortals / And intoxicate those on the throne with the blood of their subjects."[82]

Kniazhnin's play addresses what was seen in the eighteenth century as the irreconcilable conflict between the individual's desire for freedom and the necessity of his being ruled. Vadim berates his people's servility to a king but observes that, without a monarch, Novgorodians fell to quarrelling, and "pride, envy, malice, unrest were abroad in the city."[83] In the last scene, Riurik explains to Vadim that in Rus', the "fruit of freedom" was "disarray, robbery, murder, and violence," and in the mêlée, "sons arose against fathers, and fathers against their children"; it was a tyranny "of another kind."[84] Indeed, Vadim is forced to admit Riurik's legitimacy; he "came by invitation of the whole people" and saved the city by bringing it "peace."

None of the writers in eighteenth-century Russia—not Kniazhnin, Novikov, Radishchev, or the hundreds of other members of the publishing public—could resolve the conflict between freedom and power and the potential of both for abuse. But one should not denigrate the hard thought that went into this conundrum. As Anton Chekhov has pointed out, one must not confuse "two concepts: *solving the problem* and *formulating it correctly*. Only the latter is obligatory for an author."[85] Despite Catherine's edginess, she need not have feared for her life and reign since her rule, overall, was that of a good tsar, and she had earned reserves of good will. Those who were dissatisfied with the policies of the aging empress assumed the problems would be resolved when her son mounted the throne, which Paul did in early November of 1796, after his mother died of a stroke.

PAUL I

The many criticisms levied against Catherine during her last years in power meant that writers greeted the new ruler with relief and expectation. Paul seemed to embody the Masonic ideals of political morality and social reform and hence should have proved the "good tsar" of every Russian's dreams. The thirty-year-old Nikolai Karamzin, already a respected prose writer, reflected the general mood in an ode to Paul on the occasion of Muscovites' taking the oath of loyalty. Joining the ranks of advice littérateurs, Karamzin imitated the established formulae by welcoming the end of capriciousness in the royal office and offering suggestions for guiding the new reign. Paul, he intoned, would resurrect the concept of a legal sovereign: "With him enthroned, justice reappears, / Conscience is reconciled with law." To rectify other abuses, the new ruler would choose worthy counselors and stop the persecution of Masons through a return of "freedom with mercy."[86]

Karamzin very quickly lost his enthusiasm. In 1802, chastened by Paul's reign, he published another hymn of praise, 187 pages in length, but dedicated to the resplendence of Catherine, "the Great one whom we all worshipped." The speech defended every aspect of the empress's foreign and domestic policy, in particular her "wise laws" that protected person and property. Summarizing the *Nakaz,* Karamzin now extolled Catherine as a legal sovereign who demonstrated that "autocracy was no enemy of freedom."[87] A memoirist recalled that the son did the mother a favor: "Never was Catherine held in such glory among her people" as after Paul ascended the throne; in contrast, her rule appeared "golden."[88] The father and son acted like two grim bookends whose homeliness ensured the glitter of the embossed works of Catherine that they flanked.

During his four-year reign, Emperor Paul seemed almost genetically driven to become a bad tsar; he certainly committed the same mistakes as his father. Like Peter III, he felt so secure as a legally appointed male Romanov that he neither justified his power nor forged a consensus of support among the educated elite.[89] Paul's accession manifesto, just like Peter's, announced a conception of monarchy that differed markedly from the thrust of the past century. Paul proclaimed that he was ascending the "throne of our forefathers, which we have inherited."[90] The emphasis on heredity was confirmed in the new succession law that Paul, in a dramatic gesture, promulgated at his coronation; it established male primogeniture, with women able to accede only in the absence of male heirs. To accentuate paternal lineage and displace Catherine, a female monarch, Paul engaged in bizarre behavior just after she died: he disinterred Peter III, crowned him posthumously, laid him in state next to his wife, and removed the crown from her coffin.[91] Clearly, the new monarch wanted to inherit the throne from his father, not his mother, who he believed had kept them both from power.

Heading even further backward in political time, Paul not only elevated hereditary right in his accession manifesto, but he also resurrected its correlative, divine right, by speaking of his throne as a "God-given burden." At a stroke, he thus abolished the atmosphere of secularism and the criteria of fitness and election that had developed over the course of the century. The new emperor intended such a revolution. He thought of himself as a kind of godhead and aspired to gird his imperial office with religious underpinnings, for instance through his odd quest to become Grand Master of the Order of Malta.[92]

The new succession law also aimed generally at eroding the partnership between crown and nobility and specifically at preventing the elite from interfering in the succession process. The Slavophile scholar Boris Glinskii claimed that the establishment of heredity as the sole criterion for accession eliminated the need for "sanctification" by any representative group and resulted in a dynasty that rested on the military and the bureaucracy rather than the will of the people.[93] Parades, soldierly discipline, uniforms, administrative centralization, and religious ceremony became emblematic of the reign.[94] Furthermore, Paul described himself as an "unlimited autocrat" *(neogranichennyi Samoderzhets),* which carried the meaning of despot among the educated elite. Even in distant provinces, people began murmuring that "he won't rule long."[95]

Paul's attempts at being a good tsar backfired. He knew he should act like a reforming tsar, but his execution of policies, like his father's, engendered only fiasco and opposition.[96] Wanting to signal his concern for the lower orders, rather than vested interests, he insisted that everyone, including serfs, take the oath, but some peasants took this as a sign of emancipation, ceased obeying their masters, and the army had to be mobilized to quell disturbances.[97] In the first calendar year of Paul's reign, roughly 48,000 edicts gave an impression of a new broom sweeping clean; however,

Paul I. D. G. Levitskii, *Russkaia zhivopis'* . . . St. Petersburg, 1902, vol. 1

he presented no coherent plan except to undo his mother's system, so that the administration appeared inept and erratic.[98] He spoke vigorously about rule of law but looked backward to the regulated state of Peter the Great, at a moment when thinkers were looking forward to the concept of equality before a set of fundamental laws.

As grand duke, Paul had always enunciated the principles of a model enlightened monarch, but his government reproduced instead the barracks atmosphere of his old court at Gatchina.[99] Like his father, he worshipped Frederick the Great with the result that "the ancien régime, organized according to Prussian military principles, became the essence of Paul's vision for Russia."[100] Lack of direction likewise characterized Paul's foreign policy. He estranged erstwhile allies like Austria and Britain and after crusading against the revolution ended up in the orbit of Napoleonic France. Wanting to play the arbiter in European affairs, he switched from policies of nonintervention to planning aggressive campaigns in Italy, Switzerland, and India.[101] Unpublished works satirized Paul and his officials as blind, deaf, and dumb, as men who consult gypsies about how to direct policy.[102]

The characteristics of a bad tsar surfaced insistently. The erratic nature of Paul's policies and his willful shifts in opinion led to questions about his personality; some argued he was a megalomaniac, others that he was clinically insane.[103] While Roderick E. McGrew's biography lays to rest charges of insanity, Paul possessed the character of a despot: he was impetuous, capricious, brash, petty, violent, lacked judgment, and demanded total obedience even as his will lurched from one radical solution to another.[104] McGrew has provided a portrait that is unsettling: "Paul in action was the frightened martinet, unpredictable, inconsistent, and above all, uncontrolled. . . . [H]is obvious inability to control the power which he wielded destroyed whatever confidence his more enlightened policies might have won him."[105] One of Paul's contemporaries, Ivan Dolgorukii, was equally acerbic in his memoirs: "Without the smallest shred of a sense of justice or humanity, he only dressed in the skin of a man, underneath he was an evil and predatory beast."[106]

Many among the elite held Paul in contempt and fear, much like Radishchev's picture of a despot. Literature concerning monarchy lost its richness since the number of publications fell, and an atmosphere charged with insecurity prevented dialogue between monarch and subject.[107] Although scion of a clan that for centuries sought access to the throne, Dolgorukii remarked: "I felt very lucky that he [Paul] forgot absolutely all about me."[108] Less fortunate were the twelve thousand people who were arrested, exiled, or dismissed without trial during the reign. In an obsessive effort to stave off a revolution, Paul established a myriad of restrictions: on dress, on socializing, on travel abroad, on private printing presses, on the importation of foreign books and sheet music, and on the use of such words as society *(obshchestvo)* or citizens *(grazhdane)*. In addition, he nullified many of the guarantees enunciated in the Charter of 1785, which was regarded as a fundamental law in the empire; for instance, he rescinded the nobility's rights to assemble, elect a marshal, appeal directly to the monarch, and be free of corporal punishment.

Paul came to personify the bad tsar, whose policies failed any moral test. At least since the 1760s, many among the elite had sought in vain for some constitutional arrangement that might prevent an absolute monarch from slipping into despotism, and the century's last ruler proved the urgency.[109] However, as is known in hindsight, Russian sovereigns would not consent even to the vaguest restrictions on their power. At the time of Paul, the good citizens, while hoping for a better solution, felt obliged to stop the tyrant with the most readily available alternative to constitutionalism—assassination. In his memoirs, Prince Adam Czartoryski wrote that the outcome was expected: "Everyone felt it coming, wished for it, feared it, and was sure of it."[110] The sixty-eight men directly involved in the act of regicide on the night of March 11, 1801, were acting against tyranny.[111] The elite judged that this was a deliverance, and they released a collective sigh of relief.[112]

Paul's son, the future Alexander I, made the tortured decision to acquiesce in the overthrow (but not assassination), because he too recognized that his father had become a classic bad tsar:

> When he mounted the throne my father sought to reform everything. He began brilliantly enough, but he did not carry through. Everything was turned upside down, which only added to the great confusion that already existed in affairs. The military wastes nearly all of its time parading. No plan is followed anywhere. Orders are given that a month later are countermanded. Remonstrances of any sort, even if the harm is obvious, are never tolerated. In short, the welfare of the State counts for nothing in the direction of affairs; there is only the capriciousness of absolute power. It would be impossible to enumerate for you all of the mad things which have taken place, severity without justice, great partiality, and total inexperience in affairs. Employment is assigned by force, merit counts for nothing. Finally my poor country is in an indefensible state. The peasant is burdened, commerce is impeded, and individual liberty and personal security are at an end.[113]

Alexander came to the throne promising to rule "according to the laws and spirit of Our Most August Grandmother . . . whose wise policies" brought greatness and prosperity.[114] The young man did indeed promote an atmosphere of consensus and reform, but he would also shatter the hopes of those who strove for a regime founded on fundamental laws and encompassing some form of representative body, a regime where a monarch, in Dashkova's words, is invested "with power to do good, but prevented from doing the least evil."[115]

The Significance of the Eighteenth-Century Political Dialogue

*T*he public dialogue between ruler and ruled changed and charged the whole atmosphere of political power in eighteenth-century Russia. After 1613, Romanov rulers had projected their legitimacy by donning religious garb, recalling the elective origins of their dynasty, and vowing to preserve ancient traditions. Peter the Great cast aside the Muscovite justifications for power, seized upon the modern vision of a monarch as secular reformer, and appropriated the role with more vigor than any other European ruler. In the great work of modernization, Peter sought from the elite not mere acquiescence but active involvement, and he therefore not only lectured these subjects but also, like an effective teacher, engaged them in public discourse about his right and duty to perform the tasks that lay ahead. Under Peter's successors, especially Catherine II, the dialogue continued, finding a venue in the various publications that appeared during the print explosion that marked her reign.

This discourse centered on the definition and feasibility of monarchy and thus took place within the context of the various "enlightenments" that challenged educated men and women throughout Europe and demanded the reassessment of accepted institutions. The literature of political engagement—both justification literature, primarily written by monarchs and their entourage and directed toward members of the educated elite, and advice literature, primarily written by members of the educated elite and directed toward rulers—reaffirmed that monarchy in Russia was a necessity, and every generation discovered additional reasons for the utility and desirability of the institution.

The Russian dialogue drew upon the unbroken continuity of discourse on monarchy that dated back to the classical era. Both discussions concluded that democracy and aristocracy were unreasonable or ruinous as alternatives in large states with unprotected borders. The same classical conventions further agreed that monarchy best complemented the workings of the physical universe or the social world and assumed that certain innate attributes of royal persons assured the well-being of their people.

Eighteenth-century Russians put new sparkle in these age-old arguments by blending them with Enlightenment thinking: rulers discovered new justifications for their office, and their subjects devised new ways of determining legitimacy. Peter the Great identified monarchy with the idea of progress, used the ability to effect rapid change as the primary justification for his absolute power, and made reform an essential duty of a Russian tsar. Driven by an uncertain law of succession, post-Petrine claimants to the throne buttressed their cases by going through an elective process and emphasizing dynastic descent, while always promising to act as reforming tsars. In 1762, Catherine II acknowledged the new cry of philosophes for monarchs to abide by laws, and she justified her ascent and reign on the basis of election and reform but also on her vow to act as a sovereign bound by legal restraints.

Members of the educated elite participated in negotiating and establishing the new justifications as signs of legitimacy. Practitioners of advice literature challenged monarchs to ever greater heights of reform and encouraged readers to present their own projects. Writers celebrated the Romanov dynasty, but especially the elective element that accompanied most monarchs' ascent to the throne and the contractual ties that thereby bound them to their subjects. Other authors urged the issuance of law codes that would apply to both citizen and ruler. Russian historians read these new or reworked signs of legitimacy back to the first of the Riurikids and all of the Romanovs, reconfiguring Russian history to match the new criteria that had recently emerged. Belletrists added to the liveliness of advice literature by mythologizing the good tsar, whose personal moral sense would ennoble the population, and by excoriating the bad tsar, whose evil conduct would doom him and his state.

As each succeeding generation of writers elaborated its criteria for royal conduct and rulers expanded upon the justifications for power, both sets of interlocutors spoke in the language of the Enlightenment and achieved a consensus about monarchy that integrated state and elite society in a new sense of cohesion. Indeed, this is a major aim of dialogue. According to Plato, it stands as a type of intercourse that should logically end in a single truth.[1] Perhaps for this reason, during her reign, Catherine began writing advice literature, and Russian writers often used the rhetoric of justification.

Toward the end of the century, the arguments in favor of monarchy possessed great force because each generation's contribution to the dialogue existed alongside the newer views, while reverence for the office based on custom and religion never fully disappeared. Hence, the collection of concepts on monarchy resembled a palimpsest, and rulers could lie secure under multiple layers of legitimacy: as dynamic reformers; as elected by the people; as ruling according to established legal procedures; as members of a dynasty destined to lead Russia forward along a European path; and as people who understood the precepts of behavior ordained by God, nature, duty, and morality. The rules of this elaborate construct also dictated that those who failed to measure up should be ousted, and they were.

The existence and nature of political dialogue in eighteenth-century Russia belies three long-held contentions. First, the underlying assumptions of the public discourse gainsay "the traditional equation of autocracy with despotic power."[2] Unlike despots, the monarchs who wrote justification literature believed it was necessary to win the support of the elite if they wanted to ascend and keep the throne; they recognized that they could not reign or rule by fiat alone. Unlike subjects in a despotic state, the writers of advice literature practiced their craft because they recognized an accepted web of restrictions governing policy and behavior that limited the power of their rulers. For them, an "unlimited autocrat" meant a tyrant.

Second, the Russian educated elite has often been described as fearful, masochistic, and politically paralyzed. And yet, in 1730, that elite debated abrogating absolutism and later acted to overthrow two regents and two monarchs on charges of tyranny, that is, of not conforming to the standards of conduct that writers, in dialogue with their monarchs, had so carefully articulated. In the context of the Enlightenment, continued support of monarchy came to rest not on servility but on conscious choice achieved through critical analysis. These actions and beliefs suggest a group determinedly *engagé* and willing to act on their convictions.

A third contention holds that Russian development is unique and stands outside the normal European framework. One scholar has complained that "too often, historians are inclined to view Russia as sui generis, appended to Europe but almost entirely different in its societies and institutions."[3] The vigor of a political dialogue that reflected the ongoing penetration of Enlightenment thought among Russia's own philosophes should work to normalize the history of the easternmost of the European nations. In addition, discovering that Russian conceptions of monarchy resemble Western traditions and ideals can guide historians to other political parallels.

Eighteenth-century Russian writers and monarchs certainly regarded themselves as moving along a path of European development. The dialogue that took place between Catherine II and her subjects, especially in the earlier part of her reign, resonated with the hope that Russia was rapidly on its way to establishing both rule by law and some type of institution permitting the elite to share its opinions with the ruler, not only through the written word but by actual participation in governance. Indeed, the practice of giving public advice to monarchs is only one step removed from a legally established advisory council, similar to the one Nakita Panin suggested in 1762 and that Catherine at first approved—and the latter could lay the foundation for a representative legislative assembly. Neither of these steps was taken, despite the fervent hopes and suggestions of dozens of men and women like Dashkova, Fonvizin, Kniazhnin, Shcherbatov, and Radishchev. They supported monarchy but remained fearful that without such institutions monarchy could degenerate into despotism—the nightmare that haunted all of advice literature—and the reign of Paul I proved the case.

Paul's abuse of power did not shatter the belief in monarchy, but confirmed the desire for the institution to move, even if slowly, in the direction of a constitutional order. After his father was overthrown, Alexander I rekindled the hopes for a limited monarchy, and the time was ripe, but absolutism remained. Another opportunity occurred after the War of 1812; never had the country been so unified, and never were expectations higher that Alexander would introduce a constitution. Geoffrey Hosking described the lost moment.

> It [after 1818] was a time when government, society, and the masses might have been drawn into a closer association resting on "regular" institutions and the rule of law. That was what many educated Russians both wished and expected to happen, and when it did not they were disappointed and embittered.[4]

The government settled into a state of arrested political development as the Romanovs stubbornly clung to their absolute power.

And yet, even most of the alienated—for instance those who stood on Senate Square in December of 1825 or on Palace Square in January of 1905— continued to accept the idea of monarchy, albeit in a limited form. Nonetheless, absolute monarchy lasted into the twentieth century, and here Russia was indeed unique; all the other European absolutist states had become victims of revolution and/or had evolved into limited monarchies. The longevity of absolute monarchy in Russia has variously been attributed to fear, paralysis, servility, the belief in divine right, the heavy weight of tradition, lack of intermediary bodies, or the Russian soul. More realistically, economic and social backwardness certainly prolonged political stasis; roughly 90 percent of Russia's population remained rural, isolated, and often illiterate and impoverished.

This book offers another reason for the survival of absolutism. Dialogue implicates its participants in the conclusions it reaches more firmly than does tradition or proselytism. The eighteenth-century discourse had animated political life and persuasively argued in favor of monarchy. The strength of this conclusion lasted well into the nineteenth century. Writers had avowed that Russia without monarchy was inconceivable, indeed doomed; therefore, in the face of the Romanovs' intransigence, an absolute ruler was preferable to no monarch at all. In addition, nineteenth-century monarchs and their subjects drew from the deep well of legitimacy that their eighteenth-century ancestors had constructed. Of all the justifications, only election disappeared. Paul I, by passing a new succession law, ended the elective element that had played such a prominent and empowering role for the elite; as a palliative he reinforced the ever popular dynastic justification. The other signs of legitimacy remained. Above all, Russian monarchs continued to reform—whether renovating the law code and the courts, the administrative structure, the military, and the educational system, or emancipating the serfs—and writers, especially historians, continued to establish the connection between their rulers and progress. Only monarchy itself remained unreformed, but many patiently waited for this ultimate act of a reforming tsar. In the meantime, the institution was sustained by the hopes and expectations with which monarchy had been invested during the eighteenth-century dialogue this book has described.

Abbreviated Romanov Family Tree to 1801

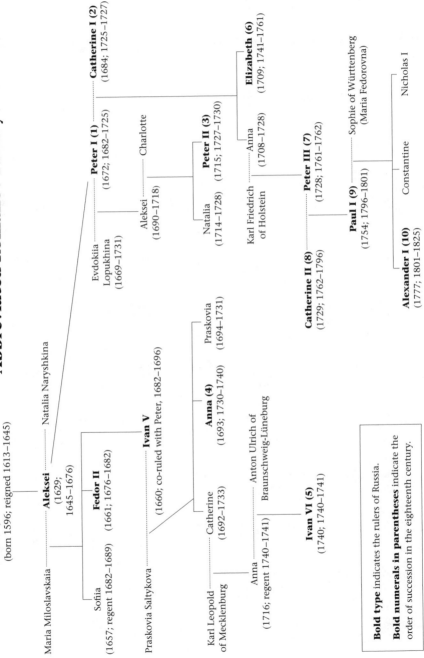

Bold type indicates the rulers of Russia.

Bold numerals in parentheses indicate the order of succession in the eighteenth century.

Mikhail, the first Romanov ruler (born 1596; reigned 1613–1645)

Maria Miloslavskaia ···· **Aleksei** ···· Natalia Naryshkina
(1629; 1645–1676)

Sofia (1657; regent 1682–1689)

Fedor II (1661; 1676–1682)

Ivan V (1660; co-ruled with Peter, 1682–1696)

Praskovia Saltykova

Catherine (1692–1733)

Karl Leopold of Mecklenburg ···· Anna (1716; regent 1740–1741)

Anton Ulrich of Braunschweig-Lüneburg

Ivan VI (5) (1740; 1740–1741)

Anna (4) (1693; 1730–1740)

Praskovia (1694–1731)

Peter I (1) (1672; 1682–1725) ···· **Catherine I (2)** (1684; 1725–1727)

Evdokiia Lopukhina (1669–1731)

Aleksei (1690–1718) ···· Charlotte

Natalia (1714–1728)

Peter II (3) (1715; 1727–1730)

Anna (1708–1728) ···· Karl Friedrich of Holstein

Elizabeth (6) (1709; 1741–1761)

Peter III (7) (1728; 1761–1762) ···· **Catherine II (8)** (1729; 1762–1796)

Paul I (9) (1754; 1796–1801) ···· Sophie of Württemberg (Maria Fedorovna)

Alexander I (10) (1777; 1801–1825)

Constantine

Nicholas I

NOTES

ABBREVIATIONS

PSZ   *Polnoe sobranie zakonov Rossiiskoi imperii*, Sobranie I, 45 vols. St. Petersburg, 1830. The Complete Collection of the Laws of the Russian Empire

BE   *Entsiklopedicheskii slovar'*. Published by F. A. Brokgauz and I. A. Efron. Leipzig and St. Petersburg, 1890–1907. Reprint, Iaroslavl, 1990–1994. The Encyclopedic Dictionary

BRAN   Biblioteka Rossiiskoi akademii nauk. The Library of the Russian Academy of Sciences. St. Petersburg

RGADA   Rossiiskii gosudarstvennyi arkhiv drevnykh aktov. The Russian State Archive of Ancient Acts. Moscow

RO   Rukopisnyi otdel. Manuscript Division of the Russian State Library. Moscow

SOII   Sankt-Peterburgskoe otdelenie Instituta istorii. Archive of the St. Petersburg filial of the Institute of Russian History of the Russian Academy of Sciences

PSS   Polnoe sobranie sochinenii. Complete Collection of Works

SK   *Svodnyi katalog russkoi knigi grazhdanskoi pechati XVIII veka, 1725–1800.* 6 vols. Moscow, 1962–1975. Cumulative Catalog of Eighteenth-Century Russian Secular Books

M   Moscow

Spb   St. Petersburg

L   Leningrad

NY   New York

INTRODUCTION: LITERATURE ON MONARCHY

1. For a discussion of this term, see O. G. Usenko, "Ob otnoshenii narodnykh mass k tsariu Alekseiu Mikhailovichu," in *Tsar' i tsarstvo v russkom obshchestvennom soznanii,* ed. A. A. Gorskii, A. I. Kuprianov, and L. N. Pushkarev (M, 1999), 70.

2. Richard Pipes, *Russia under the Old Regime* (NY, 1974), 24. The italics are part of the quote from J. Kürst, *Geschichte des Hellenismus* (Leipzig-Berlin, 1926), 2:335–36.

3. See especially, Reinhart Koselleck, *Critique and Crisis: Enlightenment and the*

Pathogenesis of Modern Society (Cambridge, Mass., 1988); Jürgen Habermas, *The Structural Transformation of the Public Sphere: An Inquiry into a Category of Bourgeois Society,* trans. T. Burger (Cambridge, Mass., 1998); *Sociabilité et société bourgeoise en France, en Allemagne, et en Suisse, 1750–1850,* ed. Étienne François (Paris, 1986). Also see Richard Firth Green, *Poets and Princepleasers: Literature and the English Court in the Late Middle Ages* (Toronto, 1980).

4. Daniel Gordon, "'Public Opinion' and the Civilizing Process in France: The Example of Morellet," *Eighteenth-Century Studies* 22 (1989): 303; also see the statement by Yutaka Takenaka, "Land-Owning Nobles and Zemstvo Institutions: The Post-Reform Estate System in Political Perspective," in *Empire and Society: New Approaches to Russian History,* ed. Teruyuki Hara and Kimitaka Matsuzato (Sapporo, Japan, 1997), 132–50.

5. The quotations are from Mona Ozouf, "L'Opinion publique," in *The French Revolution and the Creation of Modern Political Culture,* vol. 1, *The Political Culture of the Old Regime,* ed. Keith Michael Baker (Oxford, 1987), 423–25; and Anthony J. La Vopa, "Conceiving a Public: Ideas and Society in Eighteenth-Century Europe," *Journal of Modern History* 64 (1992): 112. Also consult Diethelm Klippel, "The True Concept of Liberty: Political Theory in Germany in the Second Half of the Eighteenth Century," in *The Transformation of Political Culture: England and Germany in the Late Eighteenth Century,* ed. Eckhart Hellmuth (Oxford, 1990), 447–66; Gary Marker, *Publishing, Printing, and the Origins of Intellectual Life in Russia, 1700–1800* (Princeton, 1985).

6. Joan M. Afferica has made a similar point in "The Political and Social Thought of Prince M. M. Shcherbatov" (Ph.D. diss., Harvard University, 1967), 313–14.

7. I have also utilized the standard sources: P. N. Berkov, *Istoriia russkoi zhurnalistiki XVIII veka* (M, 1952); *SK,* 6 vols. (M, 1962–1975); S. P. Luppov, *Kniga v Rossii v pervoi chetverti XVIII veka* (L, 1973); and the various tables in Marker, *Publishing.*

8. For example, slightly over 300 children's books were published in the century; of these, 50 were original Russian publications, as opposed to translations, and of those, 2 dozen spoke of monarchs and monarchy. See O. V. Alekseeva, "Khronologicheskii ukazatel'," *Materialy po istorii russkoi detskoi literatury (1750–1855),* ed. A. K. Pokrovskaia (M, 1929), 137–38. Of 600 sermons and odes, 112 featured monarchy, *SK* (1964), 2:338–47, and (1967), 5:238–42. Twenty of 77 biographies concerned monarchs, W. Gareth Jones, "Biography in Eighteenth-Century Russia," *Oxford Slavonic Papers,* New Series 22 (1989), passim. In addition, 94 memoirs and diaries discussed monarchs: A. G. Tartakovskii, *Russkaia memuaristika, XVIII–pervoi poloviny XIX v.* (M, 1991), 244–61, 262–70. About 100 novels contained political themes: V. V. Sipovskii, *Politicheskiia nastroeniia v russkom romane XVIII v.* (Spb, 1905).

9. A. N. Medushevskii, *Utverzhdenie absoliutizma v Rossii* (M, 1994), 291–99; Marker, *Publishing,* 25, 60.

10. Robert Wuthnow, *Communities of Discourse: Ideology and Social Structure in the Reformation, the Enlightenment, and European Socialism* (Cambridge, Mass., 1989), 15; Norbert Elias, *The Court Society,* trans. Edmund Jephcott (NY, 1983), 5; Richard Wortman, *Scenarios of Power: Myth and Ceremony in Russian Monarchy,* vol. 1, *From Peter the Great to the Death of Nicholas I* (Princeton, 1995), 3. On the difficulties of constructing an "image" of monarchy, see Michel Vovelle, "La représentation populaire de la monarchie," in *The French Revolution and the Creation of Modern Political Culture,* vol. 1, *The Political Culture of the Old Regime,* ed. Keith Michael Baker (Oxford, 1987), 77–86.

11. These numbers represent the counts I made in the course of my research. I have used letters that were printed in the century, but for private correspondence consult E. N. Marasinova, *Psikhologiia elity rossiiskogo dvorianstva poslednei treti XVIII veka (Po materialam perepiski)* (M, 1999).

12. Sipovskii, *Politicheskiia nastroeniia,* 3.

13. T. V. Artem'eva makes the same case for the "cultural texts" she uses in her monograph, *Russkaia istoriosofiia XVIII veka* (Spb, 1996), 5–6.

14. Wortman, *Scenarios of Power*, 9; Edward L. Keenan, "Muscovite Political Folkways," *Russian Review* 45 (1986): 158.

15. Stephen L. Baehr, *The Paradise Myth in Eighteenth-Century Russia: Utopian Patterns in Early Secular Russian Literature and Culture* (Stanford, 1991), 158; Antony Lentin, introduction to *Prince M. M. Shcherbatov: On the Corruption of Morals in Russia,* ed. and trans. Antony Lentin (Cambridge, 1969), 74; Harold B. Segel, ed. and trans., *The Literature of Eighteenth-Century Russia* (NY, 1967), 2:396.

16. A. Iu. Samarin, *Chitatel' v Rossii vo vtoroi polovine XVIII veka* (M, 2000), 209, but also see the charts, 211–69.

17. On the traditionalism of most members of the provincial nobility, see Wilson R. Augustine, "Notes Toward a Portrait of the Eighteenth-Century Russian Nobility," *Canadian Slavic Studies* 4 (1970): 373–425. On the breakdown by social strata of those who subscribed to books and journals in the second half of the century, see Samarin, *Chitatel' v Rossii,* 135; about 5 percent were noblewomen.

18. Marc Raeff has estimated that the elite as a whole represented about .5 to 1 percent of the population in the eighteenth century, *Origins of the Russian Intelligentsia: The Eighteenth-Century Nobility* (NY, 1966), 12; a more precise study calculates that the group comprised .5 percent of the population in 1719 and .7 percent in 1795: V. M. Kabuzan, "Naselenie Rossiiskoi imperii v XVIII veke," in *Issledovaniia po istorii Rossii XVI–XVIII vv.: Sbornik statei v chest' 70–letiia Ia. E. Vodarskogo* (M, 2000), 42–75. Overall, an estimation of the numbers of educated elite remains a guessing game, but Samarin in his study, *Chitatel' v Rossii,* has taken a significant step forward by identifying about ten thousand people and organizations who subscribed to books and journals in the second half of the eighteenth century.

19. A. P. Sumarokov, "Tragediia. Dmitrii Samozvanets," *Polnoe sobranie vsekh sochinenii* (M, 1781), 4:61.

20. Habermas, *Structural Transformation of the Public Sphere*, 27–28, 52; Hans Erich Bödeker, "Journal and Public Opinion: The Politicization of the German Enlightenment in the Second Half of the Eighteenth Century," in *The Transformation of Political Culture: England and Germany in the Late Eighteenth Century,* ed. Eckhart Hellmuth (Oxford, 1990), 444.

21. Douglas Smith, *Working the Rough Stone: Freemasonry and Society in Eighteenth-Century Russia* (DeKalb, 1999), 55. Throughout his book, Smith equates the terms civil society and the public; I would agree with John LeDonne that the nobility and civil society were "coterminous," because only they possessed the rights and privileges without which it is difficult to speak of a civil society, except in a loose sense. See John LeDonne, *Absolutism and Ruling Class: The Formation of the Russian Political Order, 1700–1825* (Oxford, 1991), viii.

22. Marker, *Publishing,* 11, 75.

23. David Cannadine, "Introduction: Divine Rites of Kings," in *Rituals of Royalty: Power and Ceremonial in Traditional Societies,* ed. D. Cannadine (Cambridge, 1987), 3.

24. Irina Reyfman, *Vasilii Trediakovsky: The Fool of the "New" Russian Literature* (Stanford, 1990), 1; T. H. Breen, *The Character of the Good Ruler: Puritan Political Ideas in New England, 1630–1730* (NY, 1970), xx.

25. Paul Veyne, *Les grecs, ont-ils cru à leurs mythes? Essai sur l'imagination constituante* (Paris, 1983), 89–102; also see Ralph E. Giesey, "The King Imagined," in *The*

French Revolution and the Creation of Modern Political Culture, vol. 1, *The Political Culture of the Old Regime*, ed. Keith Michael Baker (Oxford, 1987), 41–59.

26. Michel Foucault, *The Archaeology of Knowledge and the Discourse on Language*, trans. A. M. Sheridan Smith (NY, 1972), 32, 120, 136; also see Roger Chartier, *Cultural History: Between Practices and Representations* (Ithaca, 1988).

27. Richard van Dülmen, *The Society of the Enlightenment: The Rise of the Middle Class and Enlightenment Culture in Germany*, trans. Anthony Williams (Cambridge, 1992), 82; Franz Hubert Robling, "Political Rhetoric in the German Enlightenment," in *The Transformation of Political Culture: England and Germany in the Late Eighteenth Century*, ed. Eckhart Hellmuth (Oxford, 1990), 413.

28. L. S. Mercier, *Notions claires sur les gouvernements* (Amsterdam, 1797), vi–vii, as quoted in Habermas, *Structural Transformation of the Public Sphere*, 95–96.

29. The situation was somewhat similar in the German states. See James van Horn Melton, "From Enlightenment to Revolution: Hertzberg, Schlözer, and the Problem of Despotism in the Late *Aufklärung*," *Central European History* 12 (1979): 103–23.

30. On the connection between absolute monarchy and public opinion, consult Mona Ozouf, "'Public Opinion' at the End of the Old Regime," in *The Rise and Fall of the French Revolution*, ed. T. C. W. Blanning (Chicago, 1996), 97; Keith Michael Baker, "Political Thought at the Accession of Louis XVI ," in Blanning, *Rise and Fall of the French Revolution*, 73; and Alan S. Kahan, *Aristocratic Liberalism: The Social and Political Thought of Jacob Burckhardt, John Stuart Mill, and Alexis de Tocqueville* (Oxford, 1992), 20.

31. Both are quoted in Keith Michael Baker, "Politics and Public Opinion under the Old Regime: Some Reflections," in *Press and Politics in Pre-Revolutionary France*, ed. J. Censer and J. Popkin (Berkeley, 1987), 241–46.

32. Ibid., 212, 243.

33. Marker, *Publishing*, 233.

34. Consult, for instance, Judith Ferster, *Fictions of Advice: The Literature and Politics of Counsel in Late Medieval England* (Philadelphia, 1996). On "mirrors," please see chap. 1. Another use of the term "advice literature" is to delineate self-help books such as etiquette manuals, household guides, or tracts on raising children. See Catriona Kelly, *Refining Russia: Advice Literature, Polite Culture, and Gender from Catherine to Yeltsin* (Oxford, 2001); and Kathleen Ashley and Robert L. A. Clark, eds., *Medieval Conduct* (Minneapolis, 2001).

35. In contrast, for instance, Robert Darnton has analyzed a process of "delegitimization" in the literature he studied in *The Forbidden Best Sellers of Prerevolutionary France* (NY, 1994).

36. Max Weber, *Economy and Society: An Outline of Interpretive Sociology*, ed. Guenther Roth and Claus Wittich (Berkeley, 1978), 36.

37. Baehr, *Paradise Myth*, passim; Wortman, *Scenarios of Power*, 1–192.

38. Valerie A. Kivelson, *Autocracy in the Provinces: The Muscovite Gentry and Political Culture in the Seventeenth Century* (Stanford, 1996), 1–3.

39. David L. Ransel, *The Politics of Catherinian Russia: The Panin Party* (New Haven, 1975), 1. Keenan claims that the "true secret" of Muscovite Russia was that it was an oligarchy, but it needed the monarch for legitimacy, "Muscovite Political Folkways," 118, 132, 142; Nancy Shields Kollmann, *Kinship and Politics: The Making of the Muscovite Political System, 1345–1547* (Stanford, 1987), 146; also see her *By Honor Bound: State and Society in Early Modern Russia* (Ithaca, 1999), 17–20.

40. Nicholas Henshall, *The Myth of Absolutism: Change and Continuity in Early Modern European Monarchy* (London, 1992), 210–11. For an insightful discussion of the term absolutism, see H. M. Scott, "Introduction: The Problem of Enlightened Ab-

solutism," in *Enlightened Absolutism: Reform and Reformers in Later Eighteenth-Century Europe* (Ann Arbor, 1990), 1–36. For a good discussion of the term "oriental despotism," see Donald Ostrowski, *Muscovy and the Mongols: Cross-Cultural Influences on the Steppe Frontier, 1304–1589* (Cambridge, 1998), 85–107.

41. Isabel de Madariaga, "Autocracy and Sovereignty," in *Politics and Culture in Eighteenth-Century Russia: Collected Essays by Isabel de Madariaga* (London, 1998), 40–56; originally published in *Canadian-American Slavic Studies* 16 (1982): 369–87.

42. *O gosudarstvennom pravlenii i raznykh rodakh onago iz Entsiklopedii,* trans. I. Tumanskii (Spb, 1770), 72.

43. For instance, in Radishchev's *Journey, tsar'* was used 31 times, *gosudar'* 12 times, *imperator* 4 times (but only once in relation to a Russian ruler, Peter the Great), and *samoderzhets* once, to describe Frederick II the Great of Prussia. Yasuo Urai, ed., *A Lemmatized Concordance to A Journey from Petersburg to Moscow of A. N. Radishchev* (Sapporo, Japan, 1998), 128, 508, 645.

For general studies, please consult A. Lakier, "Istoriia titula gosudarei Rossii," *Zhurnal Ministerstva narodnago prosveshcheniia* 56 (1847): 81–156; B. B. Glinskii, "K voprosu o titule 'samoderzhets'," *Istoricheskii vestnik* 2 (1913): 567–603; Iu. N. Shchapov, "Dostoinstvo i titul tsaria na Rusi do XVI veka," in Gorskii, *Tsar' i tsarstvo,* 7–16; A. A. Gorskii, "Predstavleniia o 'tsare' i 'tsarstve' v srednevekovoi Rusi (do serediny XVI veka)," in Gorskii, *Tsar' i tsarstvo,* 17–37.

44. Karamzin was quoted by S. S. Uvarov, "Mnenie Uvarova ob 'Istorii gosudarstva rossiiskogo' Karamzina (March 1816)," Pushkinskii dom, *fond* 265, *opis'* 2, no. 2907; F. R. de Chateaubriand, "De Buonaparte et des Bourbons (1814)," *Oeuvres complètes de Chateaubriand* (Paris, 1928), 3:16.

45. M. S. Anderson, *Europe in the Eighteenth Century, 1713–1783* (London, 1987), 160–61, 175.

46. Franco Venturi, *Utopia and Reform in the Enlightenment* (Cambridge, 1971), 26.

47. The extent of the penetration of the Enlightenment in Russia remains a debated issue; for instance, Keenan recognizes its rapid assimilation, as do I, but Baehr disagrees. See Keenan, "Trouble with Muscovy," 104; Baehr, *Paradise Myth,* xi.

48. Marc Raeff, "Seventeenth-Century Europe in Eighteenth-Century Russia? (Pour prendre congé du dix-huitième siècle russe)," *Slavic Review* 41 (1982): 612. For a definition of "language" in semiotic terms, see B. A. Uspenskii, "Historia sub specie semioticae," in *Soviet Semiotics,* ed. Daniel P. Lucid (Baltimore, 1977), 107–8; Wuthnow, *Communities of Discourse,* 312–13.

49. Martin Malia, *Russia under Western Eyes: From the Bronze Horseman to the Lenin Mausoleum* (Cambridge, Mass., 1999), 10, 56.

50. Nicholas V. Riasanovsky, *A Parting of the Ways: Government and the Educated Public in Russia, 1801–1825* (Oxford, 1976); Raeff, *Origins of the Russian Intelligentsia.*

51. Isaiah Berlin, "Alleged Relativism in Eighteenth-Century European Thought," in *The Crooked Timber of Humanity: Chapters in the History of Ideas,* ed. Henry Hardy (NY, 1992), 82, 85, 87.

52. Perry Anderson, *Lineages of the Absolutist State* (London, 1974), 328.

1: WRITING ABOUT MONARCHY

1. Milton V. Anastos, "Byzantine Political Theory: Its Classical Precedents and Legal Embodiment," in *The Past in Medieval and Modern Greek Culture,* ed. S. Vryonis, Jr. (Malibu, 1978), 18.

2. John Procopé, "Greek and Roman Political Theory," in *The Cambridge History of*

Medieval Political Thought, c. 350–c. 1450, ed. J. H. Burns (Cambridge, 1988), 26; for seventeenth-century repetitions of the arguments, see J. P. Sommerville, "Absolutism and Royalism," in *The Cambridge History of Political Thought, 1450–1700,* ed. J. H. Burns (Cambridge, 1991), 347–73. For a discussion of Robert Hinton's "ideal" and "real" cultural patterns, see Robert C. Tucker, "Culture, Political Culture, and Communist Society," *Political Science Quarterly* 88 (1973): 173–90.

3. Rudolf Vierhaus, *Germany in the Age of Absolutism* (Cambridge, 1988), 113; Anastos, "Byzantine Political Theory," 17.

4. "To the Emperor Arcadius," *The Letters of Synesius of Cyrene, Bishop of Ptolemais,* trans. Augustine Fitzgerald (Oxford, 1926), 381 (c. 400).

5. Aristotle, *Politics,* book 3, trans. Benjamin Jowett (NY, 1943), chap. 14, p. 158.

6. Homer, *The Iliad,* book 2, trans. Richmond Lattimore (Chicago, 1962), 81, lines 204–5.

7. Bossuet is quoted in Sommerville, "Absolutism and Royalism," 350; the other quotations are from Burns, *Lordship, Kingship, and Empire: The Idea of Monarchy, 1400–1525* (Oxford, 1992), 146; and Vivian R. Gruder, "Bourbon Monarchy: Reforms and Propaganda at the End of the Old Regime," in *The French Revolution and the Creation of Modern Political Culture,* vol. 1, *The Political Culture of the Old Regime,* ed. Keith Michael Baker (Oxford, 1987): 365–66.

8. George H. Sabine, *A History of Political Theory* (NY, 1937), 249; D. M. Nicol, "Byzantine Political Thought," *Cambridge History, c. 350–c. 1450,* 51; Sommerville, "Absolutism and Royalism," 352.

9. Aristotle, *Politics,* book 3, chap. 15, p. 159, 1. 1285b; *Sedulius Scottus: On Christian Rulers,* trans. Edward G. Doyle (Binghamton, 1983), 59.

In Russia, particularly in Muscovy, a patrimonial, rather than a paternal, image prevailed until the seventeenth century, with the ruler viewing Russia as his hereditary property or himself as the master over his slaves rather than his family writ large. Nonetheless, there is a natural parallel between a ruler and a father, and the term *otechestvo* (fatherland) had long been used to describe the native land; thus, evidence may be cited that the strongest conception of the ruler in Muscovite times was, despite the contradictions, the "stern yet beneficent . . . father-tsar." See Kivelson, *Autocracy in the Provinces,* 13; also see the excellent discussion by Marshall Poe, "What Did Russians Mean When They Called Themselves 'Slaves of the Tsar'?" *Slavic Review* 57 (1998): 585–608; "Otechestvo," *Slovar' russkogo iazyka XI–XVII vv.* 13 (M, 1987): 238.

10. Polybius, *The Histories,* book 6, trans. W. R. Paton (Cambridge, Mass., 1966), chap. 4, p. 275. For this time-honored reason, Russians did not acknowledge the legitimacy of Mongol rule. On this point, consult Charles J. Halperin, *Russia and the Golden Horde: The Mongol Impact on Medieval Russian History* (Bloomington, Ind., 1985), 61–74; and Ostrowski, *Muscovy and the Mongols,* 144–63.

11. The last phrase is from Jean de Terre-Rouge's *Disputatio de controversia successionis regia,* in Roland E. Mousnier, *Institutions of France under the Absolute Monarchy, 1598–1789,* vol. 2, *The Organs of State and Society,* trans. Arthur Goldhammer (Chicago, 1984), 649. All the rest were used by Sir Francis Theobald in his pamphlet, *A Discourse Concerning . . . the Best, Most Ancient, and Legal Form of Government* (London, 1660), 20–21.

12. Sabine, *History of Political Theory,* 211, 297; Janet Nelson, "Kingship and Empire," *Cambridge History, c. 350–c. 1450,* 217; Elias made the same point about elites in *Court Society,* 16–17.

13. Anastos, "Byzantine Political Theory," 27, 30. The statement was written by the third-century jurist Ulpian and incorporated into the code three hundred years later.

14. Ernst Kantorowicz, *The King's Two Bodies: A Study in Medieval Political Theology* (Princeton, 1957).

15. Francis Dvornik, *Early Christian and Byzantine Political Philosophy: Origin and Background* (Dumbarton Oaks, 1966), 2:623 ff.

16. Michel Foucault, *The History of Sexuality: An Introduction*, vol. 2, *The Use of Pleasure*, trans. R. Hurley (NY, 1978), 88. Russian writers also share this emphasis on "masks" of power. See M. A. Reisner, "Obshchestvennoe blago i absoliutnoe gosudarstvo," *Vestnik prava za 1902*, nos. 9–10: 1–128, especially 123–24; I. O. Tarnopol'skaia, "'Bozhestvennoe pravo korolei' i 'kontraktnaia teoriia': Monarkhicheskaia ideia na zapade i vostoke Evropy v XVI–XVII vekakh," in Gorskii, *Tsar' i tsarstvo*, 56–58.

17. From his *On Law and Justice*, as quoted in Anastos, "Byzantine Political Theory," 21.

18. Dio Chrysostom, "The Second Discourse on Kingship," *Dio Chrysostom*, trans. J. W. Cohoon (London, 1932), 2:99–100.

19. Jean Dunbabin, "Government, c. 1150–c. 1450," *The Cambridge History of Medieval Political Thought, c. 350–c. 1450*, ed. J. H. Burns (Cambridge), 495.

20. Christine de Pizan, *The Book of the Body Politic*, ed. and trans. Kate Langdon Forhan (Cambridge, 1994), 493; also see Dietrich Gerhard, *Old Europe: A Study of Continuity, 1000–1800* (NY, 1981), 17–19.

21. Plato, *The Republic*, book 5, trans. Desmond Lee (Baltimore, 1955), 263, l. 473cd; Procopé, "Greek and Roman Political Theory," 25; Sabine, *History of Political Theory*, 249–51; Dunbabin, "Government," 482–88; John of Salisbury's *Policratus* (1159) is quoted in Edwin R. Goodenough, "The Political Philosophy of Hellenistic Kingship," *Yale Classical Studies* 1 (1928): 100.

22. The quotation is from a sixteenth-century English chronicle, as found in Breen, *Character of the Good Ruler*, 7.

23. *Scottus*, 63–64; also see Gabor Klaniczay, "Representations of the Evil Ruler in the Middle Ages," in *European Monarchy*, ed. Heinz Duchhardt (Stuttgart, 1992), 69.

24. Goodenough, "Political Philosophy of Hellenistic Kingship," 69; Nelson, "Kingship and Empire," 217–18; Virgil, "Eclogue IV," *Eclogues and Georgics*, trans. T. F. Royds (NY, 1946), 24–27; Pliny, "Panegyricus," *Letters and Panegyricus*, trans. Betty Radice (London, 1969), 2:329–33 (c. 100); Polybius, *Histories*, book 6, chap. 5, p. 279; Synesius, "Arcadius," 385–86.

25. The quotations are from Barker, "Kingship," in *From Alexander to Constantine: Passages and Documents Illustrating the History of Social and Political Ideas, 336 B.C.–A.D. 337*, ed. and trans. Ernest Barker (Oxford, 1956), 89; and Sabine, *History of Political Theory*, 147. Also consult A. M. Hocart, *Kings and Councillors: An Essay in the Comparative Anatomy of Human Society* (Chicago, 1936), 86–101. On the "inherent sacredness of sovereign power," see Clifford Geertz, "Centers, Kings, and Charisma: Reflections on the Symbolics of Power," in *Culture and Its Creators: Essays in Honor of Edward Shils*, ed. Joseph Ben-David and Terry Nichols Clark (Chicago, 1977), 151.

26. "A Decree of the Cities of the Province of Asia, 48 B.C.," in Barker, *From Alexander to Constantine*, 209.

27. Francis Dvornik, "The Emperor Julian's 'Reactionary' Ideas on Kingship," in *Late Classical and Mediaeval Studies*, ed. Kurt Weitzmann (Princeton, 1955), 72; H.

Hunger, *Die hochsprächliche profane Literatur der Byzantiner* (Vienna, 1978), 2:127–28.

28. See, for instance, on eleventh- and fifteenth-century practices, K. Yusuf, *A Turko-Islamic Mirror for Princes* (Chicago, 1983); and *Lo Specchio del Principe* (Rome, 1991); as well as Thomas Lister, *A Mirror for Princes* (London, 1797). For the best survey of "mirror" literature, see W. Berges, *Fürstenspiegel des hohen und späten Mittelalters* (Leipzig, 1938).

29. Judith Ferster, *Fictions of Advice: The Literature and Politics of Counsel in Late Medieval England* (Philadelphia, 1996), 2–3, 132, 160.

30. "An Egyptian Papyrus of the First Century B.C. on Constitutions, Alexandria, and Kingship," in Barker, *From Alexander to Constantine*, 100.

31. Ferster sees most Western "mirrors" as modeled on the ninth-century pseudo-Aristotelian Arabic *Kitah sirr al-asrar*, commonly called the *Secretum Secretorum;* she also provides a good analysis of Chaucer's *Tale of Melibee* and Machiavelli's *The Prince* as prime examples of advice literature. See her *Fictions of Advice*, 2–3, 89–107, 160–73.

32. Foucault, *History of Sexuality*, 172. An excellent example of depicting a reigning monarch as ideal is de Pizan's two-volume paean, *Livre des fais et bonnes moeurs du sage roy Charles V* (c. 1400). Also consult Peter Burke, *The Fabrication of Louis XIV* (New Haven, 1992), 37; R. H. Jones, *The Royal Policy of Richard II: Absolutism in the Later Middle Ages* (London, 1968), 144; and, for just one non-Western example, Maxwell K. Hearn, *Splendors of Imperial China* (NY, 1996), 346–47.

33. P. Stafford, *Queens, Concubines, and Dowagers: The King's Wife in the Early Middle Ages* (Athens, Ga., 1981), 240–41.

34. Diotogenes, "Treatise on Kingship," in Barker, *From Alexander to Constantine*, 365; for these traits as universally applied to monarchs, see Hocart, *Kings and Councillors*, 140–44, 198–99.

35. The *Book of Emperors* is quoted in Henry A. Myers, *Medieval Kingship* (Chicago, 1982), 261; the ideal is repeated in Mousnier, *Institutions of France*, 2:20, but as one lost in the more modern, bureaucratic era.

36. This phrase is from the title of the pamphlet published in London in 1660 by Theobald, *A Discourse Concerning.`. . .*

37. Georges Florovsky, "The Problem of Old Russian Culture," *Slavic Review* 21 (1962): 1–15.

38. *The Russian Primary Chronicle: Laurentian Text,* trans. and ed. S. H. Cross and O. P. Sherbowitz-Wetzor (Cambridge, Mass., 1953), 59–60, 130, 133. Much scholarship has debated the authenticity of this version of history, for instance, George Vernadsky, *Ancient Russia* (New Haven, 1943), 51, 59, 69; and his *Kievan Russia* (New Haven, 1947), 288–90; G. Tel'berg, *Istoricheskiia formy monarkhii v Rossii* (M, 1914), 9; Francis Dvornik, *The Slavs: Their Early History and Civilization* (Boston, 1956), 23–38; Nicholas Riasanovsky, "The Norman Theory of the Origin of the Russian State," *Russian Review* 7 (1947): 98–99. A. K. Tolstoi in 1868 wrote an amusing "history" of Russia in verse based on these lines in the *Chronicle:* "Istoriia gosudarstva rossiiskago ot Gostomysla do Timasheva," *Polnoe sobranie stikhotvorenii v dvukh tomakh* (L, 1984), 1:325–38.

39. N. Rozhkov, *Proiskhozhdenie samoderzhaviia v Rossii* (M, 1906), 204–5; V. I. Sergeevich, *Lektsii i izsledovaniia po istorii russkago prava* (Spb, 1883).

40. "The Lay of Igor's Campaign," in *Medieval Russia's Epics, Chronicles, and Tales,* ed. S. A. Zenkovsky (NY, 1963), 155, 160. Although the famous controversy over the authenticity of the *Lay* is still being waged, I share the conviction that it is a medieval masterpiece and not an eighteenth-century forgery.

41. Keenan, "Muscovite Political Folkways," 142, 147.

42. Omelian Pritsak, "The Invitation to the Varangians," *Harvard Ukrainian Studies* 1 (1977): 7, and *The Origin of Rus'* (Cambridge, Mass., 1981), 1:3–7.

43. Ilarion, "Sermon on Law and Grace," in *Sermons and Rhetoric of Kievan Rus'*, trans. Simon Franklin (Cambridge, Mass., 1991), 18, 23. Also see the exegesis of Ellen Hurwitz, "Metropolitan Hilarion's *Sermon on Law and Grace:* Historical Consciousness in Kievan Rus'," *Russian History* 7 (1980): 322–33; *Russian Primary Chronicle*, 122.

44. Charles J. Halperin, "The Concept of the Russian Land from the Ninth to the Fourteenth Centuries," *Russian History* 2 (1975): 29–38; for one example, see Ellen Hurwitz, "Andrei Bogoliubskii: An Image of the Prince," *Russian History* 2 (1975): 68–80.

45. Vernadsky, *Kievan Russia*, 9, 178–81; M. Tikhomirov, *The Towns of Ancient Rus'* (M, 1959), 233.

46. As quoted in J. L. I. Fennell, "The Dynastic Crisis of 1497–1502," *Slavonic and East European Review* 39 (1960–1961): 6; on the same topic, see John V. A. Fine, Jr., "The Muscovite Dynastic Crisis of 1497–1502," *Canadian Slavonic Papers* 8 (1966): 198–215; and Kollmann, *Kinship and Politics*, 155–59.

47. L. Ermolaev, "Kniga o postanovlenii blagochestivykh tsarei i velikikh kniazei na tsarstvo," in *Gosudarstvo i tserkov v ikh vsaimnykh otnosheniiakh v moskovskom gosudarstve*, ed. A. Ia. Shpakov (Kiev, 1904), appendix 2: 96–126; David Miller, "The Coronation of Ivan IV of Moscow," *Jahrbücher für Geschichte Osteuropas* 15 (1967): 561–74; Leonid Ignatieff, "Rights and Obligations in Russia and the West," *Canadian Slavonic Papers* 2 (1957): 26–37; Daniel Rowland, "Did Muscovite Literary Ideology Place Limits on the Power of the Tsar (1540s–1660s)?" *Russian Review* 49 (1990): 125–55.

48. Miller, "Coronation of Ivan IV," 559–74.

49. Ihor Ševčenko, "A Neglected Byzantine Source of Muscovite Ideology," *Harvard Slavic Studies* 2 (1954): 141–80.

50. As quoted in Francis Dvornik, "Byzantium, Muscovite Autocracy, and the Church," in *Rediscovering Eastern Christemdom*, ed. A. H. Armstrong and E. J. B. Fry (London, 1963), 110 n. 5.

51. Ivan Timofeev, *Vremennik Ivana Timofeeva*, ed. O. A. Derzhavina (M, 1951), 298.

52. *Russian Primary Chronicle*, 131.

53. As quoted in Dvornik, "Byzantium," 110 n. 5.

54. Iosif Volotskii, *Prosvetitel'*, ed. A. Volkov (Kazan, 1896), 287; M. D"iakonov, *Vlast' moskovskikh gosudarei: Ocherki iz istorii politicheskikh idei drevnei Rusi do kontsa XVI veka* (Spb, 1889), 99–100.

55. D"iakonov, *Vlast' moskovskikh gosudarei*, 94, 110–11, 117–19, 125; "The Testament of Vladimir Monomach," in *Russian Primary Chronicle*, appendix 1, 206–15.

56. Although the usual combined role of priest and chieftain was absent in the native version of paganism, the Varangians had a tradition that Odin sacrificed himself for his people: Edward S. Reisman, "The Cult of Boris and Gleb: Remnant of a Varangian Tradition?" *Russian Review* 37 (1978): 141–57. Also see Norman W. Ingham, "The Sovereign as Martyr, East and West," *Slavic and East European Journal* 17 (1973): 1–16.

57. On these themes, consult Michael Cherniavsky, *Tsar and People: Studies in Russian Myths* (New Haven, 1961), 5–127; Dmitri Obolensky, "Popular Religion in Medieval Russia," in *The Religious World of Russian Culture*, ed. Andrew Blane (The Hague, 1975), 2:43–47; George P. Fedotov, *Kievan Christianity: The Tenth to the Thirteenth Centuries* (NY, 1946); Franklin Sciacca, "In Imitation of Christ: Boris and Gleb

and the Ritual Consecration of the Russian Land," *Slavic Review* 49 (1990): 253–60; Charles Halperin, "The Russian Land and the Russian Tsar: The Emergence of Muscovite Ideology, 1380–1408," (Ph.D. diss., Columbia University, 1973).

58. V. M. Zhivov and B. A. Uspenskii, "Tsar' i bog: Semioticheskie aspekty sakralizatsii monarkha v Rossii," in *Iazyki kul'tury i problemy perevodimosti*, ed. B. A. Uspenskii (M, 1987), 47–61.

59. Michael Cherniavsky, "Khan or Basileus: An Aspect of Russian Medieval Political Theory," in *The Structure of Russian History*, ed. Michael Cherniavsky (NY, 1970), 71, and "Ivan the Terrible and the Iconography of the Kremlin Cathedral of Archangel Michael," *Russian History* 2 (1975): 3–28. Also see R. P. Dmitrieva, *Skazanie o kniaziakh vladimirskikh* (M, 1955); Dvornik, "Byzantium," 106–18.

Concerning Mongol influence, some tantalizing sources include Halperin, *Golden Horde;* Ostrowski, *Muscovy and the Mongols;* Elizabeth Endicott-West, *Mongolian Rule in China* (Cambridge, Mass., 1989); Beatrice Forbes Manz, "The Office of *Darugha* under Tamerlane," *Journal of Turkish Studies* 9 (1985): 59–69; Edward L. Keenan, "Muscovy and Kazan, 1445–1552: A Study in Steppe Politics" (Ph.D. diss., Harvard University, 1965).

60. Gustav Alef, "The Political Significance of the Inscriptions on Muscovite Coinage in the Reign of Vasili II," *Speculum* 34 (1959): 1–19; Marc Szeftel, "The Title of the Muscovite Monarch up to the End of the Seventeenth Century," *Canadian-American Slavic Studies* 13 (1979): 61, 65–66; Ian Grey, *Ivan III and the Unification of Russia* (NY, 1964), 38, 52; William K. Medlin, *Moscow and East Rome* (Geneva, 1952); John Meyendorff, *Byzantium and the Rise of Russia* (Crestwood, NY, 1989), and *The Byzantine Legacy in the Orthodox Church* (Crestwood, NY, 1982). On the nettlesome issue of titles, consult Vernadsky, *Ancient Russia*, 253–54; Madariaga, "Autocracy and Sovereignty," 369–87; W. Vodoff, "Remarques sur la valeur du terme 'tsar' appliqué aux princes russes avant le milieu du XVe siècle," *Oxford Slavonic Papers* 9 (1978): 1–41; Ostrowski, *Muscovy and the Mongols*, 164–98.

61. Gustav Alef, "The Adoption of the Muscovite Two-Headed Eagle: A Discordant View," *Speculum* 41 (1966): 1–21; D"iakonov, *Vlast' moskovskikh gosudarei*, v–vi, 54–57, 77, 87–88; Miller, "Coronation of Ivan IV"; Robert O. Crummey, *The Formation of Muscovy, 1304–1613* (NY, 1987), 147; Wortman, *Scenarios of Power*, 25–27.

62. V. Malinin, *Starets Eleazarova monastyria Filofei i ego poslaniia* (Kiev, 1901), 50, 55. The literature on this topic is vast and controversial; some examples include Nikolay Andreyev, "Filofey and his Epistle to Ivan Vasil'yevich," *Slavonic and East European Review* 38 (1959–1960): 1–31; Robert Lee Wolf, "The Three Romes: The Migration of an Ideology and the Making of an Autocrat," *Daedalus* 88 (1959): 291–311; Dmitri Stremoouukhoff, "Moscow the Third Rome: Sources of the Doctrine," *Speculum* (1953): 84–101; Ostrowski, *Muscovy and the Mongols*, 219–43; and the classic by Hildegard Schaeder, *Moskau das dritte Rom* (Hamburg, 1929).

63. Cherniavsky, *Tsar and People*, 63.

64. Rowland, "Muscovite Literary Ideology," 125–55.

65. Bjarne Nørretranders, *The Shaping of Czardom under Ivan Groznyi* (Copenhagen, 1964), 175; Marc Raeff, "An Early Theorist of Absolutism: Joseph of Volokolamsk," *American Slavic and East European Review* 8 (1949): 79–89; V. V. Leontovich, *Istoriia liberalizma v Rossii, 1762–1914* (Paris, 1980), 1–3; Thomas G. Masaryk, *The Spirit of Russia* (London, 1919), 1:24–25.

The literature on Iosif of Volokolamsk is extensive: D"iakonov, *Vlast' moskovskikh gosudarei*, 98–99; George Vernadsky, "The Heresy of the Judaizers and the Policies of Ivan III of Moscow," *Speculum* 8 (1933): 436–54; A. A. Zimin, "O politicheskoi doktrine Iosifa Volotskogo," *Trudy otdela drevnerusskoi literatury* 9 (1953): 159–77; George P. Majeska, "The Moscow Coronation of 1498 Reconsidered," *Jahrbücher für Geschichte Osteuropas* 26 (1978): 353–61.

66. Paul Bushkovitch, "The Formation of a National Consciousness in Early Modern Russia," *Harvard Ukrainian Studies* 10 (1986): 365–66.

67. Timofeev, *Vremennik*, 42; S. F. Platonov, *Drevnerusskiia skazaniia i povesti o smutnom vremeni* (Spb, 1913), 104–5; Halperin, "Russian Land and the Russian Tsar," 188–32.

68. Bushkovitch, "National Consciounsess," 364–66. The first text that idealized this vision of harmony was the early fifteenth-century "Slovo o zhitii i prestavlenii velikogo kniazia Dmitriia Ivanovicha," *Pamiatniki starinnoi russkoi literatury* 8 (1856): 53–60. Also see Hunger, *Literatur der Byzantiner*, 120–45; V. Valdenberg, *Drevnerusskiia ucheniia o predelakh tsarskoi vlasti* (Petrograd, 1916), 5–6, 438–41.

69. *Russian Primary Chronicle*, 61–69, 81–86, 94, 131. Also see Ihor Ševčenko, *On a Kiev Edition of a Byzantine Mirror of Princes* (Cambridge, Mass., 1974).

70. *The Domostroi: Rules for Russian Households in the Time of Ivan the Terrible*, ed. and trans. Carolyn Johnston Pouncy (Ithaca, 1994); on this concept see Cherniavsky, *Tsar and People*, 54–59. I disagree with Keenan that the concern with good and bad rulers was part of a "dissenting tradition": "Muscovite Political Folkways," 146, 150–51.

71. His rule has been interpreted in a variety of ways. See Joel Raba, "The Authority of the Muscovite Ruler at the Dawn of the Modern Era," *Jahrbücher für Geschichte Osteuropas* 24 (1976): 321–44; Cherniavsky, "Ivan the Terrible and Iconography"; Alexander Yanov, *The Origins of Autocracy: Ivan the Terrible in Russian History* (Berkeley, 1981).

72. *Poslaniia Ivana Groznogo*, ed. D. S. Likhachev (M, 1951), 15.

73. Bjarne Nørretranders, "Ivan Groznyj's Conception of Tsarist Authority," *Scando-Slavica* 9 (1963): 238–48; Steven Runciman, "Byzantium, Russia, and Caesaropapism," *Canadian Slavonic Papers* 2 (1957): 1–10; S. M. Shpilevskii, *Vlast' moskovskikh gosudarei* (Spb, 1889).

74. Rowland, "Muscovite Literary Ideology," 142–48. The literature on this topic is substantial and controversial. See *Perepiska Ivana Groznogo s Andreem Kurbskim*, ed. Ia. S. Lur'e and Iu. D. Rykov (L, 1979); Edward Keenan, *The Kurbskii-Groznyi Apocrypha: The Seventeenth-Century Genesis of the Correspondence Attributed to Prince A. M. Kurbskii and Tsar Ivan IV* (Cambridge, Mass., 1971); I. Zil'berman, *Politicheskie vzgliady Ivana Groznogo* (L, 1953).

75. "Skazanie o Makhmete-Saltane," *Sochineniia I. Peresvetova*, ed. A. Zimin (M, 1956), 152–54; Timofeev, *Vremennik*, 14–20, 24, 202, 207; *Kazanskaia istoriia*, ed. G. N. Moiseeva ((M, 1954); A. S. Lappo-Danilevskii, "Ideia gosudarstva i glavneishie momenty eia razvitiia v Rossii so vremen smuty do epokhi preobrazovanii," *Golos minuvshago* 2 (1914): 7–8; R. G. Skrynnikov, *Ivan the Terrible*, trans. Hugh F. Graham (Gulf Breeze, Fla., 1981), 25–26; Dmitri Obolensky, "Russia's Byzantine Heritage," *Selection II*, ed. Cecily Hastings and Donald Nicholl (London, 1954), 87–123; Marc Szeftel, "The Epithet *Groznyi* in Historical Perspective," in *The Religious World of Russian Culture*, ed. Andrew Blane (The Hague, 1975), 101–15. For a selection of Muscovite political literature, see *Moskovskaia politicheskaia literatura XVI veka*, ed. M. Kovalenskii (Spb, 1914), especially pp. 85–133. In addition, consult Maureen Perrie, "The Popular Image of Ivan the Terrible," *Slavonic and East European Review* 56 (1978): 275–86, and her *Image of Ivan the Terrible in Russian Folklore* (Cambridge, 1987). Also see V. K. Sokolova, *Russkie istoricheskie predaniia* (M, 1970), 49–96. Rowland provides a superb discussion in "Muscovite Literary Ideology," 132–34.

76. The most accessible source is S. F. Platonov, *The Time of Troubles: A Historical Study of the Internal Crisis and Social Struggle in Sixteenth- and Seventeenth-Century Muscovy*, trans. John T. Alexander (Lawrence, Kansas, 1970).

77. Marc Szeftel, "L'Autocratie moscovite et l'absolutisme français au XVIIe siècle: Parallèles et divergences," *Canadian-American Slavic Studies* 16 (1982): 54–58; M. N. Tikhomirov, "Soslovno-predstavitelnye uchrezhdeniia (zemskie sobory) v Rossii XVI veka," *Voprosy istorii* (1958): 4–9; L. V. Cherepnin, "Zemskie sobory i utverzhdenie absoliutizma v Rossii," in *Absoliutizm v Rossii, XVII–XVIII vv.*, ed. N. M. Druzhinin (M, 1964), 94–95; V. A. Iakushkin, *Gosudarstvennaia vlast' i proekty gosudarstvennoi reformy v Rossii* (Spb, 1906), 1–10.

78. Donald J. Bennett, "The Idea of Kingship in Seventeenth-Century Russia," (Ph.D. diss., Harvard University, 1967), 15–19; Mousnier, *Institutions of France*, 2:653–54.

79. Among many others, one might consult R. G. Skrynnikov, *Boris Godunov*, trans. Hugh F. Graham (Gulf Breeze, Fla., 1982) and Caryl Emerson, *Boris Godunov: Transpositions of a Russian Theme* (Bloomington, Ind., 1986).

80. On pretenders' constant claims to being the "true" tsar, see Paul Avrich, *Russian Rebels, 1600–1800* (NY, 1972).

81. *Skazanie Avraamiia Palitsyna*, ed. O. A. Derzhavina and E. V. Kolosova (M, 1955), 9. Also, see Daniel Rowland, "The Problem of Advice in Muscovite Tales about the Time of Troubles," *Russian History* 6 (1979); and I. I. Polosin, "Ivan Timofeev—russkii myslitel', istorik, i d"iak XVII v.," in *Sotsial'no-politicheskaia istoriia Rossii XVI–nachala XVII v.* (M, 1963), 263–352.

82. P. G. Liubomirov, *Ocherk istorii nizhegorodskogo opolcheniia 1611–1613 gg.* (M, 1939), 14–17, 176–80, 205–22; B. B. Glinskii, *Bor'ba za konstitutsiiu, 1612–1861 gg.* (Spb, 1908), 3–7.

83. These are compiled in S. A. Belokurov, ed., "Utverzhdennaia gramota ob izbranii na Moskovskoe gosudarstvo Mikhaila Fedorovicha Romanova," *Chteniia v Imp. Obshchestve istorii i drevnostei rossiiskikh pri Moskovskom universitete* 218 (1906): 1–110; Platonov, *Drevnerusskiia skazaniia*; L. V. Cherepnin, "Smuta i istoriografiia XVII v.," *Istoricheskie zapiski* 14 (1945): 81–128; "Novyi letopisets," *Polnoe sobranie russkikh letopisei*, 14:23–24.

84. Fedor Griboedov, "Istoriia o tsariakh i velikikh kniaziakh zemli russkoi," in *Pamiatniki drevnei pis'mennosti*, ed. S. F. Platonov and V. V. Maikov (M, 1896), 121:26; also see L. N. Pushkarev, "Bogoizbrannost' monarkha v mentalitete russkikh predbornykh deiatelei rubezha novogo vremeni," in Gorskii, *Tsar' i tsarstvo*, 59–69.

85. Platonov, *Drevnerusskiia skazaniia*, 327–33, 428–29; A. S. Vatveev, *Kniga ob izbranii na tsarstvo velikago Gosudariia Mikhaila Fedorovicha* (1672; M, 1856), 2.

86. Platonov, *Drevnerusskiia skazaniia*, 219.

87. Belokurov, "Utverzhdennaia gramota," 49–50; Grigorii Kotoshikhin, *O Rossii v tsarstvovanie Alekseia Mikhailovicha*, ed. A. Barsukov (Spb, 1906), 126; Platonov, *Drevnerusskiia skazaniia*, 428–29.

88. V. V. Mavrodin, "Nekotorye voprosy evoliutsii russkogo samoderzhaviia v XVII–XVIII vv.," in *Voprosy genezisa kapitalizma v Rossii: Sbornik statei* (L, 1960), 79–81; for an overall examination of the boyars in this century, consult the classic study by Robert O. Crummey, *Autocrats and Servitors: The Boyar Elite in Russia, 1613–1689* (Princeton, 1983); and Hugh Ragsdale, *The Russian Tragedy: The Burden of History* (Armonk, NY, 1996), 35–36.

89. Iakushkin, *Gosudarstvennaia vlast'*, 11–13.

90. Please consult Rowland, "Problem of Advice," 271–72; the quotations are located in *The Muscovite Law Code (Ulozhenie) of 1649*, part 1, *Text and Translation*, trans. and ed. Richard Hellie (Irvine, 1988), 2; Robert O. Crummey, "Constitutional Reform During the Time of Troubles," in *Reform in Russia and the U.S.S.R.: Past and Prospects*, ed. Robert O. Crummey (Urbana, 1989), 37. Zhivov and Uspenskii believe that Aleksei was trying consciously to imitate the Byzantine concept of the monarch as Animate Law. See "Tsar' i bog," 63.

91. Kivelson, *Autocracy in the Provinces*, 247.

92. S. Polotskii, *Izbrannye sochineniia* (M, 1953), 16–17, 97–107; I. Pushkarev, "Gosudarstvo i vlast' v obshchestvenno-politicheskoi mysli kontsa XVII v." in *Obshchestvo i gosudarstvo feodal'noi Rossii*, ed. V. T. Pashuto (M, 1975), 189–92; A. I. Beletskii, "Stikhotvoreniia Simona Polotskogo na temy iz vseobshchei istorii," in *Sbornik statei v chest' prof. V. P. Buzeskula* (Khar'kov, 1914), 596–605; L. N. Maikov, *Ocherki iz istorii russkoi literatury XVII i XVIII stoletii* (Spb, 1889), 1–162; I. Tatarskii, *Simon Polotskii, ego zhizn' i deiatel'nost'* (M, 1886).

93. "The Life of Archpriest Avvakum by Himself," in Zenkovsky, *Medieval Russia's Epics*, 363; Pushkarev, "Gosudarstvo i vlast'," 194–96.

94. Jean Bodin, *The Six Books of the Commonwealth*, trans. M. J. Tooley (1576; NY, 1967); Julian H. Franklin, *Jean Bodin and the Rise of Absolutist Theory* (Cambridge, Mass., 1972); Mousnier, *Institutions of France*, 2:659–65.

95. Richelieu is most succinct in *Mémoires du Cardinal de Richelieu* 9 (Paris, 1929): 14–59; William F. Church, *Richelieu and Reason of State* (Princeton, 1972). On Bodin, Richelieu, and Louis XIV, see Daniel Engster, *Divine Sovereignty: The Origins of Modern State Power* (DeKalb, 2001), 47–149.

96. Jacques-Bénigne Bossuet, *Politique tirée des propres paroles de l'Écriture sainte* (1678; Geneva, 1967), quotation on p. 65; James I wrote the *Trew Law of Free Monarchies* in 1598.

97. The best treatment remains John Neville Figgis, *The Divine Right of Kings* (1896; Cambridge, 1967).

98. Consult, for example, David Ogg, *Louis XIV* (Oxford, 1967); John B. Wolf, *Louis XIV* (NY, 1968); John C. Rule, ed., *Louis XIV and the Craft of Kingship* (Columbus, Ohio, 1969).

99. In England, Hobbes dispensed with the god-king analogy but also removed politics from the domain of private standards of morality and thereby nullified the right to resist. Carl Schmitt, *The Leviathan in the State Theory of Thomas Hobbes: Meaning and Failure of a Political Symbol* (Westport, Conn., 1996), 53.

100. Leonard Krieger, *The Politics of Discretion: Pufendorf and the Acceptance of Natural Law* (Chicago, 1965); George N. Clark, *The Seventeenth Century* (Oxford, 1929), 124 ff.

101. The best single study is Marc Raeff, *The Well-Ordered Police State: Social and Institutional Change through Law in the Germanies and Russia, 1600–1800* (New Haven, 1983).

102. On the ceremonial changes that accompanied this, see Wortman, *Scenarios of Power*, 31–41.

103. Of the wealth of material, consult J. L. H. Keep, "The Decline of the Zemsky Sobor," *Slavonic and East European Review* 36 (1957): 100–152.

104. Here, I disagree with Crummey, who says Aleksei would have conceived this as "unimaginable blasphemy." See his "Court Spectacles in Seventeenth-Century Russia: Illusion and Reality," in *Essays in Honor of A. A. Zimin* (Columbus, Ohio,

1985), 135. On the Muscovite image of the tsar, see Tarnopol'skaia, "'Bozhestvennoe pravo," 49–58; Rowland, "Muscovite Literary Ideology," 125–55; and Bennett, "Idea of Kingship." Aleksei's quotations are reprinted in *Zapiski otd. russkoi i slavianskoi arkheologii Imp. russkago arkheologicheskago obshchestva* 2 (1861): 772–73.

105. The quote is from Polotskii, *Sochineniia*, 19. V. O. Kliuchevskii considered the paternal image a profound change; under the *votchina* concept, "Muscovite people of the sixteenth century regarded their sovereign as the owner of the state territory rather than as the guardian of public weal, and thought of themselves as strangers and sojourners, dwelling on that territory by political accident." *A Course in Russian History: The Seventeenth Century,* trans. Natalie Duddington (Armonk, NY, 1994), 70. Also see G. Olšr, "La Chiesa e lo Stato nel cerimoniale d'incoronazione degli ultimi sovrani Ririkidi," *Orientalia Christiana Periodica* 16 (1950): 268–79.

106. On this topic, please consult Valerie Kivelson, "The Constitutional Crisis of 1730 and the Evolution of Noble Political Culture," in *Imperial Russia: New Histories for the Empire,* ed. Jane Burbank and David L. Ransel (Bloomington, Ind., 1998), 5–31.

107. *PSZ* 2, no. 905 (12 January 1682). The term appeared in the 1682 edict abolishing *mestnichestvo,* the archaic system for filling official positions according to precedence. Also see A. Liutsh, "Russkii absoliutizm XVIII veka," in *Itogi XVIII veka v Rossii* (M, 1910); and M. M. Bogoslovskii, *Iz istorii verkhovnoi vlasti v Rossii* (Nizhnii Novgorod, 1905).

108. "Privilegii na Akademiiu," *Drevniaia rossiiskaia vivliofika* 6 (1788): 390–420; Mirosław Frančić, "Juraj Križanić, Ideolog Absolutyzmu," *Zeszyty naukowe uniwersytetu Jagiellonskiego. Prace historyczne* 51 (1974): 127–28; B. D. Datsiuk, *Iurii Krizhanich: Ocherk politicheskikh i istoricheskikh vzgliadov* (M, 1946), 106–8; I. Pushkarev, *Iurii Krizhanich: Ocherk zhizni i tvorchestva* (M, 1984); Iu. V. Kurskov, *Vedushchie . . . mysli i proekty . . . 40–60kh godov XVII veka* (Chita, 1973).

109. Crummey, "Court Spectacles," 141.

110. I. K. Shusherin, *Zhitie sviateishago patriarsha Nikona, pisannoe nekotorym byvshim pri niem klirikom* (Spb, 1784), 216.

111. Raeff, *Police State,* 187; Nicol, "Political Thought," 62.

112. *PSZ* 2, no. 619 (30 January 1676); no. 622 (3 February 1676); no. 624 (10 February 1676).

113. Marc Raeff, *Understanding Imperial Russia: State and Society in the Old Regime,* trans. Arthur Goldhammer (NY, 1984), 1–33.

114. *PSZ* 2, no. 914 (27 April 1682); I. A. Zheliabuzhskii, "Dnevnyia zapiski," *Russkii arkhiv* 3 (1910): 2–3.

115. *PSZ* 2, no. 920 (26 May 1682); A. A. Matveev, *Zapiski* (Spb, 1841), 2–10. The "people" included the patriarch, metropolitans, archbishops, bishops, and the entire Holy Sobor; the tsareviches of Siberia and Kasim; boyars, *okol'nichie* (lords-in-waiting, one rank below boyars), members of the Boyar Duma, *stol'niki* (courtiers), *striapchie* (officers of the tsar's household), Moscow nobility, *zhil'tsy* (a rank below the former but higher than provincial nobility), city nobility; all ranks of service people, *gosti* (wealthy merchants), lesser traders, artisans, and free villagers; only the enserfed peasantry were excluded. On these ranks, consult Richard Hellie, *Enserfment and Military Change in Muscovy* (Chicago, 1971), 22–25, 168, 199–200; and Joseph T. Fuhrmann, *Tsar Alexis: His Reign and His Russia* (Gulf Breeze, Fla., 1981), 96–101. By 1685, Peter, Ivan, and Sophia were all to be called "Autocrats of All the Russias": RGADA, *f.* 2, *op.* 1, *ed. khr.* 1, *l.* 5 (1682–1685).

116. *PSZ* 2, no. 931 (25 June 1682). French kings also promised "to maintain our subjects in a tranquil condition." See *Recueil général des anciennes lois françaises* 21 (Paris, 1821–1833), no. 1 (1 September 1715).

117. Lindsey A. J. Hughes, *Sophia: Regent of Russia, 1657–1704* (New Haven, 1990), 52–88; and her *Russia and the West: The Life of a Seventeenth-Century Westernizer, Prince Vasily Vasil'evich Golitsyn (1643–1714)* (Newtonville, Mass., 1984). For more details, consult S. M. Soloviev, *History of Russia*, trans. and ed. Lindsay A. J. Hughes (Gulf Breeze, Fla., 1989), 25:99–150. Prince I. B. Kurakin heaped lavish praise on her qualities as a ruler and her secularism. See "Gistoriia o Tsare Petre Alekseeviche, 1682–1694," *Arkhiv Kn. F. A. Kurakina*, ed. M. I. Semevskii (Spb, 1890), 1:50; also, E. D. Lermontov, *Pokhval'noe slovo Likhudova Tsarevne Sof'e Alekseevne* (M, 1910).

2: THE REFORMING TSAR

1. For a study of the "fledglings," see N. I. Pavlenko, *Ptentsy gnezda petrova* (M, 1984).

2. *PSZ* 3, no. 1611 (22 December 1697); *PSZ* 6, no. 3893 (5 February 1722); L. N. Maikov, *Rasskazy Nartova o Petre Velikom* (Spb, 1891), 53 (c. 1701). Even earlier, Fedor II decreed that petitioners should cease addressing him as though he were God. *PSZ* 2, no. 826 (8 June 1680).

3. See, for instance, the law of 8 December 1718, "O vziat'e shtrafa, kto v tser'kve govorit' stanet," in *Ukazy Petra Velikago* (Spb, 1777).

4. N. A. Voskresenskii, *Zakonodatel'nye akty Petra I* (M, 1945), 156 (22 October 1721); V. A. Nashchokin, *Zapiski* (Spb, 1842), 12.

5. James Cracraft, "Empire versus Nation: Russian Political Theory under Peter I," *Harvard Ukrainian Studies* 10 (1986): 527.

6. On this topic, consult M. I. Semevskii, *Slovo i delo, 1700–1725* (Spb, 1884).

7. Concerning the generational pattern, one can assume that both Talitskii and Tsikler were born before 1660. Talitskii has usually been identified as an Old Believer, but N. B. Golikova convincingly disproved this in *Politicheskie protsessy pri Petre I: Po materialam Preobrazhenskogo prikaza* (M, 1957), 135–37. Talitskii (d. 1701) received a death sentence that was commuted after he recanted. *Russkii biograficheskii slovar'* (Spb, 1912), s.v. "Talitskii, G."; E. F. Shmurlo, *Petr Velikii v otsenke sovremennikov i potomstva* (Spb, 1912); B. I. Syromiatnikov, *"Reguliarnoe" gosudarstvo Petra Pervogo i ego ideologiia* (M, 1943), 6, 155; *BE*, s.v. "Tsikler (Ivan Eliseevich)." Also see Gyula Szvák, *False Tsars*, trans. Peter Daniel (NY, 2000), 7–25.

8. "Manifest o vyzove inostrantsev v Rossiiu," in *Pis'ma i bumagi Imperatora Petra Velikago* 2, no. 421 (16 April 1702); I. Smolitsch, "Zur Frage der Periodisierung der Geschichte der russischen Kirche," *Kyrios* 5 (1940–1941): 79.

9. G. Esipov, *Raskol'nich'i dela* (Spb, 1863), 2:76–77.

10. S. Iavorskii, *Znameniia prishestviia antikhristova i konchiny veka* (M, 1703); P. O. Morozov, *Feofan Prokopovich kak pisatel'* (Spb, 1880), 86–87; J. Šerech, "Stefan Yavorsky and the Conflict of Ideologies in the Age of Peter I," *Slavic and East European Review* 30 (1951): 40–62.

11. Peter refused to allow the publication of Stefan's major work, *Rock of Faith*, which challenged the Petrine view of the supremacy of the monarch in ecclesiastical matters: "Christ did not entrust his Church to the Emperor Tiberius but to the Apostle Peter." Iavorskii, *Kamen' very* (Spb, 1728), 443. The work was written between 1713 and 1718. Also consult S. Benson, "The Role of Western Political Thought in

Petrine Russia," *Canadian-American Slavic Studies* 8 (1974): 254–74; Iu. Samarin, *Stefan Iavorskii i Feofan Prokopovich* (M, 1844), 119–21; F. Ternovskii, "Mitropolit Stefan Iavorskii: Biograficheskii ocherk," *Trudy Kievskoi dukhovnoi akademii* (1864): 254–55.

12. On Peter's admiration of Luther, please see Morozov, *Feofan Prokopovich*, 166.

13. A. N. Pypin, "Nachatki novago dvizheniia: Literatura vremen Petra Velikago," *Vestnik Evropy* 12 (1894): 752–54; N. S. Tikhonravov, "Moskovskie vol'nodumtsy nachala XVIII veka i Stefan Iavorskii," in *Sochineniia* (M, 1898) 2:180–82.

14. Samarin, *Stefan Iavorskii*, 383–86.

15. Šerech, "Stefan Yavorsky," 55.

16. Never a profile in courage, the Acting Patriarch invariably backed down in a confrontation and opportunistically clung to his positions. In the case of the Muscovite "free thinkers," for example, he at first claimed ecclesiastical jurisdiction over the "heresy" but then admitted that it threatened the stability of the state and warranted secular surveillance. Tikhonravov, "Moskovskie Vol'nodumtsy," 156–304.

17. *PSZ* 6, no. 3718 (25 January 1721). For European influences in the law, consult G. Bissonnette, "Pufendorf and the Church Reforms of Peter the Great" (Ph.D. diss., Columbia University, 1962). Also see James Cracraft, *The Church Reform of Peter the Great* (Stanford, 1971); and *The Spiritual Regulations of Peter the Great*, ed. and trans. Alexander V. Muller (Seattle, 1972).

18. I. A. Shliapkin, "Sv. Dmitrii Rostovskii i ego vremia, 1651–1709," *Zapiski Istoriko-filologicheskago fakul'teta Imp. S-Peterburgskogo universiteta* 25 (1891): 395.

19. *PSZ* 5, no. 3006 (30 March 1716).

20. On Peter, Pufendorf, and natural law, consult A. P. Piatkovskii, "Osmnadtsatyi vek v russkoi istorii," in *Iz istorii nashago literaturnago i obshchestvennago razvitiia* 1 (Spb, 1889): 52–55; Alfred Dufour, "Pufendorf," in *The Cambridge History of Political Thought, 1450–1700* (Cambridge, 1991), 561–88.

21. This evidence contradicts Michael Cherniavsky's conclusion that secularization resulted in a vision of a sovereign emperor in which only "power sanctified power." *Tsar and People*, 89, 99.

22. Voskresenskii, *Zakonodatel'nye akty Petra I*, no. 213 (22 October 1721); "Manifest," *Pis'ma i bumagi Petra Velikago*, no. 421 (16 April 1702).

23. *Pis'ma Petra Velikago, pisannyia k grafu B. P. Sheremetevu* (M, 1774), 11 (9 September 1702).

24. Feofan Prokopovich, *Slova i rechi* (Spb, 1760), 1:7–8. The medieval theorist, Christine de Pizan, wrote that rulers should serve God "with good deeds rather than spending time withdrawn in long prayers." *Book of the Body Politic*, 11.

25. *PSZ* 6, no. 3718 (25 January 1721). Prokopovich was probably familiar with chap. 19 of Spinoza's *Tractatus Theologico-Politicus*, which makes the same point.

26. Peter is quoted from a letter of 1717 in S. M. Solov'ev, *Istoriia Rossii* (M, 1963), 9:141–42.

27. Frederick II, "An Essay on Forms of Government," *Posthumous Works* (London, 1789), 5:5–33, and his *Refutation of Machiavelli's Prince or Anti-Machiavel*, trans. Paul Sonnino (Athens, Ohio, 1981), 34.

28. For Peter's ideas on monarchy, see Evgenii V. Anisimov, *The Reforms of Peter the Great: Progress through Coercion in Russia*, trans. John T. Alexander (Armonk, NY, 1993); V. O. Kliuchevskii, *Peter the Great*, trans. Liliana Archibald (NY, 1961); Syromiatnikov, *Gosudarstvo Petra Pervogo*; N. I. Pavlenko, "Petr I (K izucheniiu sotsial'no-politicheskikh vzgliadov)," in *Rossiia v period reform Petra I*, ed. N. I. Pavlenko (M, 1973), 40–102; Ernst Winter, "Josefinismus und Petrinismus: Zur vergleichenden Geschichte der österreichischen und

russischen Aufklärung," *Canadian-American Slavic Studies* 16 (1982): 357–68; Lindsey Hughes, *Russia in the Age of Peter the Great* (New Haven, 1998), 92–100.

29. Please see my article, "The Reforming Tsar: The Redefinition of Autocratic Duty in Eighteenth-Century Russia," *Slavic Review* 51 (1992): 77–98.

30. Wortman has demonstrated that his "symbolic language" was already in place before he embarked on his reforms. See *Scenarios of Power*, 43–44.

31. I. Golikov, *Zhizn' Leforta i Gordona* (M, 1800), 53–61.

32. V. O. Kliuchevskii, "Petr Velikii sredi svoikh sotrudnikov," *Ocherki i rechi* (M, n.d.), 475.

33. For some European ramifications, see Lionel Rothkrug, *Opposition to Louis XIV: The Political and Social Origins of the French Revolution* (Princeton, 1965); and Franco Venturi, "History and Reform in the Middle of the Eighteenth Century," in *The Diversity of History: Essays in Honor of Sir Herbert Butterfield*, ed. John H. Elliott and Helmut G. Koenigsberger (Ithaca, 1970), 223–44. However, Reisner sees the simpler notion of the common good as the sole justification for the Russian monarchy in "Obshchestvennoe blago i absoliutnoe gosudarstvo," 1–128.

34. Barker, *From Alexander to Constantine*, 83.

35. Larry Wolff, *Inventing Eastern Europe: The Map of Civilization on the Mind of the Enlightenment* (Stanford, 1994), 202.

36. Voltaire, *Russia under Peter the Great*, trans. M. F. O. Jenkins (Rutherford, N.J., 1983), 65, 251; the book is a paean to the monarch's policies. As another example, Antoine Thomas (d. 1785) began an epic, the *Petreid*, modeled on the *Aeneid*, that demonstrated that "enlightened despotism and accelerated progress were interdependent parts of Peter's myth." While the verse is not brilliant, the myth is expressed clearly: "Je vois le despotisme en tes heureuses mains, / Etonné de servir au bonheur des humains . . . / Et, du trop lent destin changeant l'ordre commun, / Que dix siècles pressés viennent s'unir en un" (Fortunate to be in your hands, despotism / Astonished to be serving the happiness of man, and, / Changing the usual slow movement of destiny, / I see ten centuries compressed into one). The French verse is reproduced in Albert Lortholary, *Le Mirage russe en France au XVIIIe siècle* (Paris, 1951), 74–76; Dmitri von Mohrenschildt, *Russia in the Intellectual Life of Eighteenth-Century France* (NY, 1936), 275–80.

37. P. P. Shafirov, *Razsuzhdenie, kakie zakonnyia prichiny Ego velichestvo Petr Velikii . . .* (Spb, 1722); Wortman, *Scenarios of Power*, 42–78. On Peter and the foreign press, see Astrid Blome, *Das deutsche Russlandbild im frühen 18. Jahrhundert* (Wiesbaden, 2000). Also consult Cracraft, "Empire versus Nation," 524–41; Evgenii V. Anisimov, "Russia in Search of a New National Ethos," *Meeting Report: Kennan Institute for Advanced Russian Studies* 8, no. 16 (lecture of 14 May 1991, as reported by P. McInerny); O. G. Ageeva, "Imperskii status Rossii: K istorii politicheskogo mentaliteta russkogo obshchestva nachala XVIII veka," in Gorskii, *Tsar' i tsarstvo*, 112–40.

38. Peter is quoted in Solov'ev, *Istoriia*, 9:141.

39. *Pis'ma i bumagi Petra Velikago* 9, no. 3251 (27 June 1709).

40. "Opisannoe samovidtsem torzhestvo . . . 22 oktiabria 1721 . . . ," *Syn otechestva* 11 (1849): 2.

41. Golikov, *Zhizn' Leforta*, 53–61; *Pis'ma i bumagi Petra Velikago* 2, no. 421 (16 April 1702); Maikov, *Rasskazy Nartova*, 101–3 (c. 1718); *PSZ* 5, no. 3151 (3 February 1718).

42. Arthur Young, *Travels in France during the Years 1787, 1788, 1789* (London, 1913), 43.

43. Voskresenskii, *Zakonodatel'nye akty Petra I*, 150 (5 December 1724); Baehr, *Paradise Myth*, 19.

44. Prokopovich's *Bukvar', ili pervoe uchenie otrokam* is translated in Cracraft, *Church Reform,* 284–85.

45. Medushevskii, *Utverzhdenie absoliutizma v Rossii,* 291–99; Marker, *Publishing,* 25, 60.

46. *PSZ* 5, no. 3006 (30 March 1716).

47. *PSZ* 5, no. 3466 (11 December 1719).

48. *PSZ* 5, no. 3298 (4 February 1719); no. 3318 (3 March 1719); no. 2707 (25 August 1713).

49. *PSZ* 6, no. 3708 (16 February 1721).

50. Raeff, *Understanding Imperial Russia,* 45.

51. *PSZ* 7, no. 4345 (5 November 1723).

52. *PSZ* 7, no. 4540 (4 August 1724).

53. *PSZ* 5, no. 3464 (10 December 1719); *PSZ* 7, no. 4378 (3 December 1723); *PSZ* 5, no. 3464 (10 December 1719).

54. *Ukazy Petra Velikago:* 42 (1 August 1715), 471 (17 April 1722), 866 (22 January 1724).

55. F. B. Berkgol'ts, *Dnevnik vedennyi s 1721–1725 g.* (M, 1858), 2:83–85 (6 February 1722).

56. See the discussion in William C. Fuller, Jr., *Strategy and Power in Russia, 1600–1914* (NY, 1992), 35–84.

57. As quoted in Solov'ev, *Istoriia,* 9:141; also see P. N. Miliukov, *Gosudarstvennoe khoziaistvo Rossii v pervoi chetverti XVIII stoletiia i reforma Petra Velikago* (Spb, 1905), 545–46.

58. From the *Dukhovnyi reglament, PSZ* 6, no. 3718 (25 November 1721).

59. Kliuchevskii, "Petr Velikii," 506–9; Ia. Ia. Shtelin, *Liubopytnyia i dostopamiatnyia skazaniia o Imp. Petre Velikom* (Spb, 1786), 121, 368.

60. Kliuchevskii, *Sochineniia* (M, 1958), 4:221, as translated by John T. Alexander in Anisimov, *Reforms of Peter the Great,* 39.

61. Anisimov, *Reforms of Peter the Great,* and *Empress Elizabeth: Her Reign and Her Russia, 1741–1761,* trans. John T. Alexander (Gulf Breeze, Fla., 1995), 144.

62. On this point, see Raeff, "Seventeenth-Century Europe in Eighteenth-Century Russia?" 611–19.

63. James Cracraft, "Opposition to Peter the Great," in *Imperial Russia 1700–1917: State, Society, Opposition,* ed. E. Mendelsohn and M. Shatz (DeKalb, 1988), 22; Golikova, *Politicheskie protsessy pri Petre I.* The files are to be found in RGADA.

64. Leonard Krieger, *Kings and Philosophers, 1689–1789* (NY, 1970), 247–59. However, he concluded that "the tyrannical brutality of the Romanov . . . would seem antithetical to the notion of an enlightened ruler in any of its ususal connotations," p. 243. Also see his *Essay on the Theory of Enlightened Despotism* (Chicago, 1975). Those who agree he should be ranked among "enlightened" rulers include Reinhard Wittram, "Formen und Wandlungen des europäischen Absolutismus," in *Glaube und Geschichte: Festschrift für Friedrich Gogarten,* ed. Heinrich Kunte (Giessen, 1948), 295; M. S. Anderson, *Peter the Great* (London, 1995); Medushevskii's *Utverzhdenie absoliutizma v Rossii* makes an especially strong case.

65. Anastos, "Byzantine Political Theory," 17; also see Edward Shils, *The Intellectuals and the Powers and Other Essays* (Chicago, 1972), 5–6.

66. Voskresenskii, *Zakonodatel'nye akty Petra I,* 150 (5 December 1724); also see Yoshihide Tanaka, "Tsar and the Elite at the Beginning of the Eighteenth Century," *Slavic Studies* 46 (1999), 122–24.

67. However, one may find twelfth-century versions of a similar recognition.

Robert L. Benson, "Political *Renovatio:* Two Models from Roman Antiquity," in *Renaissance and Renewal in the Twelfth Century,* ed. Robert L. Benson and Giles Constable (Toronto, 1991), 339–86. Peter even revolutionized the language of communication: V. M. Zhivov, *Iazyk i kul'tura v Rossii XVIII veka* (M, 1996), 69–154.

68. Two of Peter's guides in politics, Pufendorf and Wolff, explored the idea that the assent of citizens served as a limit on a monarch's rule. See Walter Gleason, "Political Ideals and Loyalties of Some Russian Writers of the Early 1760s," *Slavic Review* 34 (1975): 563. Also see K. A. Papmehl, *Freedom of Expression in Eighteenth-Century Russia* (The Hague, 1971), 1–7. Peter himself had a library of about 1,600 volumes: E. I. Bobrova, *Biblioteka Petra I* (Leningrad, 1978). And consult Raeff, "Seventeenth-Century Europe in Eighteenth-Century Russia?" 612–15.

69. Byzantine emperors also wrote prefaces to their decrees, but Peter's rhetoric had little precedent in an absolutist state: Herbert Hunger, *Prooimion: Elemente der byzantinischen Kaiseridee in den Arengen der Urkunden* (Vienna, 1964); Liutsh, "Russkii absoliutizm XVIII veka," 41.

70. Anderson, *Europe in the Eighteenth Century,* 185.

71. Iu. M. Lotman, "Agreement and Self-Giving as Archetypal Models of Culture," in *The Semiotics of Russian Culture,* ed. Ann Shukman (Ann Arbor, 1984), 134.

72. Maikov, *Rasskazy Nartova,* 53 (c. 1701).

73. N. P. Pavlov-Sil'vanskii, *Proekty reform v zapiskakh sovremennikov Petra Velikago* (Spb, 1897), 80.

74. M. Ia. Volkov, "Monakh Avraamii i ego poslanie Petru I," in *Rossiia v period reform Petra I,* ed. N. I. Pavlenko (M, 1973), 336; F. Sushintskii, "Iz literatury epokhi Petra Velikago: Starets Avraamii i ego poslanie Petru Velikomu," *Filologicheskiia zapiski* 1 (Voronezh, 1914): 112–40.

75. Folk legends also depicted tsars as advice seekers: "Legenda o vziatii Oreshka," *Petr Velikii v anekdotakh,* ed. M. Shevliakov and Ia. Shchegolev (Spb, 1901), 201.

76. The manuscript is transcribed in N. A. Baklanova, "Tetradi startsa Avraama," *Istoricheskii arkhiv* 6 (1951): 143–55.

77. "1697: Delo o podannykh tsariu tetradiakh stroitelem Andreevskogo monastyria Avraamiem. Donosy Avraamiia, Pososhkova, i dr.," in *I. T. Pososhkov: Zhizn' i deiatel'nost',* ed. B. B. Kafengauz (M, 1950), 173–81; M. M. Bogoslovskii, *Petr I: Materialy dlia biografii* (M, 1940), 385–87.

78. On his participation in Avraamii's circle, see K. A. Papmehl, "Pososhkov as a Thinker," *Slavic and East European Studies* 6 (1961): 81; Kafengauz, *Pososhkov,* 20–36. Other "projectors" similar to Pososhkov are discussed in Pavlov-Sil'vanskii, *Proekty reform,* 88–97. Also see Uspenskii, "Historia sub specie semioticae," 107–14.

79. When not writing book-length attacks on Protestantism and Old Believers, he was involved with vodka distilleries, minting, mining, textiles, and weapons development; typically, he submitted several other projects to government authorities relating to monetary policy, education, and military affairs. I. T. Pososhkov, "O ratnom povedenii" in *Materialy dlia russkoi istorii,* ed. S. Belokurov (M, 1888), 522–29; *Sbornik pisem I. T. Pososhkova k Mitropolitu Stefanu Iavorskomu,* ed. V. I. Sreznevskii (Spb, 1910); Kafengauz, *Pososhkov,* 183–84; A. Tsarevskii, *Pososhkov i ego sochineniia* (M, 1883). It was long thought his family were peasants. See I. S. Beliaev, *Krest'ianin-pisatel' nachala XVIII veka, I. T. Pososhkov* (M, 1902).

80. His works were not published until the nineteenth and twentieth centuries: I. T. Pososhkov, *Sochineniia,* ed. M. P. Pogodin (M, 1842); *Zerkalo ochevidnoe,*

ed. A. Tsarevskii, 2 vols.(Kazan, 1895–1900); *Zaveshchanie otecheskoe k synu*, ed. A. Popov (M, 1873); *Kniga o skudnosti i bogatstve*, ed. B. B. Kafengauz (M, 1951). Pososhkov has been called a mercantilist, a cameralist, a physiocrat, and a forebear of Adam Smith. See A. Brikner, *Ivan Pososhkov*, vol. 1, *Pososhkov kak ekonomist* (Spb, 1876); M. Klochkov, "Pososhkov o krest'ianakh," in *Velikaia reforma*, vol. 1 (Spb, 1911); Charles B. O'Brian, "Ivan Pososhkov: Russian Critic of Mercantilist Principles," *American Slavic and East European Review* 14 (1955): 503–11. *The Domostroi: Rules for Russian Households in the Time of Ivan the Terrible*, ed. and trans. Carolyn Johnston Pouncy (Ithaca, 1994).

81. Ivan Pososhkov, *The Book of Poverty and Wealth*, ed. and trans. A. P. Vlasto and L. R. Lewitter (London, 1987), pp. 379, 155, 363.

82. Ibid., 377, 259, 379, 154.

83. For an analysis of why he may have been imprisoned, see Barbara J. Merguerian, "Political Ideas in Russia During the Reign of Peter the Great (1682–1739)" (Ph.D. diss., Harvard University, 1970), 321–25.

84. Pavlov-Sil'vanskii, *Proekty reform*, 17–78; M. O. Blamberg, "The Publicists of Peter the Great" (Ph.D. diss., Indiana University, 1974), 35.

85. Brenda Meehan-Waters, *Autocracy and Aristocracy: The Russian Service Elite of 1730* (New Brunswick, N.J., 1982), 149; Kliuchevskii, *Peter the Great*, 244; also see Raeff, "Seventeenth-Century Europe in Eighteenth-Century Russia?" 611–19.

86. This topic has been well researched: Shmurlo, *Petr Velikii*; Nicholas V. Riasanovsky, *The Image of Peter the Great in Russian History and Thought* (Oxford, 1985).

87. A. I. Mankiev (d. 1723), *Iadro rossiiskoi istorii* (Spb, 1770), also published in 1784, 1791, and 1799.

88. See my "The Idea of Autocracy Among Eighteenth-Century Russian Historians," *Russian Review* 55 (1996): 156–57; Mankiev, *Iadro rossiiskoi istorii*, 181, 384.

89. Mankiev, *Iadro rossiiskoi istorii*, 383; I. K. Kirilov (1691–1737), *Tsvetushchee sostoianie vserossiiskogo gosudarstva*, ed. V. A. Rybakov (M, 1977); the original was published in 1727–1730; Feofan Prokopovich, *Istoriia Imperatora Petra Velikago, ot rozhdeniia ego do Poltavskoi batalii . . .* , 2nd ed. (M, 1788).

90. Gavriil (Buzhinskii, 1680–1731) gave a special series of sermons read in Peter's presence, for instance, *Slovo o promysle Bozhii* (11 October 1720) (Spb, 1776); *Polnoe sobranie pouchitel'nykh slov* (M, 1784).

91. Likhachev is quoted in William Edward Brown, *A History of Eighteenth-Century Russian Literature* (Ann Arbor, 1980), 22.

92. He had received theological training in Poland and Italy, where he adopted the critical and skeptical posture of the early Enlightenment. At the Kievan Academy, he was professor of theology but introduced the teaching of new courses such as physics and mathematics, at which he also excelled. He had access to rich private libraries in Kiev, for instance that of Prince Dmitrii M. Golitsyn. Peter's generosity also enabled Feofan to become a man of means, and he amassed his own library of 30,000 volumes, which "in its wealth has no equal in Russia." As quoted from contemporaries in G. V. Plekhanov, *History of Russian Social Thought*, trans. B. M. Bekkar (NY, 1967), 73–74; and R. Stupperich, "Feofan Prokopovich in Rom," *Zeitschrift für Osteuropäische Geschichte* 5 (1931): 327–39.

93. Plekhanov, *History of Russian Social Thought*, 44. Feofan eulogized Peter at that time and also for his victory at Poltava. Prokopovich, "Slovo (1706)," *Slova i rechi* (Spb, 1760), 1:1–11; and "Slovo (1709)," *Sochineniia*, ed. I. P. Eremin (M, 1961), 23–38. For similar attitudes, consult Walter Ullmann, *The Carolingian Renaissance and the Idea of Kingship* (London, 1969), 35–37.

94. B. Titlinov, "Feofan Prokopovich," *Russkii biograficheskii slovar'* (Spb, 1913), vol. Prituits-Reis, pp. 399–448; I. A. Chistovich, "Feofan Prokopovich i ego vremia," *Sbornik statei chitannykh v otdelenii russkago iazyka i slovesnosti Akademii nauk* 4 (Spb, 1868).

95. Prokopovich, "Slovo (1716)," *Slova i rechi*, 44; and "Slovo (1725)," *Slova i rechi*, 131.

96. Prokopovich, "Slovo (1717)," *Sochineniia*, 63; "Slovo (1722)," *Sochineniia*, 119; and "Slovo (1725)," *Sochineniia*, 137.

97. *BE*, s.v. "Gavriil Buzhinskii"; Jury Šerech, "On Feofan Prokopovic as Writer and Preacher in his Kiev Period," *Harvard Slavic Studies* 2 (1954): 222; Prokopovich, "Slovo (1716)," *Slova i rechi*, 44–45.

98. Prokopovich, "Slovo (1725)," *Slova i rechi*, 126–27; see the discussion in Iu. M. Lotman and B. A. Uspenskii, "Myth-Name-Culture," in *Semiotics and Structuralism: Readings from the Soviet Union*, ed. Henryk Baran (White Plains, NY, 1976), 17–32.

99. Peter on his trips abroad became enchanted with theatre, a passion he shared with his beloved and progressive sister, Natalia, who died in 1716. P. O. Morozov, "Russkii teatr pri Petre Velikom," *Ezhegodnik Imperatorskikh teatrov* 4 (1893–1894): 52–80, quotations on pp. 78 and 80.

100. Henshall, *Myth of Absolutism*, 32.

101. François de Lamothe Fénelon, *The Adventures of Telemachus, the Son of Ulysses*, trans. E. W. S. (London, 1857), 1:115 (book 5).

102. Esipov, *Raskol'nich'i dela*, 2:11; Morozov, *Feofan Prokopovich*, 166–71, 190–91.

103. As quoted in Kliuchevskii, "Petr Velikii," 475.

104. Nikolai Kostomarov, "Tsarevich Aleksei Petrovich," in *Istoricheskiia monografii i izsledovaniia* (M, 1881), 14:213.

105. Solov'ev, *Istoriia Rossii*, 9:141–42. Usually, for instance in the Swedish formulation, an "autocratic monarch" would rule "according to his wish." See Miliukov, *Gosudarstvennoe khoziaistvo*, 500 n. 1.

106. Voskresenskii, *Zakonodatel'nye akty Petra I*, no. 220 (3 February 1718); RGADA, f. 140, ed. khr. 51 (1718); *PSZ* 5, no. 3151 (3 February 1718). Peter also spoke of the need for an heir to have a broad education: knowledge of Russian, training "in the fear of God and in our Orthodox Christian faith," the "best knowledge of military and political or civil affairs and of foreign governments," and an ability in foreign languages in order to read history and other subjects.

107. The son, according to Alain Besançon's intriguing study, embodied in Peter's mind all those who were against his reforms or the path he took to reform; Aleksei became the sacrificial lamb, whose death saved Russia from being plunged back into the darkness from which it had so recently emerged. *Le Tsarévitch immolé* (Paris, 1967).

At the trial, Aleksei was ordered to name all his accomplices in getting abroad, and torture, floggings, execution, or deportation to Siberia awaited those on the list he provided. The literature on this episode is extensive. See O. F. Kozlov, "Delo Tsarevicha Alekseia," *Voprosy istorii* 9 (1969): 86–91; R. Wittram, *Peter I, Czar und Kaiser* (Göttingen, 1964), 2:346–405; M. P. Pogodin, ed., "Tsarevich Aleksei Petrovich po svidetel'stvam vnov' otkrytym," *Chteniia v Imp. Obshchestve istorii i drevnostei rossiiskikh pri Moskovskom universitete* 3 (1861): 1–374; N. G. Ustrialov, *Istoriia tsarstvovaniia Petra Velikago* 6 (Spb, 1863).

108. B. B. Kafengauz, *Ocherki istorii SSSR: Period feodalizma* (M, 1954), 633; Sokolova, *Russkie istoricheskie predaniia*, 64–96.

109. B. H. Sumner, *Peter the Great and the Emergence of Russia* (NY, 1962), 96; D. E. Izbekov, "Odin iz maloizvestnykh literaturnykh protivnikov Feofana Prokopovicha (Dmitrii Kantemir)," in *Pamiatniki novoi russkoi istorii*, ed. V. Kashpirev (Spb, 1871), 1–35.

110. Prokopovich, "Slovo o vlasti i chesti tsarskoi," *Sochineniia*, 76–93.

111. Lotman, "Agreement and Self-Giving," 134.

112. *PSZ* 6, no. 3893 (5 February 1722). The decree demonstrated Feofan's tactic of using examples from both scripture and precedent: it cited the example of Isaac, who—although through trickery—gave his blessing to his second-born son, and of Ivan III, who bequeathed the throne to his grandson over his son although he later changed his mind; neither of these was convincing.

113. Anisimov, *Empress Elizabeth*, 144.

114. Baron de Montesquieu, *The Spirit of the Laws*, trans. T. Nugent (NY, 1949), 61 (bk. 5, sect. 14).

115. *Pravda* was reprinted in *PSZ* 7, no. 4870 (21 April 1726), pp. 602–43, double-columned. Cracraft has cast doubt on Feofan's authorship, but I believe that the document bears his authorial signature in terms of rhetoric, style, and structure of argument. See his "Did Feofan Prokopovich Really Write *Pravda voli monarshei?*" *Slavic Review* 40 (1981): 173–93.

116. P. P. Pekarskii, *Nauka i literatura v Rossii pri Petre Velikom* (1862; reprint, Leipzig, 1972), 2:664–65.

117. *Pravda*, 606.

118. *Pravda*, 604–6, 619.

119. G. Gurvich, *"Pravda voli monarshei" Feofana Prokopovicha i eia zapadno-evropeiskie istochniki* (Iur'ev, 1915), viii; Antony Lentin, "Some Reflections on *Pravda voli monarshei*," *Study Group on Eighteenth-Century Russia Newsletter* 24 (1996), 3–7; Marc Raeff, "Review of *The Spiritual Regulations of Peter the Great*, trans. and ed. Alexander Muller," *Canadian-American Slavic Studies* 8 (1974): 327–28.

120. Weber, *Economy and Society*, 215.

121. *Pravda*, 604–5, 619, 624–26, 628; also see Gurvich, *"Pravda voli monarshei,"* 12; Feofan made many of these same points in his sermon, "Slovo o vlasti i chesti tsarskoi."

122. *Pravda*, 617, 629, 622, 606.

3: THE ELECTED MONARCH

1. On this issue, see Procopé, "Greek and Roman Political Theory," 21–36.

2. Montesquieu, *Spirit of the Laws*, 61 (bk. 5, section 14). Also see A. Lentin, "Did Montesquieu Know *Pravda voli monarshei?*" *Study Group on Eighteenth-Century Russia Newsletter* 27 (1999): 18–25.

3. S. A. Belokurev, ed., "Utverzhdennaia gramota ob izbranii na Moskovskoe gosudarstvo Mikhaila Fedorovicha Romanova," *Chteniia v Imp. Obshchestve istorii i drevnostei rossiiskikh pri Moskovskom universitete* 218 (1906): 1–110; Szeftel, "L'Autocratie moscovite," 45–62; Bogoslovskii, *Iz istorii verkhovnoi vlasti v Rossii*, 14–19.

4. V. A. Bil'basov, *Istoriia Ekateriny Vtoroi* (Spb, 1890), 1:437.

5. M. D. Chulkov, *Peresmeshnik, ili Slavenskiia skazki* (M, 1767), 2:11; F. A. , *Prikliucheniia Femistokla* (Spb, 1781), 19; Kvint Kurtsii Ruf [Quintus Curtius Rufus], *Istoriia o Aleksandre Velikom* (Spb, 1767), 2:513; P. A. Plavil'shchikov, "Riurik," *Sochineniia* (Spb, 1816), 1:6 (act 1, scene 3).

6. Sumarokov, *Polnoe sobranie*, 6:284.

7. M. M. Shcherbatov, "Raznyiia razsuzhdeniia o pravlenii," *Sochineniia Kniazia M. M. Shcherbatova*, ed. E. P. Khrushchov (Spb, 1896–1898), 1:337.

8. V. T. Zolotnitskii, ed. *Sokrashchenie estestvennago prava* (Spb, 1764), 105; I. Tumanskii, *O gosudarstvennom pravlenii* (Spb, 1770), 4.

9. Iu. S. Sorokin et al., "Izbiratel'nyi," *Slovar' russkogo iazyka XVIII veka* (Spb, 1997), 9:9; Feofan Prokopovich used the term "consensual government" in a sermon, "Slovo (1722)," *Sochineniia*, 119. On the importance of consensus in Russian history, consult Keenan, "Muscovite Political Folkways," 115–81.

10. Sabine, *History of Political Theory*, 211, 297; Nelson, "Kingship and Empire," 217; Elias, *Court Society*, 16–17.

11. Shcherbatov, "Raznyia razsuzhdeniia," 1:367.

12. I will not fight the temptation to note that this body was roughly the size of the Central Committee of the Communist Party of the Soviet Union, which ousted Nikita Khrushchev in 1964.

13. LeDonne, *Absolutism and Ruling Class*, viii; Nelson, "Kingship and Empire," 217; Sabine, *History of Political Theory*, 297.

14. Michael T. Florinsky pointed out that these regiments "took the place of colleges and universities as training schools where the youth of the upper class prepared for their professional career." See his *Russia: A History and an Interpretation* (NY, 1961), 1:419, 481. Also see Christopher Duffy, "The Age of Marshal Münnich, 1725–1741," in *Russia's Military Way to the West* (London, 1981), 42–43; Iu. N. Smirnov, "Rol' gvardii v ukreplenii organov vlasti rossiiskogo absoliutizma v pervoi polovine XVIII veka," in *Pravitel'stvennaia politika i klassovaia bor'ba v Rossii v period absoliutizma* (Kuibyshev, 1985), 15–31; I. Pushkarev, *Istoriia Imperatorskoi Rossiiskoi gvardii* (Spb, 1844), 1:60–61, 130; and M. M. Shtrange, *Demokraticheskaia intelligentsiia v XVIII veke* (M, 1965), 9–28.

15. Meehan-Waters, *Autocracy and Aristocracy*, 148–60, quotations on pp. 148–49. On the origin of the term *vremenshchik*, see A. A. Vasil'chikov, *Semeistvo Razumovskikh* (M, 1869), 4.

16. Marc Raeff, "Review Article: Autocracy Tempered by Reform or by Regicide?" *American Historical Review* 98 (1993): 1147; Liutsh, "Russkii absoliutizm XVIII veka," 50–57.

17. Florinsky, *Russia*, 432–95 (the three chapters covering this epoch are entitled "The Era of Palace Revolutions"; also see S. M. Troitskii, "Istoriografiia 'dvortsovykh perevorotov' v Rossii XVIII v.," *Voprosy istorii* 2 (1966): 38–53.

18. F. Prokopovich, "O smerti Imperatora Petra Vtorago i o vozshestvii na prestol Gosudaryni Imperatritsy Anny Ioannovny," *Moskovskii vestnik* 1 (1830): 66.

19. RGADA, *f.* 156, *op.* 1, *ed. khr.* 88 (27 May 1682), and *f.* 140, *op.* 1 (1718). The unused blank forms are still stored in the archives.

20. *Manifesty, ukazy, i drugiia pravitel'stvennyia rasporiazheniia* (Spb, 1895), 137.

21. Wortman, *Scenarios of Power*, 89–90.

22. LeDonne, *Absolutism and Ruling Class*, viii; LeDonne also alerted me to the importance of consensus in Japanese society, as described in Chie Nakane, *Japanese Society* (Berkeley, 1970).

23. The quote is from Prokopovich, "Pravda voli monarshei," reprinted in *PSZ* 7, no. 4870 (21 April 1726), 627. On one statesman's reaction to the problem, see Ransel, *Politics of Catherinian Russia*, 67–69.

24. On the problems of women and power, see Leslie P. Peirce, *The Imperial Harem: Women and Sovereignty in the Ottoman Empire* (Oxford, 1993), 267–85; Louise

Olga Fradenburg, "Introduction: Rethinking Queenship," in *Women and Sovereignty,* ed. Louise Olga Fradenburg (Edinburgh, 1992), 1–13.

25. For details consult Soloviev, *History of Russia,* 25:99–150; and, especially, Hughes, *Sophia: Regent of Russia,* 52–88. Also see the chapters on life in the *terem* and on Sofiia's rule in Isolde Thyrêt, *Between God and Tsar: Religious Symbolism and the Royal Women of Muscovite Russia* (DeKalb, 2001), 118–69.

26. On Catherine, consult Ia. K. Grot, "Bibliograficheskiia i istoricheskiia zametki: Proiskhozhdenie Ekateriny I," *Sbornik otdelenii russkago iazyka i slovesnosti Imperatorskoi Akademii nauk* 18 (1877): 7–9; M. I. Semevskii, *Tsaritsa Katerina Alekseevna, Anna, i Villem Mons, 1692–1724* (Spb, 1884).

27. Feofan Prokopovich, *Kratkaia povest' o smerti Petra Velikogo . . .* (Spb, 1819), 17–19; F. M. Azanchevskii, *Istoriia Preobrazhenskago polka* (M, 1859), 229–30. On the debate among the political elite, consult N. Kostomarov, "Ekaterina Alekseevna, pervaia russkaia imperatritsa," *Istoricheskiia monografii i izsledovaniia* 14 (1881): 315–18; and I. I. Ditiatin, "Verkhovnaia vlast' v Rossii XVIII stoletiia," in his *Stat'i po istorii russkago prava* (Spb, 1895), 598–99. In the words of a cynical commentator, remarking on both Menshikov's and Catherine's humble origins, "A scullery maid [was] placed on the throne by a pastry cook": Fitzgerald Molloy, *The Russian Court in the Eighteenth Century* (NY, 1905), vii.

28. Peter placed great importance on this coronation. He gathered descriptions of the coronations of Louis XV, Frederika I of Sweden, and Holy Roman Emperor Charles VI and his wife Elizabeth in order to make sure his and Catherine's conformed to European norms: RGADA, *f.* 2, *op.* 1, *ed. khr.* 15 (7 May 1724). Prince M. M. Shcherbatov believed the coronation was in part a result of the fact Catherine was "prone to luxury." Shcherbatov, *On the Corruption of Morals,* 159. On the coronation itself, see Wortman, *Scenarios of Power,* 66–75; and on placing Peter's court in the context of his reign, see Lindsay Hughes, "The Courts at Moscow and St. Petersburg, c. 1547–1725," in *The Princely Courts of Europe: Ritual, Politics, and Culture under the Ancien Régime, 1500–1750,* ed. John Adamson (London, 1999), 302–13.

29. *PSZ* 7, no. 4366 (15 November 1723); no. 4643 (28 January 1725). Wortman intriguingly suggests that "only [women rulers] could claim to defend Peter's heritage without threatening a return of his punitive fury": *Scenarios of Power,* 85 and also 66.

30. *PSZ* 7, no. 4646 (2 February 1725). The edited copies of the oath are located in RGADA, *f.* 156, *ed. khr.* 218 (2 February 1725). P. A. Tolstoi had the idea of linking the coronation oath to Catherine's legitimacy. See P. N. Durin, *Istoriia Leibgvardii Semenovskago polka* (Spb, 1883), 1:182–83.

31. *PSZ* 7, no. 4870 (21 April 1726); P. P. Pekarskii, *Opisanie slaviano-russkikh knig i tipografii, 1698–1725 godov* (Spb, 1862; reprint, Leipzig, 1972), 664–65.

32. The anonymous letters continued throughout the reign: RGADA, *f.* 7, *op.* 1, *ed. khr.* 215–16, 224, 229, 241, 247–49 (1727).

33. Shcherbatov, *On the Corruption of Morals,* 163; E. Karpovich, "Zamysli verkhovnikov i chelobitchikov v 1730 godu," *Otechestvennyia zapiski* 1 (1872): 212–13.

34. Its original members included Menshikov, Admiral F. M. Apraksin, Chancellor G. I. Golovkin, Vice Chancellor Baron A. I. Osterman, Privy Councillor P. A. Tolstoi, and Prince D. M. Golitsyn. *PSZ* 7, no. 4842 (26 February 1726); and no. 4862 (28 March 1726). See also A. N. Filippov, *Istoriia senata v pravlenie Verkhovnago tainago soveta i kabineta* (Iu'rev, 1895); a rebuttal to the former book is A. S. Alekseev, "Legenda ob oligarkhicheskikh tendentsiiakh v tsarstvovanii Ekateriny I," *Russkoe obozre-*

nie 1 (1896): 76–129, 755–75; and William Slany, "Russian Central Governmental Institutions, 1725–1741," (Ph.D. diss., Cornell University, 1958), vol. 1: 37–55.

35. *BE,* s.v. "Ekaterina I Alekseevna"; P. P. Pekarskii, ed., "Ukaz Ekateriny I," *Istoricheskiia bumagi sobrannyia K. I. Arsen'evym. Sbornik otd. russkago iazyka i slovesnosti
Imperatorskoi Akademii nauk* 9 (Spb, 1872): 85–86, 98. On Catherine's respect for Peter's reforms, see N. P. Pavlov-Sil'vanskii, "Mneniia verkhovnikov o reformakh Petra
Velikogo," *Sochineniia* (Spb, 1910), 2:373–410.

36. Several plots, each acknowledging the legitimacy of Peter's grandson as the
successor, had played themselves out before the moment of Catherine's death. Menshikov, at first in league with the German faction, planned to assassinate young Peter and veil his sister Natalia, so that the Holstein family could seize the throne.
Once they fell out, Menshikov succeeded in getting Catherine's approval to let his
daughter and son marry Peter and Natalia. Another proposal suggested marrying Peter to his half-aunt, Elizabeth, but church authorities objected. Walther Kirchner,
"The Death of Catherine I," *American Historical Review* 5 (1946): 254–61; "Protokoly
Verkhovnago tainago soveta," *Chteniia v Imperatorskom Obshchestve istorii i drevnostei
rossiiskikh pri Moskovskom universitete* 3 (1858): 11–12.

37. *Zapiska o konchine Gosudaryni Imperatritsy Ekateriny Alekseevny i o vstuplenii
na prestol Gosudaria Imperatora Petra II Alekseevicha* (Spb, 1913), 1–2.

38. The document, the signature appended by Cabinet Minister A. B. Makarov,
and the attestations of relatives are found in RGADA, *f.* 2, *op.* 1, *ed. khr.* 21 (7 May 1727).

39. Durin, *Istoriia Leib-gvardii Semenovskago polka,* 190. The Duke of Holstein's
obsession with obtaining Schleswig was passed on to his son, who reigned briefly (in
part because of the Schleswig quest) as Peter III. During Catherine's reign, it caused
friction with a number of Russia's allies, but the country remained at peace from
1725 to 1733.

40. *PSZ* 8, no. 5007 (7 May 1727); and no. 5072 (8 May 1727).

41. Annotation in *PSZ* 6, no. 3893 (5 February 1722), 496; Pavlov-Sil'vanskii,
"Mneniia verkhovnikov," 373–401; Cracraft, *Church Reform of Peter the Great,* 130–32;
PSZ 8, no. 5179 (10 October 1727); *Detstvo, vospitanie, i leta iunosti russkikh imperatorov* (Spb, 1914), 24–25; F. Prokopovich, "Rech' . . . po koronatsii . . . (25 February
1728)," *Slova i rechi* 2 (Spb, 1760): 225–27.

42. Nashchokin, *Zapiski,* 29.

43. An apocryphal story claimed that Aleksei pushed his daughter into bed
with the sick Peter in order that she become impregnated with the precious Romanov seed.

44. The hostility to Peter among the members of this "boyar" party centered
not on his westernization but on his "way of life," treatment of the tsarevich, marriage to a commoner, and the subjection of church to state. See M. D. Khmyrov,
Grafinia E. I. Golovkina i ee vremia (Spb, 1867), 113.

45. Prince D. M. Golitsyn (1663–1737) owned a fine library of 2,600 volumes.
Pekarskii, *Nauka i literatura,* 1:257–63. On his political influences, see Isabel de
Madariaga, "Portrait of an Eighteenth-Century Russian Statesman: Prince Dmitry
Mikhaylovich Golitsyn," in her *Politics and Culture in Eighteenth-Century Russia,*
57–77; M. M. Bogoslovskii, *Konstitutsionnoe dvizhenie 1730 g.* (M, 1906), 7–9; Glinskii,
Bor'ba za konstitutsiiu, 50–53; P. N. Miliukov, "Verkhovniki i shliakhetsvo," in *Iz is-
torii russkoi intelligentsii* (Spb, 1903), 1–51; A. S. Lappo-Danilevskii, "L'Idée de l'état et
son évolution en Russie depuis les troubles du XVIIe siècle jusqu'aux réformes du
XVIIIe," in *Essays in Legal History,* ed. P. Vinogradoff (London, 1913), 380–81.

46. The two drafts of the Conditions are reprinted in D. A. Korsakov, *Votsarenie Imperatritsy Anny Ioannovny* (Kazan, 1880), 8–9, 17–18; the codicil is quoted in N. A. Protasov, "'Konditsii' 1730 g. i ikh prodolzhenie," *Uchenye zapiski Tambovskogo gosudarstvennogo pedagogicheskogo instituta* 15 (1957): 226.

47. Meehan-Waters, *Autocracy and Aristocracy*, 148–60.

48. Prokopovich, "Slovo (1718)," *Sochineniia*, 79.

49. On this point, I disagree with David Ransel's contention that the council was empowered to deal with the crisis. See "The Government Crisis of 1730," in *Reform in Russia and the U.S.S.R.: Past and Prospects*, ed. Robert O. Crummey (Urbana, 1989), 60–61. Also see "Rondeau to Lord Viscount Townshead," *Sbornik Imperatorskago russkago istoricheskago obshchestva* 66 (1889): 151 (26 February 1730).

50. Both Korsakov and Miliukov believed he possessed such a plan, but others disagree. N. A. Protasov, "Sushchestvoval li politicheskii plan D. M. Golitsyna?" *Istochnikovedcheskie raboty* 3 (1973): 90–107; W. Recke, "Die Verfassungspläne der russischen Oligarchen im Jahre 1730 und die Thronbesteigung der Kaiserin Anna Ivanovna," *Zeitschrift für Osteuropäische Geschichte* 2 (1911–1912): 11–64; Madariaga, "Portrait of Golitsyn," 71–72, 76.

51. Opinions are wildly divided over interpreting this episode in Russian history; please consult the bibliographical essays of David Ransel, "Political Perceptions of the Russian Nobility: The Constitutional Crisis of 1730," *Laurentian University Review* 3 (1972): 20–38; and of Troitskii, "Istoriografiia," 38–53.

52. *PSZ* 8, no. 5499 (4 February 1730). Indeed, Prokopovich was not allowed to conduct a thankgiving service in the Uspenskii Sobor, presumably because he would naturally have referred to Anna as autocrat. See F. Prokopovich, "Pozdravitel'noe pis'mo Imperatritse Anne Ioannovne," *Zhurnal Ministerstva narodnago prosveshcheniia* 9 (1836): 577–78.

53. The entire *generalitet* at this time consisted of 126 Russians and 53 foreigners.

54. Procurator-General Pavel Iaguzhinskii, one of Peter the Great's closest associates, had informed Anna in Mitau that the council was acting on its own behalf, and he was arrested. Korsakov, *Votsarenie*, 9, 121; Chistovich, *Feofan Prokopovich*, 258.

55. F. Prokopovich, "Iz"iasnenie, kakovy byli nekikh lits umysli, zateiki i deistviia v prizov na prestol Eia Imperatorskago Velichestva," in *Pamiatniki novoi russkoi istorii*, vol. 1, pt. 2, ed. P. Kashpirev (Spb, 1871), 12; Duke de Liria, *Zapiski . . . 1727–1730 gg.* (Spb, 1845), 81. For the various texts, see Korsakov, *Votsarenie*, 9–11 (Project of the Fifteen) and 170 (Project of the Society); Kashpirev, *Pamiatniki*, 4–5 (Project of the 361); and N. A. Protasov, "Dvorianskie proekty 1730 goda," *Istochnikovedcheskie raboty* 2 (1971): 61–102. Protasov makes a convincing case that the Project of the Society appeared in late January in "Zapiska Tatishcheva o proizvol'nom rassuzhdenii dvorianstva v sobytiiakh 1730 g.," *Problemy istochnikovedeniia* 11 (1963): 250–51. For some translations, see Marc Raeff, *Plans for Political Reform in Imperial Russia, 1730–1905* (Englewood Cliffs, N.J., 1966), 44–52.

56. "Rondeau," 134 (2 February 1730); "Extraits des dépêches de M. Magnan," in N. Tourgueneff, *La Russie et les russes* (Bruxelles, 1847), 3:258 (2 February 1730).

57. Meehan-Waters, *Autocracy and Aristocracy*, 137.

58. N. P. Zagoskin, *Verkhovniki i shliakhetstvo 1730 goda* (Kazan, 1881), 45; Ransel, "Political Perceptions," 32–35; Kashpirev, "Zapiski neizvestnago," *Pamiatniki*, 10–11; and his "Sobytiia 1730 goda i izvlechenie iz depesh frantsuzskikh rezidentov v Moskve," *Pamiatniki*, 366.

59. Many scholars see a strong Swedish influence in all the projects. See H. Hjärne, "Ryska konstitutionsproject år 1730 efter svenska förebilder," *Svensk historisk tid-*

skrift 4 (1884): 189–272; Korsakov, *Votsarenie*, 280–86; Miliukov, "Verkhovniki," 1–51; and Madariaga, "Portrait of Golitsyn," 36–60. Also see Recke, "Verfassungpläne," 36–38; Brenda Meehan-Waters, "The Russian Aristocracy and the Reforms of Peter the Great," *Canadian-American Slavic Studies* 8 (1974): 298; Zagoskin, *Verkhovniki*, 36–38.

60. On the service aims of the nobility in 1730, consult Raeff, *Origins of the Russian Intelligentsia*, 63–83.

61. Although they represented the service nobility, the circle was chaired by Prince Cherkasskii, and it met at the palace of Senator V. I. Novosil'tsov. See Liutsh, "Russkii absoliutizm XVIII veka," 96. See also V. N. Tatishchev (1686–1750), "Dve zapiski Tatishcheva, otnosiashchiiasia k tsarstvovaniiu Imperatritsy Anny: Proizvol'noe i soglasnoe razsuzhdenie i mnenie sobravshagosia shliakhetstva russkago o pravlenii gosudarstvennom," *Utro* (1859): 375–77. The preamble may have been written later; see Protasov, "Zapiska Tatishcheva," 237–65. On his role in 1730, consult S. C. Feinstein, "V. N. Tatishchev and the Development of the Concept of State Service in Petrine and Pre-Petrine Russia," (Ph.D. diss., New York University, 1971), 134–96; and R. L. Daniels, "V. N. Tatishchev and the Succession Crisis of 1730," *Slavic and East European Review* 49 (1971): 550–59.

62. As translated by Paul Dukes in *Russia under Catherine the Great*, vol. 1, *Select Documents on Government and Society* [hereafter *Select Documents*](Newtonville, Mass., 1978), 25–27. On Tatishchev's loyalty to absolute monarchy, consult Miliukov, "Verkhovniki," 20, 28, 32.

63. Protasov, "'Konditsii' 1730 g.," 226, and "Verkhovnyi tainyi sovet i proekty 1730 goda," *Istochnikovedcheskie raboty* 1 (1970): 69–70, 85–86, 100–101; Ransel, "Government Crisis of 1730," 48; Tourgueneff, *Russie et les russes*, 266 (18 February 1730).

64. Prokopovich, "Iz"iasnenie," 11–16; N. V. Golitsyn, "Feofan Prokopovich i votsarenie Imp. Anny Ioannovny," *Vestnik Evropy* 2 (1907): 520; I. A. Chistovich, "Uchenyi kruzhok Feofana Prokopovicha," in *A. D. Kantemir, ego zhizn' i sochineniia*, ed. V. Pokrovskii (M, 1910), 18.

65. Iaguzhinskii is quoted in Korsakov, *Votsarenie*, 6.

66. Meehan-Waters, *Autocracy and Aristocracy*, 145.

67. Korsakov, *Votsarenie*, 264–65; as translated by Ransel, "Political Perceptions," 27.

68. L. Cassels, *The Struggle for the Ottoman Empire, 1717–1740* (London, 1966), 31.

69. Korsakov, *Votsarenie*, 274; Protasov believes that the proposal of the aristocrats was written by the council, but my textual analysis reveals a different vocabulary and rhetoric from all their other documents: "Proekty reform," 88–89. For an insightful reading of the Cherkasskii petition, please see Valerie A. Kivelson's "Kinship Politics/Autocratic Politics: A Reconsideration of Early Eighteenth-Century Political Culture," in *Imperial Russia: New Histories for the Empire*, ed. Jane Burbank and David L. Ransel (Bloomington, Ind., 1998), 5–31.

70. Korsakov, *Votsarenie*, 274.

71. Feofan's plan with the suggestion is reprinted in Golitsyn, "Feofan Prokopovich," 524–25.

72. As quoted in Ransel, "Nikita Panin's Imperial Council Project and the Struggle of Hierarchy Groups at the Court of Catherine II," *Canadian Slavic Studies* 4 (1970): 448.

73. Korsakov, *Votsarenie*, 275–77; I. M. Dolgorukii, "Povest' o rozhdenii moem," *Sochineniia Dolgorukago* (Spb, 1849), 2:11–14.

74. "Rondeau," 168 (12 March 1730). Korsakov and Miliukov share this interpretation with many others. See Merguerian, "Political Ideas in Russia"; Madariaga,

"Portrait of Golitsyn," 36; A. Yanov, "The Drama of the Time of Troubles, 1725–1730," *Canadian-American Slavic Studies* 12 (1978): 1–59; S. A. Sedov, "Plany ogranicheniia samoderzhaviia v 1730 godu i pozitsiia dvorianstva," in *Sosloviia i gosudarstvennaia vlast' v Rossii, XV–seredina XIX vv. Chteniia pamiati Akad. L. V. Cherepnina. Tezisy dokladov* (M, 1994), 2:94; Ia. Gordin, *Mezh rabstvom i svobodoi* (Spb, 1994).

75. Meehan-Waters, *Autocracy and Aristocracy,* 145; James Cracraft, "The Succession Crisis of 1730: A View from the Inside," *Canadian-American Slavic Studies* 12 (1978): 84.

76. Henshall, *Myth of Absolutism,* 30.

77. Krieger, *Kings and Philosophers,* 57.

78. Harold A. Ellis, *Boulainvilliers and the French Monarchy: Aristocratic Politics in Early Eighteenth-Century France* (Ithaca, 1988), 1–15.

79. Benson, "Western Political Thought in Petrine Russia," 264; Raeff, *Understanding Imperial Russia,* 84.

80. This "change in the understanding of autocratic power" is the theme in Karpovich, "Zamysli verkhovnikov," 209–37. Nicholas V. Riasanovsky has noted: "But, whatever its exact nature, Russian eighteenth-century constitutionalism proved to be abortive, and it did not supplant, or apparently even affect, the triumphant image of a crowned reformer bringing light into the Russian darkness." See his *Image of Peter the Great in Russian History and Thought* (Oxford, 1985), 25.

81. Ransel, "Panin's Imperial Council Project," 448.

82. *PSZ* 8, no. 5509 (28 February 1730); no. 5510 (4 March 1730); no. 5517 (16 March 1730); *Opisanie koronatsii Eia Velichestva Imperatritsy . . . 28 Aprelia 1730* (M, 1730), 18–23; B. Titlinov, "Feofan Prokopovich," 417; Korsakov, *Votsarenie,* 298–303; for a poetic and heroic account of exile, see N. B. Dolgorukaia, *Pamiatnyia zapiski, 1714–1771* (M, 1867).

83. *PSZ* 8, no. 5909 (17 December 1731); V. Stroev, *Bironovshchina i kabinet ministrov* (M, 1909–1910), 1:34; Alexander Lipski, "A Re-examination of the 'Dark Era' of Anna Ioannovna," *American Slavic and East European Review* 15 (1956): 477–88, and "Some Aspects of Russia's Westernization During the Reign of Anna Ioannovna," *American Slavic and East European Review* 18 (1959): 1–11; Arcadius Kahan, "Continuity in Economic Activity and Policy During the Post-Petrine Period in Russia," *Journal of Economic History* 25 (1965): 61–85. Russia enjoyed victories in the War of the Polish Succession (1733–1735) and the Turkish War (1735–1739) and cast its net to the Americas. See Duffy, "Marshal Münnich," 43; Lewis A. Tambs, "Anglo-Russian Enterprises Against Hispanic South America," *Slavonic and East European Review* 48 (1970): 360.

84. Wortman, *Scenarios of Power,* 82; A. P. Sumarokov, ". . . Anne Ioannove . . ." (1 Jan 1740), *Izbrannye proizvedeniia* (L, 1957), 51.

85. Chistovich, "Uchenyi kruzhok," 17–49; P. P. Epifanov, "'Uchenaia druzhina' i prosvetitel'stvo XVIII veka," *Voprosy istorii* 3 (1963): 37–53; G. V. Plekhanov, *Istoriia russkoi obshchestvennoi mysli* (M, 1914), 98–160.

86. F. Prokopovich, *Istoriia o izbranii i vosshestvii na prestol . . . Anny Ioannovny* (Spb, 1837), first published in May 1730 and distributed widely, and *Slovo v den' vosshestviia na . . . prestol . . . Anny Ioannovny* (Spb, 1733), p. 2 and 14 (9 January 1733).

87. F. Prokopovich, "Slovo v den' koronatsii Anny Ioannovny (28 april 1731)," *Slova i rechi* (Spb, 1765), 78–81, and "Slovo v den' vospominaniia koronatsii Imp. Anny Ioannovny (28 April 1734)," *Slova i rechi,* 209–10.

88. V. N. Tatishchev, *Razgovor o pol'ze nauk i uchilishch (1733)* (M, 1887), 138. He developed this theme in his histories, which will be discussed in chapter 5.

89. A. D. Kantemir, "Satira I and II," in *Satiry i drugiia stikhotvorcheskiia sochineniia* (Spb, 1762), 55–67, 66–88, "Petrida," in *Sobranie stikhotvorenii* (L, 1956), 241–47, and "Zhitie," in *Satiry*, 1–14. Also see the essays in *A. D. Kantemir*, ed. Pokrovskii: Belinskii, "Obshchii obzor vos'mi satir i drugikh sochinenii Kantemira," 62–63, and Galakhov, "Podrobnyi analiz satir Kantemira," 73 (no initials were given in the book for the authors' names); and I. Serman, "Vozmozhna li rekonstruktsiia zamysla Petridy Kantemira?" *Study Group on Eighteenth-Century Russia Newsletter* 21 (1993): 17–21.

90. V. K. Trediakovskii, *Panegirik . . . Anne . . . Ioannovne* (Spb, 1732).

91. For typical indictments, see Soloviev, *History of Russia* 34, trans. Walter J. Gleason, Jr. (Gulf Breeze, Fla., 1984): 71–78; V. O. Kliuchevskii, *Kurs russkoi istorii* (M, 1908), 4:390–93; Ia. P. Shakhovskoi, "Zapiski," *Russkaia starina* 24 (1872): 10–24 (he lived from 1705 to 1777); S. Androsov, "Ivan Nikitin i 'Delo Rokyshevskogo'," *Study Group on Eighteenth-Century Russia Newsletter* 21 (1993): 22–35; O. F. Kozlov, "K voprosu o politicheskoi bor'be v Rossii v pervoi polovine XVIII v.," *Ezhegodnik Gosudarstvennogo istoricheskogo muzeia* (1965–1966): 119–28.

92. N. P. Luzhin, "Dva pamfleta vremen Anny Ioannovny," *Izvestiia Imperatorskoi Akademii nauk po otd. russkago iazyka i slovesnosti* 8 (1858): 49–64.

93. Chistovich, "Uchenykh kruzhok," 124–36; Esipov, *Raskol'nich'i dela*, 2:433.

94. Some estimates hold Biron responsible for sending as many as 20,000 people into Siberian exile, 5,000 of whom disappeared. See P. N. Miliukov et al., *Histoire de Russie*, vol. 2 (Paris, 1932): 464; K. Stählin [Shtellin], *Geschichte Russlands von den Anfängen bis zur Gegenwart* (1930; reprint, Graz, 1931), 2:231; A. Sleptsov, *Bironovshchina* (Petrograd, n.d.).

95. This contrasts sharply with a theme in Wortman's *Scenarios of Power* that "displaying themselves as foreigners" affirmed monarchs' hold on the throne: p. 5 and *passim*. While many Russians were prominent in the administration, Andrei Osterman ran the foreign office; Baron Burckhardt Münnich headed the War College; Count Reinhold Löwenholde oversaw court matters; and German officers dominated the two new guards' regiments, the Izmailovskii and Horse Guards, whose creation threatened to offset the influence of the Semenovskii and Preobrazhenskii units.

96. As quoted in Iakushkin, *Gosudarstvennaia vlast'*, 48; the best summation of the "Project" is in Iu. V. Got'e, "Proekt o popravlenii gosudarstvennykh del Artemiia Petrovicha Volynskago," *Dela i dni* 3 (1922): 1–30.

The literature is extensive. See "Zapiska ob Artemii Volynskom," *Chteniia v Imp. Obshchestve istorii i drevnostei rossiiskikh* 2 (1858): 135–70; D. A. Korsakov, "Artemii Petrovich Volynskii: Biograficheskii ocherk" [hereafter "Volynskii"], *Drevniaia i novaia Rossiia* 2 (1876): 45–60; A. N. Filippov, "A. P. Volynskii, kak kabinet-ministr," *Istoricheskii vestnik* 84 (1901): 552–68; and "Materialy dlia biografii A. P. Volynskago," *Starina i novizna* 6 (1903): 243–92.

97. D. A. Korsakov, "Artemii Petrovich Volynskii i ego 'konfidenty'," *Russkaia starina* 10 (1885): 17–18. The article was occasioned by the dedication of a monument on June 27, 1885, for the three, Volynskii, P. M. Eropkin, and A. F. Khrushchov. Volynskii's tongue was torn out, and he was so badly tortured that on the scaffold his arm hung lifeless, and his head was covered in bloody bandages; the executioners first cut off the hand and then the head. His proposals were normal, but he earned the enmity (he was not a likeable fellow) of both the Biron and Osterman factions at court.

98. Kireevskii, P. V. *Piesni, sobrannyia* (M, 1871), 8:291.

99. Ernst-Ioann Biron, "Obstoiatel'stva . . . ," *Vremia* 6 (1861): 522–39.

100. Feofan, though, had overseen Anna's conversion to Orthodoxy, when she was fifteen: *BE*, s.v. "Anna Leopol'dovna."

101. M. V. Lomonosov, "Oda . . . v prazdnik . . . Ioanna Tretiiago . . . (12 Aug 1741)," *PSS* (M, 1959), 8:34–42.

102. *PSZ* 11, no. 8262 (23 October 1740) and no. 8286 (11 November 1740); RGADA, *f.* 2, *op.* 1, *ed. khr.* 52 (9 November 1740), and "Dela Preobrazhenskogo i Tainoi kantseliarii," *f.* 7, *op.* 699–855 (1740–1742). Also see Durin, *Istoriia Leib-Gvardii Semenovskago polka*, 234–38; V. V. Andreev, *Predstaviteli vlasti v Rossii posle Petra I* (Spb, 1870), 87–89.

103. *Vnutrennii byt russkago gosudarstva s 17-go oktiabria 1740 g. po 25-e noiabria 1741 goda po dokumentam . . .* (M, 1886), 546–50 (17 April 1741); Christoph H. von Manstein, *Contemporary Memoirs of Russia from the Year 1727 to 1744* (London, 1968), 327; *BE*, s.v. "Anna Leopol'dovna."

104. "Proekt grafa I. A. Osterman o prevedenii v blagosostoianie Rossii," *Arkhiv kniazia Vorontsova* 25 (1880): 10–11; *Vnutrennii byt*, 546 (12 January 1741); RGADA, *f.* 2, *op.* 1, *ed. khr.* 55, *l.* 2; John L. H. Keep, "The Secret Chancellery, the Guards, and the Dynastic Crisis of 1740–1741," *Forschungen zur Osteuropäischen Geschichte* 25 (1978): 169–93.

105. Solov'ev, in his *History,* suggested the possiblity. See Lentin, "Montesquieu," 24 n. 15.

106. Elizabeth had to sign a separate, personal oath to Ivan: RGADA, *f.* 2, *op.* 1, *ed. khr.* 51–54 (7 October 1840). On the Braunschweig clan, see M. Korf, *Braunshveigskoe semeistvo* (Spb, 1917; reprint, M, 1993). Elizabeth was groomed to become the wife of Louis XV of France, but the match did not occur because of her illegitimacy at birth. See Albert Vandal, *Louis XV et Elisabeth de Russie* (Paris, 1896). For biographical details, consult Anisimov, *Empress Elizabeth;* and Tamara Talbot Rice, *Elizabeth, Empress of Russia* (NY, 1970); most other biographies are combinations of history and gossipy romance.

107. *Vnutrennii byt,* 534–35 (17 October 1741). The protocols and drafts of manifestoes are located in RGADA: *f.* 3, *ed. khr.* 8 (1741), 1–35, and *f.* 2, *op.* 1, *ed. khr.* 55 (2–7 November 1741), 1–50.

108. The phrase is a chapter title in Hans Rogger, *National Consciousness in Eighteenth-Century Russia* (Cambridge, Mass., 1960); also see F. Kh. Etse, "Poezdka imp. Elizavety Petrovny v Estliandskuiu guberniiu," *Russkii arkhiv* (1895): 6.

109. *PSZ* 11, no. 8473 (25 November 1741).

110. *PSZ* 11, no. 8474 (25 November 1741). The numbers were carefully tabulated as well: RGADA, *f.* 2, *op.* 1, *ed. khr.* 61 (1741–1742 gg.).

111. Catherine II, "Antidot," in *Osmnadtsatyi vek*, ed. P. I. Bartenev (M, 1869), 4:303.

112. "Avtobiografiia Grafa A. R. Vorontsova," *Arkhiv kniazia Vorontsova* 5 (1872): 9. LeDonne has also demonstrated her leadership of the Naryshkin-Trubetskoi network in "Frontier Governors General, 1772–1825, [part] II. The Southern Frontier," *Jahrbücher für Geschichte Osteuropas* 48 (2000): 183.

113. Catherine II, "Antidot," 303; "Rondeau," 155; Durin, *Istoriia Leib-gvardii Semenovskago polka*, 239; Pushkarev, *Istoriia Rossiiskoi gvardii*, 205–6; Anisimov, *Empress Elizabeth*, 21–27; RGADA, *f.* 3, *op.* 1, *ed. khr.* 9 (1741).

114. RGADA, *f.* 2, *op.* 3, *ed. khr.* 59 (14 February 1742); Ia. Ia. Shtelin, *Vsepoddanneishee pozdravlenie . . . (18 December 1741)* (Spb, 1741), 2.

115. *PSZ* 11, no. 8476 (28 November 1741).

116. *PSZ* 11, no. 8480 (12 December 1741) and no. 8506 (22 January 1742).

117. Nonetheless, the reign continues to fascinate. Dostoevskii planned to write a play on the theme. See F. M. Dostoevskii, "Nabroski i plany," *PSS* (L, 1974), 9:113–14. And three novels, written by E. P. Karnovich (1823–1885), G. P. Danilevskii (1828–1890), and V. A. Sosnora (b. 1936), are collected in the volume, *Romanovy: Dinastiia v romanakh: Ioann Antonovich* (M, 1994).

118. *PSZ* 11, no. 8478 (3 December 1741); RGADA, *f. 2, op. 1, ed. khr.* 62 (18 October 1742).

119. The number of serfs given as gifts to the regiments totaled 7,482; Pushkarev, *Istoriia Rossiiskoi gvardii,* 244. Also consult N. N. Firsov, *Vstuplenie na prestol imperatritsy Elizavety Petrovny* (Kazan, 1888); A. B. Kamenskii, "Catherine the Great," in *The Emperors and Empresses of Russia,* ed. Donald J. Raleigh (Armonk, NY, 1996), 145; and Evgenii V. Anisimov, *Rossiia v seredine XVIII veka: Bor'ba za nasledie Petra* (M, 1986), 25–29.

120. Wortman, *Scenarios of Power,* 89–109; *Obstoiatel'noe opisanie . . . koronovaniia . . . Elisavety Petrovny (25 aprelia 1742)* (Spb, 1744); "O koronatsii Imperatritsy Elizavety," RGADA, *f. 2, op. 3, ed. khr.* 59 (14 February 1742); "Opisanie vosshestviia na prestol Elizavety Petrovny," RO, *f. 17, no.* 1070, *ll.* 104–17. For examples of the rhetoric, see Lomonosov, "Oda . . . po koronatsii (1742)," *PSS* 8:82–102; V. K. Trediakovskii, "Imperatritse Elizavete Petrovne v den' ee koronovaniia," *Panegirik i stikhotvoreniia* (L, 1935), 135–40.

121. *PSZ* 11, no. 8560 (12 November 1742); RGADA, *f. 2, op. 1, ed. khr.* 67 (November 1742).

122. Max Weber, *The Theory of Social and Economic Organization,* trans. A. M. Henderson and T. Parsons (NY, 1947), 328; Karen Malvey Rasmussen, "Catherine II and Peter I: The Idea of a Just Monarch. The Evolution of an Attitude in Catherinian Russia" (Ph.D. diss., University of California, Berkeley, 1973), 41–56.

123. A. Florov, "Slovo . . . na . . . den' koronatsii . . . Elisavety Petrovny," in *Rechi . . . russkimi professorami* (M, 1819), 18–34 (26 April 1756).

124. Some examples might include A. Demidov, "Perevod rechi," *Ezhemesiachnyia sochineniia* 1 (1756): 14–30; and Ia. F. Verner, "Rech' o tom, chto Monarshee imia liuboviiu k poddannym bezsmertie sebe priobretaet," in *Sochineniia i perevody* (Spb, 1758), 291–308 (7 September 1758). Scholarship has long reflected this emphasis. See R. Nisbet Bain, *The Daughter of Peter the Great* (NY, 1900); Melvin Wren, "The Daughter of Peter the Great," in his *The Western Impact upon Tsarist Russia* (Chicago, 1971), 73–82; K. Valishevskii (elsewhere Waliszewski), *Doch' Petra Velikago* (M, 1990); this is also one of many interesting themes in Rasmussen, "The Idea of a Just Monarch."

125. A. S. [Sumarokov], "Slovo pokhval'noe o Petre Velikom," *Trudoliubivaia pchela* (1759): 579–92.

126. Anisimov, *Empress Elizabeth,* 47; Rogger, *National Consciousness,* 30–32; Trediakovskii: *Panegirik i stikhotvoreniia,* 135–40 (1742); Lomonosov, *PSS* 8:55 (1742); Verner, "Rech'," 294; G. Kuz'menskii, *Pokhval'naia rech' Petru Velikomu* (Spb, 1744), 33 (22 August 1744); Kantemir, *Satiry,* 33–34.

127. For a point by point analysis of Elizabeth's continuation of her father's policies, see Anisimov, *Rossiia v seredine XVIII veka;* also see S. V. Eshevskii, "Ocherk tsarstvovaniia Elizavety Petrovny," *Otechestvennyia zapiski* (1868): no. 5, 17–58; no. 6, 337–419; no. 7, 9–62.

128. Viktor P. Naumov, "Elizabeth I," in *The Emperors and Empresses of Russia: Rediscovering the Romanovs,* ed. Donald J. Raleigh and comp. A. A. Iskenderov (Armonk, NY, 1996), 69–100.

129. Lomonosov, "Oda (1748)," *PSS* 8:217, and "Slovo pokhval'noe . . . Petru Velikomu (1755)," p. 593.

130. Naumov, "Elizabeth I," 97. For a similar view, see N. D. Chechulin, *Russkoe provintsial'noe obshchestvo vo vtoroi polovine XVIII veka* (Spb, 1889), 54–57.

131. A. B. Kamenskii, "Reformy v Rossii XVIII veka v istoricheskoi retrospektive," in *Sosloviia i gosudarstvennaia vlast' v Rossii, XV–seredina XIX vv.* (M, 1994), 1:146–48; Slany, "Russian Institutions," 567.

132. Raeff, *Understanding Imperial Russia*, 59–62; S. O. Schmidt, "La Politique intérieure du tsarisme au milieu du XVIIIe siècle," *Annales, Economies, Sociétés, Civilisation* 21 (1966): 101–3; Paul Dukes, *Catherine the Great and the Russian Nobility* (Cambridge, 1967), 36–37; Walter J. Gleason, *Moral Idealists, Bureaucracy, and Catherine the Great* (New Brunswick, 1981), 31–52; Venturi, *Utopia and Reform*, 127; Afferica, "Shcherbatov," 26–46.

133. Kantemir, for instance, translated and commented on Horace, Fontenelle, Boileau, and Aesop; he befriended philosophes while ambassador to France and England; and he was thoroughly familiar with Newton, Locke, Hobbes, Milton, Pope, Swift, and Addison and Steele. On Trediakovskii, consult Reyfman, *Vasilii Trediakovsky*. Also see Papmehl, *Freedom of Expression*, 13–32.

134. Lomonosov composed seventeen odes addressed to five monarchs. See Pierre R. Hart, "Neoclassicism," in *The Handbook of Russian Literature*, ed. Victor Terras (New Haven, 1985), 299; and "Zhizn' M. V. Lomonosova," in *Sobranie raznykh sochinenii M. V. Lomonosova* (Spb, 1778), iii. On the connections between the poet and politics in another epoch, see V. J. Scattergood, *Politics and Poetry in the Fifteenth Century* (London, 1971).

135. M. V. Lomonosov, *Mogushchestvo i slava . . . Elizavety . . . na novoi 1758 god* (Spb, 1758); Baehr, *Paradise Myth*.

136. Peter Burke, *The Fabrication of Louis XIV* (New Haven, 1992), 37.

137. Raeff, *Origins of the Russian Intelligentsia*, 73. The penetration of the Enlightenment is a theme that dominates the literature. See P. P. Pekarskii, *Istoriia Imperatorskoi Akademii nauk v Peterburge*, 2 vols. (Spb, 1870–1873); G. A. Vasetskii, "Filosofskie vzgliady Mikhaila Lomonosova," in *Iz istorii russkoi filosofii* (M, 1951); *Izbrannye proizvedeniia russkikh myslitelei vtoroi poloviny XVIII v.*, ed. I. Ia. Shchipanov (M, 1952); Z. A. Kamenskii, *Filosofskie idei russkogo prosveshcheniia* (M, 1971).

The various problems connected with the Russian Enlightenment are beyond the scope of this study, for instance the differentiation between French and Central European influences or the extent of assimilation, but see David M. Griffiths, "In Search of Enlightenment: Recent Soviet Interpretations of Eighteenth-Century Russian Intellectual History," *Canadian-American Slavic Studies* 16 (1982): 317–56. Edward L. Keenan believes, as do I, in the force of Enlightenment in this era, but Stephen L. Baehr does not. See Keenan, "The Trouble with Muscovy," 104; and Baehr, *Paradise Myth*, xi.

138. Kantemir, "Elizavete pervoi," *Satiry*, stanzas 65–73; Sumarokov, "Slovo," *Polnoe sobranie*, 9:229–38; N. N. Popovskii in *Poety XVIII veka*, vol. 1 (L, 1972): "Oda," 98–99 (1754); "Stikhi," 103 (1755); "Oda," 105 (1756).

139. The polymath addressed monarchs on the birth of an heir, accessions to the throne, coronations, and name days. The pieces are reproduced in *Ody i pokhval'nyia slova Lomonosova* (M, 1837); the best were his paeans to Elizabeth (1749) and Peter (1755). For Lomonosov as a believer in enlightened absolutism, see G. A. Gukovskii, *Russkaia literatura XVIII veka* (M, 1939), 98–104; also see Sementkovskii, "Lomonosov i Kantemir, kak edinomyshlenniki," in *D. A. Kantemir*, ed. Pokrovskii, 128–31 (no initials given for Sementkovskii).

140. Lomonosov, *Ody i pokhval'nyia slova:* "Slovo," 200, 217 (1749); "Oda," 93–102 (1747); "Oda," 196–207 (1747); and "Oda," 154–73 (1762). "Ukaz ob uchrezhdenii v Moskve universiteta i dvukh gimnazii," *Ezhemesiachnyia sochineniia* 1 (1755): 98–104. Also see G. M. Vasnetskii, *V. Lomonosov: Ego filosofskie i sotsial'no-politicheskie vzgliady* (M, 1954), 14–18; Walter J. Gleason, "The Two Faces of the Monarch: Legal and Mythical Fictions in Lomonosov's Ruler Imagery," *Canadian-American Slavic Studies* 16 (1982): 391–93.

141. V. N. Tatishchev, "Kratkoe iz"iatie iz velikikh del Petra Velikogo, imperatora vserossiiskogo," in P. P. Pekarskii, "Novye izvestiia o V. N. Tatishcheve," *Zapiski Imperatorskoi Akademii nauk* 4 (1864): 18–19; V. K. Trediakovskii, "Plach' o konchine . . . Petra Velikago," *Sochineniia Trediakovskago* (Spb, 1849), 1:570–77; Verner, "Rech'," 300; Lomonosov, "Oda," *PSS* 8:749 (1761). The theme was also repeated in speeches. See A. Demidov, "Perevod rechi v pamiat' . . . rozhdeniia . . . Pavla Petrovicha," *Ezhemesiachnyia sochineniia* (1756): 14–30.

142. Lomonosov, "Oda . . . na vziatie Khotina," *PSS* 8:16–30 (1739).

143. Sumarokov, "Oda," *Izbrannye proizvedeniia*, 58 (1743).

144. Sumarokov, *Polnoe sobranie*, vol. 2: "Oda . . . Elisavete . . . ," 13 (1755) and "O prusskoi voine," 20.

145. Lomonosov, *PSS* 8: "Oda", 196–207 (1747); "Oda," 215–25 (1748); "Oda," 632–38 (1757); and "Oda," 647–48 (1759).

146. S. G. Domashnev (1742–1796), "Son," *Poleznoe uveselenie* (1761): 209–20.

147. See, for instance, "Rech' kotoruiu odin razumnoi chelovek iz garamantov k Aleksandru velikomu," trans. D. Anichkov, *Poleznoe uveselenie* (1761): 81–91; A. Vershnitskii, "Rech' Marka Avreliia . . . k synu svoemu i nasledniku prestola," *Dobroe namerenie* (September 1764), pp. 429–32, and (October 1764), pp. 449–75. See the discussion in Gleason, "Political Ideals," 567–68 n. 5.

148. John Barclay, *Argenis* (London, 1621). It was translated into all European languages and was among the favorite books of Leibniz and Richelieu. I have read this novel of 3,000 pages only in the French and Russian translations: *L'Argénis*, trans. Abbé Josse (Paris, 1754), 3 vols., quotation in 1:160; *Agenida, povest' geroicheskaia*, trans. Trediakovskii (Spb, 1751), 32.

149. The empress attended theatre twice a week and allowed home theatres to function. See Anisimov, *Empress Elizabeth*, 193–94.

150. Gleason, *Moral Idealists*, 1–31, and "The Two Faces of the Monarch," 388–409; A. A. Morozov, "M. V. Lomonosov i teleologiia Kristiana Vol'fa," in *Literaturnoe tvorchestvo M. V. Lomonosova*, ed. P. N. Berkov and I. Serman (M, 1962), 163–96. Among dozens of examples, see Lomonosov, *PSS* 8: "Oda," 30 (1739); "Oda," 45 (1742); "Oda," 79 (1746); "Oda," 93 (1747); and "Oda," 220 (1748).

151. Lomonosov, "Tamira i Selim," *PSS* 8:292–364.

152. Lomonosov, "Demofont," *PSS* 8:411–86.

153. Sumarokov, "Posviashchenie," *Trudoliubyvaia pchela* (January 1759): 3.

154. Gukovskii, *Russkaia literatura XVIII veka*, 135–36.

155. Sumarokov, "Khorev," *Polnoe sobranie*, 3:47 (act 5, scene 1); Kantemir had earlier praised Peter for "knowing all the natural laws by heart": *Satiry*, 32.

156. Sumarokov, "Hamlet," *Polnoe sobranie*, 3:78 (act 1, scene 2); for a warning not to read political messages into the work, consult Marcus C. Levitt, "Sumarokov's Russianized Hamlet: Texts and Contexts," *Slavonic and East European Journal* 38 (1994): 319–41. This play marked the first appearance of a Shakespeare play on the Russian stage.

157. Sumarokov, *Polnoe sobranie* 3: "Aristona," 185–254; "Sinav i Truvor," 121–83.

158. From 1755 to 1757, he published articles in *Ezhemesiachnyia sochineniia* that recommended measures to increase trade and commerce, to provide for fairer distribution of the wealth, and to provide better conditions for university professors.

159. Sumarokov, "Son. Shchastlivoe obshchestvo," *Trudoliubyvaia pchela* (December 1759): 740–47; in the same issue, his discontent is expressed in "Rastavanie s muzami," 768.

160. Other journal articles captured similar themes and crictisms; see, for instance, the unattributed "Nekotorykh persidskikh tsarei, po vostochnym pisateliam," *Sochineniia i perevody k pol'ze i uveseleniiu sluzhashchiie* (1759): 58.

161. On Peter's idealization in peasant tales, see *Petr Velikii v anekdotakh*, 192–246; P. K. Alefirenko, *Krest'ianskoe dvizhenie i krest'ianskii vopros v Rossii v 30–50 godakh XVIII veka* (M, 1958), 292–325; Luzhin, "Dva pamfleta," 49–64.

4: The Legal Sovereign

1. *The Travels of Olearius in Seventeenth-Century Russia*, trans. and ed. Samuel H. Baron (Stanford, 1967), 174–75.

2. *PSZ* 11, no. 8658 (7 November 1742); "Opisanie obriada . . . ," RGADA, f. 2, op. 1, ed. khr. 67 (6–7 November 1742).

3. Raeff, "Autocracy Tempered by Reform or by Regicide?" 1149.

4. Ia. Ia. Shtelin, "Zapiski . . . o Petre Tret'em . . . ," *Chteniia v Imp. Obshchestve istorii i drevnostei rossiskikh pri Moskovskom universitete* 4 (1866): 95.

5. *PSZ* 15, no. 11,390 (25 December 1761) and no. 11,391 (25 December 1761).

6. A. Brikner, "Anton-Fridrikh Biushing (1724–1795)," *Istoricheskii vestnik* 7 (July 1886): 13.

7. A. T. Bolotov, *Zhizn' i prikliucheniia Andreia Bolotova* (L, 1931; reprint, 1973), 2:173.

8. Only three weeks before the overthrow, Peter called her a "fool" in public and seemed intent on getting himself free to marry his mistress. A. B. Kamenskii, "Ekaterina II," *Voprosy istorii* 3 (1989): 69–70.

9. Riasanovsky, *The Image of Peter the Great*, 34.

10. Most major historians have accepted Catherine's assessment, including N. M. Karamzin, S. M. Solov'ev, and V. O. Kliuchevskii; the most recent example is Anisimov, *Rossiia v seredine XVIII veka*, 210–23.

11. For both a summary and an example of the tendency to side either with Peter or Catherine, see Carol S. Leonard, "The Reputation of Peter III," *Russian Review* 47 (1988): 263–92.

12. Carol S. Leonard, *Reform and Regicide: The Reign of Peter III of Russia* (Bloomington, Ind., 1993); A. S. Myl'nikov, "Peter III," in *The Emperors and Empresses of Russia*, ed. Donald J. Raleigh; S. O. Shmidt, "Vnutrenniaia politika Rossii serediny XVIII veka," *Voprosy istorii* (1987): 42–58. Earlier efforts at presenting a positive picture of Peter III's reign include J.-Ch. T. de Laveaux, *Histoire de Pierre III, Empereur de Russie*, 2 vols. (Paris, 1798); R. Nisbet Bain, *Peter III: Emperor of Russia* (London, 1902); N. N. Firsov, *Petr III i Ekaterina II: Pervye gody eia tsarstvovaniia. Opyt kharakteristiki* (Petrograd, 1915); H. Fleischacker, "Porträt Peters III," *Jahrbücher für Geschichte Osteuropas* (1957): 127–89.

13. This is the main theme in Leonard, "Reputation of Peter III," and see especially p. 264 n. 4; Shmidt, "Vnutrenniaia politika," 42–58.

14. Lomonosov, "Oda . . . Petru Feodorovichu na vosshestvie na prestol (1 January 1762)," *PSS* 8:751–60 (the Petrine theme was evident as early as his odes of 1742 and 1743 in *PSS* 8:59–68 and 103–10); Sumarokov, " . . . Petru Feodorovichu, na vozshestvie Ego na prestol (25 December 1761)," *Polnoe sobranie,* 2:29–32; I. S. Barkov, "Oda . . . [early 1762]," *Poety XVIII veka* (M, 1936), 172–76; I. F. Bogdanovich, "Oda . . . ," *Poleznoe uveselenie* (January 1762): 1–5.

15. G. Helbig, *Biographie Peters des Dritten* (Tübingen, 1809), 2:6; "Predstavlenie grafa M. D. Vorontsova Imperatoru Petru Tret'emu," *Arkhiv kniazia Vorontsova* 15 (1882): 251; the edict is quoted in Myl'nikov, "Peter III," 115; for his references to his forebears see, for instance: *PSZ* 15, no. 11,442 (16 February 1762); no. 11,445 (21 February 1762); no. 11,849 (28 March 1762).

16. Consult volume 15 of *PSZ*. On his varied interests, see "Dnevnik statskago sovetnika Mizere o sluzhbe pri Petre Tret'em," *Russkii arkhiv* (1911), 2: 12 and 16; "Imperator Petr Tretii: Zapiski D. P. Siversa," *Russkii arkhiv* 7 (1909): 519; Shtelin, "Zapiski," 97–99; A. S. Myl'nikov (same as Mylnikov), "Petr III," *Voprosy istorii* 4–5 (1991): 43–58; Bain, *Peter III,* 47–49.

17. *PSZ* 15, no. 11,445 (21 February 1762). One scholar maintains that these measures aided the introduction of free speech and cleared the way "for the new ideas which were to be planted in the next reign." See Papmehl, *Freedom of Expression,* 31.

18. Brikner, "Biushing," 13; Leonard, *Reform and Regicide,* passim; Firsov, *Petr i Ekaterina,* 25. Because of these rumors, over a dozen pretenders subsequently claimed to be Peter III. See K. V. Sivkov, "Samozvanstvo v Rossii v poslednei treti XVIII v.," *Istoricheskie zapiski* 31 (1950): 88–135.

19. Marc Raeff, "The Domestic Policies of Peter III and his Overthrow," *American Historical Review* 65 (1970): 1291–94; Leonard, *Reform and Regicide,* 40–72; "Stikhi pokhvalnye . . . ," RGADA, *f.* 156, *ed. khr.* 237 (1762). On his popularity, see Molloy, *Russian Court,* 247.

20. Raeff, "Domestic Policies of Peter III," 1302.

21. D. V. Volkov, "Avtobiograficheskiia zapiski," *Russkaia starina* 11 (1874): 481–87.

22. Raeff, "Domestic Policies of Peter III," 1287–1310.

23. Bil'basov, *Istoriia Ekateriny Vtoroi,* 1:424–25.

24. Ransel, *Politics of Catherinian Russia,* 58–62, quotation on p. 59.

25. Mylnikov, "Peter III," 128.

26. This was Bolotov's opinion in his *Zhizn',* 2:169–71.

27. F. N. Golitsyn, "Zhizn' ober-kamergera Ivana Ivanovicha Shuvalova," *Moskvitianin* 6 (1853): 92; Raeff, "Domestic Policies of Peter III," 1303–7.

28. Shtelin, "Zapiski," 98. In fact, of the inner circle of nine, two generals and three statesmen were Russian, but they were regarded as less powerful than the Germans.

29. Lomonosov, "Oda (1 ianvaria 1762)," *PSS* 8:751–60. By June, the poet had lost any enthusiasm for Peter, as was evident in the name day ode he prepared but never delivered. See S. N. Chernov, "M. V. Lomonosov v odakh 1762 g.," *XVIII vek* (1935): 153–54.

30. Anderson, *Europe in the Eighteenth Century,* 171.

31. Many writers believe the Holstein problem was the main reason for his downfall. See S. M. Soloviev, *History of Russia,* vol. 42, *A New Empress: Peter III and Catherine II, 1761–1762,* trans. N. Lupinin (Gulf Breeze, Fla., 1990), 54–66; Leonard, *Reform and Regicide;* Stanley B. R. Poole, "Peter III and Pugachev," *Royal Mysteries and Pretenders* (London, 1969), 67–80; G. P. Gooch, *Catherine the Great and Other Studies*

(Hamden, Conn., 1966), 20; John T. Alexander, *Catherine the Great: Life and Legend* (NY, 1989), 35–47. The quotation is from A. Goudar, *Mémoires pour servir à l'histoire de Pierre III, Empereur de Russie* (Frankfurt, 1763), 21.

32. Firsov, *Petr i Ekaterina*, 29, 39.

33. Peter's tutor admitted that when his pupil turned from domestic to foreign policy, the results were disastrous. See Shtelin, "Zapiski," 98.

34. Golitsyn, "Zhizn' Shuvalova," 92; Shtelin, *Opisanie feierverka . . . o zakli-uchennom mire . . .* (Spb, 1762). Peter III worshipped the Prussian king in a way that suggests the king had become a father figure; Peter called him "my master," wore a signet ring with his picture on it, and dressed in a Prussian uniform with the Order of the Black Eagle. Peter turned the official celebration of the end of the war with Prussia into a childish celebration of the person of Frederick the Great and the glories of his army.

35. Anisimov, *Rossiia v seredine XVIII veka*, 25–29; Golitsyn, "Zhizn' Shuvalova," 92.

36. Leonard, *Reform and Regicide*, 117–37.

37. His lack of sense and judgment constituted the chief criticism levied against him by Isabel de Madariaga in *Russia in the Age of Catherine the Great* (New Haven, 1981), 2–3; also see Leonard, *Reform and Regicide*, 144. Even Peter's portraits seem to display a lack of judgment or maturity. See Viktor Magids, "Ego vysochestvo v originale i na portrete," *Tvorchestvo* 10 (1990): 31–32; Nikolai Prozhogin, "Sud'ba odnogo portreta," *Nashe nasledie* 2 (1990): 34–35.

38. His personality has long been a source of interest: E. Lawrence, "Catherine II," *Harper's Monthly* 38 (1869): 624–35; Brikner, "Biushing," 14; Laveaux, *Histoire de Pierre III* 1:228; Ransel, *Politics of Catherinean Russia*, 62–63; Anisimov, *Empress Elizabeth*, 233–37.

39. As quoted in Bil'basov, *Istoriia Ekateriny Vtoroi*, 1:23.

40. "Zapiska sovremennika, gruzinskogo arkhiereia, o vstuplenii na prestol Imp. Ekateriny II," *Chteniia v Imp. Obshchestve istorii i drevnostei rossiiskikh pri Moskovskom universitete* 4 (1900): 23.

41. *Zapiski Imperatritsy Ekateriny Vtoroi* (Spb, 1907), 505; Bil'basov, *Istoriia Ekateriny Vtoroi*, 1:429.

42. *PSZ* 16, no. 11,582 (28 June 1762).

43. Bil'basov, *Istoriia Ekateriny Vtoroi*, 1:429.

44. A. P. Sumarokov, "Eia Imperatorskomu Vysochestvu Gosudaryne Velikoi Kniagine, Ekaterine Alekseevne," *Trudoliubyvaia pchela* (1759): 3.

45. "Mnenie . . . Ekateriny II o poslednykh mysliakh Imp. Elizavety . . . , kasatel'no togo, komu nasledovat' . . . prestolom," RGADA, *f.* 2, *op.* 1, *ed. khr.* 65, *ll.* 1–4.

46. Ia. Ia. Shtelin, "Zapiska," *Russkii arkhiv* 2 (1909): 527.

47. L.-Ph. de Segur, *Mémoires, ou Souvenirs et anecdotes* (Paris, 1826), 1:292.

48. "Tri pis'ma Petra III-go iz Ropshi k Ekaterine II-oi," *Russkii arkhiv* 2 (1911): 20–21.

49. This phrase was part of Catherine's second accession manifesto, which is reprinted in *Osmnadtsatyi vek*, 4:216–33.

50. Apparently, this was a substantial fear, and rhetoric and flattery aside, Catherine was greeted as "the liberator of Russia from inevitable danger, the near destruction of the Empire." See "Proekt Grafa Bestuzheva-Riumina o podnesenii Ekaterine II titula materi otechestva s sobstvennoruchnym otkazom eia," RGADA, *f.* 10, *op.* 1, *ed. khr.* 7 (18 September 1762).

51. See the discussion in Gleason, "Political Ideals," 565–66.

52. Lomonosov, "Oda . . . Ekaterine Alekseevne (28 June 1762)," *PSS* 8:772–81.

53. Peter was probably killed in a drunken brawl on July 5, while under guard at Ropsha; a manifesto claimed that Peter had suffered a violent hemorrhoidal attack and that medical help had been summoned, but to no avail; his death provided "evidence of the divine intention of God": *PSZ* 16, no. 11,599 (7 July 1762).

54. *PSZ* 16, no. 11,582 (28 June 1762). The second manifesto was deleted from the law books in 1797 by Paul, presumably because of its indictment of his father; it is reprinted in *Osmnadtsatyi vek* 4:216–23. The same sentiments were repeated in less elaborate formation in her coronation manifesto: *PSZ* 16, no. 11,598 (7 July 1762).

55. "Sobstvennoruchnyia vospominaniia Imp. Ekateriny II ob odnom iz pervykh zasedanii eia v senate posle vosshestviia na prestol," RGADA, *f.* 10, *op.* 1, *ed. khr.* 2 (n.d.)

56. Verner, "Rech'," 292.

57. As quoted in John T. Alexander, "Catherine II's Efforts at Liberalization and Their Aftermath," in *Reform in Russia and the U.S.S.R.: Past and Prospects*, ed. R. O. Crummey (Urbana, 1989), 73.

58. See the excellent discussion in Gleason, *Moral Idealists*, 88–91.

59. Bolotov, *Zhizn'*, 131; Trubetskoi, "Zametki Trubetskago v kalendare v 1762 godu," *Russkaia starina* 73 (1892): 446.

60. Catherine II, "Antidot (Protivoiadie)," in *Osmnadtsatyi vek* 4:125, 299, 302–3.

61. Chernov, "Lomonosov v odakh," 161.

62. A. Barsov, "Po koronovaniia . . . Ekateriny Alekseevny (3 October 1762)," in *Sobranie rechei, govorennykh v Imperatorskom Moskovskom universitete* (M, 1788), 17–33.

63. *PSZ* 16, no. 11,583 (28 June 1762).

64. See, for instance, V. A. Maikov, "Oda po vosshestvii ee velichestva na . . . prestol (1762)," *Izbrannye proizvedeniia* (M, 1966), 185–90; "Obstoiatel'noe opisanie . . . koronovaniia . . . Ekateriny Vtoroi," *Zhurnal kamer-fur'erskii* (1762): 30–34; Sumarokov, "Gosudaryne . . . Ekaterine Vtoroi (28 June 1762)," *Polnoe sobranie*, 2:37–45; M. M. Kheraskov, *Tvoreniia vnov' ispravlennyia i dopolnennyia* (n.d., n.p.), 29–32, and "Oda . . . 1763 goda," *Izbrannye proizvedeniia* (L, 1961), 59–64.

65. On Catherine presenting herself at her coronation as a legislatrix, please see Wortman, *Scenarios of Power*, 122–28.

66. As quoted in Franco Venturi, *The End of the Old Regime in Europe*, trans. R. Burr Litchfield (Princeton, 1991), 2:816.

67. The concept was most recently developed by O. A. Omel'chenko in his *"Zakonnaia monarkhiia" Ekateriny II* (M, 1993); he quotes the Russian translation of Fénelon's *Télémaque* on p. 19. David Griffiths believes that the fear of despotism only arose in the 1780s, but I think it emerged earlier. See his "Catherine II: The Republican Empress," *Jahrbücher für Geschichte Osteuropas* 21 (1973): 342.

68. Sumarokov, "O proiskhozhdenii slova Tsar'," *Polnoe sobranie*, 10:158.

69. See, for instance, *O gosudarstvennom pravlenii*, 13; S. E. Desnitskii, "Rassuzhdenie o roditel'skoi vlasti . . . ," *Izbrannye proizvedeniia russkikh myslitelei vtoroi poloviny XVIII* (M, 1952), 1:232–33.

A professor of jurisprudence at Moscow University suggested another common argument: "In a monarchical government great public deeds and important undertakings are brought to fruition more quickly and successfully than in a republic." See

I. A. Tret'iakov, *Slovo o rimskom pravlenii i o raznykh onogo peremenakh* . . . (M, 1769), 23 (30 June 1769).

70. Shcherbatov, "Raznyia razsuzhdeniia," 339–40. This work was originally written in French in about 1760. Also consult Marc Raeff, "State and Nobility in the Ideology of M. M. Shcherbatov," *American Slavic and East European Review* 19 (1960): 363–79.

71. *O gosudarstvennom pravlenii,* 72.

72. N. Panin, "Spisok s chernago sobstvennoruchnago doklada," *Sbornik russkago istoricheskago obshchestva* 7 (1871): 209; for this document, I am generally using the translation in Raeff, *Plans for Political Reform,* 63–68.

73. Afferica, "Shcherbatov," 48–49.

74. This is the main theme in Rasmussen, "The Idea of a Just Monarch."

75. Leonard Krieger provides a brilliant overview of the topic in *An Essay on the Theory of Enlightened Despotism* (Chicago, 1975). In my view, the term enlightened despotism, as opposed to enlightened absolutism—whose first use is traced to 1847—is not appropriate because the word despotism, Montesquieu's "perversion" of monarchy, was equated with tyranny, an "authority not subject to the restraint of any laws." See Scott, "The Problem of Enlightened Absolutism," quote on p. 4.

76. As quoted in A. A. Kizevetter, "Portrait of an Enlightened Autocrat," in *Catherine the Great,* ed. Marc Raeff (NY, 1972), 16.

77. D. I. Ilovaiskii, "Graf Iakov Sivers," in *Sochineniia* (M, 1884), 1: 465–66, 474; also consult K. L. Blum, *Ein Russischer Staatsmann: Denkwürdigkeiten des Grafen J. J. Sievers,* 2 vols. (Leipzig, 1857).

78. On Catherine in all her aspects, consult the encyclopedic work of Madariaga, *Catherine the Great,* in which the phrase "reforming zeal" is often used.

79. Alexander, "Catherine II's Efforts at Liberalization," 72, 76–78; also see James A. Duran, Jr. "The Reform of Financial Administration in Russia during the Reign of Catherine II," *Canadian Slavic Studies* 4 (1970): 464–96; Robert E. Jones, "Catherine II and the Provincial Reform of 1775: A Question of Motivation," *Canadian Slavic Studies* 4 (1970): 497–512; John P. LeDonne, "The Provincial and Local Police under Catherine the Great, 1775–1796," *Canadian Slavic Studies* 4 (1970): 513–28.

80. For a balanced estimate of Catherine as an enlightened monarch, please see Madariaga, "Catherine II and Enlightened Absolutism," in *Politics and Culture in Eighteenth-Century Russia,* 195–214.

81. Voltaire, letter to Catherine, as quoted in Wolff, *Inventing Eastern Europe,* 232.

82. Lomonosov, "Oda (28 June 1762)," *PSS* 8:775.

83. David Griffiths, "To Live Forever: Catherine II, Voltaire, and the Pursuit of Immortality," *Russia and the World of the Eighteenth Century,* ed. R. P. Bartlett, A. G. Cross, and Karen Rasmussen (Columbus, Ohio, 1988), 458–59.

84. *O gosudarstvennom pravlenii,* 1.

85. *PSZ* 16, no. 11,616 (18 July 1762). On these themes, consult Geoffrey Hosking, *Russia and the Russians: A History* (Cambridge, Mass., 2001), 213–18.

86. As quoted in Dukes, *Catherine the Great,* 42.

87. Rasmussen, "The Idea of a Just Monarch," 191–380.

88. N. D. Chechulin sees hatred of favorites as a central motivating force for instituting rule by law. See his *Proekt Imperatorskago soveta v pervyi god tsarstvovaniia Ekateriny II* (Spb, 1894), 8. Please see the pioneering article by John T. Alexander, "Favourites, Favouritism, and Female Rule in Russia, 1725–1796," in *Russia in the Age of the Enlightenment,* ed. Roger Bartlett and Janet M. Hartley (London, 1990), 106–24. The problem was pandemic in early modern Europe. See *The World of the Favourite,* ed. J. H. Elliott and L. W. B. Brockliss (New Haven, 1999).

89. The quotations are drawn from men usually placed in different political camps: Panin, "Spisok," 204–10; Shcherbatov, "Opravdanie moikh myslei (1789)," *Sochineniia* (Spb, 1898), 2:249–51, and "Raznye razsuzhdeniia," 344.

90. Richard S. Wortman, *The Development of a Russian Legal Consciousness* (Chicago, 1976), 16.

91. Upon learning of Catherine's *Nakaz*, the Rt. Hon. Henry Seymour Conway of the British Foreign Office thought the empress would be the first in history to relinquish absolute power. See Dukes, *Catherine the Great*, 9.

92. V. A. Petrova, "Politicheskaia bor'ba vokrug senatskoi reformy 1763 goda," *Vestnik Leningradskogo universiteta* 14 (1967): 61. Catherine also tried to reverse some despotic actions. For instance, she pardoned Artemii Volynskii in 1765: "Volynskii," she said, "was arrogant and impertinent in his deeds, but certainly not a traitor; on the contrary, he was a good and zealous patriot and enthusiastic supporter of useful reforms in his Fatherland. Although he suffered capital punishment, he was innocent." See Korsakov, "Volynskii," 54.

93. Panin was tutor to Paul from 1760 and head of the College of Foreign Affairs from 1763 to 1781; in 1762, he supported Catherine but expected her to act as regent for her son. See Ransel, *Politics of Catherinian Russia*, 6, 44.

94. G. P. Makogonenko, *Nikolai Novikov i russkoe prosveshchenie XVIII v.* (M, 1951); G. A. Gukovskii, *Ocherki po istorii russkoi literatury XVIII veka: Dvorianskaia fronda v literature 1750kh–1760kh godov* (M, 1936).

95. Petrova, "Politicheskaia bor'ba," 63–65; the quotation is from Ransel, *Politics of Catherinian Russia*, 87; the text of the project is found in Panin, "Spisok," 209–13.

96. Ransel, "Panin's Imperial Council Project," 443–63, quotation on p. 446.

97. "Zamechaniia neizvestnago na manifest ob uchrezhdenii Imperatorskago soveta i razdelenie Senata na departamenty," *Sbornik Imperatorskago russkago istoricheskago obshchestva* 7 (1871): 218. In "Panin's Imperial Council Project" (p.448), Ransel has claimed that the statesman A. P. Bestuzhev is the author.

98. As quoted in Ransel, *Politics of Catherinian Russia*, 121. From the vantage point of the Revolution of 1905, V. E. Iakushkin rues that the council was not set up for it would have been a first step "toward the introduction of a constitution on foundations similar to the Swedish constitution." See his *Gosudarstvennaia vlast'*, 52–53.

99. Walter J. Gleason, "Pufendorf and Wolff in the Literature of Catherinian Russia," *Germano-Slavica* 2 (1978): 427–37. Even Panin gave up the idea of a council when it would no longer be dominated by himself and his clique. On this tendency, see Ransel, *Politics of Catherinian Russia*, 134.

100. I. F. Bogdanovich, "Primechaniia o Germanskikh pravakh," *Sobranie novostei* (December 1776): 14–15; Wortman, *Russian Legal Consciousness*, 8–31.

101. Catherine founded and funded the Russian Academy in 1768 for the translation of foreign books; in its first four years, over 40 titles were published, and it continued its activity until 1783; the project brought to fruition 112 separate translations, running to 174 volumes and involving over forty-four people. W. Gareth Jones, *Nikolay Novikov: Enlightener of Russia* (Cambridge, 1984), 82; V. P. Semennikov, *Sobranie . . . o perevode inostrannykh knig, uchrezhdennoe Ekaterinoi II, 1768–1783 gg.* (Spb, 1913), 64. Many volumes were also published by private presses such as Novikov's, for example, G. Blekston [Blackstone], *Istolkovaniia aglinskikh* [*sic*] *zakonov* (M, 1780).

102. *O gosudarstvennom pravlenii;* Victor Kamendrowsky, "Catherine II's *Nakaz*, State Finances, and the *Encyclopédie*," *Canadian-American Slavic Studies* 13 (1979): 545–54; *SK*, 3: 165–66 (nos. 6840–46).

103. *Sokrashchenie estestvennago prava vybrannoe iz raznykh avtorov dlia pol'zy rossiiskago obshchestva*, ed. and trans. V. T. Zolotinskii (Spb, 1764), 100; for commentary on this work, consult A. N. Makarov, *Uchenie ob osnovnykh zakonakh v russkoi iuridicheskoi literature XVIII i pervoi treti XIX veka* (Spb, 1913), 1–4.

104. Marker, *Publishing*, 198; A. Artem'ev confirmed the public's great interest in the idea of law in the preface to his *Kratkoe nachertanie rimskikh i rossiiskikh prav* (M, 1777), 2.

105. F. Blagovidov, "Otnoshenie sovremennikov i istorii k Nakazu . . . Ekateriny II," *Nabliudatel'* 10 (1895): 57–85.

106. *PSZ* 17, no. 12,801 (14 December 1766). The manifesto went through seven drafts and involved Catherine's personal participation. See A. V. Florovskii, *Sostav zakonodatel'noi komissii* (Odessa, 1915), 8.

107. Catherine had a copy of the *Ulozhenie* placed in a silver shrine before the Legislative Commission met; she especially admired its clear, simple, and concise language. *PSZ* 18, no. 12,877 (20 April 1767).

108. On the Legislative Commission, please see Dukes, *Catherine the Great;* and Florovskii, *Sostav.*

109. Kerry R. Morrison, "Catherine II's Legislative Commission: An Administrative Interpretation," *Canadian Slavic Studies* 4 (1970): 482.

110. One of the leading Russian philosophes, S. E. Desnitskii, constantly praised this Mother of the Fatherland for her work in improving the system of justice. The quote is in his "Predstavlenie ob uchrezhdenii zakonodatel'noi, suditel'noi, i nakazatel'noi vlasti v rossiiskoi imperii," ed. A. Uspenskii, *Zapiski Imperatorskoi Akademii nauk po istoriko-filologicheskomu otdeleniiu* 7 (1905): 23. Also see Desnitskii's *Slovo na den' tezoimenitstva Imperatritsy Ekateriny II . . . noiabria 29 dnia 1775* (M, 1775), and *Iuridicheskoe razsuzhdenie o pol'ze znaniia otechestvennago zakonoiskusstva . . . aprelia 22 dnia 1778* (M, 1778).

111. Later, 129 articles were supplemented. I am using the translation found in *Catherine the Great's Instruction (Nakaz) to the Legislative Commission, 1767* [hereafter *Nakaz*], ed. and trans. Paul Dukes (Newtonville, Mass., 1977).

112. The comment on Quesnay is found in Habermas, *Structural Transformation of the Public Sphere*, 99.

Throughout her reign, Catherine lavishly subsidized the publication of the books upon which she relied. See, for instance, *Nastavleniia politicheskiia barona Vil'fel'da i Uchenie o gosudarstvennom upravlenii*, trans. F. Shakhovskoi (M, 1768); *Sushchestvennoe izobrazhenie estestva narodnykh obshchestv i vsiakago roda zakonov, sochinennoe gospodinom Iusti*, trans. A. S. Volkov (M, 1770); and Justi's *Osnovanie sily i blagosostoianiia tsarstv, ili Podrobnoe nachertanie vsekh znanii kasaiushchikhsia do gosudarstvennago blagochiniia* (Spb, 1778). Please consult N. D. Chechulin, "Ob istochnikakh Nakaza," *Zhurnal Ministerstva narodnago prosveshcheniia* (April 1902): 290–302; Ragsdale, *The Russian Tragedy*, 63; M. D"iakonov, "Vydaiushchiiisia russkii publitsist XVIII veka," *Vestnik prava* 7 (1904): 5.

113. Marker, *Publishing*, 91.

114. V. Bogoliubov, *N. I. Novikov i ego vremia* (M, 1916), 33; Venturi, *Utopia and Reform*, 127.

115. Jones, *Nikolay Novikov*, 15.

116. The quotation is from G. S. Vinskii, *Moe vremia* (Spb, 1914), 40–43, 103; his memoir covers from the 1750s to 1793. For an excellent introduction and bibliography, consult Madariaga, *Catherine the Great*, 139–83.

117. "Materialy, otnosiashchiesia k Zakonodatel'noi Komissi 1767 g.," in V. N. Bochkarev, *Voprosy politiki v russkom parlamente XVIII veka: Opyt izucheniia politicheskoi ideologii XVIII veka. Po materialam Zakonodatel'noi komissii 1762–1768 gg.* (M, 1923), 47–48, 54.

118. *PSZ* 18, no. 12,978 (27 September 1767). There was also a movement to erect a statue of her as the Great Legislatrix. See Ilovaiskii, "Graf Iakov Sivers: Biograficheskii ocherk," *Russkii vestnik* 45 (1865): no. 2, p. 640.

119. Bochkarev, "Materialy," 47–49, 52–54.

120. Ibid., 47.

121. P. S. Gratsianskii, *Politicheskaia i pravovaia mysl' v Rossii vtoroi poloviny XVIII v.* (M, 1984), 53.

122. *Nakaz*, art. 625, p. 118. The first two articles mention Christianity and the precepts of religion that guide people's actions, and article 351 (p. 89) advises parents to raise their children in the "fear of God."

123. Catherine II, *Sochineniia Imperatritsy Ekateriny II,* ed. A. N. Pypin (Spb, 1907), 12:663–74; *Nakaz*, art. 9, pp. 44–45. Also please see Isabel de Madariaga, "Catherine II and Montesquieu Between Prince M. M. Shcherbatov and Denis Diderot," in *Politics and Culture in Eighteenth-Century Russia,* 235–61.

124. Dukes, *Select Documents,* 41–42; *Nakaz*, art. 9–12, pp. 44–45.

125. Stephen L. Baehr sees this as evidence of the "paradise myth" in Russian literature, with the state "providing writers with a text for their eutopias." See his *Paradise Myth,* 121; *Nakaz*, art. 15, p. 44; art. 346, p. 89; arts. 520–21, pp. 107–8.

126. The *Nakaz* mentioned the other monarchical obligations of "defense of the whole Community," increasing the size of the dominions and maintaining an army, but like Peter in his official pronouncements, considered domestic duties, especially the system of justice, more important. *Nakaz*, art. 149, p. 59; art. 452, p. 9; art. 519, p. 107.

127. *Nakaz*, arts. 512 and 523, p. 107–8.

128. For Catherine's ideas on the monarch being subject to the laws, see E. S. Vilenskaia, "Ob osobennostiakh formirovaniia russkoi osvoboditel'noi mysli v XVIII veke," *Voprosy filosofii* 2 (1951): 114–17; also consult Papmehl, *Freedom of Expression,* 47–70.

129. *Nakaz*, arts. 19, 21, 34, pp. 44–46; Ia. P. Kozel'skii, *Filosofskie predlozheniia* (Spb, 1768); reprinted as "Filosofskie predlozheniia," in *Izbrannye proizvedeniia russkikh myslitelei vtoroi poloviny XVIII veka* (M, 1952), 1:520 (arts. 389–91).

130. *Nakaz*, art. 18, p. 44.

131. *Nakaz*, art. 149, pp. 59–60; art. 224, p. 72.

132. On this rich topic, consult Elise Wirtschafter, *Social Identity in Imperial Russia* (DeKalb, 1997).

133. P. K. Shchebal'skii, "Perepiska Ekateriny II s gr. N. I. Paninym," *Russkii vestnik* 45 (1863): 753.

134. F. V. Taranovskii, "Politicheskaia doktrina v Nakaze Imperatritsy Ekateriny II," in *Sbornik statei po istorii prava, posviashchennyi M. F. Vladimirskomu-Budanovu* (Kiev, 1904), 84; *Nakaz*, arts. 18, 20–21, pp. 44–45; art. 149, pp. 59–60.

135. On Catherine and the concept of civil rights, please see Isabel de Madariaga, "The Eighteenth-Century Origin of Civil Rights," in *Politics and Culture in Eighteenth-Century Russia,* 78–94.

136. *Nakaz*, art. 3, p. 43.

137. *Nakaz*, art. 63, p. 49; arts. 477, 484, 494, pp. 102–4.

138. Gruder, "The Bourbon Monarchy," 367. Also see the discussions in Klippel, "True Concept of Liberty," 447; and Jean L. Cohen and Andrew Arato, "Civil Society and Political Theory," in *The Transformation of Political Culture: England and Germany in the Late Eighteenth Century,* ed. Eckhart Hellmuth (Oxford, 1990), 86–89.

139. Shcherbatov expressed the Hobbesian view in his first published article on government, "O nadobnosti i o pol'ze grazhdanskikh zakonov," *Ezhemesiachnyia sochineniia* (July 1759): 37–54.

140. Griffiths, "Catherine II: The Republican Empress," 325–26. Her citizens shared this view as well. See D. I. Fonvizin, "Naidennoe v bumagakh pokoinago Grafa Nikity Ivanovicha Panina razsuzhdenie o nepremennykh Gosudarstvennykh Zakonakh," in E. S. Shumigorskii, *Imperator Pavel I: Zhizn' i tsarstvovanie* (Spb, 1907), appendix, 4–13.

141. Occasionally, though, the monarch must "prepare" the minds of the people or open them up to outside influences. *Nakaz,* arts. 57–58, 62, pp. 48–49.

142. *Nakaz,* arts. 29, 36–39, pp. 45–46. Montesquieu made the same distinctions in book 11 of *Spirit of the Laws,* and they were often repeated. See, for instance, Metropolitan Platon (Levshin), "V den' . . . tezoimenitstva Ego Imp. Velichestva," in *Prodolzhenie pouchitel'nykh slov pri vysochaishem dvore . . . Ekateriny. . . .* (Spb, 1769), 3:46–48, 54; Catherine II, "Grazhdanskoe nachal'noe uchenie," *Sochineniia Imperatritsy Ekateriny II* (Spb, 1849), 1:174; I. F. Bogdanovich, "Predislovie," in *Istoriia o byvshikh peremenakh v rimskoi respublike Verto d'Obüfa* (Spb, 1771), no pp.; Kozel'skii, *Filosoficheskiia predlozheniia,* as reproduced in P. Stolpianskii, "Odin iz nezametnykh deiatelei Ekaterinskoi epokhi: Iakov Pavlovich Kozel'skii," *Russkaia starina* 12 (1906): 525 (arts. 370–71); Kozel'skii, "Predislovie," to L. Kol'berg, *Istoriia datskaia,* 2 vols., trans. Ia. Kozel'skii (Spb, 1765–1766), no pp.; S. Venitseev, "Predislovie," *Nachal'nyia osnovaniia filosoficheskiia o grazhdanine Fomy Gobbeziia,* from the Latin (Spb, 1776), no pp.

143. *Nakaz,* art. 511, pp. 106–7; art. 43, p. 47.

144. Raeff, *Origins of the Russian Intelligentsia,* 27–29, 97–98; also consult Brenda Meehan-Waters, "The Development and the Limits of Security of Noble Status, Person, and Property in Eighteenth-Century Russia," in *Russia and the West in the Eighteenth Century,* ed. A. G. Cross (Newtonville, Mass., 1983), 294–305.

145. Alexander, "Catherine II's Efforts at Liberalization," 79.

146. "Kriticheskiia zametki po istorii politicheskikh idei v Rossii," *Nauchnye trudy russkago narodnago universiteta v Prage* (Prague, 1928), 1:75–77.

147. N. D. Chechulin, *Nakaz Imperatritsy Ekateriny II, dannyi komissii o sochinenii proekta novago ulozheniia* (Spb, 1907), cxliv–cxlvii. For instance, the young Nikolai Novikov, an officer in the Izmailovskii Regiment, was called to Moscow to take minutes at the meetings. See Jones, *Nikolay Novikov,* 14–16.

148. Venturi, *End of the Old Regime,* 1:164–65.

149. N. M. Druzhinin, "Prosveshchennyi absoliutizm v Rossii," in *Absoliutizm v Rossii, XVII–XVIII vv.* (M, 1964), 430–37; L. A. Derbov, *Istoricheskie vzgliady russkikh prosvetitelei vtoroi polovine XVIII veka* (Saratov, 1987), 97.

150. Kozel'skii, *Filosoficheskiia predlozheniia,* 530–31 (art. 400).

151. Desnitskii, "Predstavlenie o uchrezhdenii zakonodatel'noi, suditel'noi, i nakazatel'noi vlasti v rossiiskoi imperii," especially 4–7 and 22. "Nakazatel'noi," or penal, is often mistranslated as "executive." See Dukes, *Catherine the Great,* 47; and A. H. Brown, "The Father of Russian Jurisprudence: The Legal Thought of S. E. Desnitskii," in *Russian Law: Historical and Political Perspectives,* ed. W. E. Butler (Leyden, 1977), 133. For his enthusiasm on Britain, see his "Posviashchenie k perevodu knigi T. Boudena," *Nastavnik zemledel'cheskii . . .* (M, 1780), no pp., dedicated to Paul.

152. Baehr, *Paradise Myth,* 2, 38.

153. "Predislovie," in Peter's *Tetrady zapisnyia* . . . *1704–1706* (Spb, 1774), 1–4.

154. E. I. Kostrov, "Oda (1780)," *Poety XVIII veka* (L, 1972), 2:139; "Razmyshlenie uedinennago potekhontsa," *Ezhemesiachnyia sochineniia* (1786): 3–6.

155. I. Ia., *Zrelishche sveta, ili Vsemirnoe zemleopisanie* (Spb, 1789), 14; Ia. A. Komeniia [J. A. Comenius], *Vidimyi svet* (M, 1768), 422–23; Catherine's primer emphasized the same theme: *O dolzhnostiakh cheloveka i grazhdanina. Kniga k chteniiu opredelennaia v narodnykh gorodskikh uchilishchakh Rossiiskoi imperii* (Spb, 1787), 129.

156. A. M. Turgenev, "Zapiski . . . 1772–1863," *Russkaia starina* 62 (1889): 61–62.

157. On the view of the rest of Europe toward the interplay in Russia among despotism, reforms, and liberty, see Venturi, *End of the Old Regime*, 2:764–853.

158. Montesquieu mentioned Russia about ten times in *Spirit of the Laws;* on true monarchies, see bk. 2, chaps. 1, 4, and 5; bk. 3, chap. 10; bk. 13, chap. 6; bk. 19, chaps. 15 and 21; on Russia's despotic features, see bk. 2, chap. 5; bk. 5, chap. 14; bk. 19, chap. 14; also see bk. 17, chap. 4, for the influence of climate. Kozel'skii repeated the same sentiments in his *Filosoficheskiia predlozheniia*, arts. 379–81, p. 527.

159. Desnitskii, *Slovo o priamom i blizhaishem sposobe k naucheniiu iurisprudentsiiam* (M, 1768), and *Iuridicheskoe razsuzhdenie*, esp. 10–11; S. A. Pokrovskii, *Politicheskie i pravovye vzgliady . . . Desnitskogo* (M, 1955), 51–53; I. A. Tret'iakov also shared this view: *Slovo o proisshestvii i uchrezhdenii universitetov v Evrope na gosudarstvennykh izhdiveniiakh* (M, 1768).

On Desnitskii's major importance in jurisprudence, consult B. I. Syromiatnikov, "S. E. Desnitskii—Osnovatel' nauki russkogo pravovedeniia," *Izvestiia Akademii nauk SSSR, otdeleniia ekonomiki i prava* 3 (1945): 33–40; Brown, "The Father of Russian Jurisprudence," 117–41; M. D. Zagriatskov sees him as a "bourgeois ideologue" because he defended the interests of the merchant class from which he sprang, "Obshchestvenno-politicheskie vzgliady S. E. Desnitskogo," *Voprosy istorii* 7 (1949): 101.

160. Montesquieu, *Spirit of the Laws*, bk. 15, chap. 1; D. Didro, "Zamechaniia na Nakaz," *PSS* (M, 1947), 10:417.

161. Rasmussen, "The Idea of a Just Monarch," 91; before she became empress, she wrote of plans to free the serfs: "Sobstvennoruchnyia zametki Velikoi kniagini Ekateriny Alekseevny," *Sbornik Imperatorskago russkago istoricheskago obshchestva* 7 (1871): 84; Sivers is quoted in V. I. Semevskii, *Krest'ianskii vopros v Rossii v XVIII i pervoi polovine XIX veka* (Spb, 1888), 1:180–81; also see D. A. Golitsyn, "Pis'ma," in *Izbrannye proizvedeniia russkikh myslitelei vtoroi poloviny XVIII veka* (M, 1952), 2:34–35, 40, 37. For caveats on the interpretations of serfdom during Catherine's reign, please see Isabel de Madariaga, "Catherine II and the Serfs: A Reconsideration of Some Problems," *Politics and Culture in Eighteenth Russia*, 124–49.

162. Griffiths, "Catherine II: The Republican Empress," 323–44; G. Z. Eliseev, "Nakaz Imperatritsy Ekateriny o sochinenii proekta novago ulozheniia," *Otechestvennyia zapiski* 176 (1868): 78–80.

163. *The Political and Legal Writings of Denis Fonvizin*, ed. and trans. Walter J. Gleason (Ann Arbor, Mich., 1985), 201–2.

164. Kheraskov, *Polidor*, as quoted in Stephen Baehr, "From History to National Myth: *Translatio imperii* in Eighteenth-Century Russia," *Russian Review* 27, no. 1 (January 1978): 7; Betskoi's comment is found in *PSZ* 18, no. 12,957 (11 August 1767).

165. Catherine II, *Antidot*, 289.

166. Ibid., 242. The passage is translated in the engaging article by Marcus C. Levitt, "An Antidote to Nervous Juice: Catherine the Great's Debate with Chappe d'Auteroche over Russian Culture," *Eighteenth-Century Studies* 32 (1998): 55.

167. Catherine II, *Antidot,* 242–43. Also see George E. Munro, "Politics, Sexuality, and Servility: The Debate Between Catherine II and the Abbé Chappe D'Auteroche," in *Russia and the West,* ed. A. G. Cross, 124–31; A. N. Pypin, "Kto byl avtorom 'Antidota'?" in *Sochineniia Imperatritsy Ekateriny II* (Spb, 1901), 7:i–lvi.

168. P. I. Panin: "Pribavlenie k razsuzhdeniiu . . . sochinennoe Generalom Grafom Paninym, o chem . . . imet' poleznym dlia Rossiiskoi Imperii fundamental'nye prava, ne peremeniaemyia na vse vremena nikakoiu vlastiiu"; "Pis'mo k Nasledniku prestola . . ."; "Formy manifesty, kakoi razsuzhdaiutsia, ne mozhet li byt' ugoden k izdaniiu pri zakonnom po predopredeleniiu Bozheskomu vozshestvii na prestol Naslednika"; "Punkty," in Shumigorskii, *Pavel I,* appendix, 13–35.

169. M. M. Shcherbatov, "Razmyshleniia," *Sochineniia,* 1:390.

170. Ibid.; Shcherbatov, "O porokah i samovlastii Petra I (c.1782)," *Sochineniia,* 2: passim, and "Statistika v razsuzhdenii Rossii (1776)," *Sochineniia,* 1:564.

171. Shcherbatov, "Raznyia razsuzhdeniia," 337–38, 348, and "Opravdanie," *Sochineniia,* 1:259; and see the discussion in D"iakonov, "Vydaiushchiisia russkii publitsist," 21–22.

172. Catherine herself understood the disarray in the running of the empire; see, for instance, her *Règlements de Sa Majesté impériale Catherine II impératrice et autocratrice de toutes les russes, etc., pour l'administration des gouvernements de l'empire des Russies* (Spb, 1788).

173. Panin, "Formy manifesty," 22–24.

174. Shcherbatov, "O porokakh," 34, 46–48.

5: The Agent of History

1. John B. Bury noted that this generational pattern lends histories their "permanent interest," because each work arises "at a given epoch and is characteristic of the tendencies and ideas of that epoch," *The Ancient Greek Historians* (NY, 1909), 252.

2. On Tatishchev's contributions, consult S. N. Valk, "V. N. Tatishchev i nachalo novoi russkoi istoricheskoi literatury," *XVIII vek* 7 (1966): 71–72; I. N. Boltin, as another example, edited a model edition of *Pravda russkaia* (Spb, 1792).

3. See, for instance, J. B. Black, *The Art of History: A Study of Four Great Historians of the Eighteenth Century* (NY, 1965); and Preserved Smith, *The Enlightenment, 1687–1776* (NY, 1962), 202–30.

4. The three professional historians who were at work in Russia in the century—Gottlieb Baier (1694–1738), Gerhard Müller (1705–1783), and August-Ludwig Schlözer (1735–1809)—are not included in this study because they were imported German academicians, and therefore their works might not necessarily reflect Russian perspectives on the autocracy, but see A. B. Kamenskii, "Akademik G.-F. Miller i russkaia istoricheskaia nauka XVIII veka," *Istoriia SSSR* 1 (1989): 144–59. Also consult S. M. Solov'ev, "Pisateli russkoi istorii XVIII veka," *Arkhiv istoriko-iuridicheskikh svedenii* 2 (1855): 3–82; P. N. Miliukov, *Glavnyia techeniia russkoi istoricheskoi mysli* (M, 1897), 17–19, 70–146; S. A. Peshtich, *Russkaia istoriografiia XVIII veka* (L, 1961), 1:194, 222–62.

5. Mankiev, *Iadro rossiiskoi istorii.*

6. V. N. Tatishchev (1686–1750), *Istoriia rossiiskaia,* 6 vols. (M, 1768–1784), and *Istoriia rossiiskaia,* 7 vols. (M, 1962–1968).

7. M. V. Lomonosov (1711–1765), *Kratkii rossiiskii letopisets s rodosloviem* (Spb, 1759), and *Drevniaia rossiiskaia istoriia ot nachala rossiiskago naroda do konchiny velik-*

ago kniazia Iaroslava Pervago ili do 1054 goda (Spb, 1766), written from 1754 to 1758.

8. Catherine II (1729–1796) is the only writer of history in this group who is not Russian-born. See her "Zapiski kasatel'no rossiiskoi istorii," *Sobesednik liubitelei rossiiskago slova*, nos. 1–11 (1783) and nos. 12–15 (1784). Published anonymously, the "Zapiski" take up roughly seventy pages of each issue of the journal, which Catherine and Princess E. R. Dashkova edited. Catherine followed an outline prepared for her by Professor Kh. A. Chebotarev (1746–1815) of Moscow University, *Vstuplenie v nastoiashchuiu istoriiu o Rossii* (M, 1847). Also consult A. N. Pypin, "Istoricheskie trudy Ekateriny II," *Vestnik Evropy* 5 (September 1901): 170–202, and 6 (December 1901): 760–803.

9. M. M. Shcherbatov (1733–1790), *Istoriia rossiiskaia ot drevneishikh vremen*, 7 vols. (Spb, 1774–1791); the quotation is located in *Pis'mo kniazia Shcherbatova k priiateliu* (M, 1788), 140.

10. I. N. Boltin (1735–1792), *Primechaniia na istoriiu drevniia i nyneshniia Rossii Leklerka* [hereafter *Leklerk*], 2 vols. (Spb, 1788), and *Kriticheskiia primechaniia na istoriiu kn. Shcherbatova* [hereafter *Shcherbatov*], 2 vols. (Spb, 1793–1794).

11. T. S. Mal'gin (1752–1819), *Zertsalo rossiiskikh gosudarei ot rozhdestva Khristova s 862 po 1791 godu* (Spb, 1791).

12. In order of date of birth: V. K. Trediakovskii (1703–1769), *Tri razsuzhdeniia o trekh glavneishikh drevnostiakh rossiiskikh* (Spb, 1773); A. P. Sumarokov (1718–1777), "Kratkaia Moskovskaia letopis' (1774)," "Kratkaia istoriia Petra Velikago (n.d.)" and "Streletskii bunt (1768)," *Polnoe Sobranie* (M, 1781), 6:161–79, 234–42, and 185–228; I. P. Elagin (1725–1794), *Opyt povestvovaniia o Rossii* (Spb, 1803); I. S. Barkov (1732–1768), "Sokrashchennaia rossiiskaia istoriia," in *Sokrashchennaia universal'naia istoriia*, ed. Gil'mar Kuras (Spb, 1762), 357–90; F. A. Emin (1735–1770), *Rossiiskaia istoriia* (Spb, 1767–1769); and N. I. Novikov (1744–1818), *Opyt istoricheskago slovaria o rossiiskikh pisateliakh* (Spb, 1772).

13. I have read, as far as I can judge, all the extant major histories of Russia. The manuscripts are located in SOII, BRAN, RO, and RGADA. I have not included the hundreds of chronologies and genealogies for they offer little interpretation. I am grateful to Dr. E. B. Beshenkovskii, a bibliographer and scholar of the eighteenth century, for sharing with me his inventory and deep knowledge of these manuscript collections.

14. In the tradition of Pierre Bayle's *Dictionnaire historique et critique* (1697) and J. G. Walch's *Philosophisches Lexicon* (1726), Tatishchev attempted an alphabetical compendium of knowledge but only reached the entry "kliuchnik" in his *Leksikon rossiiskoi. Istoricheskoi, geograficheskoi, politicheskoi, i grazhdanskoi*, 3 vols. (Spb, 1793). Shcherbatov translated works on legal, ethical, and philosophical themes; see M. D'iakonov, "Vydaiushchiisia russkii publitsist XVIII veka," *Vestnik prava* 7 (1904): 1–27. Boltin had a superb library of Enlightenment books and translated the *Encyclopédie* to the letter *k*; see V. Iushkov, *Ocherk iz istorii russkago samosoznaniia XVIII-go veka. Obshchie istoricheskie vzgliady I. N. Boltina* (Kiev, 1912). Elagin was typical in the sources he used and cited throughout his *Opyt povestvovaniia*: Mably, Rousseau, Robertson, Hume, d'Alembert, Voltaire, and Pufendorf. Keenan agrees that Western culture was rapidly assimilated in this century, while Baehr disagrees: "The Trouble with Muscovy," 104; *Paradise Myth*, xi.

15. On this topic, please see Derbov, *Istoricheskie vzgliady*, 26–28.

16. Iu. M. Lotman and B. A. Uspenskii, "The Role of Dual Models in the Dynamics of Russian Culture," in Lotman and Uspenskii, *Semiotics of Russian Culture*, 35.

17. P. G. Daniel, *Histoire de France* (Paris, 1713), 1:xxiii, as quoted in Mousnier, *Institutions of France,* 2:3.

18. Emin, *Rossiiskaia istoriia,* 1:1–2.

19. The quotation is found in *Russkaia istoriografiia* (M, 1941), 138. On the broader implications of this topic, consult Rogger, *National Consciousness.*

20. As quoted in Mankiev, *Iadro,* i; and P. P. Shafirov, *Razsuzhdenie kakie zakon-nyia prichiny ego velichestvo Petr Velikii . . . k nachatiiu voiny protiv korolia Karla XII shvedskago 1700 godu imel* (Spb, 1722). For similar injunctions, see "Istoriia rossiiskaia s 1450 po 1617 (c. 1711)," SOII, *f.* 115, *n.* 543:45; Tatishchev, *Istoriia rossiiskaia* (1962), 1:81.

21. Lomonosov: "Report (21 June 1750)," *PSS* 6:79–80, "Zamechaniia na dissertatsiiu G.-F. Millera 'Proiskhozhdenie imeni i naroda rossiiskogo'," *PSS* 6:17–79, and *Drevniaia rossiiskaia istoriia,* 173–216. See also Walter Gleason, "The Course of Russian History According to an Eighteenth-Century Layman," *Laurentian University Review* 10 (1977): 17–29.

22. Catherine II, "Zapiski", and "Mnenie Gosudaryni Ekateriny II o tom, kak dolzhno pisat' Russkuiu istoriiu," *Ruskoi vestnik* 5 (1816): 4.

23. Boltin, *Leklerk,* 1:1. See also V. O. Kliuchevskii, "Lektsii po russkoi istoriografii," *Sochineniia* (M, 1959), 7:426; and K. A. Papmehl, "The Quest for the Nation's Cultural Roots in Russian Historiography Before Karamzin," in *Russia and the World of the Eighteenth Century,* ed. R. P. Bartlett, A. G. Cross, and Karen Rasmussen (Columbus, Ohio, 1988), 22–35. On Fréret, see G. P. Gooch, *History and Historians in the Nineteenth Century* (Boston, 1959), 13.

24. On this issue, consult Venturi, "History and Reform," 225–44.

25. Koselleck, *Critique and Crisis,* 130–31.

26. Voltaire, *Collection complète des oeuvres* (Geneva, 1768–1777), vol. 12:52 ("*L'Esprit des Lois* de M. de Montesquieu"), and vol. 30:455 ("Sommaire de l'histoire"); Émile Haumant, *La Culture française en Russie* (Paris, 1910), 110.

27. See, for instance, Hurwitz, "Metropolitan Hilarion's *Sermon,*" 322–33; and M. N. Tikhomirov, "Razvitie istoricheskikh znanii v Kievskoi Rusi . . . X–XVII vv.," in *Ocherki istorii istoricheskoi nauki v SSSR,* ed. M. N. Tikhomirov (M, 1955), 89–105.

28. "Istoriia o nachale russkoi zemli (1760–1761)," RO, *f.* 735, *n.* 178, *ll.* 41–46; "Nashestvie tatar v Rossiiu i rodoslovie velikikh kniazei rossiiskikh," SOII, *f.* 36, *op.* 1, *ll.* 451–61; SOII, "Letopisets, 1222–1555," *f.* 36, *op.* 1, *ll.* 129–440; "Letopisets kratkii do 1659 goda: Sbornik 1754 g.," Rumiantsev, RO, *f.* 256, *n.* 374, *ll.* 252–57; "Kratkii letopisets: Khronograf Dorofeia Monemvasiiskogo (1731)," RO, *f.* 178, *n.* 1256, *ll.* 334–56; "Vypiski iz letopistsa za 1154–1571 gg. (1784–1791)," RO, *f.* 151: 40–42 .

29. The exception was P. A. Zakhar'in (1750–1800), *Novyi sinopsis* (Nikolaev, 1798); for instance, "Russkaia istoriia (1758)," by Likhachev, *f.* 238, *n.* 1, SOII; "Letopisets rossiiskii (1756)," BRAN, 4.1: 1–660.

30. See, for instance, S. P. Sokovnin, *Opyt istoricheskago slovaria o vsekh v istinnoi pravoslavnoi greko-rossiiskoi vere sviatoiu neporochnuiu zhizniiu proslavivshikhsia muzhakh* (M, 1784); of the 177 saints, 34 were rulers.

31. Innokenti Gizel', *Sinopsis* (published in Kiev in 1674, 1678, 1680, and 1683; and in St. Petersburg in 1823, 1836, and 1861).

32. This brief book contains a wealth of insight. See T. V. Artem'eva, *Russkaia istoriosofiia XVIII veka* (Spb, 1996).

33. "Predislovie" to Feofan Prokopovich, *Istoriia Imperatora Petra Velikago ot rozhdeniia ego do Poltavskoi batalii* (Spb, 1773), n.p. For instance, the works of Peter

Krekshin (d. 1763) on Peter's birth and his glorious life and deeds all saw publication in the 1780s as did books of anecdotes and biographies of his chief aides. For just three examples, see Petr Velikii, *Tetrady i zapisnyia . . . 1704–1706* (Spb, 1774); F. O. Tumanskii, *Sobranie raznykh zapisok i sochinenii, sluzhashchikh k dostavleniiu polnago svedeniia o zhizni i deianiiakh gosudaria Imp. Petra Velikago*, 10 vols. (Spb, 1787–1788); and I. I. Golikov, *Deianiia Petra Velikago, mudrago preobraziteliia Rossii, sobrannyia iz dostovernykh istochnikov i raspolozhennyia po godam*, 30 vols. (M, 1788–1797).

34. Mal'gin, *Zertsalo*, 3.

35. G. Vasnetskii, *M. V. Lomonosov: Ego filosofskie i sotsial'no-politicheskie vzgliady* (M, 1954), 14–18.

36. Catherine II, "Istoricheskoe predstavlenie iz zhizni Riurika: Podrazhanie Shekspiru," *PSS* (Spb, 1893), 1:133; Mankiev, *Iadro*, 180–81; Mal'gin, *Zertsalo*, 28.

37. Tatishchev, "Kratkoe iz"iatie," 18–19; and Tatishchev's *Istoriia rossiiskaia* (1962), 1:87. Also consult A. I. Iukht, "V. N. Tatishchev o reformakh Petra I," *Obshchestvo i gosudarstvo feodal'noi Rossii*, ed. V. T. Pashuto (M, 1975), 209–18; in a similar vein, see Prokopovich, *Istoriia Petra Velikago*, written at the beginning of the century, not truly a history but a chronology.

38. Sumarokov, "Streletskii bunt," 179; Mal'gin, *Zertsalo*, 141–43; A. L. Shletser [Schlözer], *Izobrazhenie rossiiskoi istorii*, trans. N. Nazimov (Spb, n.d.).

39. As translated in Afferica, "Shcherbatov," 162.

40. Taken from the prologue of Otto of Freising's *Deeds of Frederick Barbarossa*, as quoted in Keenan, "The Trouble with Muscovy," 108.

41. Tatishchev, *Istoriia rossiiskaia* (1773), 2:460.

42. *Russkii biograficheskii slovar'* (NY, 1962), s.v. "Boltin."

43. "Predislovie k istoricheskoi knige, sostavlennoi po poveleniiu Tsaria Fedora Alekseevicha," in E. Zamyslovskii, *Tsartvovanie Fedora Alekseevicha* (Spb, 1871), appendix 4: xxxix. See also David Das, "History Writing and the Quest for Fame in Late Muscovy: Andrei Lyzlov's *History of the Scythians*," *Russian Review* 51 (1992): 502–9.

44. Lomonosov, *Drevniaia rossiiskaia istoriia*, 171, and "Posviashchenie k pervomu tomu 'Istorii rossiiskoi' V. N. Tatishcheva," *PSS* 6:15–16. See also P. Hoffmann, "Lomonosov als Historiker," *Jahrbücher für Geschichte der UdSSR und Volksdemokratischen Länder Europas* 5 (1961): 361–73. Tatishchev, *Istoriia rossiiskaia* (1768), 1:i–iv, and *Razgovor o pol'ze nauk i uchilishch* (M, 1887), 65 (written in 1733). Also consult Miliukov, *Glavnyia techeniia*, 21–30, 122–33.

45. Novikov, *Opyt istoricheskago slovaria*, 1–3.

46. D. E. Shoffen, *Istoriia slavnykh gosudarei i velikikh generalov* (Spb, 1765), 1.

47. Catherine II, "Zapiski," 50–51.

48. D. D. Shampai, "O tirazhakh 'Kratkogo rossiiskogo letopistsa s rodosloviem'," in *Literaturnoe tvorchestvo M. V. Lomonosova*, 282–85 (it was published in a *tirage* of 2,400, the largest in the century); on Novgorod, see "Gistoriia drevniaia rossiiskaia o kniazhei (1756)," BRAN, l6.4.1.

49. Children's literature was a new genre that appeared in the 1700s and, late in the century, began centering on Russian history. See F. O. Tumanskii, *Novyi detskii mesiatsoslov . . .* (Spb, 1787); *Nachertanie vseobshchei istorii v pol'zu . . . iunoshestva . . .* (M, 1794); *Istoricheskaia igra dlia detei . . .* (M, 1795); *Detskaia rossiiskaia istoriia, izdannaia v pol'zu obuchaiushchagosia iunoshestva* (Smolensk, 1797); *Kratkaia rossiiskaia istoriia . . . v pol'zu narodnykh uchilishch* (Spb, 1799); M. Berlinskii, *Kratkaia rossiiskaia istoriia, dlia upotrebleniia iunoshestvu . . .* (M, 1800).

50. For example, "Rodoslovie gosudarei rossiiskikh ot pervogo Riurika do tsaria

Feodorova Ivanovicha (c. 1750)," RGADA, *f.* 187, *op.* 2, *ed. khr.* 115, *l.* 2; "Sbornik: Otryvok iz rodoslovnoi velikikh kniazei i gosudarei do Ekateriny (1776)," RO, *f.* 218, *n.* 695, *ll.* 1–114; "Kniga rodoslovnaia (1765)," BRAN, 4.1.36: 182 pages of graphs; and "Nachalo kniazheniia rossiiskikh kniazei do Elizavetoi Petrovnoi," RO, *f.* 218, *n.* 676, *ll.* 26–52 .

51. Mankiev, *Iadro*, 181.

52. G. Baier, *O variagakh* (Spb, 1767). One might recall that when Andrei Amalrik espoused the Normanist theory in the Soviet era, it led to his arrest and exile.

53. On this question, consult the brief discussion in Artem'eva, *Istoriosofiia*, 16–25.

54. Catherine II, "Zapiski," 2:75, 78–79, 87–89, and her "Istoricheskoe predstavlenie," 120–21. On Riurik's new language, see Zakhar'in, *Novyi sinopsis*, 26; Mal'gin, *Zertsalo*, 2. Also consult A. S. C. Ross, "Tatishchev's 'Joachim Chronicle,'" *University of Birmingham Historical Journal* 3 (1951): 53–54.

55. "O tsariakh," SOII, *f.* 36, *op.* 1, *n.* 644, *ll.* 5–31; "Letopisets ot nachala russkoi zemli do tsaria Alekseia Mikhailovicha," RO, *f.* 310, *n.* 1283, *l.* 5; "Rodoslovnaia kniga velikikh i udel'nykh kniazei: 81 glava s tablitsami (1768)," RGADA, *f.* 181, *op.* 1, *ed. khr.* 176, *ll.* 1–7.

56. Lomonosov, *Letopisets*, 291–96, and *Drevniaia rossiiskaia istoriia*, 214–16; an anonymous historian claimed that Riurik built "over 100 cities" in "O prishestvii velikago kniazia Riurika na velikoe novogorodskoe kniazhenie i o velikikh kniaziakh i tsariakh prezhde byvshikh v Rossii (1768)," BRAN, 31.4.16: 23; similarly, Artem'ev, *Kratkoe nachertanie*, 121. See, for instance, the classic by Kirilov, *Tsvetushchee sostoianie*.

57. Gruder, "The Bourbon Monarchy," 364.

58. "Istoriia russkaia (c.1750)," BRAN, 32.13.1: 372–671; another allots 138 of its 213 pages to Peter, "Drevniaia rossiiskaia istoriia do 1710 goda (1786)," SOII, *f.* 11, *ed. khr.* 19; the anonymous historian wrote "Russkaia istoriia svodnaia (c.1750)," BRAN, 25.1.3: 42–179.

59. Mankiev, *Iadro*, 383–84.

60. Lomonosov is quoted in F. Ia. Priima, "Lomonosov i 'Istoriia rossiskoi imperii pri Petre Velikom' Vol'tera," *XVIII vek* 3 (1958): 183. Lomonosov was tutored by Christian Wolff but his views remained pedestrian; consult A. A. Morozov, "M. V. Lomonosov i teleologiia Kristiana Vol'fa," in *Literaturnoe tvorchestvo M. V. Lomonosova*, 163–96; M. I. Sukhomlinov, "Lomonosov, student Marburgskogo universiteta," *Russkii vestnik* 31 (1861), 127–65; Gleason, "Two Faces of the Monarch," 399–409; I. D. Martysevich, *Voprosy gosudarstva i prava v trudakh M. V. Lomonosova* (M, 1861), 127–65.

61. Foreigners who wrote histories of Russia tended to see Peter as a culmination of Russian history (for instance, Voltaire's *Histoire de l'empire de Russie sous Pierre le Grand*) or, later, Catherine in the same light (for instance Schlözer's *Tableau de l'histoire de Russie* of 1769).

62. Mankiev, *Iadro*, xi–xii; I. F. Bogdanovich (1743–1803), "Istoricheskoe izobrazhenie Rossii," *Sochineniia* (Spb, 1848), 2:169–70.

63. Lomonosov, *Letopisets*, 300, 319. Aleksandr Radishchev's preoccupation with Novgorod is evident in his historical jottings: "K rossiiskoi istorii," PSS (Spb, 1907), 3:31–40.

64. "Razsuzhdenie o rossiiskom i rimskom pravitel'stvakh," RO, *f.* 17, *n.* 343; E. K. Putnyn', *Istoki russkoi istoriografii antichnosti: M. V. Lomonosov, A. N. Radishchev* (Saratov, 1968); Allen McConnell, "Radishchev and Classical Antiquity," *Canadian-American Slavic Studies* 16 (1982): 469–90; Baehr, "From History to National Myth," 1–14.

65. Lomonosov, *Drevniaia rossiiskaia istoriia*, 171, 214–16, 220; for the monarch-legislator as a common theme, see Vilenskaia, "Ob osobennostiakh formirovaniia russkoi osvoboditel'noi mysli," 116–17.

66. Lomonosov, "Idei dlia zhivopisnykh kartin iz rossiiskoi istorii," *PSS* 6:371.

67. In 1993, I delivered an address on this topic to historians at the Academy of Sciences in Moscow, and the audience saw profound similarities between Boris Godunov and Boris Yeltsin.

68. "Russkaia letopis' s drevneishikh vremen do 1700 g. (1741)," RGADA, *f.* 181, *op.* 1, *ed. khr.* 358, *ll.* 1176–1255; Lomonosov, "Opisanie streletskikh buntov i pravleniia tsarevny Sof'i," *PSS* 6:100–131.

69. On his strange career, consult Beshenkovskii, "Zhizn' Fedora Emina," *XVIII vek* 11 (1976): 186–203, and his "Istoriograficheskaia sud'ba 'Rossiiskoi istorii' F. A. Emina," *Istoriia i istoriki* (M, 1973).

70. Epifanov, "'Uchenaia druzhina,'" 37–53; L. A. Petrov, *Obshchestvenno-politicheskie vzgliady Prokopovicha, Tatishcheva, i Kantemira* (Irkutsk, 1959).

71. P. Znamenskii, "Tatishchev i ego istoriia," *Trudy Kievskoi dukhovnoi akademii* 1 (1862): 197–228.

72. For instance, Pierre Louis Claude Gin's *Les Vrais principes de gouvernement* was published three times in the 1780s and offered a rationalist justification of absolutism.

73. Tatishchev, *Istoriia rossiiskaia* (1962), 1:359. On Prokopovich, see A. B. Prosina, "Teoreticheskoe obosnovanie F. Prokopovichem reform Petra I," *Vestnik Moskovskogo universiteta* 6 (1969): 63–71.

74. S. P. Rumiantsev, "Petr Velikii," *Sobesednik* 7 (1783): 173.

75. Pekarskii, *Nauka i literatura*, 255–57; Ustrialov, *Istoriia tsarstvovaniia Petra Velikago*, 298–304; Kantemir, *Satiry*, 32.

76. Tatishchev, *Razgovor*, 136–37, and *Istoriia rossiiskaia* (1962), 1:362, 371. In *Select Documents*, the editor, Paul Dukes, claims that Tatishchev influenced Montesquieu in this view, 18–19.

77. S. Pufendorf, *L'Introduction à l'histoire générale . . . où l'on voit . . . les interêts des souverains* (Amsterdam, 1743), translated into Russian and published in 1718, 1723, 1767, and 1777.

78. Tatishchev, *Istoriia rossiiskaia* (1962), 1:359–61, *Razgovor*, 135–40, and "Dve zapiski Tatishcheva," 371. Also see Emin, *Rossiiskaia istoriia*, 1:x.

79. Mankiev, *Iadro*, 18–27; Tatishchev, *Istoriia rossiiskaia* (1963), 2:33–34; Emin, *Rossiiskaia istoriia*, 1:38–39.

80. "Drevniaia rossiiskaia istoriia do 1710 goda (1786)," SOII, *f.* 11, *ed. khr.* 19, *l.* 35.

81. "Russkaia letopis' s drevneishikh vremen do 1700 g. (1741)," RGADA, *f.* 181, *op.* 1, *ed. khr.* 358, *l.* 707.

82. *The Antidote* (London, 1772), 110, 118, 120, 125.

83. Tatishchev, *Istoriia rossiiskaia* (1963), 2:33–34; Emin, *Rossiiskaia istoriia*, 1:38–39; "Russkaia istoriia ot Riurika do Ekateriny (c. 1735)," BRAN, 32.6.1: 1–16.

84. Tatishchev, "Razsuzhdenie," 369–79, *Istoriia rossiiskaia* (1962), 1:87, "Kratkoe iz"iatie," 18–19, and "Dve zapiski Tatishcheva," 369–71; Emin, *Rossiiskaia istoriia*, 1:27.

85. Tatishchev, *Istoriia rossiiskaia* (1768), 1:18, and *Istoriia rossiiskaia* (1963), 2:137–43.

86. Tatishchev, *Istoriia rossiiskaia* (1962), 1:366–67; Emin, *Rossiiskaia istoriia*, 2:522.

87. Korsakov, "Volynskii i ego 'konfidenty'," 28. Tatishchev made his argument in four places. See his *Istoriia rossiiskaia* (1962), 1:366–68, *Istoriia rossiiskaia*

(1964), 4: passim, *Razgovor,* 138–39, and "Razsuzhdenie," 370–73. On his commitment to enlightenment, see *Istoriia rossiiskaia* (1963), 2:78–81. In contrast, the older ecclesiastical histories were more concerned about the threat of Roman Catholicism replacing Russian Orthodoxy if Poland had succeeded in conquering Russia. See "Istoriia rossiiskaia 1740 g.," BRAN, 16.13.6: 396–419; "Gistoriia drevnyia rossiiskaia o kniazhiakh (1756)," BRAN, 16.4.1: 81–96; "Istoriia rossiiskaia (1715)," RO, 4698: 106–245.

88. For instance, I. V. Nekhachin never once used the title in 222 pages of a dictionary of Russia's rulers, *Istoricheskoi slovar' rossiiskikh gosudarei, kniazei, tsarei, imperatorov, i imperatrits* (M, 1793).

89. The question of whether there were limitations on the tsar's power has its own long history. See, for instance, Rowland, "Muscovite Literary Ideology," 125–55.

90. Gruder, "The Bourbon Monarchy," 364–65.

91. Boltin, *Leklerk,* 2:464, 471; also see V. S. Ikonnikov, *Istoricheskiia trudy Boltina* (St. Petersburg, 1902), 18–20. He attacked Nicholas LeClerc, *Histoire physique, morale, civile, et politique de la Russie ancienne et moderne,* 6 vols. (Paris, 1783–1794), which was based on P. S. Levecque, *Histoire de Russie,* 5 vols. (Paris, 1782–1783).

92. Catherine II, "Zapiski," I: 105, and her "Mnenie," 3–11; Boltin, *Leklerk* 2:1, 82–87, 172–73, 423–24.

93. Boltin, *Leklerk,* 1:306–10 and 2:17. Michael Cherniavsky makes much the same argument in "Ivan the Terrible as Renaissance Prince," *Slavic Review* 27 (1968), 195–211. Catherine II, *Antidot,* 296–97.

94. Catherine II, *Antidot,* 289–90.

95. For another example of this mentality, see Kol'berg, *Istoriia datskaia.*

96. Shcherbatov, *Istoriia rossiiskaia,* 1 (1794), xv, 280–81, and 2 (1805), 257; also see I. A. Fedosov, *Iz istorii russkoi obshchestvennoi mysli XVIII stoletiia: M. M. Shcherbatov* (M, 1967), 44–68.

97. Shcherbatov, *Istoriia rossiiskaia,* 2 (1783), 541–42; 5, pt. 2 (1786), 111; 6 (1790), 50–53; and 7, pt. 1 (1790), 262–64; and "Istoriia rossiiskaia (1766)," BRAN, 45.8.268: 9.

98. M. M. Shcherbatov, "Razsmotrenie o porokakh i samovlastii Petra Velikago," in "Raznyia sochineniia," *Chteniia v Imperatorskom obshchestve istorii i drevnostei rossiiskikh pri Moskovskom universitete* 1 (1860): 5–22; "Sostoianie Rossii do Petra Velikago," in "Raznyia sochineniia," 23–28. Shcherbatov calculates that, without Peter, Russia would have remained backward for another 210 (sic) years.

99. Shcherbatov, *Istoriia rossiiskaia,* 7 (1790), 131; 1 (1794), n.p.

100. The quotations are Elagin's, *Opyt povestvovaniia o Rossii,* 81, 166–67. Similar sentiments are expressed in "Istoriia rossiiskaia ot Ivana Groznago do kontsa XVII veka," SOII, *f.* 115, *ed. khr.* 91, *l.* 80; "Ob izbranii na tsarskii prestol Mikhaila Feodorovicha," SOII, *f.* 36, *op.* 1, *n.* 645, *ll.* 107–9; Boltin, *Shcherbatov,* 1:230–31, and *Leklerk,* 1:250–51; 2:289–90, 464, 471–75.

101. Shcherbatov, *Istoriia rossiiskaia,* 1 (1794), 191–92, 225; and 2 (1805), 5; Boltin, *Shcherbatov,* 1:176–78. For Boltin on Vladimir, see *Otvet general maiora Boltina na pis'mo kniazia Shcherbatova* (Spb, 1789), 129–30; E. A. Bolkhovitinov [Mitropolit Evgenii, 1767–1837], *Istoricheskoe obozrenie rossiiskago zakonopolozheniia* (Spb, 1826), v (originally published in 1797). Chebotarev, *Vstuplenie,* 19; "Svedeniia rossiiskoi imperii Professora Kharitona Chebotareva iz kabinetnykh bumag Imp. Ekaterine II," RGADA, *f.* 10, *op.* 1, *ed. khr.* 363 (n.d.), *ll.* 1–35.

102. Chebotarev, *Vstuplenie,* 4; Boltin, *Leklerk,* 2:476–78.

103. Kozel'skii, "Predislovie," in *Istoriia datskaia,* 2:40–42, 56–59.

104. Boltin, *Leklerk*, 1:316–18; 2:22–23, 104, 172, 206–9, 233–37, 251, 254–55, 330, 360–62.

105. Elagin, "Opyt povestvovaniia o Rossii (1790)," RGADA, *f.* 181, *ed. khr.* 34, pt. 1:1–28.

106. Bogdanovich, *Izobrazhenie*, 203. His history, he said, intended to "depict good examples," 153.

107. Zakhar'in, *Novyi sinopsis*, v.

108. Sumarokov, "Streletskii bunt," 192–97, 205, 218–19.

109. Catherine II, *Antidot*, 295.

110. Shcherbatov, *Istoriia rossiiskaia*, 5, pt. 3 (1786), 217.

111. Mankiev, *Iadro*, 190; "Istoriia rossiiskaia (1740)," BRAN, 16.13.6:386.

112. Shcherbatov, *Istoriia rossiiskaia*, 5, pt. 2 (1786), 91, 287–89; and pt. 3, 222–23, and "O samoderzhavstve gosudarei i tsarei vseia Rossii (1768)," BRAN, 31.4.16, II: 45–367.

113. Boltin, *Leklerk*, 2:467–71, 476–78, 522–23; Mal'gin, *Zertsalo*, 117.

114. Lomonosov, *Drevniaia rossiiskaia istoriia*, 233; Tatishchev, "Razsuzhdenie," 373; Boltin, *Leklerk*, 2:476–78, 355.

6: THE GOOD TSAR

1. Gorbachev made the impromptu remark while addressing a meeting of Soviet editors in 1988; he was quoted by Philip Taubman, "A Soviet Paradox," *New York Times*, 3 October 1988.

2. Please consult the introduction for numbers of publications, esp. notes 7, 8, 9, and 11.

3. Marker, *Publishing*, 11–12, 103; also see Bogoliubov, *Novikov*, 31–32.

4. For a discussion of the Russian "sacralization of the enlightened worldview," see Raffaella Faggionato, "From a Society of the Enlightened to the Enlightenment of Society: The Russian Bible Society and Rosicrucianism in the Age of Alexander I," *Slavonic and East European Review* 79 (2001): 461–87, quotation on p. 461. Also see Koselleck, *Critique and Crisis*, 130–31.

5. On these influences, consult Gleason, *Moral Idealists*, especially pp. 53–85; on the varieties of Pietist attitudes toward absolute rule, see Mary Fulbrook, "Religion, Revolution, and Absolutist Rule in Germany and in England," *European Studies Review* 12 (July 1982): 301–21.

6. Marker estimates that over 8,000 titles appeared, *Publishing*, 105; another scholar states that from 1725 to 1800, there were 8,952 books published, of these 3,591 were belles-lettres: V. V. Sipovskii, *Ocherki iz istorii russkago romana* (Spb, 1909), 1:34–35.

7. In the process, according to late-twentieth-century theorists, groups like the bourgeoisie were busily creating "social spaces," "public spheres," and "fellowships of discourse" that created "enunciative modalities" to communicate with "the sphere of public authority." Despite the lack of a sizeable bourgeoisie in Russia, many of these concepts may have some relevance to the Russian scene, which I hope future scholars might address. See Foucault, *Archaeology of Knowledge;* Habermas, *Structural Transformation of the Public Sphere;* Koselleck, *Critique and Crisis;* Wuthnow, *Communities of Discourse;* and Dülmen, *Society of the Enlightenment.*

8. Sipovskii, *Politicheskiia nastroeniia*, 35.

9. Raeff, *Origins of the Russian Intelligentsia*, 154.

10. Marker, *Publishing*, 206. For instance, Catherine herself published a primer that consisted of roughly two hundred maxims. See Catherine II, "Grazhdanskoe nachal'noe uchenie," *Sochineniia* (1849), 1:177–78.

11. "The Empress Catherine II's Notes on the *Journey*," in A. N. Radishchev, *A Journey from St. Petersburg to Moscow*, trans. Leo Weiner (Cambridge, Mass., 1958), 242.

12. Marcus Aurelius, *Zhitie i dela Marka Avreliia Antoniia, tsesaria rimskago* [hereafter *Zhitie . . . Avreliia*], trans. and annotated by S. Volchkov (Spb, 1789), 161; this biography was published by the Academy of Sciences in 1740, 1760, 1775, 1789, and 1798.

13. "Zvezda na lbu, ili znak dobrykh del," *Raznyia povestvovaniia: Sochinnenyia nekotoroiu rossiiankoiu* (Spb, 1779), 114.

14. N. Bulich, *Sumarokov i sovremennaia emu kritika* (Spb, 1854), 1.

15. As quoted in Arthur O. Lovejoy, *Reflections on Human Nature* (Baltimore, 1961), 197; also consult N. D. Chechulin, *Russkii sotsial'nyi roman XVIII veka* (Spb, 1900), 14.

16. M. M. Kheraskov, *Numa Pompilii, ili protsvetaiushchii Rim* (M, 1768), 161, and "Predislovie," n.p. Consult chap. 6, "The Rise of the Russian Utopia," in Baehr, *Paradise Myth*, 112–44.

17. Marker, *Publishing*, 233.

18. Jones, *Nikolay Novikov*, 61.

19. *SK*, 2:338–47 and 5:238–42; Paul Bushkovitch, *Religion and Society in Russia: The Sixteenth and Seventeenth Centuries* (Oxford, 1992), 150, 175.

20. P. R. Hart, "Neoclassicism," in *A Handbook of Russian Literature*, ed. Victor Terras (New Haven, 1985), 299.

21. Brown, *Eighteenth-Century Russian Literature*, 340.

22. "O teatre," *Zritel'* (June 1792): 126, 129.

23. It was published in 1747, 1767, and 1782 under the title *Pokhozhdenie Telemaka [The Adventures of Télémaque]*; appeared in verse by V. K. Trediakovskii in 1766, 1786, and 1788 as *Stranstvovaniia Telemaka* [The Travels of Télémaque] (in *Vsiakaia vsiachina*, Catherine recommended the latter as an antidote for insomnia); and in 1788, 1797, and 1800 it came out under the title *Prikliucheniia Telemaka [The Adventures of Télémaque]*. Bolotov's memoir is quoted in Bogoliubov, *Novikov*, 29. Soviet authors suggested Catherine saw the book as a threat, but she allowed its publication. See Gukovskii, *Russkaia literatura XVIII veka*, 69; also, please see A. S. Orlov, "'Tilemakhida' V. K. Trediakovskogo," *XVIII vek* (1935): 5–11.

24. Iu. D. Levin, "The English Novel in Eighteenth-Century Russia," in *Literature, Lives, and Legality in Catherine's Russia*, ed. A. G. Cross and G. S. Smith (Nottingham, England, 1994), 159. See M. Komarov, *Starinnyia pis'ma kitaiskago imperatora k rossiiskomu gosudariu* (M, 1787).

25. W. Gareth Jones, "Novikov's Naturalized *Spectator*," in *The Eighteenth Century in Russia*, ed. J. G. Garrard (Oxford, 1973), 151. Forty-two journals appeared during the reign; before 1762, Russia had only three newspapers (*Viedomosti*, 1702–1727, continued as *Sankt-Peterburgskiia viedomosti*, 1728–October 1917, and *Moskovskiia viedomosti*, 1756–1917) and two journals (*Ezhemesiachnyia sochineniia*, 1755–1764, and *Trudoliubivaia pchela*, 1759).

26. *Rastushchii vinograd*, which began publication in April 1785, is a good example. See "Domovaia zapiska o zaraze novomodnoi eresi i o sredstvakh iztseliagoshchikh ot onoi," *Rastushchii vinograd* (July 1786); O. P. Kozodavlev, "Razsuzhdenie o narodnom prosveshchenii," *Rastushchii vinograd* (April 1785): 64–100, (June 1785): 67–77, (July 1785): 61–75, and "Rech' o pol'ze matematiki," *Rastushchii vinograd* (June 1785): 16–39. Makogonenko describes the journal as organized propaganda in *Nikolai Novikov*, 6.

27. Jones, "Biography," 63, 67. *Lives* appeared in 1765, 1771, and 1789; also see Griffiths, "To Live Forever," 452.

28. S. N. Glinka , *Zapiski* (Spb, 1895); the memoir covers the years 1776 to 1825. D. I. Fonvizin, *Zhizn' grafa Nikity Ivanovicha Panina* (Spb, 1786). The definitive guide lists 96 memoirs, 60 of which covered Catherine's reign, and 57 diaries, 34 recording the empress's three-decade rule, Tartakovskii, *Russkaia memuaristika*, 244–61; 262–70.

29. Lortholary, *Le Mirage russe*, 106–7; also consult J. Renwick, "Marmontel, Voltaire, and the Bélisaire Affair," *Studies on Voltaire and the Eighteenth Century* 121 (1974): 397 pp., passim.

30. Marmontel, letter to Catherine, as quoted in Papmehl, *Freedom of Expression*, 35.

31. Venturi, *Utopia and Reform*, 127.

32. Marker, *Publishing*, 214–16, 233.

33. Papmehl, *Freedom of Expression*, 35.

34. See the discussion in Marc Raeff, "The Heterogeneity of the Eighteenth Century in Russia," in *Russia and the World*, 666–79.

35. Scholars who maintain the strength of the sacral image of the tsar include Cherniavsky, *Tsar and People;* Zhivov and Uspenskii, "Tsar' i bog," 47–154; and Uspenskii, *Tsar' i patriarkh: Kharizma vlasti v Rossii* (M, 1998). Baehr, who examines principally odes, likewise overemphasizes the godlike image of the Russian ruler in his *Paradise Myth*. On the complexities of the issue, consult I. F. Khudushina, *Tsar'. Bog. Rossiia: Samosoznanie russkogo dvorianstva (konets XVIII—pervaia tret' XIX vv.)* (M, 1995).

36. See, for instance, A. P. Sumarokov, "Son. Shchastlivoe obshchestvo," *Trudoliubivaia pchela* (December 1759): 740–41.

37. *Detskoe uchilishche* (Spb, 1783), 1–21, 235–36, quotations on pp. 21 and 236. From the French of Prince Bomont [de Beaumont], but redone and supplemented by Petr Svistunov.

38. "O teatre," *Zritel'* (August 1792): 273–74.

39. G. R. Derzhavin, *Stikhotvoreniia* (L, 1957); I have modified the translation in Segel, *Literature*, 261. Depending on the edition of the Old Testament, the psalm is 81 or 82.

40. G. Marmontel', *Velizer* (M, 1768). This edition, published by Moscow University Press, was republished twice more; another translation, *Velisarii*, sponsored by the Academy of Sciences, had four editions. For the quotations, I am using an English edition, M. Marmontel, *Belisarius* (London, 1773), 72. Another dozen of Marmontel's works were published in Russia during the century.

41. F. A. Emin, *Prikliucheniia Femistokla i raznyia politicheskiia, grazhdanskiia, filosoficheskiia, fizicheskiia, i voennyia ego s synom razgovory,* 2nd ed. (Spb, 1781), 29, italics in the original.

42. "Zvezda na lbu," 111.

43. G. R. Derzhavin, "Videnie murzy (1783)," *Stikhotvoreniia Derzhavina* (M, 1941), 35–37.

44. Ia. Kniazhnin, "Vadim Novgorodskii," *Sankt-Peterburgskii merkurii* 3 (August 1793), 138.

45. Sumarokov, "Son," 739.

46. Kheraskov, *Numa*, 161.

47. Bolotov, *Zhizn'*, 3:413.

48. N. Novikov, "Predislovie," *Moskovskoe ezhemesiachnoe izdanie* 2 (1781): 257–58.

49. I. A. Krylov, "Kaib: Vostochnaia povest'," *PSS* (Spb, 1847), 1:173–213. The tale was originally published in 1792 in the journal, *Zritel'*.

50. *PSZ* 18, no. 12,978 (27 September 1767); for nearly identical praise at nearly the same time, see V. A. Maikov, "Oda na novyi 1768 god," *Izbrannye proizvedeniia,* 190–94.

51. Marmontel, *Belisarius,* 171; M. M. Shcherbatov, "Puteshestvie v zemliu Ofirskuiu g'na S . . . Shvetskago dvorianina," *Sochineniia* (Spb, 1896), 1:979.

52. E. R. Dashkova, *The Memoirs of the Princess Daschkaw, Lady of Honour to Catherine II,* ed. Mrs. W. Bradford (London, 1840), 1:27, and "Nadpis'," *Sobesednik liubitelei rossiiskago slova* 1 (1783): 14.

53. N. M. Karamzin, *Pis'ma russkogo puteshestvennika* (L, 1984), 199. Published in 1789.

54. I. M. Shaden, *Slovo o dushe zakonov* (M, 1767), 14 (23 April 1767); Kh. A. Chebotarev, *Velichie, mogushchestvo i slava Rossii* (M, 1795), 21 (30 June 1795); *Noveishee povestvovatel'noe zemleopisanie . . . dlia maloletnykh detei . . .* (Spb, 1795), 135–38; Tikhon (Malinin), *Slovo na den' tezoimenitstva . . . Ekateriny. . . .* (Spb, 1790).

55. Plavil'shchikov, "Riurik," *Sochineniia,* 1:14 (act 2, sc. 1).

56. Sumarokov, "Dmitrii," *Polnoe sobranie,* 4:101 (act 3, sc. 5).

57. *Zhitie . . . Avreliia,* 77.

58. Tikhon, *Slovo na . . . den' vosshetsviia na prestol . . .* (Spb, 1791), 1–5; Radishchev put this even more starkly in his *Journey,* 199–201; Kheraskov's third novel also makes the same points, *Polidor, syn Kadma i Garmonii* (M, 1794), republished in 1801 and 1806.

59. V. Levshin, "Noveishee puteshestvie," *Sobesednik liubitelei rossiiskago slova* (1784), 13:138–66; 14:5–33; 15:35–47.

60. Catherine II, "Istoricheskoe predstavlenie iz zhizni Riurika," 1:136 (act 4, sc. 1), 132 (act 3, sc. 3).

61. Bogdanovich, *Sochineniia,* vol. 1 (Spb, 1848), "Sugubnoe blazhenstvo," 169–96, and "Poema, Blazhenstvo narodov," 199–212. The dedications are on pp. 171–74 and 200–203.

62. Bogdanovich, "Sugubnoe blazhenstvo," 181, 192, 196, and "Blazhenstvo narodov," 212; similarly, see his "Oda . . . Ekaterine . . . na novyi 1765 god," *Sochineniia,* 1:252–56, and "Stikhi k muzam na tsarskoe selo," 1:291–92.

63. A. I. Zaozerskii, "A. R. Vorontsov: K istorii byta i nravov XVIII v.," *Istoricheskie zapiski* 23 (1947): 120–25.

64. A. M. Turgenev, "Zapiski," *Russkaia starina* 61 (1889): 210, and 62 (1889): 61.

65. Soviet scholars constantly complained about immaturity, tsarist illusions, and naïve monarchism; even Western scholars saw "little more than a vehicle for 'enlightened' propaganda" in the literature. See L. A. Derbov, *Obshchestvennopoliticheskie i istoricheskie vzgliady N. I. Novikova* (Saratov, 1974), 215; Brown, *Eighteenth-Century Russian Literature,* 340. A very recent example of this tendency to rue the elite's support for monarchy can be found in E. N. Marasinova, "Obraz imperatora v soznanii elity rossiiskogo dvorianstva poslednei treti XVIII veka (po materialam epistoliarnykh istochnikov)," in Gorskii, *Tsar' i tsarstvo,* 141–77.

66. P. Gol'bakh, *Sistema prirody* (M, 1940), 430. Published in Paris in 1770, *Le Système de la nature ou des lois du monde physique et du monde morale.*

67. Derzhavin, "Felitsa (1782)," *Sochineniia Derzhavina* (1831), 2:2; also see Shcherbatov, "Puteshestvie," 946.

68. "Biblioteka Korolia indiiskogo," *Rastushchii vinograd* (January 1786): 90.

69. *Zhitie . . . Avreliia,* 3.

70. T. Kipiiak, "Predislovie," in Zh. Giber, *Zhizn' i deianiia Fridrika Velikago, korolia prusskago,* trans. T. Kipiiak, from the German (Spb, 1788), xliii.

71. S. N. Glinka, *Selim i Roksana, ili Prevratnost' zhizni chelovecheskoi* (M, 1798), 13–23, quotation on p. 21.

72. P. Iu. L'vov, *Rossiiskaia Pamela, ili Istoriia Marii* (Spb, 1789), 127–28, 131.

73. Fonvizin, "Naidennoe v bumagakh . . . Panina," in Shumigorskii, *Imperator Pavel I*, appendix, 11.

74. N. P. Nikolev, "Sorena i Zamir (1784)," in *Stikhotvornaia tragediia kontsa XVIII–nachala XIX v.*, ed. V. A. Bochkarev (L, 1964), 309 (act 5, sc. 2).

75. Catherine II, "Skazka o Tsareviche Khlore," in Pypin, ed., *Sochineniia*, 1:279–96.

76. The literature on Russian Masonry is enormous, but the classics include A. N. Pypin, *Russkoe masonstvo XVIII i pervaia chetvert' XIX v.* (Petrograd, 1916); G. V. Vernadskii, *Russkoe masonstvo v tsarstvovanie Ekateriny II* (Petrograd, 1917); T. Bakounine, *Le Répertoire biographique des francs maçons russes (XVIIIe et XIXe siècles)* (Brussels, 1940). Also consult a new and first-rate addition: Douglas Smith, *Working the Rough Stone: Freemasonry and Society in Eighteenth-Century Russia* (DeKalb, Il, 1999).

77. Vernadskii, *Russkoe masonstvo*, 125–26; also see the excellent article of Isabel de Madariaga, "Freemasonry in Eighteenth-Century Russian Society," in her *Politics and Culture in Eighteenth-Century Russia*, 150–67; for other membership statistics see p. 156.

78. In-Ho L. Ryu, "Moscow Freemasons and the Rosicrucian Order: A Study in Organization and Control," in *The Eighteenth Century in Russia*, p. 198, 200–201; M. N. Longinov, *Novikov i moskovskie martinisty* (M, 1867), 6–7; a typical title would be A. Izmailov, *Evgenii, ili Pagubnyia sledstviia durnago vospitaniia i soobshchestva [Evgenii, or The Pernicious Results of a Bad Upbringing and Keeping Bad Company]* (Spb, 1799).

Catherine, with her rational and skeptical mind, denigrated Masonry's mystical bent as the "ravings of the insane" and "clear nonsense," and its penchant for secret ceremony as a "mixture of ritual and children's games." See A. O. Kruglyi, "I. P. Elagin: Biograficheskii ocherk," *Ezhegodnik imperatorskikh teatrov* 2 (1893–1894): 109; "Pis'ma Ekateriny Vtoroi k baronu Grimmu (12 January 1794)," *Russkii arkhiv* 3 (1878): 62, and 10 (1878): 208. The empress also distrusted the Masons' transnational network as a competing political allegiance. However, the group posed no threat to monarchy, for an essential part of the dogma stipulated a "trust in authority," and members "never dreamed of going against the existing order." See Longinov, *Novikov*, 6–7; Pypin, *Russkoe masonstvo*, 6–7.

79. M. M. Kheraskov, *Vladimir vozrozhdennyi. Epicheskaia poema* (M, 1785); Kheraskov is quoted in Brown, *Eighteenth-Century Russian Literature*, 262.

80. Baehr, *Paradise Myth*, 104–6, also see his discussion of Kheraskov's "Golden Wand," 100–103.

81. Raeff, "Ideology of M. M. Shcherbatov," 376–77. In the late 1770s, some Russian Masons abandoned natural law theories and the contract theory of government for the dreamy political thought of Louis Claude de St. Martin; although officials regarded his teachings with hostility, he preached adherence to a patriarchal authority, who because of his higher qualities could alone "establish the felicity of his subjects." St. Martin's book, *Des erreurs et de la vérité*, was published in Russia in 1785 by Ivan Lopukhin, under the title *O zabluzhdeniiakh i istine*. It was withdrawn from sale, along with five other titles of a Masonic content, by an edict of 27 March 1786. See Vernadskii, *Russkoe masonstvo*, 163–66, 223; *SK*, 3:108.

A publishing partner of Novikov, Ivan Lopukhin, in a Masonic catechism, asked: "What is the responsibility of the true Freemason in regard to his sovereign? He ought to respect the tsar, hold him in awe, and obey him, not only if he is good and gentle, but even if he is difficult." In fact, Lopukhin's views iterated Catherine's; he revered rule by law but, because sovereigns remained the source of law, he warned subjects not to demand constitutional guarantees: The catechism is quoted in Bogoliubov, *Novikov,* 221; I. V. Lopukhin, *Blagost' i preimushchestvo edinonachalia* (M, 1795), 9. The book was also published in 1794 under the titles, *Izobrazhenie mechty ravenstva* and *Izliianie serdtsa.* Lopukhin also published *Izobrazhenie mechty ravenstva i buinoi svobody, s pagubnymi ikh plodami* (M, 1794). His *Novoe nachertanie istinnyia teologii* (Spb, 1784) presents the outline of a utopia similar to Ophir, but headed by a "holy tsar."

82. P. Iu. L'vov, *Khram istiny, ili Videnie Sezostrisa, tsaria egipetskago* (Spb, 1790), 8.

83. Please see the superb discussion in Lovejoy, *Reflections,* passim.

84. Griffiths, "To Live Forever," 447, 449, 453, and also see his "Catherine II: The Republican Empress," 340.

85. "Zvezda na lbu," 101–14.

86. Montesquieu, *Spirit of the Laws,* 24–25 (book 3, chaps. 6–7). Levshin also told the story of one Balamir, sovereign of the Unny, who did good deeds but only "to glorify his own name"; he is forgiven for not operating from higher motives, see V. A. Levshin, *Russkiia skazki* (M, 1780–1783), 10:3–8.

87. Baehr, *Paradise Myth,* 112. The story is told that someone asked Prime Minister Benjamin Disraeli how much to praise Queen Victoria's actions in order to please her; he responded, "Lay it on with a trowel."

88. *Drevniaia rossiiskaia vivliofika* (1773), 1; the journal was published until 1775.

89. Shcherbatov, "Puteshestvie," 979–80, 889–90, and *On the Corruption of Morals,* 241.

90. Children's books, though, tended to offer uncritical praise and, when enumerating Russian rulers, only stressed their positive qualities. See, for instance, *Iunosti chestnoe zertsalo, ili Pokazanie k zhiteiskomu obkhozhdeniiu* (Spb, 1717), the first children's book printed in Russia; *Nastavlenie mladentsam. Moral', istoriia, i geografiia* (Spb, 1774); *Detskii magazin, ili Sobranie poleznykh sochinenii, sootvetstvuiushchikh detskomu vozrastu* (M, 1788), from the French; P. Zakhar'in, *Put' k blagonraviiu, ili Sokrashchennoe nastavlenie obuchaiushchemusia iunoshestvu* (M, 1793).

91. See, for instance, V. P. Petrov: "K . . . iz Londona," *Poety XVIII veka* (L, 1936), 273–74, and "Oda na karusel'," *Poety,* 258. Please see the chapter on Petrov's ode celebrating the Treaty of Kuchuk-Kainardji (1774) in Andrei Zorin, *Kormia dvuglavogo orla: Literatura i gosudarstvennaia ideologiia v Rossii v poslednei treti XVIII— pervoi treti XIX veka* (M, 2001), 67–94. Also consult Brown, *Eighteenth-Century Russian Literature,* 271–74; and Gukovskii, *Russkaia literatura XVIII veka,* 283–87.

92. G. R. Derzhavin, "Videnie murzy (1783)," *Stikhotvoreniia Derzhavina,* 35–37.

93. "Zapiski Derzhavina (1743–1812)," *Sochineniia Derzhavina* (Spb, 1871), 6:631, 635, 650, 653, 677, 681. The cycle included "Felitsa (1782)," *Sochineniia,* 2:1–9; "Videnie murzy (1782)," *Stikhotvoreniia Derzhavina,* 32–37; "Blagodarnost' Felitse (1783)," *Sochineniia,* 2:9–10; and "Izobrazhenie Felitsy (1789)," *Sochineniia,* 2:36–51.

94. Fonvizin, "Lisitsa-koznodei: Basnia," *PSS* (Spb, 1914), 141–42; I have relied upon the translation in Brown, *Eighteenth-Century Russian Literature,* 221–22. All the conceits were common at the time; for instance, Sumarokov praised Catherine as "a woman worthy of altars" in "Oda na pervyi den' 1767 goda," *Polnoe sobranie,* 2:90.

95. Chechulin, *Memuary, ikh znachenie i mesto v riadu istoricheskikh istochnikov* (Spb, 1891), 9.

96. Kliuchevskii, "Imperatritsa Ekaterina II," as quoted in Bogoliubov, *Novikov,*

8. See, for instance, A. A. Poletika, "Dnevnik," *Syn otechestva* 3 (1842): 14, 18 (1787); I. M. Dolgorukii, "Zapiski," *Sochineniia* (Spb, 1849), 2:490–92 (1760–1806).

97. Examples abound: Platon (Levshin), *Slovo pri zalozhenii Imp. Akademii khudozhestv i pri nei tserkvi* (Spb, 1765) and *Slovo . . . nad grobom Petra Velikago . . .* (Spb, 1770); F. G. Karin, *Slovo na torzhestvo mira s Portoiu Otomanskoiu* (M, 1775); A. A. Barsov, "Slovo (2 July 1771)," in *Rechi . . . russkimi professorami*, 50–72; A. Perepechin, *Oda . . . Ekaterine* (M, 1767), unpaginated (28 January 1767); I. Iankovich de Mirievo, *Oda . . . Ekaterine* (Spb, 1791), unpaginated (1 January 1791).

98. I. Vinogradov, "Oda . . . Ekaterine Velikoi na uchrezhdenie gosudarstvennago zaemnago banka," *Rastushchii vinograd* (August 1786): 1–8; Platon (Levshin), "V den' . . . v prekhozhdenii ospy . . . ," *Prodolzhenie* (Spb, 1769), 3:32–43 (22 Nov 1768); I. Teil's, *Slovo na den' vseradostnago ot previvaniia ospy . . .* (n.p., 1771); Mirievo, *Oda . . . Ekaterine*. The most typical journals include: *Sobranie novostei* (1775–1776), ed. I. F. Bogdanovich; *Sankt-Peterburgskii vestnik* (1778–1781), ed. G. L. Braiks; *Sobesednik liubitelei rossiiskago slova* (1783–1784), ed. O. P. Kozodavlev; *Lekarstvo ot skuki i zabot* (1786–1787), published by F. O. Tumanskii; *Rastushchii vinograd* (1785–1787), ed. E. V. Syreishchikov; *Sankt-Peterburgskii merkurii* (1793), ed. I. A. Krylov.

99. Gavriil (Shaposhnikov), *Slovo na . . . den' koronovaniia . . . Ekateriny . . .* (Spb, 1773), 7–8, 12; G. Lukashevich, *Oda . . . Ekaterine . . .* (M, 1775); Amvrosii (Podobedov), *Slovo v den' Preobrazheniia Gospodnia* (M, 1774); Ioasaf (Zabolotskii), *Slovo vo vtoruiu nedeliu velikago posta* (Spb, 1779). Professors, more than other writers, referred to the empress as "chosen by God" and praised her more often for conquests: "Slovo pokhval'noe . . . Ekaterine . . . ," in *Rechi . . . russkimi professorami*, 244 (22 April 1773); M. I. Afonin, *Slovo pokhval'noe . . . Ekaterine . . .* (M, 1774), (24 April 1774); S. G. Zybelin, "Pokhval'noe slovo . . . Ekaterine. . . . (30 June 1787), in *Rechi . . . russkimi professorami*, 131–69; Barsov, "Slovo," 50–72.

100. This was a theme in an entire issue of *Sobranie novostei* (September and October, 1775); A. Fialkonskii, "Tsvetushchee sostoianie Rossii," *Rastushchii vinograd* (January 1786): 6–13.

101. F. A. Emin, *Nepostoiannaia fortuna, ili Pokhozhdenie Miramonda* (Spb, 1763), 3:349–51.

102. Emin, *Prikliucheniia Femistokla*, passim, quotations on pages 240 and 325. Republished in 1781.

103. The poem attracted Dashkova's attention, and she published it in a journal dedicated to instilling among readers the notion of the progressive role of monarchy. See "Oda k premudroi Kirgizkaisatskoi Tsarevne Felitse," *Sobesednik liubitelei rossiiskogo slova* 1 (1783): 6–14.

104. Derzhavin, "Felitsa," 6–7.

105. The book was read in every classroom and awarded as a school prize and hence became part of most libraries. Catherine II, *O dolzhnostiakh cheloveka i grazhdanina*, 133.

106. Marmontel, *Belisarius*, 90–93, 132–33, 146.

107. L. N. Engel'gardt, *Zapiski, 1766–1836* (M, 1867), 192–93; I. M. Dolgorukii, *Kapishche moego serdtsa, ili Slovar' vsekh tekh lits, s koimi ia byl v raznykh otnosheniiakh . . .* (M, 1890), 2. Catherine II is the first entry in the *Dictionary*.

108. Chulkov, *Peresmeshnik* (1789), 3:11 (published previously in 1766–1768 and 1783–1785).

109. Kheraskov, *Numa*, 46, and *Rossiada: Iroicheskaia poema* (M, 1779), 172–73; Shcherbatov, "Puteshestvie," 980.

110. *Zhitie . . . Avreliia*, 84–85.

111. I. I. Khemnitser, "Dobryi tsar'," *Polnoe sobranie basen' i skazok* (Spb, n.d.), 88–89, as translated in Segel, *Literature*, 2:252; on the many problems facing judicial reform, consult Wortman, *Russian Legal Consciousness*, 8–33.

112. "Sobranie parliamentskikh chlenov" (April 1776): 37–75; "Primechaniia sobrannie I. Bogdanovichem o Germanskikh pravakh" (November 1776): 3–24; "Rech'" (November 1776): 40–45; all from *Sobranyia novostei*.

113. *Zhizn' Imperatritsy Marii Terezii, materi tsarstvuiushchago nyne Imperatora Iosifa II* (Spb, 1789), 33–36.

114. A. S. Shishkov, "Dostopamiatnyia skazaniia ob Imperatritse Ekaterine Velikoi," RO, *f.* 862, *ed. khr.* 4, pp. 26, 37.

115. V. A. Maikov, "Oda na sluchai izbraniia deputatov . . . 1767 goda," *Izbrannye proizvedeniia*, 198–201.

116. "Pis'mo," *Zhivopisets* (1772). In just two issues of this weekly, four poems in praise of Catherine appeared; they are reprinted in P. N. Berkov, *Satiricheskie zhurnaly N. I. Novikova* (M, 1951), 361–65, 371–78, 386–92, 443.

117. "Pis'mo," *Zhivopisets* (1772), reprinted in Berkov, *Zhurnaly*, 359–60; also see "Perevod . . . iz Neapolia 1771 goda," *Zhivopisets* (1772), reprinted in Berkov, *Zhurnaly*, 324–26.

118. Levshin, *Skazki*, 10:9–12.

119. *Istoriia Elisavety, korolevy angliiskoi*, trans. from the French by A. Roznotovskii (Spb, 1795), 1:14–15. Journals also set up Catherine as an example of European women having more extensive freedom than, say, their sisters in Muslim countries. See "Noveishiia izvestiia o zhenshchinakh," *Sankt-Peterburgskii merkurii* 3 (August 1793): 243–66.

120. M. M. Kheraskov, *Kadm i Garmoniia* (M, 1789), 25–26, and "Oda eia Imperatorskomu Velichestvu (28 June 1764), *Tvoreniia*, 7:99–108; Catherine II, *O dolzhnostiakh*, 166–69; *Poleznoe uprazhnenie iunoshestva, sostoiashchee v raznykh sochineniiakh i perevodakh, izdannykh pitomtsami Vol'nago blagorodnago pansiona, uchrezhdennago pri Imperatorskom Moskovskom universitete* (M, 1789), 308.

121. *Poleznoe uprazhnenie*, 313; *Nravouchenie* (M, 1790), 2, 165–70, from the French.

122. *Polnyi vseobshchii pis'movnik*, 3rd edition (M, 1805), 36, 39, 41.

123. Levshin, *Skazki*, 5:116.

124. Sumarokov, "Son." Three such "dreams" appeared soon after in other journals. See Gleason, "Political Ideals," 567–68 and n. 45.

125. *Nravouchenie*, 146–49; similarly, see "Iskusstvo pravit' gosudarstvom, ili Nastavlenie prestarelago Persidskago Monarkha synu ego," *Pokoiashchiisia trudoliubets* 1 (1784): 117–23.

126. *Nizverzhennyi Zelul, obrazets zloby, ili Zhizn' i redkiia prikliucheniia vostochnago printsa Kleoranda i printsessy Zefizy* (M, 1794), 1:18–25; 2:153.

127. Radishchev, *Journey*, 198.

128. Ioasaf (Zabolotskii), *Slovo v den' novago goda* (Spb, 1781), 9 (read in front of Catherine at the Winter Palace on New Year's Day); N. Kurganov, "Kratkiia zamyslovatiia povesti," *Pis'movnik* 2: 178; *Zhitie . . . Avreliia*, passim. Journals also carried short biographies of laudable kings who were always handsome, just, good warriors, and loved children. See "Istoriia Karla Velikago," *Rastushchii vinograd* (April 1785): 44–50, and (May 1785): 25–34.

129. Kheraskov, *Numa*, 38–40, 49; Iakov Kozel'skii, the Russian philosopher, also translated, for Paul's benefit, a book devoted largely to the elevation of Numa as

an ideal. See *Istoriia slavnykh gosudarei i velikikh generalov,* comp. E. Shofin, trans. Ia. Kozel'skii (Spb, 1765).

130. Chulkov, *Peresmeshnik,* 3:6–11.

131. F. O. Tumanskii, *Sozertsanie slavnyia zhizni sviatago blagovernago velikago kniazia Aleksandra Iaroslavicha Nevskogo* (Spb, 1789), 5, 8.

132. Kheraskov, *Kadm,* 25–26, 34–35, 51–53; also published in 1786, 1793, 1801, and 1807.

133. Arsenii [V. I. Vereshchagin], *Slovo o istinnoi slave* (M, 1779), 5–6 (24 November 1779). This theme was commonplace in sermons, for example, Gennadii [Chelnokov], *Slovo . . . pri otkrytii Imp. Vospitatel'nago doma v Moskve* (M, 1764), 4–5; L. Fedotovich, *Slovo na den' rozhdeniia . . . Pavla . . .* (Spb, 1790); Damaskin, *Slovo v . . . den' vozshestviia na . . . prestol . . . Ekateriny Alekseevny* (Spb, 1792); Platon, "Slovo v den' rozhdeniia . . . Vysochestva," 5–7, and "Slovo v den' . . . tezoimenitstva . . . Vysochestva," 30–31, in *Prodolzhenie,* 2 (Spb, 1767). A prelate who called for imperial expansionism in a sermon of 1787 was noted as an exception in Poletika, "Dnevnik," 14, 18. Also see *Razgovory o fizicheskikh i nravstvennykh predmetakh* (M, 1800), 256; the book was intended for the children of the University Noble Pension.

134. Fénelon, *Adventures of Telemachus,* 1:133 (book 4).

135. *Dvorianskoe uchilishche, ili Nravouchil'nye razgovory . . . v pol'zu blagorodnago rossiiskago iunoshestva* (Spb, 1764), 15–17; G. Mabli [Mably], *Razmyshleniia o grecheskoi istorii, ili o prichinakh blagodenstviia i neschastii grekov,* trans. A. Radishchev (Spb, 1773), 167; Glinka, *Selim,* 21; "O teatre," 273–74.

136. *Istoriia, ili Opisanie zhizni Karla XII, korolia shvedskago,* trans. P. Pomerantsev (Spb, 1777), 93, from the German. V. P. Petrov, "Istoriia Karla Velikago," *Rastushchii vinograd* (April 1785): 44–50 and (May 1785): 25–34.

137. L'vov, *Khram istiny,* 12.

138. Levshin, *Skazki,* 6:85.

139. V. A. Maikov, "Voina," *Izbrannye proizvedeniia,* 229–33, as translated in Brown, *Eighteenth-Century Russian Literature,* 278.

140. M. Popov, *Slavenskiia drevnosti, ili Prikliucheniia slavenskikh kniazei* (M, 1771), 2:3. The novel was republished in 1778, 1793, and 1794 under the title *Starinnyia dikovniki.*

141. "Pis'mo XX," *Pochta dukhov* 2 (1789): 108–17.

142. Khemnitser, "Pes i l'vy," *Polnoe sobranie stikhotvorenii* (M, 1963), 149–50. Khemnitser wrote over 100 fables and tales, and collections were published in 1779 and 1782. They feature a number of stories about lion/monarchs.

143. Desnitskii, *Slovo na . . . den' vosshestviia . . . ,* republished in *Rechi . . . russkimi professorami,* 2:325–37. Also see E. I. Kostrov, *Oda na . . . den' vosshestviia. . . .* (M, 1780), 5, 8 (28 June 1780); Gennadii, *Slovo,* 4–5; Fedotovich, *Slovo;* Damaskin, *Slovo;* Sumarokov, "Oda v den' koronovaniia Eia (22 September 1770)," *Polnoe sobranie* 2: 101–4.

144. Domashnev, "Son."

145. Shcherbatov, "Puteshestvie," 980, 1004. For similar sentiments, see "Rech' kotoruiu odin razumnoi chelovek iz garamantov k Aleksandru velikomu," trans. D. Anichkov, *Poleznoe uveselenie* (September 1761): 81–91; A. Vershnitskii, "Rech' Marka Avreliia . . . k synu svoemu i nasledniku prestola," *Dobroe namerenie* (September 1764): 429–32 and (October 1764): 449–75.

146. This, I think, is the earliest version of Sergei Uvarov's famous tripartite formula, which he coined in 1832, "Orthodoxy, Autocracy, Nationality." Besides using the formula, Teil's was one of the few to refer to Catherine as an autocrat, rather

than empress, sovereign, or tsar, in his *Slovo na den'*, 17; Zabelin, a professor of chemistry at Moscow University, was another whose work expressed such a point of view, in his "Pokhval'noe slovo." For praise of Catherine's conquests, see Iu. I. Kanits, *Slovo v publichnom sobranii pri kazanskikh gimnaziiakh po vosstanovlenii obshchago pokoia* (M, 1775); a similar fountain of praise is Afonin's *Slovo pokhval'noe . . . Ekaterine. . . .* On these issues, consult Zorin, *Ideologiia*, 33–94.

147. Kheraskov, *Rossiada*. The epic was republished in 1786 and dedicated to Catherine also for her generosity to all her subjects and to the poet in particular; the 1786 printing was subtitled *Poema epicheskaia*. Also see Zorin, *Ideologiia*, 95–156.

148. Baehr, "From History to National Myth," 6.

149. Kheraskov, *Numa*, 1 and 176, the same thoughts are expressed on pp. 24, 49, 55, 109–14.

150. Derzhavin, *Zapiski iz izvestnykh vsem proisshestvii i podlinnykh del, zakli-uchaiushchie v sebe zhizn'* (M, 1860), 319 and passim.

151. In the seventeenth century, the most popular book and the model for *Télémaque* was a political allegory whose theme attacked favorites in Europe in general but in the French courts in particular. See John Barclay, *Argenis* (London, 1621); it was translated into all European languages. Trediakovskii translated it into Russian in 1751, and it was published by the Academy of Sciences as *Argenida, povest' geroich-eskaia* (Spb, 1751).

152. L'vov, *Pamela*, 128.

153. Khemnitser, "Lev, uchredivshii sovet," *Polnoe sobranie*, 79–80.

154. P. Zakhar'in, *Arfakad, Khaldeiskaia vymyshlennaia povest'* (M, 1793–1796), 2:233–34 and 5:102. Published again in Nikolaev in 1798.

155. "Razgovor: Ia i *Truten'*," *Truten'* 32 (1 December 1769), reprinted in Berkov, *Zhurnaly*, 163; for instance, Novikov criticized courtiers stridently twice in one issue, "Portrety," and "V novoi god novoe shchastie," *Truten'* (January 1770): 230, 241.

156. Levshin, *Skazki*, 10:216.

157. Baker, "French Political Thought," 66.

158. A small sampling of such tales might include *Detskoe uchilishche* (Spb, 1783), 1–21; I. I. Dmitriev, "Tsar' i dva pastukha. Basn' XX," *Sochineniia* (M, 1810), 123; Krylov, "Kaib," 173–213; "Alibei, vostochnaia povest'," *Sankt-Peterburgskii vest-nik* (June 1778): 448–55; "Amelige, vostochnaia povest'," *Sankt-Peterburgskii vestnik* (December 1779): 403–10; "Pis'mo XLV," *Pochta dukhov* 4 (1789): 103–28.

159. Shcherbatov, "Puteshestvie," 847.

160. Khemnitser, "Slepoi lev," *Basni i skazki* (Spb, 1811), 132–33.

161. "Chenzia, kitaiskogo filosofa, dannoi ego gosudariu," *Truten'*, trans. A. L. Leont'ev (23 February 1770), reprinted in Berkov, *Zhurnaly*, 209–10; "Pis'mo XLV," *Pochta dukhov* 4 (1789): 103–28, quotation on p. 128.

162. "Skazka," *Detskoe uchilishche*, 1–21.

163. "Amelige," *Sankt-Peterburgskii vestnik*, 403–10.

164. D. V. and I. V. Nekhachin, *Novoe kratkoe poniatie o vsekh naukakh, ili Det-skaia nastol'naia uchebnaia kniga* (M, 1796–1797), 3:7–8.

165. Marmontel, *Belisarius*, 95–96.

166. Kheraskov, *Rossiada*, passim.

167. "Predislovie," in Giber, *Zhizn' Fridrika*, xx.

168. P. Zakhar'in, *Prikliuchenie Kleandra* (Nikolaev, 1788), 1–3; republished in 1793 and 1798.

169. Novikov, "O dobrodeteli," *Utrennii svet* 9 (July 1780).

170. Maksim Tirskii, "Platonicheskago filosofa: Chetvertoe razsuzhdenie," *Trudoliubyvaia pchela* (July 1759): 408–10; Shcherbatov, "Puteshestvie," 751.

171. "Chenzia," in Berkov, *Zhurnaly,* 210.

172. Marmontel, *Belisarius,* 100.

173. "Alibei," 448–55 (see n. 158 above).

174. Dmitriev, "Tsar' i dva pastukha," 123.

175. Zakhar'in, *Arfakad,* 2:233–34 and 5:102.

176. On this topic, consult Alexander, *Catherine the Great,* 201–26.

177. *Istoriia Elisavety,* 1:vi, ix; "Pechal'nye sledstviia nepostoianstva," *Moskovskoe ezhemesiachnoe izdanie* 1 (1781): 58.

178. Please see the introduction by A. V. Zapadov to Kheraskov's *Izbrannye proizvedeniia,* 34–35.

179. A. F. Voeikov, "Iz zapisok," in *Istoricheskii sbornik Vol'noi russkoi tipografii v Londone* (London, 1861), 121; he then admitted that she spent ten years each with Saltykov and Orlov.

180. Khemnitser, "Lev-svat," *Polnoe sobranie,* 142–43.

181. Vorontsov, "Avtobiograficheskaia zapiska," 8.

182. Turgenev, "Zapiski," 57–59.

183. Khemnitser, "L'vovo puteshestvie," *Polnoe sobranie,* 146–48.

184. V. V. Kapnist, "Oda na istreblenie v Rossii zvaniia raba Ekaterinoiu Vtoroiu v 15 den' fevralia 1786 goda," *Sobranie sochinenii* (M, 1960), 1:101; Catherine is quoted in Brown, *Eighteenth-Century Russian Literature,* 460.

185. Derzhavin, "Felitsa," 2–3; for other renditions of the hard-working monarch, see *Razgovory o fizicheskikh i nravstvennykh predmetakh,* 251–56; and Dolgorukii, *Povest' o rozhdenii moem. . . . ,* 30.

186. "Felitsa," in *Ob"iasneniia na sochineniia Derzhavina im samim diktovannyia . . .* (Spb, 1834), 1–9; Brown, *Eighteenth-Century Russian Literature,* 391.

187. Catherine II, "Notes," in Radishchev, *Journey,* 242.

188. Novikov, "Pis'mo redaktoru," *Truten'* 8 (June 1769), reprinted in Berkov, *Zhurnaly,* 69; Derzhavin, "Felitsa," 6–7.

189. Please see Robert E. Jones, "The Polemics of the 1769 Journals: A Reappraisal," *Canadian-American Slavic Studies* 16 (1978): 432–43; Iu. V. Stennik, "Ekaterina II—Polemist: Polemika v literaturnykh zaniatiakh imperatritsy Ekateriny II," in *Filosofskii vek. Al'manakh 11: Ekaterina i ee vremia: Sovremennyi vzgliad* (Spb, 1999): 142–64; Michael von Herzen, "Catherine II—Editor of *Vsiakaia Vsiachina?* A Reappraisal," *Russian Review* 38 (1979): 283–97.

190. As quoted in William B. Edgerton, "Ambivalence as the Key to Kniazhnin's Tragedy 'Vadim Novgorodskii'," in *Russia and the World,* 308.

7: THE BAD TSAR

1. V. K. Trediakovskii, *Telemakhida* (Spb, 1766), 1:44.

2. A. P. Sumarokov, "Oda . . . Pavlu . . . (29 June 1771)," *Polnoe sobranie,* 2 (1781): 107.

3. Nekhachin and Nekhachin, *Novoe kratkoe poniatie,* 3:7–8.

4. *Noveishee povestvovatel'noe zemleopisanie . . . ,* 135–38, italics in the original.

5. *PSZ* 18, no. 12,978 (27 September 1767).

6. Kheraskov, *Rossiada,* 168, 171–75.

7. Kheraskov, *Kadm,* 2–3 (published in 1786, 1793, 1801, and 1807).

8. *Nizverzhennyi Zelul,* 12.

9. Nikolev, "Sorena," 239 (act 1, sc. 1), 242 (act 1, sc. 2). In an Enlightenment twist, the good people are Polovtsy and pagans, while the bad are Russians and Christians.

10. Nikolev, "Sorena," 264 (act 2, sc. 5), 270 (act 3, sc. 1).

11. Fedor Emin wrote an allegorical novel, based on the event, *Nepostoiannaia fortuna.*

12. Sumarokov, "Dmitrii," *Polnoe sobranie,* 4:71 (act 1, sc. 1). Sumarokov's political plays were popular in "liberal" circles because they reflected the program of the Panin party. See Segel, *Literature,* 2:396.

13. Sumarokov, "Oda . . . Pavlu," 108.

14. As translated in Segel, *Literature,* 2:261; depending on the edition of the Old Testatment, the psalm is either 81 or 82.

15. Kheraskov, *Numa,* 39.

16. Kheraskov, *Kadm,* 2–3, 116.

17. A. N. Radishchev, *Zhitie Fedora Vasil'evicha Ushakova* (Spb, 1789), 14–17.

18. Fénelon, *Adventures of Telemachus,* 2:246 (book 2).

19. Emin, *Prikliucheniia Femistokla,* 19. First published in 1763.

20. *Niverzhennyi Zelul,* 18–25.

21. Shcherbatov, "Puteshestvie," 1024.

22. Shcherbatov, "Rech', kakovuiu by mogli govorit' shvedskiie dvoriane po vziatii pod strazhu ikh sobrat'ev," *Sochineniia* (Spb, 1898), 2:100; also consult the article by A. Lentin, "Shcherbatov, Constitutionalism, and the 'Despotism' of Sweden's Gustav III," in *Russia and the World of the Eighteenth Century,* 36–44.

23. Nikolev, "Sorena," 313–14 (act 5, sc. 5).

24. Catherine II, "Antidot," 302–3.

25. *Zhizn' i uzhasnyia deianiia rimskago imperatora Nerona,* trans. T. Mozhaiskii, from the French (Spb, 1792), 97, 112–13.

26. E. R. Dashkova, "Mnenie nekoego rossianina o edinonachalii," *Novye ezhemesiachnye sochineniia* 80 (1793): 4–7, and *Memoirs of the Princess Dashkaw,* 1:226. A similar hymn of praise to *edinonachalie* can be found in Chebotarev, *Velichie,* a speech delivered at Moscow University on June 30, 1795.

27. See, for instance, the work of the prominent Mason, I. V. Lopukhin, *Blagost' i preimyshchestvo edinonachalia.* See also chap. 6, n. 81.

28. Radishchev, "Pis'mo k drugu, zhitel'stvuiushchemu v Tobol'ske," *Izbrannye filosofskie i obshchestvenno-politicheskie proizvedeniia* (M, 1952), 218–19; also see G. I. Leonard, "Novikov, Shcherbatov, Radishchev: The Intellectual in the Age of Catherine the Great," (Ph.D. diss., SUNY Binghamton, 1980), 126–31. Nikolai Novikov was probably another exception: A. Nezelenov, *N. I. Novikov, izdatel' zhurnalov, 1769–1785 gg.* (Spb, 1875), 445.

29. Nikolev, "Sorena," 297–98 (act 4, sc. 6).

30. Plavil'shchikov, "Riurik," *Sochineniia,* 1:14 (act 2, sc. 1). The play was first staged in St. Petersburg in 1791 under the title *Vseslav;* I am grateful to Professor Irina Reyfman of Columbia University for providing me with this information.

31. P. Zakhar'in, *Arfakad,* 4:259. The novel was republished in Nikolaev in 1798.

32. Kheraskov, *Polidor,* 175–80, 213, 253–59, 444. Republished in 1801 and 1806.

33. *Zhizn' i stradanie Liudovika XVI . . . s razsmotreniem tsare-ubiistvennago opredeleniia,* trans. V. Kriazhev, from the French (M, 1793), 21–33, 48–49.

34. As quoted in Edgerton, "Ambivalence as the Key to Kniazhnin's Tragedy 'Vadim Novgorodskii'," 308.

35. N. G. Vysotskii, "Zapreshchennyia pri Ekaterine Velikoi knigi," *Russkii arkhiv* 10 (1912): 252–55.

36. On Catherine's reaction to the liberal constitution of Poland, see Jerzy Łojek, "Catherine II's Armed Intervention in Poland: Origins of the Political Decisions at the Russian Court in 1791 and 1792," *Canadian Slavic Studies* 4 (1970): 570–93.

37. The phrase is from Dashkova, "Rech' (21 October 1783)," *Drug prosveshcheniia* 1 (1804): 145.

38. *Raznyia povestvovaniia,* 105–6.

39. V. V. Kapnist, "Oda na rabstvo," *Sobranie sochinenii* (M, 1960), 1:89.

40. On the Panins, see Ransel, *Politics of Catherinian Russia;* also consult Gleason, *Moral Idealists,* 120, 134–35.

41. Fonvizin, "Naidennoe v bumagakh . . . Panina," in Shumigorskii, *Imperator Pavel I,* appendix, 4–13; please see the translation, "A Discourse on Permanent Laws of State," in *Russian Intellectual History: An Anthology,* trans. and ed. Marc Raeff (NY, 1988), 96–104. Also consult D. Fonvizin, "Slovo pokhval'noe Marku Avreliiu," *Sobranie sochinenii* (Leningrad, 1959), 1:212–13; and L. I. Kulakova, *Denis Ivanovich Fonvizin* (M, 1966), 105–6.

42. V. I. Grigorovich, *Kantsler kniaz' A. A. Bezborodko v sviazi s sobytiiami ego vremeni,* 2 vols. (Spb, 1879–1881); N. V. Minaeva, *Pravitel'stvennyi konstitutsionalizm i peredovoe obshchestvennoe mnenie v Rossii v nachale XIX veka* (Saratov, 1982); M. M. Safonov, *Problema reform v pravitel'stvennoi politike Rossii na rubezhe XVIII i XIX vv.* (L, 1988); S. V. Mironenko, *Samoderzhavie i reformy: Politicheskaia bor'ba v Rossii v nachale XIX v.* (M, 1989).

43. Dashkova, *Memoirs of the Princess Daschkaw,* 1:53.

44. Engel'gardt, *Zapiski,* 192–93.

45. Shishkov, "Dostopamiatnyia skazaniia ob Imperatritse Ekaterine Velikoi," RO, *f.* 862, *ed. khr.* 4, pp. 54–60.

46. I assume Fonvizin is referring to serfdom when he writes: "Nothing could throw His state more quickly into total ruin than suddenly giving an unprepared nation the rights of well-established European peoples." See his discourse, ". . . [R]azsuzhdenie," in Shumigorskii, *Imperator Pavel I,* 12.

47. For a discussion of Shcherbatov's sources, see Chechulin, *Russkii sotsial'nyi roman,* 17–30, 49; also see Emmanuel Waegermans, "A Russian *1984* in 1784: Shcherbatov's Vision of the Future," in *Literature, Lives, and Legality in Catherine's Russia,* ed. A. G. Cross and G. S. Smith (Nottingham, England, 1994), 45–59; and S. A. Egorov, "M. M. Shcherbatov o preobrazovanii gosudarstvennogo stroia v Rossii," *Sovetskoe gosudarstvo i pravo* 1 (1985): 112–19.

48. Shcherbatov, *On the Corruption of Morals,* 159, 235–59.

49. Shcherbatov, "Opravdanie moikh myslei (1789)," *Sochineniia,* 2:267–68.

50. A. I. Gertsen, *Sochineniia* (Petrograd, 1919), 9:270–71. Herzen probably had in mind Shcherbatov's belief in a society hierarchically arranged and Radishchev's belief in equality.

51. L'vov, *Khram istiny,* 9–12, 44–45.

52. Radishchev, *Zhitie,* 14–17. In 1789, Radishchev may also have authored a

"letter" highly critical of sovereigns in general, and especially those with the title "the Great," who during war "sacrifice millions of men like themselves . . . only to satisfy their vanity"; other monarchs "suck blood from the poor people" of their kingdoms. And yet, such observations were published. See "Pis'mo XX," *Pochta dukhov,* 108–17.

53. Princess Catherine Romanovna Dashkov, *The Memoirs of Princess Dashkov,* ed. and trans. Kyril Fitzlyon (London, 1958), 240.

54. Radishchev, *Journey,* iii, 40.

55. Ibid., 72.

56. Ibid., 74.

57. Ibid., 68–69, 197.

58. A hymn of praise that closely duplicates Radishchev's is "Razmyshlenie uedinennago potekhontsa," *Ezhemesiachnyia sochinenia* 1 (1786): 3–6.

59. Radishchev, *Journey,* 71–73.

60. Ibid., 73–74, 76.

61. Ibid., 143–63; also see McConnell, "Radishchev and Classical Antiquity," 470.

62. "Catherine's Notes," in Radishchev, *Journey,* 240, 244, 247; also see A. V. Khrapovitskii, *Dnevnik s . . . 1782 po . . . 1793 goda* (Spb, 1874), 338 (26 June 1790), Catherine's state secretary during this period.

63. Radishchev, *Journey,* 194–95; also consult the analysis by Jesse Clardy, *The Philosophical Ideas of Alexander Radishchev* (London, 1964).

64. Radishchev, *Journey,* 196–98. Radishchev had long studied these ideas; in his first book, a translation, the original author spoke about an "unwritten contract" between the sovereign and the people, which if broken "gives the people, his judges, the same or even greater power over him, as the law they gave him over criminals. *The sovereign is the first citizen of a people's society.*" In that same work, Radishchev translated the French word *despotisme* with the Russian *samoderzhavie* and gave its definition: "Autocracy is the form of government most hostile to human nature." See Mabli, *Razmyshleniia o grecheskoi istorii,* 120–21, 126. Published by the Academy of Sciences.

65. Radishchev, *Journey,* 199–201.

66. See the intriguing comments by Baehr, *Paradise Myth,* 159.

67. Catherine, "Notes," in Radishchev, *Journey,* 248.

68. This is the opinion of many scholars. See Alexander, "Catherine II's Efforts at Liberalization," 81; Allen McConnell, "The Autocrat and the Open Critic," in *Catherine the Great,* ed. Marc Raeff (NY, 1972), 177; Sara Dickinson, "The Poetics of National Landscape in Radishchev's *Journey,*" paper delivered at the National Convention of the American Association for the Advancement of Slavic Studies (September 1998), 12.

69. *PSZ* 23, no. 16,901 (4 September 1790). Emperor Paul allowed him to return to European Russia, and Alexander I fully pardoned him and returned his status, order of knighthood, and rank.

70. Putnyn', *Istoki russkoi istoriografii antichnosti,* 132.

71. A. N. Radishchev, "Os'mnadtsatoe stoletie," *PSS* (Spb, 1907), 1:334–35.

72. Khrapovitskii, *Dnevnik,* 173; on this whole issue, consult Smith, *Working the Rough Stone.*

73. Pypin, *Russkoe masonstvo,* 312–28; Gilbert H. McArthur, "Catherine II and the Masonic Circle of N. I. Novikov," *Canadian-American Slavic Studies* 4 (Fall 1970): 529–46.

74. "Ukaz Ekateriny o zatochenii Novikova v Shlissel'burgskuiu krepost'," in *N. I. Novikov i ego sovremenniki: Izbrannye sochineniia* (M, 1961), 476–78; McArthur, "Masonic Circle," 539–42; Derbov, *Obshchestvenno-politicheskie i istoricheskie vzgliady N. I. Novikova,* 214–16.

75. Kniazhnin, *Vadim novgorodskii;* it was written in 1789 and also published in *Rossiisskii featr* 39 (September 1793), but then ordered expurgated from the issue. Please see: L. N. Kulakova, "Ia. B. Kniazhnin," in *Russkie dramaturgi XVIII–XIX v.* (M, 1959), 1:327–33; V. N. Vsevolodskii-Gerngross, *Russkii teatr vtoroi poloviny XVIII veka* (M, 1960), 242–57.

76. Ilovaiskii, "Dashkova," *Sochineniia,* 1:363–64; *Materialy dlia biografii knagini* [*sic*] *E.R. Dashkovoi* (Leipzig, 1876), 93; Dashkova, *Memoirs of the Princess Daschkaw,* 1:361–66.

77. Ia. Kniazhnin, "Pis'mo eia siiatel'stvu kniagine Ekaterine Romanovne Dashkovoi," *Sobesednik liubitelei rossiiskago slova* 11 (1783): 3–9.

78. Plavil'shchikov, "Riurik," *Sochineniia;* Catherine II, "Istoricheskoe predstavlenie iz zhizni Riurika." In *Zelul,* published that same year, two monarchs are overthrown and die (albeit at their own hands, but threatened by a mob); the author was anonymous, and the work was not censored.

79. In Catherine's version, Riurik pardons Vadim, and the formerly vainglorious, power-hungry hothead agrees to assist the new ruler in his great tasks.

80. "Vadim Novgorodskii," *Sankt-Peterburgskii merkurii* 3 (August 1793): 124–44, quotation on p. 138; also see the excellent discussion by Edgerton, "Ambivalence," 309–13.

81. Kniazhnin, *Vadim Novgorodskii,* 30 (act 2, sc. 4).

82. Ibid., 30 (act 2, sc. 4).

83. Ibid., 7–9 (act 1, sc. 1).

84. Ibid., 65.

85. Chekhov's letter of 27 October 1888 is quoted in Edgerton, "Ambivalence," 311.

86. N. M. Karamzin, *Oda na sluchai prisiagi moskovskikh zhitelei ego imperatorskomu velichestvu Pavlu I* (M, 1796), 5, 8; and consult L. G. Kisliagina, "Formirovanie idei samoderzhaviia v politicheskoi kontseptsii N. M. Karamzina," in *Voprosy metodologii i istorii istoricheskoi nauki* (M, 1977), 143–44.

87. In this work, Karamzin summarized the entire range of themes used in advice literature; in this case, the Catherinian model was being presented to the young Alexander I. See *Istoricheskoe pokhval'noe slovo Ekaterine Vtoroi* (M, 1802).

88. Dolgorukii, *Kapishche moego serdtsa,* 363.

89. The best treatment of Paul's life and reign is Roderick McGrew, *Paul I of Russia, 1754–1801* (Oxford, 1992); also consult the collection of essays *Paul I: A Reassessent of His Life and Reign,* ed. Hugh Ragsdale (Pittsburgh, 1979). Another standard is Dmitrii Kobeko, *Tsesarevich Pavel Petrovich, 1754–1796* (Spb, 1883).

90. *PSZ* 24, no. 17,530 (6 November 1796).

91. *PSZ* 24, no. 17,909 (5 April 1797); the details of his coronation and the imagery he used to create a new sense of monarchy may be found in Wortman, *Scenarios of Power,* 1:169–92.

92. On Paul's turning back to Byzantine traditions of legitimization, see A. V. Skorobogatov, "Obraz monarkha v ofitsial'noi ideologii Rossii na rubezhe XVIII–XIX vekov," in *Filosofskii vek. Al'manakh 17: Istoriia idei kak metodologiia gumanitarnykh issledovanii,* ed. T. V. Artem'eva and M. I. Mikeshin (Spb, 2001), 1:229–30.

93. Glinskii, *Bor'ba za konstitutsiiu,* 12.

94. Especially on the theme of centralization, see Richard H. Warner, "The Political Opposition to Tsar Paul I" (Ph.D. diss., New York University, 1977).

95. M. V. Klochkov, *Ocherki pravitel'stvennoi deiatel'nosti vremeni Pavla I* (Petrograd, 1916), 581.

96. Opinions remain divided on the reign of Paul I. A. G. Brikner, *Kaiser Pauls I Ende, 1801* (Stuttgart, 1897) considers him a deranged despot. Shumigorskii, *Imperator*

Pavel I, sees him as a progressive reformer with character defects that wrecked his policies, an analysis similar to that made about his father, Peter III.

97. Turgenev, "Zapiski," *Russkaia starina* 61 (1889): 212; *PSZ* 24, no. 17,769 (29 January 1797). The common people and the simple soldier believed that he held their interests dear, probably because he attacked the noble elements. See R. McGrew, "A Political Portrait of Paul I from the Austrian and English Diplomatic Archives," *Jahrbücher für Geschichte Osteuropas* 18 (1970): 512–13; Klochkov, *Ocherki*, 407–33, 570–72, 583. The legend grew that a prayer on his grave provided the most effective remedy for unrequited love, an unhappy family life, job problems, and court cases.

98. McGrew, *Paul I*, 206–10.

99. For enlightened utterances by Paul, see, for instance, "Nakaz Imperatora Pavla I, 1788 g.," *Vestnik Evropy* 1 (1867): 316–22; "Tsesarevich Pavel Petrovich," *Russkaia starina* 9 (1874): 667–83. Turgenev described both moods in "Zapiski," *Russkaia starina* 47 (1885): 377–80, and 49 (1886): 55–56.

100. John L. H. Keep, "Paul I and the Militarization of Government," in *Paul I: A Reassessment of His Life and Reign*, ed. Hugh Ragsdale, 91–103; McGrew, *Paul I*, viii.

101. Because Alexander soon made peace with Britain, some have suspected that "English gold" figured in Paul's downfall. See James J. Kenney, Jr., "Lord Whitworth and the Conspiracy Against Tsar Paul I: The New Evidence of the Kent Archive," *Slavic Review* 36 (1977): 205–19.

102. I. A. Krylov, *Trumf* (Spb, 1880), a comedy in two acts, written in 1800, satirizing Paul and his entourage. Odists, though, continued to ply their craft and advised monarchs to live up to Petrine ideals, while plays counseled avoiding flatterers and enacting dynamic measures. See, for instance, M. M. Kheraskov, "Oda Ego Imperatorskomu Velichestvu . . . (12 November 1796) and "Oda Ego Imperatorskomu Velichestvu . . . (March 1797)," in *Tvoreniia vnov ispravlennyia i dopolnennyia* (n.d., n.p.), 7:193–204; V. A. Ozerov, "Iaropolk i Oleg," *Sochineniia Ozerova* (Spb, 1828), 3:3–60, first presented at the St. Petersburg Court Theatre on May 16, 1798.

103. Kasimir Waliszewski (same as Valishevskii) believed he was both. See *Le Fils de la grande Catherine: Paul I empereur de Russie: Sa vie, son règne, et sa mort, 1754–1801* (Paris, 1912).

104. Raeff, "Autocracy Tempered by Reform or by Regicide?" 1153. This characterization of Paul's reign is certainly that shared in F. Golovkin's memoirs, *Dvor i tsarstvovanie Pavla I: Portrety, vospominaniia, i anekdoty* (M, 1912), esp. 132–41; and in V. D. Davydov, "Pamiatnyia zametki," *Russkaia starina* 3 (1871): 782–92.

105. McGrew, "Portrait of Paul I," 503–29, quotation on p. 528.

106. Dolgorukii, *Kapishche moego serdtsa*, 388.

107. An anonymous Englishman, for instance, lamented the fact that in Russia, for a population of 25,000,000, there were only 500 copies of newspapers, compared to 600 in Hungary with seven million people, and one copy apiece for every Englishman and Frenchman. See "Account of the Political Journals, etc., in Russia," *Monthly Magazine* 9 (1800): 433–35.

108. Dolgorukii, *Kapishche moego serdtsa*, 72.

109. On constitutionalism and its connection with the assassination, see N. Ia. Eidel'man, *Gran' vekov: Politicheskaia bor'ba v Rossii v kontse XVIII–nachale XIX stoletiia* (M, 1982). Also consult the seminal volumes by Minaeva, *Konstitutsionalizm;* Safonov, *Problema reform;* and Mironenko, *Samoderzhavie.*

110. Adam Czartoryski, *Mémoires* (Paris, 1887), 1:237.

111. For details on the deed itself, see Leo Loewenson, "The Death of Paul I

(1801) and the Memoirs of Count Bennigsen," *Slavonic and East European Review* 29 (1950–1951): 212–32.

112. McGrew, *Paul I*, 3.

113. As quoted in Warner, "Opposition," 152, from Grand Duke Alexander's letters to LaHarpe.

114. *PSZ* 24, no. 19,779 (12 March 1801).

115. Dashkova, *Memoirs of the Princess Daschkaw*, 1: 53. Also see, for instance, "Zapiska Grafa A. P. Vorontsova o Rossii v nachale nyneshniago veka, predstavlennaia Aleksandru Pavlovichu," *Arkhiv kniazia Vorontsova* 29 (1883): 451–70; "Zapiska neizvestnago litsa o Senate i gosudarstvennom ustroistve (1801)," *Arkhiv kniazia Vorontsova* 12 (1877): 456–62.

CONCLUSION: THE SIGNIFICANCE OF THE EIGHTEENTH-CENTURY POLITICAL DIALOGUE

1. Plato, *The Republic*, book 7, 199–205.

2. Kollmann, *By Honor Bound*, 19–20.

3. Steven Merritt Miner, "Where the West Begins," *New York Times Book Review* (8 July 2001), 14. Also see Kollmann, *By Honor Bound;* and Dominic Lieven, *Empire: The Russian Empire and Its Rivals* (New Haven, 2001).

4. Hosking, *Russia and the Russians*, 247.

BIBLIOGRAPHY

PRIMARY SOURCES

Archival Sources

Materials have been used from the following archives:

Biblioteka Rossiiskoi Akademii nauk. The Library of the Russian Academy of Sciences, located in St. Petersburg (BRAN)

Rossiiskii gosudarstvennyi arkhiv drevnykh aktov. The Russian State Archive of Ancient Acts, Moscow (RGADA)

Rukopisnyi otdel. Manuscript Division of the Russian State Library, Moscow (RO)

Sankt-Peterburgskoe otdelenie Instituta istorii. Archive of the St. Petersburg branch of the Institute of Russian History of the Russian Academy of Sciences (SOII)

Sources Written before 1800

"Account of the Political Journals, etc., in Russia." *Monthly Magazine* 9 (1800): 433–35.

Afonin, M. I. *Slovo pokhval'noe . . . Ekaterine. . . .* M, 1774.

Amvrosii [Podobedov]. *Slovo v den' Preobrazheniia Gospodnia.* M, 1774.

Aristotle. *Politics.* Translated by Benjamin Jowett. NY, 1943.

Arkhiv Kn. F. A. Kurakina. Edited by M. I. Semevskii. 10 vols. Spb, 1890–1902.

Arkhiv kniazia Vorontsova. Edited by P. I. Bartenev. 40 vols. M, 1870–1895.

Arsenii [V. I. Vereshchagin]. *Slovo o istinnoi slave.* M, 1779.

Artem'ev, A. *Kratkoe nachertanie o istorii prava i chinopolozheniia rossiiskago.* M, 1777.

———. *Kratkoe nachertanie rimskikh i rossiiskikh prav.* M, 1777.

Baier, G. *O variagakh.* Spb, 1767.

Barclay, John. *Argenis.* London, 1621.

Barker, Ernest, ed. and trans. *From Alexander to Constantine: Passages and Documents Illustrating the History of Social and Political Ideas, 336 B.C.–A.D. 337.* Oxford, 1956.

Barkov, I. S. "Sokrashchennaia rossiiskaia istoriia." In *Sokrashchennaia universal'naia istoriia,* edited by Gil'mar Kuras. Spb, 1762.

Barsov, A. "Po koronovanii . . . Ekateriny Alekseevny (3 October 1762)." In *Sobranie rechei govorennykh v Imperatorskom moskovskom universitete.* M, 1788.

Belokurov, S. A. *Materialy dlia russkoi istorii.* M, 1888.

————, ed. "Utverzhdennaia gramota ob izbranii na moskovskoe gosudarstvo Mikhaila Fedorovicha Romanova." *Chteniia v Imp. Obshchestve istorii i drevnostei rossiiskikh pri Moskovskom universitete* 218 (1906): 1–110.

Berkgol'ts, F. B. *Dnevnik vedennyi s 1721–1725 g.* M, 1858.

Berkov, P. N., ed. *Satiricheskie zhurnaly N. I. Novikova.* M, 1951.

Berlinskii, M. *Kratkaia rossiiskaia istoriia dlia upotrebleniia iunoshestvu.* . . . M, 1800.

Biron, Ernst-Ioann. "Obstoiatel'stva. . . ." *Vremia* 6 (1861): 522–39.

Blackstone, William [Blekston, G.]. *Istolkovaniia aglinskikh [sic] zakonov.* M, 1780.

Bochkarev, V. N., ed. *Stikhotvornaia tragediia kontsa XVIII–nachala XIX v.* L, 1964.

Bodin, Jean. *The Six Books of the Commonwealth.* Translated by M. J. Tooley. 1576. NY, 1967.

Bogdanovich, I. F. "Predislovie." In *Istoriia o byvshikh peremenakh v rimskoi respublike Verto d'Obüfa.* Spb, 1771.

————. *Sochineniia.* 2 vols. Spb, 1848.

Bolkhovitinov, E. A. [Mitropolit Evgenii]. *Istoricheskoe obozrenie rossiiskago zakonopolozheniia.* Spb, 1826.

Bolotov, A. *Zhizn' i prikliucheniia Andreia Bolotova.* 3 vols. L, 1931. Reprint, Newtonville, Mass., 1973.

Boltin, I. N. *Kriticheskiia primechaniia na istoriiu kn. Shcherbatova.* 2 vols. Spb, 1793–1794.

————. *Otvet general maiora Boltina na pis'mo kniazia Shcherbatova.* Spb, 1789.

————. *Primechaniia na istoriiu drevniia i nyneshniia Rossii Leklerka.* 2 vols. Spb, 1788.

Beaumont [Bomont], Prince de. *Detskoe uchilishche, ili Nravouchitel'nye razgovory . . . k pol'ze rossiiskago iunoshestva.* . . . Translated and annotated by P. Svistunov. Spb, 1783.

Bossuet, Jacques-Bénigne. *Politique tirée des propres paroles de l'Écriture sainte.* 1678. Reprint, Geneva, 1967.

Catherine [Ekaterina] II. "Antidot." In *Osmnadtsatyi vek: Istoricheskii sbornik,* edited by P. I. Bartenev. Vol. 4. M, 1869.

————. *The Antidote.* London, 1772.

————. *Catherine the Great's Instruction (Nakaz) to the Legislative Commission, 1767.* Edited and translated by Paul Dukes. Newtonville, Mass., 1977.

————. "Mnenie Gosudaryni Ekateriny II o tom, kak dolzhno pisat' russkuiu istoriiu." *Russkii vestnik* 5 (1816): 3–11.

————. *O dolzhnostiakh cheloveka i grazhdanina. Kniga k chteniiu opredelennaia v narodnykh gorodskikh uchilishchakh Rossiiskoi imperii.* Spb, 1787.

————. "Pis'ma Ekateriny Vtoroi k baronu Grimmu (12 January 1794)." *Russkii arkhiv* 3 (1878): 62; 10 (1878): 208.

————. *Règlements de Sa Majesté impériale Catherine II impératrice et autocratrice de toutes les Russies, etc., pour l'administration des gourvernements de l'empire des russes.* Spb, 1788.

————. "Sobstvennoruchnyia zametki Velikoi kniagini Ekateriny Alekseevny." *Sbornik Imperatorskago russkago istoricheskago obshchestva* 7 (1871): 84.

————. *Sochineniia Imperatritsy Ekateriny II.* Edited by A. Smirdin. 3 vols. Spb, 1849–1850.

————. *Sochineniia Imperatritsy Ekateriny II.* Edited by A. N. Pypin. 12 vols. Spb, 1901–1907.

————. *Zapiski Imperatritsy Ekateriny Vtoroi.* Spb, 1907.

————. "Zapiski kasatel'no rossiiskoi istorii." *Sobesednik liubitelei rossiiskago slova* (1783): nos. 1–11; (1784): nos. 12–15.

Chateaubriand, F. R. de. "De Buonaparte et des Bourbons (1814)." In *Oeuvres complètes de Chateaubriand.* 3 vols. Paris, 1828.

Chebotarev, Kh. A. *Velichie, mogushchestvo, i slava Rossii.* M, 1795.

———. *Vstuplenie v nastoiashchuiu istoriiu o Rossii.* M, 1847.

Chrysostom, Dio. *Dio Chrysostom.* Vol. 1. Translated by J. W. Cohoon. London, 1932.

Chulkov, M. D. *Peresmeshnik, ili Slavenskiia skazki.* 3 vols. M, 1789. Published previously in 1766–1768 and 1783–1785.

Comenius, J. A. *Vidimyi svet.* M, 1768.

Curas, Hilmar [Kuras, G.], ed. *Sokrashchennaia universal'naia istoriia.* Translated by S. Volchkov. Spb, 1762.

Curtius Rufus, Quintus [Kurtsii Ruf, Kvint]. *Istoriia o Aleksandre Velikom.* 2 vols. Spb, 1767.

Czartoryski, Adam. *Mémoires.* Vol. 1. Paris, 1887.

Damaskin [Semenov-Rudnev, D. E.]. *Slovo v . . . den' vozshestviia na . . . prestol . . . Ekateriny Alekseevny.* Spb, 1792.

Daniel, P. G. *Histoire de France.* Paris, 1713.

Dashkov[a], Catherine [Ekaterina] Romanovna. *The Memoirs of Princess Dashkov.* Edited and translated by Kyril Fitzlyon. London, 1958.

———. *The Memoirs of the Princess Daschkaw, Lady of Honour to Catherine II.* Edited by Mrs. W. Bradford. 2 vols. London, 1840.

———. "Mnenie nekoego rossianina o edinonachalii." *Novyia ezhemesiachnyia sochineniia* 80 (1793): 4–7.

———. "Rech' (21 October 1783)." *Drug prosveshcheniia* 1 (1804): 145.

Davydov, V. D. "Pamiatnye zametki." *Russkaia starina* 3 (1871): 782–92.

Demidov, A. "Perevod rechi v pamiat . . . rozhdeniia . . . Pavla Petrovicha." *Ezhemesiachnyia sochineniia* 1 (1756): 14–30.

Derzhavin, G. R. *Ob"iasneniia na sochineniia Derzhavina im samim diktovannyia.* Spb, 1834.

———. *Sochineniia Derzhavina.* 3 vols. Spb, 1831.

———. *Sochineniia Derzhavina.* 6 vols. Spb, 1871.

———. *Stikhotvoreniia.* L, 1957.

———. *Stikhotvoreniia Derzhavina.* M, 1941.

———. *Zapiski iz izvestnykh vsem proisshestvii i podlinnykh del, zakliuchaiushchie v sebe zhizn'.* M, 1860.

Desnitskii, S. E. *Iuridicheskoe razsuzhdenie o pol'ze znaniia otechestvennago zakonoiskusstva. . . .* M, 1778.

———. "Posviashchenie k perevodu knigi T. Boudena." In *Nastavnik zemledel'cheskii. . . .* M, 1780.

———."Predstavlenie ob uchrezhdenii zakonodatel'noi, suditel'noi, i nakazatel'noi vlasti v rossiiskoi imperii." In *Zapiski Imperatorskoi Akademii nauk po istoriko-filologicheskomu otdeleniiu.* Vol. 7. Spb, 1905.

———."Rassuzhdenie o roditel'skoi vlasti. . ." In *Izbrannye proizvedeniia russkikh myslitelei vtoroi poloviny XVIII.* Vol. 1. M, 1952.

———. *Slovo na den' tezoimenitstva Imperatritsy Ekateriny II . . .* M, 1775.

———. *Slovo o priamom i blizhaishem sposobe k naucheniiu iurisprudentsiiam.* M, 1768.

Detskaia rossiiskaia istoriia, izdannaia v pol'zu obuchaiushchagosia iunoshestva. Smolensk, 1797.

Detskii magazin, ili Sobranie poleznykh sochinenii, sootvetstvuiushchikh detskomu vozrastu. M, 1788.

Diderot [Didro], D. "Zamechaniia na Nakaz." *PSS*. Vol. 10. M, 1947.

Dmitriev, I. I. "Tsar i dva pastukha. Basn' XX." In *Sochineniia Dmitrieva*. M, 1810.

Dobroe namerenie. Monthly. M, 1764.

Dolgorukaia, N. B. *Pamiatnyia zapiski, 1714–1771*. M, 1867.

Dolgorukii, I. M. *Kapishche moego serdtsa, ili Slovar' vsekh tekh lits, s koimi ia byl v raznykh otnosheniiakh . . .* M, 1890.

———. *Povest' o rozhdenii moem . . .* Petrograd, 1916.

———. "Zapiski." In *Sochineniia Dolgorukago*. Vol. 2. Spb, 1849.

Domashnev, S. G. "Son." *Poleznoe uveselenie* (1761): 209–20.

The Domostroi: Rules for Russian Households in the Time of Ivan the Terrible. Edited and translated by Carolyn Johnston Pouncy. Ithaca, 1994.

Drevniaia rossiiskaia vivliofika. 28 issues. Spb, 1773–1775.

Drug prosveshcheniia. M, 1804–1806.

Dvorianskoe uchilishche, ili Nravouchil'nye razgovory . . . v pol'zu blagorodnago rossiiskago iunoshestva. Spb, 1764.

Ekaterina II. See Catherine II.

Elagin, P. I. *Opyt povestvovaniia o Rossii*. Spb, 1803.

Emin, F. A. *Nepostoiannaia fortuna, ili Pokhozhdenie Miramonda*. 3 vols. Spb, 1763.

———. *Prikliucheniia Femistokla i raznyia politicheskiia, grazhdanskiia, filosoficheskiia, fizicheshkiia, i voennyia ego s synom svoim razgovory*. Spb, 1763. Also published in 1781.

———. *Rossiiskaia istoriia*. Spb, 1767–1769.

Engel'gardt, L. N. *Zapiski, 1766–1836*. M, 1867.

Ezhemesiachnyia sochineniia. Spb, 1755–1764.

Fedotovich, Luk'ian. *Slovo na den' rozhdeniia . . . Pavla. . . .* Spb, 1790.

Fénelon, François de Lamothe. *Les Avantures de Télémaque, fils d'Ulysse*. Amsterdam, 1725.

———. *The Adventures of Telemachus, the Son of Ulysses*. Translated by E. W. S. Vol. 1. London, 1857.

Fonvizin, D. I. "Lisitsa-koznodei: Basnia." In *PSS*. Spb, 1914.

———. *The Political and Legal Writings of Denis Fonvizin*. Edited and translated by Walter Gleason. Ann Arbor, 1985.

———. *Sobranie sochinenii*. 2 vols. Leningrad, 1959.

———. *Zhizn' grafa Nikity Ivanovicha Panina*. Spb, 1786.

Frederick II. "An Essay on Forms of Government." In *Posthumous Works*. Vol. 5. London, 1789.

———. *The Refutation of Machiavelli's Prince, or Anti-Machiavel*. Translated by Paul Sonnino. Athens, Ohio, 1981.

Gavriil [Buzhinskii]. *Slovo o promysle Bozhii*. Spb, 1776.

Gavriil [Shaposhnikov]. *Slovo na . . . den' koronovaniia . . . Ekateriny. . . .* Spb, 1773.

Gennadii [Chelnokov]. *Slovo . . . pri otkrytii Imp. Vospitatel'nago doma v Moskve*. M, 1764.

Gertsen [Herzen], A. I. *Sochineniia*. 9 vols. Petrograd, 1919.

Giber, Zh. *Zhizn' i deianiia Fridrika Velikago, korolia prusskago*. Translated by T. Kipiiak. Spb, 1788.

Gizel', Innokentii. *Sinopsis*. Published in Kiev in 1674, 1678, 1680, and 1683; and in St. Petersburg in 1810 (the edition used here), 1823, 1836, and 1861.

Glinka, S. N. *Selim i Roksana, ili Prevratnost' zhizni chelovecheskoi*. M, 1798.

———. *Zapiski*. Spb, 1895. Covers the years 1776–1825.

Golikov, I. I. *Deianiia Petra Velikago, mudrago preobrazitelia Rossii, sobrannyia iz dostovernykh istochnikov i raspolozhennyia po godam*. 30 vols. M, 1788–1797.

Golitsyn, D. A. "Pis'ma." In *Izbrannye proizvedeniia russkikh myslitelei vtoroi poloviny XVIII veka*. Vol. 2. M, 1952.

Golovkin, F. *Dvor i tsarstvovanie Pavla I: Portrety, vospominaniia, i anekdoty*. M, 1912.

Goudar, A. *Mémoires pour servir à l'histoire de Pierre III, Empereur de Russie.* Frankfurt, 1763.

Griboedov, Fedor. "Istoriia o tsariakh i velikikh kniaziakh zemli russkoi." In *Pamiatniki drevnei pis'mennosti,* edited by S. F. Platonov and V. V. Maikov. Vol. 121. M, 1896.

Holbach [Gol'bakh], Baron Paul d'. *Sistema prirody.* M, 1940.

Homer. *The Iliad.* Translated by Richmond Lattimore. Chicago, 1962.

Ia, I. *Zrelishche sveta, ili Vsemirnoe zemleopisanie.* Spb, 1789.

Iavorskii, S. *Kamen' very.* Spb, 1728.

————. *Znameniia prishestviia antikhristova i konchiny veka.* M, 1703.

Ilarion. "Sermon on Law and Grace." In *Sermons and Rhetoric of Kievan Rus',* translated by Simon Franklin. Cambridge, Mass., 1991.

Ioasaf [Zabolotskii]. *Slovo v den' novogo goda.* Spb, 1781.

————. *Slovo vo vtoruiu nedeliu velikogo posta.* Spb, 1779.

Istoricheskaia igra dlia detei. . . . M, 1795.

Istoriia Elisavety, korolevy angliiskoi. 2 vols. Translated by A. Roznotovskii. Spb, 1795.

Istoriia, ili Opisanie zhizni Karla XII, korolia shvedskago. Translated by P. Pomerantsev. Spb, 1777.

Istoriia slavnykh gosudarei i velikikh generalov. Compiled by E. Shofin and translated by Ia. Kozel'skii. Spb, 1765.

I. T. Pososhkov: Zhizn' i deiatel'nost'. Edited by B. B. Kafengauz. M, 1950.

Iunosti chestnoe zertsalo, ili Pokazanie k zhiteiskomu obkhozhdeniiu. Spb, 1717.

Iuridicheskoe razsuzhdenie o pol'ze znaniia otechestvennago zakonoiskusstva. M, 1778.

Ivan IV [Ivan Groznyi]. *Perepiska Ivana Groznogo s Andreem Kurbskim.* Edited by Ia. S. Lur'e and Iu. D. Rykov. L, 1979.

————. *Poslaniia Ivana Groznogo.* Edited by D. S. Likhachev. M, 1951.

Izbrannye proizvedeniia russkikh myslitelei vtoroi poloviny XVIII veka. Edited by I. A. Shchipanov. M, 1952.

Izmailov, A. *Evgenii, ili Pagubnyia sledstviia durnago vospitaniia i soobshchestva.* Spb, 1799.

Justi [Iusti], L. J. K. *Osnovanie sily i blagosostoianiia tsarstv, ili Podrobnoe nachertanie vsekh znanii kasaiushchikhsia do gosudarstvennago blagochiniia.* Spb, 1778.

————. *Sushchestvennoe izobrazhenie estestva narodnykh obshchestv i vsiakago roda zakonov, sochinennoe Gospodinom Iusti.* Translated by A. S. Volkov. M, 1770.

Kanits, Iu. I. *Slovo v publichnom sobranii pri kazanskikh gimnaziiakh po vosstanovlenii obshchago pokoia.* M, 1775.

Kantemir, A. D. *Satiry i drugiia stikhotvorcheskiia sochineniia.* Spb, 1762.

————. *Sobranie stikhotvorenii.* L, 1956.

Kapnist, V. V. "Oda na istreblenie v Rossii zvaniia raba Ekaterinoiu Vtoroiu v 15 den' fevralia 1786 goda." In *Sobranie sochinenii.* Vol. 1. M, 1960.

————. "Oda na rabstvo." In *Sobranie sochinenii.* Vol. 1. M, 1960.

Karamzin, N. M. *Istoricheskoe pokhval'noe slovo Ekaterine Vtoroi.* M, 1802.

————. *Oda na sluchai prisiagi moskovskikh zhitelei ego ImperatorskomuVelichestvu Pavlu I.* M, 1796.

————. *Pis'ma russkogo puteshestvennika.* L, 1984

Karin, F. G. *Slovo na torzhestvo mira s Portoiu Otomanskoiu.* M, 1775.

Khemnitser, I. I. *Basni i skazki.* Spb, 1811.

————. *Polnoe sobranie basen' i skazok.* Spb, n.d.

————. *Polnoe sobranie stikhotvorenii.* M, 1963.

Kheraskov, M. M. *Izbrannye proizvedeniia.* Leningrad, 1961.

———. *Kadm i Garmoniia.* M, 1789. Republished in 1786, 1793, 1801, and 1807.

———. *Numa Pompilii, ili Protsvetaiuschii Rim.* M, 1768.

———. *Oda na ustanovlenniia vnov' premudrykh zakonov.* Spb, 1767.

———. *Polidor, syn Kadma i Garmonii.* M, 1794.

———. *Rossiada. Iroicheskaia poema.* M, 1779.

———. *Tvoreniia vnov' ispravlennyia i dopolnennyia.* 7 vols. N.p., n.d.

———. *Vladimir Vozrozhdennyi. Epicheskaia poema.* M, 1785.

Khrapovitskii, A. V. *Dnevnik s . . . 1782 po . . . 1793 goda.* Spb, 1874.

Kireevskii, P. V. *Piesni sobrannyia.* 10 vols. M, 1871.

Kirilov, I. K. *Tsvetushchee sostoianie vserossiiskago gosudarstva.* Edited by V. A. Rybakov. M, 1977. Original published 1727–1730.

Kniazhnin, Ia. "Pis'mo eia siiatel'stvu kniagine Ekaterine Romanovne Dashkovoi." *Sobesednik liubitelei rossiiskago slova* 11 (1783): 3–9.

———. "Vadim Novgorodskii." *Sankt-Peterburgskii merkurii* 3 (August 1793): 124–44.

Kol'berg, L. *Istoriia datskaia.* 2 vols. Translated by Ia. Kozel'skii. Spb, 1765–1766.

Komarov, M. *Starinnyia pis'ma kitaiskago imperatora k rossiiskomu gosudariu.* M, 1787.

Kostrov, E. I. *Oda na . . . den' vosshestviia. . . .* M, 1780.

Kotoshikhin, Grigorii. *O Rossii v tsarstvovanie Alekseia Mikhailovicha.* Edited by A. Barsukov. Spb, 1906.

Kovalenskii, M., ed. *Moskovskaia politicheskaia literatura XVI veka.* Spb, 1914.

Kozel'skii, Ia. P. *Filosoficheskiia predlozheniia.* Spb, 1768. Reprinted as "Filosofskie predlozheniia" in *Izbrannye proizvedeniia russkikh myslitelei vtoroi poloviny XVIII veka.* Vol. 1, p. 520. M, 1952.

———. "Predislovie." In L. Kol'berg, *Istoriia datskaia.* 2 vols. Spb, 1765–1766.

Kozodavlev, O. P. "Razsuzhdenie o narodnom prosveshchenii." *Rastushchii vinograd* (1785): April, 64–100, June, 67–77, July, 61–75.

———. "Rech' o pol'ze matematiki." *Rastushchii vinograd* (1785): June, 16–39.

Kratkaia rossiiskaia istoriia . . . v pol'zu narodnykh uchilishch. Spb, 1799.

Krylov, I. A. "Kaib: Vostochnaia povest'." *PSS.* Vol. 1. Spb, 1847.

———. *Trumf.* Spb, 1880.

Kurganov, N. "Kratkiia zamyslovatiia povesti." In *Polnyi vseobshchii pis'movnik.* M, 1805.

Kuz'menskii, G. *Pokhval'naia rech' Petru Velikomu.* Spb, 1744.

Laveaux , J.-Ch. T. de. *Histoire de Pierre III, Empereur de Russie.* 2 vols. Paris, 1798.

"Lay of Igor's Campaign, The." In *Medieval Russia's Epics, Chronicles, and Tales,* edited by S. A. Zenkovsky. NY, 1963.

LeClerc [Leklerk], Nicolas. *Histoire physique, morale, civile, et politique de la Russie ancienne et moderne.* 6 vols. Paris, 1783–1794.

Lekarstvo ot skuki i zabot. 32 issues. Spb, 1786–1787.

Letters of Synesius of Cyrene, Bishop of Ptolemais. Translated by Augustine Fitzgerald. Oxford, 1926.

Levecque, P. S. *Histoire de Russie.* 5 vols. Paris, 1782–1783.

Levshin, V. A. *Russkiia skazki.* 10 vols. M, 1780–1783.

Liria, Duke de. *Zapiski diuka Liriiskogo i Bervikskogo vo vremia prebyvaniia ego pri imperatorskom rossiiskom dvore v zvanii posla korolia ispanskogo 1727–1730 gg.* Spb, 1845 .

Lister, Thomas. *A Mirror for Princes.* London, 1797.

Lomonosov, M. V. *Drevniaia rossiiskaia istoriia ot nachala rossiiskago naroda do konchiny velikago kniazia Iaroslava Pervago ili do 1054 goda.* Spb, 1766.

———. *Kratkii rossiiskii letopisets s rodosloviem.* Spb, 1759.

———. *Literaturnoe tvorchestvo M. V. Lomonosova.* Edited by P. Berkov and I. Serman. M, 1962.

———. *Mogushchestvo i slava . . . Elizavety . . . na novoi 1758 god.* Spb, 1758.

———. *Ody i pokhval'nyia slova Lomonosova.* M, 1837.

———. *Polnoe sobranie sochinenii.* 10 vols. M, 1959.

———. *Sobranie raznykh sochinenii.* Spb, 1778.

Lopukhin, I. V. *Blagost' i preimushchestvo edinonachalia.* M, 1795. Previously published under two different titles: *Izobrazhenie mechty ravenstva* and *Izliianie serdtsa.*

Lukashevich, G. *Oda . . . Ekaterine. . . .* M, 1775.

L'vov, P. Iu. *Khram istiny, ili Videnie Sezostrisa, tsaria egipetskago.* Spb, 1790.

———. *Rossiiskaia Pamela, ili Istoriia Marii.* Spb, 1789.

Mably, G. *Razmyshleniia o grecheskoi istorii, ili O prichinakh blagodenstviia i neschastii grekov.* Translated by A. Radishchev. Spb, 1773.

Maikov, L. N. *Rasskazy Nartova o Petre Velikom.* Spb, 1891.

Maikov, V. A. *Izbrannye proizvedeniia.* M, 1966.

Mal'gin, T. S. *Zertsalo rossiiskikh gosudarei ot rozhdestva Khristova s 862 po 1791 godu.* Spb, 1791.

Manifesty, ukazy, i drugiia pravitel'stvennyia rasporiazheniia. Spb, 1895.

Mankiev, A. I. *Iadro rossiiskoi istorii.* Spb, 1770. Also published in 1784, 1791, and 1799.

Manstein, C. H. von. *Contemporary Memoirs of Russia from the Year 1727 to 1744.* London, 1968.

Marcus Aurelius. *Zhitie i dela Marka Avreliia Antoniia, tsesaria rimskago.* Translated and annotated by S. Volchkov. Spb, 1789.

Marmontel, Jean François. *Belisarius.* London, 1773.

———. *Velizer.* M, 1768.

"Materialy dlia biografii A. P. Volynskago." *Starina i novizna* 6 (1903): 243–92.

Materialy dlia biografii knagini [sic] E. R. Dashkovoi. Leipzig, 1876.

Materialy dlia russkoi istorii. Edited by S. Belokurov. M, 1888.

"Materialy, otnosiashchiesia k Zakonodatel'noi komissi 1767 g." In *Voprosy politiki v russkom parlamente XVIII veka,* edited by V. N. Bochkarev. M, 1923.

Matveev, A. A. *Zapiski.* Spb, 1841.

Mercier, L. S. *Notions claires sur les gouvernements.* Amsterdam, 1797.

Mirievo, I. Iankovich de. *Oda . . . Ekaterine.* Spb, 1791.

Montesquieu, Baron de. *The Spirit of the Laws.* Translated by T. Nugent. NY, 1949.

Moskovskoe ezhemesiachnoe izdanie. 3 issues. M, 1781.

The Muscovite Law Code (Ulozhenie) of 1649. Translated and edited by Richard Hellie. Irvine, 1988.

Nachertanie vseobshchei istorii v pol'zu . . . iunoshestva. . . . M, 1794.

Nashchokin, V. A. *Zapiski.* Spb, 1842.

Nastavlenie mladentsam. Moral', istoriia, i geografiia. Spb, 1774.

Nekhachin, D. V., and I. V. Nekhachin. *Novoe kratkoe poniatie o vsekh naukakh, ili Detskaia nastol'naia uchebnaia kniga.* 3 vols. M, 1796–1797.

Nekhachin, I. V. *Istoricheskoi slovar' rossiiskikh gosudarei, kniazei, tsarei, imperatorov, i imperatrits.* M, 1793.

Nikolev, N. P. "Sorena i Zamir." In *Stikhotvornaia tragediia kontsa XVIII–nachala XIX v.,* edited by V. A. Bochkarev. M, 1964.

N. I. Novikov i ego sovremenniki: Izbrannye sochineniia. M, 1961.

Nizverzhennyi Zelul, obrazets zloby, ili Zhizn' i redkiia prikliucheniia vostochnago printsa Kleoranda i printsessy Zefizy. M, 1794.

Noveishee povestvovatel'noe zemleopisanie . . . dlia maloletnykh detei. . . . Spb, 1795.

Novikov, N. I. *Opyt istoricheskago slovaria o rossiiskikh pisateliakh.* Spb, 1772.

"Obstoiatel'noe opisanie . . . koronovaniia . . . Ekateriny Vtoroi." *Zhurnal kamerfur'erskii* (1762): 30–34.

Obstoiatel'noe opisanie . . . koronovaniia . . . Elisavety Petrovny (25 aprelia 1742). Spb, 1744.

O gosudarstvennom pravlenii i raznykh rodakh onago iz Entsiklopedii. Translated by I. Tumanskii. Spb, 1770.

Olearius. *The Travels of Olearius in Seventeenth-Century Russia.* Translated and edited by Samuel H. Baron. Stanford, 1967.

"O nekotorykh persidskikh tsarei, po vostochnym pisateliam." *Sochineniia i perevody* (1759): 55–59.

Opisanie koronatsii Eia Velichestva Imperatritsy i Samoderzhitsy Vserossiiskoi, Anny Ioannovny . . . 28 Aprelia 1730. M, 1730.

Osmnadtsatyi vek: Istoricheskii sbornik. Edited by P. I. Bartenev. 4 vols. M, 1869.

Osterman, I. A. "Proekt grafa I. A. Ostermana o prevedenii v blagosostoianie Rossii." In *Arkhiv kniazia Vorontsova.* Vol. 25. M, 1880.

Ozerov, V. A. *Sochineniia Ozerova.* 3 vols. Spb, 1828.

Palitsyn, A. *Skazanie Avraamiia Palitsyna.* Edited by O. A. Derzhavina and E. V. Kolosova. M, 1955.

Panin, N. "Spisok s chernago sobstvennoruchnago doklada." *Sbornik Imperatorskago russkago istoricheskago obshchestva* 7 (1871): 202–22.

Paul I. "Nakaz Imperatora Pavla I, 1788 g." *Vestnik Evropy* 1 (1867): 316–22.

Perepechin, A. *Oda . . . Ekaterine.* M, 1767.

Peresvetov, I. *Sochineniia I. Peresvetova.* Edited by A. Zimin. M, 1956.

Peter I [Petr Velikii]. *Pis'ma i bumagi Imperatora Petra Velikago.* 13 vols. Spb, 1887–.

———. *Pis'ma Petra Velikago, pisannyia k grafu B. P. Sheremetevu.* M, 1774.

———. *Tetrady zapisnyia . . . 1704–1706.* Spb, 1774.

———. *Ukazy Petra Velikago.* Spb, 1777.

Peter III. "Tri pis'ma Petra III-go iz Ropshi k Ekaterine II-oi." *Russkii arkhiv* 2 (1911): 20–21.

Petrov, V. P. "Istoriia Karla Velikago." *Rastushchii vinograd* (April 1785): 44–50 and (May 1785): 25–34.

———. "K . . . iz Londona." *Poety XVIII veka.* M, 1936.

———. "Oda na karusel'." *Poety XVIII veka.* M, 1936.

Pizan, Christine de. *The Book of the Body Politic.* Edited and translated by Kate Langdon Forhan. Cambridge, 1994.

Plato. *The Republic.* Translated by Desmond Lee. Baltimore, 1955.

Platon [Levshin]. *Prodolzhenie pouchitel'nykh slov pri vysochaishem dvore . . . Ekateriny. . . .* 3 vols. Spb, 1767–1769.

———. *Slovo . . . nad grobom Petra Velikago. . . .* Spb, 1770.

———. *Slovo pri zalozhenii Imp. Akademii khudozhestv i pri nei tserkvi.* Spb, 1765.

Plavil'shchikov, P. A. *Sochineniia Petra Plavil'shchikova.* Spb, 1816.

Pliny. *Letters and Panegyricus.* 2 vols. Translated by Betty Radice. London, 1969.

Pochta dukhov. 8 issues. Spb, 1789.

Poety XVIII veka. M, 1936.

Poety XVIII veka. 2 vols. L, 1972.

Pokoiashchiisia trudoliubets. M, 1784–1785.

Poletika, A. A. "Dnevnik." *Syn otechestva* 3 (1842): 1–24.

Poleznoe uprazhnenie iunoshestva, sostoiashchee v raznykh sochineniiakh i perevodakh, iz-

dannykh pitomtsami Vol'nago blagorodnago pansiona, uchrezhdennago pri Imperatorskom moskovskom universitete. M, 1789.

Poleznoe uveselenie. M, 1760–1762.

Politicheskie protsessy pri Petre I: Po materialam Preobrazhenskogo prikaza. M, 1957.

Polnoe sobranie pouchitel'nykh slov. M, 1784.

Polnoe sobranie zakonov rossiiskoi imperii. Sobranie 1. 45 vols. Spb, 1830.

Polnyi vseobshchii pis'movnik. 3rd edition. M, 1805.

Polotskii, S. *Izbrannye sochineniia*. M, 1953.

Polybius. *The Histories*. Translated by W. R. Paton. Cambridge, Mass., 1966.

Popov, M. *Slavenskiia drevnosti, ili Prikliucheniia slavenskikh kniazei*. 2 vols. M, 1771. The novel was republished in 1778, 1793, and 1794 under the title *Starinny dikovniki*.

Pososhkov, I. T. *The Book of Poverty and Wealth*. Edited and translated by A. P. Vlasto and L. R. Lewitter. London, 1987.

———. *Kniga o skudosti i bogatstve*. Edited by B. B. Kafengauz. M, 1951.

———. *Sbornik pisem I. T. Pososhkova k Mitropolitu Stefanu Iavorskomu*. Edited by V. I. Sreznevskii. Spb, 1910.

———. *Sochineniia*. Edited by M. P. Pogodin. M, 1842.

———. *Zaveshchanie otecheskoe k synu*. Edited by A. Popov. M, 1873.

———. *Zerkalo ochevidnoe*. Edited by A. Tsarevskii. 2 vols. Kazan, 1895–1900.

Pravda russkaia. Edited by I. N. Botlin. Spb, 1792.

Prokopovich, Feofan. *Istoriia Imperatora Petra Velikago, ot rozhdeniia ego do Poltavskoi batalii*. . . . Spb, 1773. 2nd edition published in M, 1788.

———. *Istoriia o izbranii i vosshestvii na prestol . . . Anny Ioannovny*. Spb, 1837.

———. "Iz"iasnenie, kakovy byli nekikh lits umysli, zateiki, i deistviia v prizov na prestol Eia Imperatorskago Velichestva." In *Pamiatniki novoi russkoi istorii*, edited by P. Kashpirev. Vol. 1, pt. 2. Spb, 1871.

———. *Kratkaia povest' o smerti Petra Velikogo*. Spb, 1819.

———. "O smerti Imperatora Petra Vtorago i o vozshestvii na prestol Gosudaryni Imperatritsy Anny Ioannovny." *Moskovskii vestnik* 1 (1830): 42–74.

———. "Pozdravitel'noe pis'mo Imperatritse Anne Ioannovne." *Zhurnal Ministerstva narodnago prosvesheniia* 9 (1836): 577–78.

———. *Slova i rechi*. 2 vols. Spb, 1760.

———. *Slovo v den' vosshestviia na . . . prestol . . . Anny Ioannovny*. Spb, 1733.

———. *Sochineniia*. Edited by I. P. Eremin. M, 1961.

"Protokoly Verkhovnago tainago soveta." *Chteniia v Imperatorskom Obshchestve istorii i drevnostei rossiiskikh pri Moskovskom universitete* 3 (1858): 1–124.

Pufendorf, S. *L'Introduction à l'histoire générale . . . où l'on voit . . . les interêts des souverains*. Amsterdam, 1743.

Radishchev, A. N. *A Journey from St. Petersburg to Moscow*. Translated by Leo Wiener and edited by Roderick P. Thaler. Cambridge, Mass., 1958.

———. "Pis'mo k drugu, zhitel'stvuiushchemu v Tobol'ske." In *Izbrannye filosofskie i obshchestvenno-politicheskie proizvedeniia*. M, 1952.

———. *PSS*. Spb, 1907.

———. *Zhitie Fedora Vasil'evicha Ushakova*. Spb, 1789.

Rastushchii vinograd. Monthly. Spb, 1785–1787.

Razgovory o fizicheskikh i nravstvennykh predmetakh. M, 1800.

Raznyia povestvovaniia: Sochinenyia nekotoroiu rossiiankoiu. Spb, 1779.

Rechi, proiznesennyia v torzhestvennykh sobraniiakh Imperatorskago Moskovskago univer-

siteta russkimi professorami onago. M, 1819.

Recueil générale des anciennes lois françaises. Paris, 1821–1833.

Richelieu, Armand Jean du Plessis, duc de. *Mémoires du Cardinal de Richelieu.* Vol. 9. Paris, 1929.

Rivière, P. Le Mercier de la. *L'Ordre naturel et essentiel des sociétés politiques.* London, 1767.

"Rondeau to Lord Viscount Townshead." *Sbornik Imperatorskago russkago istorichesk-ago obshchestva* 66 (1889).

Rumiantsev, S. P. "Petr Velikii." *Sobesednik* 7 (1783): 173.

Russian Primary Chronicle: Laurentian Text. Translated and edited by S. H. Cross and O. P. Sherbowitz-Wetzor. Cambridge, Mass., 1953.

Sankt-Peterburgskii merkurii. Monthly. Spb, 1793.

Sankt-Peterburgskii vestnik. 42 issues. Spb, 1778–1781.

Schlözer [Shletser], A. L. *Izobrazhenie rossiiskoi istorii.* Translated by N. Nazimov. Spb, n.d.

Scottus, Sedulius. *On Christian Rulers.* Translated by Edward G. Doyle. Binghamton, NY, 1983.

Segel, Harold B., ed. and trans. *The Literature of Eighteenth-Century Russia.* 2 vols. NY, 1967.

Ségur, L.-Ph. de. *Mémoires, ou Souvenirs et anecdotes.* Paris, 1826.

Shaden, I. M. *Slovo o dushe zakonov.* M, 1767.

Shafirov, P. P. *Razsuzhdenie, kakie zakonnyia prichiny Ego Velichestvo Petr Velikii . . . k nachatiiu voiny protiv korolia Karla XII shvedskago 1700 godu imel.* Spb, 1722.

Shakhovskoi, Ia. P. "Zapiski." *Russkaia starina* 24 (1872): 10–24.

Shcherbatov, M. M. *Istoriia rossiiskaia ot drevneishikh vremen.* 7 vols. Spb, 1774–1791.

———. *Pis'mo kniazia Shcherbatova k priiateliu.* M, 1788.

———. *Prince M. M. Shcherbatov: On the Corruption of Morals in Russia.* Edited and translated by A. Lentin. Cambridge, 1969.

———. "Raznyia sochineniia." *Chteniia v Imperatorskom Obshchestve istorii i drevnostei rossiiskikh pri Moskovskom universitete* 1 (1860): 5–22.

———. *Sochineniia kniazia M. M. Shcherbatova.* 2 vols. Edited by I. P. Khrushchov. Spb, 1896–1898.

Shoffen, D. E. *Istoriia slavnykh gosudarei i velikikh generalov.* Spb, 1765.

Shusherin, I. K. *Zhitie sviateishago Patriarsha Nikona, pisannoe nekotorym byvshim pri nem klirikom.* Spb, 1784.

Sievers, D. P. "Imperator Petr Tretii. Zapiski D. P. Siversa." *Russkii arkhiv* 7 (1909): 518–26.

"Slovo o zhitii i prestavlenii velikogo kniazia Dmitriia Ivanovicha." *Pamiatniki starin-noi russkoi literatury* 8 (1856): 53–60.

Sobesednik liubitelei rossiiskago slova. 16 issues. Spb, 1783–1784.

Sobranie novostei. Monthly. Spb, 1775–1776.

Sochineniia i perevody k pol'ze i uveseleniiu sluzhashchiie. Monthly. 1755–1764.

Sokovnin, S. P. *Opyt istoricheskago slovaria o vsekh v istinnoi pravoslavnoi greko-rossiiskoi vere sviatoiu neporochnuiu zhizniiu proslavivshikhsia muzhakh.* M, 1784.

Sokrashchenie estestvennago prava vybrannoe iz raznykh avtorov dlia pol'zy rossiiskago ob-shchestva. Edited and translated by V. T. Zolotinskii. Spb, 1764.

Stählin [Shtelen], Ia. Ia. *Geschichte Russlands von den Anfängen bis zur Gegenwart.* 1772. Reprint, Graz, 1931.

———. *Liubopytnyia i dostopamiatnyia skazaniia o Imp. Petre Velikom.* Spb, 1786.

———. *Opisanie feierverka . . . o zakliuchennom mire. . . .* Spb, 1762.

———. *Vsepoddanneishee pozdravlenie. . . .* Spb, 1741.

———. "Zapiski . . . o Petre Tret'em. . . ." *Chteniia v Imperatorskom Obshchestve istorii i drevnostei rossiskikh pri Moskovskom universitete* 4 (1866): 95.

Stikhotvornaia tragediia kontsa XVIII–nachala XIX v. Edited by V. A. Bochkarev. M, 1964.

Sumarokov, A. P. *Izbrannye proizvedeniia.* L, 1957.

———. *Polnoe sobranie vsekh sochinenii, v stikhakh i proze.* Edited by N. Novikov. 10 vols. M, 1781–1787.

Synesius. *The Letters of Synesius of Cyrene, Bishop of Ptolemais.* Translated by Augustine Fitzgerald. Oxford, 1926.

Tatishchev, V. N. "Dve zapiski Tatishcheva, otnosiashchiiasia k tsarstvovaniiu Imperatritsy Anny: Proizvol'noe i soglasnoe razsuzhdenie i mnenie sobravshagosia shliakhetstva russkago o pravlenii gosudarstvennom." *Utro* (1859): 369–77.

———. *Istoriia rossiiskaia.* 6 vols. M, 1768–1784.

———. *Istoriia rossiiskaia.* 7 vols. M, 1962–1968.

———. *Leksikon rossiiskoi. Istoricheskoi, geograficheskoi, politicheskoi, i grazhdanskoi.* 3 vols. Spb, 1793.

———. *Razgovor o pol'ze nauk i uchilishch 1733.* M, 1887.

Teil's, I. *Slovo na den' vseradostnago ot previvaniia ospy.* . . . N.p., 1771.

Theobald, Francis. *A Discourse Concerning . . . the Best, Most Ancient, and Legal Form of Government.* London, 1660.

Tikhon [Malinin]. *Slovo na den' tezoimenitstva . . . Ekateriny.* . . . Spb, 1790.

———. *Slovo na . . . den' vosshetsviia na prestol.* . . . Spb, 1791.

Timofeev, Ivan. *Vremennik Ivana Timofeeva.* Edited by O. A. Derzhavina. M, 1951.

Trediakovskii, V. K. *Panegirik . . . Anne . . . Ioannovne.* Spb, 1732.

———. *Panegirik i stikhotvoreniia.* L, 1935.

———. *Sochineniia Trediakovskago.* Spb, 1849.

———. *Telemakhida.* 2 vols. Spb, 1766.

———. *Tri razsuzhdeniia o trekh glavneishikh drevnostiakh rossiiskikh.* Spb, 1773.

———, trans. *Argenida, povest' geroicheskaia.* Spb, 1751. Translation of John Barclay's *Argenis.* London, 1621.

Tret'iakov, I. A. *Slovo o proisshestvii i uchrezhdenii universitetov v Evrope na gosudarstvennykh izhdiveniiakh.* M, 1768.

———. *Slovo o rimskom pravlenii i o raznykh onago peremenakh.* . . . M, 1769.

Trubetskoi. "Zametki Trubetskago v kalendare v 1762 godu." *Russkaia starina* 73 (1892): 443–48.

Truten'. Weekly. Spb, 1769–1770.

Tumanskii, F. O. *Novyi detskii mesiatsoslov.* . . . Spb, 1787.

———. *Sobranie raznykh zapisok i sochinenii, sluzhashchikh k dostavleniiu polnago svedeniia o zhizni i deianiiakh Gosudaria Imp. Petra Velikago.* 10 vols. Spb, 1787–1788.

———. *Sozertsanie slavnyia zhizni sviatago blagovernago velikago kniazia Aleksandra Iaroslavicha Nevskogo.* Spb, 1789.

Turgenev, A. M. "Zapiski Aleksandra Mikhailovicha Turgeneva: 1772–1863." *Russkaia starina* 48 (1885): 55–82; 53 (1887): 77–106; 61 (1889): 209–30; 62 (1889): 57–62.

Turgenev [Tourgueneff], N. *La Russie et les russes.* 3 vols. Paris, 1847.

Utrennii svet. 36 issues. Spb/M, 1770–1780.

Vatveev, A. S. *Kniga ob izbranii na tsarstvo Velikago Gosudariia Mikhaila Fedorovicha.* 1672. M, 1856.

Venitseev, S. "Predislovie." In *Nachal'nyia osnovaniia filosoficheskiia o grazhdanine Fomy Gobbeziia.* Spb, 1776. N. p.

Verner, Ia. F. "Rech' o tom, chto monarshee imia liuboviiu k poddannym bezsmertie sebe priobretaet." In *Sochineniia i perevody.* Spb, 1758.

Vershnitskii, A. "Rech' Marka Avreliia . . . k synu svoemu i nasledniku prestola." *Dobroe namerenie* (1764): 429–432; 449–475.

Vil'fel'd, Baron. *Nastavleniia politicheskiia barona Vil'fel'da i Uchenie o gosudarstvennom upravlenii*. Translated by F. Shakhovskoi. M, 1768.

Vinogradov, I. "Oda . . . Ekaterine Velikoi na uchrezhdenie gosudarstvennago zaemnago banka." *Rastushchii vinograd* (1786): August, 1–8.

Vinskii, G. S. *Moe vremia*. Spb, 1914.

Virgil. *Eclogues and Georgics*. Translated by T. F. Royds. NY, 1946.

Vnutrennii byt russkago gosudarstva s 17-go oktiabria 1740 g. po 25-e noiabria 1741 goda po dokumentam. . . . M, 1886.

Volkov, D. V. "Avtobiograficheskiia zapiski." *Russkaia starina* 11 (1874): 481–87.

Volotskii, Iosif. *Prosvetitel'*. Edited by A. Volkov. Kazan, 1896.

Voltaire. *Collection complète des oeuvres*. Geneva, 1768–1777.

———. *Russia under Peter the Great*. Translated by M. F. O. Jenkins. Rutherford, NJ, 1983.

Vorontsov, A. R. "Avtobiografiia grafa A. R. Vorontsova." In *Arkhiv kniazia Vorontsova*. Vols. 5, 29. M, 1872, 1883.

Voskresenskii, N. A. *Zakonodatel'nye akty Petra I*. M, 1945.

Young, Arthur. *Travels in France during the Years 1787, 1788, 1789*. London, 1913.

Yusuf, K. *A Turko-Islamic Mirror for Princes*. Chicago, 1983.

Zakhar'in, P. *Arfakad, Khaldeiskaia vymyshlennaia povest'*. 4 vols. M, 1793–1796.

———. *Novyi sinopsis*. Nikolaev, 1798.

———. *Prikliuchenie Kleandra*. Nikolaev, 1788. Republished in 1793 and 1798.

———. *Put' k blagonraviiu, ili Sokrashchennoe nastavlenie obuchaiushchemusia iunoshestvu*. M, 1793.

"Zamechaniia neizvestnago na manifest ob uchrezhdenii Imperatorskago soveta i razdelenie Senata na departamenty." *Sbornik Imperatorskago Russkago istoricheskago obshchestva* 7 (1871): 218.

"Zapiska ob Artemii Volynskom." *Chteniia v Imperatorskom Obshchestve istorii i drevnostei rossiiskikh* 2 (1858): 135–70.

Zapiska o konchine Gosudaryni Imperatritsy Ekateriny Alekseevny i o vstuplenii na prestol Gosudaria Imperatora Petra II Alekseevicha. Spb, 1913.

"Zapiska sovremennika, gruzinskogo arkhiereia, o vstuplenii na prestol Imp. Ekateriny II." *Chteniia v Imperatorskom Obshchestve istorii i drevnostei rossiiskikh* 4 (1900): 17–24.

Zaveshchanie otecheskoe k synu. Edited by A. Popov. M, 1873.

Zenkovsky, S. A., ed. *Medieval Russia's Epics, Chronicles, and Tales*. NY, 1963.

Zhivopisets. Weekly. 1772–1773.

Zhizn' Imperatritsy Marii Terezii, materi tsarstvuiushchago nyne Imperatora Iosifa II. Spb, 1789.

Zhizn' i stradanie Liudovika XVI . . . s razsmotreniem tsare-ubiistvennago opredeleniia. Translated by V. Kriazhev. M, 1793.

Zhizn' i uzhastnyia deianiia rimskago imperatora Nerona. Translated by T. Mozhaiskii. Spb, 1792.

Zritel'. 11 issues. Spb, 1792.

"Zvezda na lbu, ili znak dobrykh del." *Raznyia povestvovaniia: Sochinennyia nekotoroiu rossiiankoiu*. Spb, 1779.

SECONDARY SOURCES

Afferica, Joan M. "The Political and Social Thought of Prince M. M. Shcherbatov." Ph.D. diss., Harvard University, 1967.

Ageeva, O. G. "Imperskii status Rossii: K istorii politicheskogo mentaliteta russkogo obshchestva nachala XVIII veka." In *Tsar' i tsarstvo v russkom obshchestvennom soznanii. Mirovospriiatie i samosoznanie russkogo obshchestva,* edited by A. A. Gorskii et al. M, 1999.

Alef, Gustav. "The Adoption of the Muscovite Two-Headed Eagle: A Discordant View." *Speculum* 41 (1966): 1–21.

———. "The Political Significance of the Inscriptions on Muscovite Coinage in the Reign of Vasili II." *Speculum* 34 (1959): 1–19.

Alefirenko, P. K. *Krest'ianskoe dvizhenie i krest'ianskii vopros v Rossii v 30–50 godakh XVIII veka.* M, 1958.

Alekseev, A. S. "Legenda ob oligarkhicheskikh tendentsiiakh v tsarstvovanii Ekateriny I." *Russkoe obozrenie* 1 (1896): 76–129, 755–75.

Alekseeva, O. V. "Khronologicheskii ukazatel'." In *Materialy po istorii russkoi detskoi literatury (1750–1855),* edited by A. K. Pokrovskaia. M, 1929.

Alexander, John T. "Catherine II's Efforts at Liberalization and Their Aftermath." In *Reform in Russia and the U.S.S.R.,* edited by Robert O. Crummey. Urbana, 1989.

———. *Catherine the Great: Life and Legend.* NY, 1989.

———. "Favourites, Favouritism, and Female Rule in Russia, 1725–1796." In *Russia in the Age of the Enlightenment,* edited by Roger Bartlett and Janet M. Hartley. London, 1990.

Anastos, Milton V. "Byzantine Political Theory: Its Classical Precedents and Legal Embodiment." In *The Past in Medieval and Modern Greek Culture,* edited by S. Vryonis, Jr. Malibu, 1978.

Anderson, M. S. *Europe in the Eighteenth Century, 1713–1783.* London, 1987.

———. *Peter the Great.* London, 1995.

Anderson, Perry. *Lineages of the Absolutist State.* London, 1974.

Andreev, V. V. *Predstaviteli vlasti v Rossii posle Petra I.* Spb, 1870.

Andreyev, Nikolay. "Filofey and his Epistle to Ivan Vasil'yevich." *Slavonic and East European Review* 38 (1959–1960): 1–31.

Androsov, S. "Ivan Nikitin i 'Delo Rokyshevskogo.'" *Study Group on Eighteenth-Century Russia Newsletter* 21 (1993): 22–35.

Anisimov, Evgenii V. *Empress Elizabeth: Her Reign and Her Russia, 1741–1761.* Translated by John T. Alexander. Gulf Breeze, Fla., 1995.

———. *Reforms of Peter the Great: Progress through Coercion in Russia.* Translated by John T. Alexander. Armonk, NY, 1993.

———. *Rossiia v seredine XVIII veka: Bor'ba za nasledie Petra.* M, 1986.

———. "Russia in Search of a New National Ethos." *Meeting Report: Kennan Institute for Advanced Russian Studies* 8, no. 16 (lecture of 14 May 1991, as reported by P. McInerny).

Artem'eva, T.V. *Russkaia istoriosofiia XVIII veka.* Spb, 1996.

———, ed., and M. I. Mikeshin. *Filosofskii vek. Al'manakh 17: Istoriia idei kak metodologiia gumanitarnykh issledovanii.* 2 vols. Spb, 2001.

Ashley, Kathleen, and Robert L. A. Clark, eds. *Medieval Conduct.* Minneapolis, 2001.

Augustine, Wilson R. "Notes Toward a Portrait of the Eighteenth-Century Russian Nobility." *Canadian Slavic Studies* 4 (1970): 373–425.

Avrich, Paul. *Russian Rebels, 1600–1800.* NY, 1972.

Azanchevskii, F. M. *Istoriia Preobrazhenskago polka.* M, 1859.

Baehr, Stephen L. "From History to National Myth: *Translatio imperii* in Eighteenth-Century Russia." *Russian Review* 27, no. 1 (1978): 1–14.

———. *The Paradise Myth in Eighteenth-Century Russia: Utopian Patterns in Early Secular Russian Literature and Culture.* Stanford, 1991.

Bain, R. Nisbet. *The Daughter of Peter the Great.* NY, 1900.

———. *Peter III: Emperor of Russia.* London, 1902.

Baker, Keith Michael. "Political Thought at the Accession of Louis XVI." In *The Rise and Fall of the French Revolution,* edited by T. C. W. Blanning. Chicago, 1996.

———. "Politics and Public Opinion under the Old Regime: Some Reflections." In *Press and Politics in Pre-Revolutionary France,* edited by J. Censer and J. Popkin. Berkeley, 1987.

———, ed. *The French Revolution and the Creation of Modern Political Culture.* Vol. 1, *The Political Culture of the Old Regime.* Oxford, 1987.

Baklanova, N. A. "Tetradi startsa Avraama." *Istoricheskii arkhiv* 6 (1951): 143–55.

Bakounine, T. *Le Répertoire biographique des francs maçons russes (XVIIIe et XIXe siècles).* Brussels, 1940.

Baran, H., ed. *Semiotics and Structuralism: Readings from the Soviet Union.* White Plains, NY, 1976.

Bartlett, R. P., A. G. Cross, and Karen Rasmussen, eds. *Russia and the World of the Eighteenth Century.* Columbus, Ohio, 1988.

Bartlett, Roger, and Janet M. Hartley, eds. *Russia in the Age of the Enlightenment.* London, 1990.

Beletskii, A. I. "Stikhotvoreniia Simeona Polotskago na temy iz vseobshchei istorii." In *Sbornik statei v chest' Prof. V. P. Buzeskula.* Khar'kov, 1914.

Beliaev, I. S. *Krest'ianin-pisatel' nachala XVIII veka, I. T. Pososhkov.* M, 1902.

Ben-David, Joseph, and Terry Nichols Clark, eds. *Culture and Its Creators: Essays in Honor of Edward Shils.* Chicago, 1977.

Bennett, Donald J. "The Idea of Kingship in Seventeenth-Century Russia." Ph.D. diss., Harvard University, 1967.

Benson, Robert L. "Political *Renovatio:* Two Models from Roman Antiquity." In *Renaissance and Renewal in the Twelfth Century,* edited by Robert L. Benson and Giles Constable. Toronto, 1991.

Benson, S. "The Role of Western Political Thought in Petrine Russia." *Canadian-American Slavic Studies* 8 (1974): 254–74.

Berges, W. *Die Fürstenspiegel des hohen und späten Mittelalters.* Leipzig, 1938.

Berkov, P. N. *Istoriia russkoi zhurnalistiki XVIII veka.* M, 1952.

Berlin, Isaiah. "Alleged Relativism in Eighteenth-Century European Thought." In *The Crooked Timber of Humanity: Chapters in the History of Ideas,* edited by Henry Hardy. NY, 1992.

Besançon, Alain. *Le Tsarévitch immolé.* Paris, 1967.

Beshenkovskii, E. B. "Istoriograficheskaia sud'ba 'Rossiiskoi istorii' F. A. Emina." *Istoriia i istoriki.* (1973): 186–203.

———. "Zhizn' Fedora Emina." *XVIII vek* 11 (1976): 186–203.

Bil'basov, V. A. *Istoriia Ekateriny Vtoroi.* 2 vols. Spb, 1890.

Bissonnette, G. "Pufendorf and the Church Reforms of Peter the Great." Ph.D. diss., Columbia University, 1962.

Black, J. B. *The Art of History: A Study of Four Great Historians of the Eighteenth Century.* NY, 1965.

Blagovidov, F. "Otnoshenie sovremennikov i istorii k Nakazu . . . Ekateriny II." *Nabliudatel'* 10 (1895): 57–85.

Blamberg, M. O. "The Publicists of Peter the Great." Ph.D. diss., Indiana University, 1974.

Blanning, T. C. W., ed. *The Rise and Fall of the French Revolution.* Chicago, 1996.

Blome, Astrid. *Das deutsche Russlandbild im frühen 18. Jahrhundert.* Wiesbaden, 2000.

Blum, K. L. *Ein Russischer Staatsmann: Denkwürdigkeiten des Grafen J. J. Sievers.* 2 vols. Leipzig, 1857.

Bobrova, E. I. *Biblioteka Petra I.* L, 1978.

Bochkarev, V. N. *Voprosy politiki v russkom parlamente XVIII veka: Opyt izucheniia politicheskoi ideologii XVIII. Po materialam Zakonodatel'noi komissii 1762–1768 gg.* M, 1923.

Bödeker, Hans Erich. "Journal and Public Opinion: The Politicization of the German Enlightenment in the Second Half of the Eighteenth Century." In *The Transformation of Political Culture: England and Germany in the Late Eighteenth Century,* edited by Eckhardt Hellmuth. Oxford, 1990.

Bogoliubov, V. *N. I. Novikov i ego vremia.* M, 1916.

Bogoslovskii, M. M. *Iz istorii verkhovnoi vlasti v Rossii.* Nizhnii Novgorod, 1905.

———. *Konstitutsionnoe dvizhenie 1730 g.* M, 1906.

———. *Petr I: Materialy dlia biografii.* M, 1940

Breen, T. H. *The Character of the Good Ruler: Puritan Political Ideas in New England, 1630–1730.* NY, 1970.

Brikner, A. "Anton-Fridrikh Biushing (1724–1795)." *Istoricheskii vestnik* 7 (July 1886): 5–26.

———. *Ivan Pososhkov.* Vol. 1, *Pososhkov kak ekonomist.* Spb, 1876.

———. *Kaiser Pauls I Ende, 1801.* Stuttgard, 1897.

Brown, A. H. "The Father of Russian Jurisprudence: The Legal Thought of S. E. Desnitskii." In *Russian Law: Historical and Political Perspectives,* edited by W. E. Butler. Leyden, 1977.

Brown, William Edward. *A History of Eighteenth-Century Russian Literature.* Ann Arbor, 1980.

Bulich, N. *Sumarokov i sovremennaia emu kritika.* Spb, 1854.

Burbank, Jane, and David L. Ransel, eds. *Imperial Russia: New Histories for the Empire.* Bloomington, Ind., 1998.

Burke, Peter. *The Fabrication of Louis XIV.* New Haven, 1992.

Burns, J. H. *Lordship, Kingship, and Empire: The Idea of Monarchy, 1400–1525.* NY, 1992.

———, ed. *The Cambridge History of Medieval Political Thought, c. 350–c. 1450.* Cambridge, 1988.

———, ed. *The Cambridge History of Political Thought, 1450–1700.* Cambridge, 1991.

Bury, John B. *The Ancient Greek Historians.* NY, 1909.

Bushkovitch, Paul. "The Formation of a National Consciousness in Early Modern Russia." *Harvard Ukrainian Studies* 10 (1986): 355–76.

———. *Religion and Society in Russia: The Sixteenth and Seventeenth Centuries.* Oxford, 1992.

Butler, W. E., ed. *Russian Law: Historical and Political Perspectives.* Leyden, 1977.

Cannadine, David, ed. *Rituals of Royalty: Power and Ceremonial in Traditional Societies.* Cambridge, 1987.

Cassels, L. *The Struggle for the Ottoman Empire, 1717–1740.* London, 1966.

Censer, J., and J. Popkin, eds. *Press and Politics in Pre-Revolutionary France.* Berkeley, 1987.

Chartier, Roger. *Cultural History: Between Practices and Representations.* Ithaca, 1988.

Chechulin, N. D. *Memuary, ikh znachenie i mesto v riadu istoricheskikh istochnikov.* Spb, 1891.

———. *Nakaz Imperatritsy Ekateriny II, dannyi komissii o sochinenii proekta novago ulozheniia.* Spb, 1907.

———. "Ob istochnikakh Nakaza." *Zhurnal Ministerstva narodnago prosveshcheniia* (April 1902): 290–302.

———. *Proekt Imperatorskago soveta v pervyi god tsarstvovaniia Ekateriny II.* Spb, 1894.

———. *Russkii sotsial'nyi roman XVIII veka.* Spb, 1900.

———. *Russkoe provintsial'noe obshchestvo vo vtoroi polovine XVIII veka.* Spb, 1889.

Cherepnin, L. V. "Smuta i istoriografiia XVII v." *Istoricheskie zapiski* 14 (1945): 81–128.

———. "Zemskie sobory i utverzhdenie absoliutizma v Rossii." In *Absoliutizm v Rossii, XVII–XVIII vv.,* edited by N. M. Druzhinin. M, 1964.

Cherniavsky, Michael. "Ivan the Terrible and the Iconography of the Kremlin Cathedral of Archangel Michael." *Russian History* 2 (1975): 3–28.

———. "Ivan the Terrible as Renaissance Prince." *Slavic Review* 27 (1968): 195–211.

———. "Khan or Basileus: An Aspect of Russian Medieval Political Theory." In *The Structure of Russian History,* edited by M. Cherniavsky. NY, 1970.

———. *Tsar and People: Studies in Russian Myths.* New Haven, 1961.

———, ed. *The Structure of Russian History.* NY, 1970.

Chernov, S. N. "M. V. Lomonosov v odakh 1762 g." *XVIII vek* (1935): 133–79.

Chistovich, I. A. "Feofan Prokopovich i ego vremia." In *Sbornik statei chitannykh v otdelenii russkago iazyka i slovesnosti Akademii nauk.* Vol. 4. Spb, 1868.

———. "Uchenyi kruzhok Feofana Prokopovicha." In *A. D. Kantemir, ego zhizn' i sochineniia,* edited by V. Pokrovskii. M, 1910.

Church, William F. *Richelieu and Reason of State.* Princeton, 1972.

Clardy, Jesse. *The Philosophical Ideas of Alexander Radishchev.* London, 1964.

Clark, George N. *The Seventeenth Century.* Oxford, 1929.

Cohen, Jean L., and Andrew Arato. "Civil Society and Political Theory." In *The Transformation of Politial Culture: England and Germany in the Late Eighteenth Century,* edited by Eckhart Hellmuth. Oxford, 1990.

Coleman, Janet. *Medieval Readers and Writers, 1350–1400.* NY, 1981.

Cracraft, James. *The Church Reform of Peter the Great.* Stanford, 1971.

———. "Did Feofan Prokopovich Really Write *Pravda voli monarshei?*" *Slavic Review* 40 (1981): 173–93.

———. "Empire Versus Nation: Russian Political Theory under Peter I." *Harvard Ukrainian Studies* 10 (1986): 524–21.

———. "Opposition to Peter the Great." In *Imperial Russia 1700-1917: State, Society, Opposition,* edited by E. Mendelsohn and M. Shatz. DeKalb, 1988.

———. "The Succession Crisis of 1730: A View from the Inside." *Canadian-American Slavic Studies* 12 (1978): 61–84.

Cross, A. G., ed. *Russia and the West in the Eighteenth Century.* Newtonville, Mass., 1983.

Cross, A. G., and G. S. Smith, eds. *Literature, Lives, and Legality in Catherine's Russia.* Nottingham, England, 1994.

Crummey, Robert O. *Autocrats and Servitors: The Boyar Elite in Russia, 1613–1689.* Princeton, 1983.

———. "Court Spectacles in Seventeenth-Century Russia: Illusion and Reality." In *Essays in Honor of A. A. Zimin.* Columbus, Ohio, 1985.

———. *The Formation of Muscovy, 1304–1613.* NY, 1987.

———, ed. *Reform in Russia and the U.S.S.R.: Past and Prospects.* Urbana, 1989.

Daniels, R. L. "V. N. Tatishchev and the Succession Crisis of 1730." *Slavic and East European Review* 49 (1971): 550–59.

Darnton, Robert. *The Forbidden Best Sellers of Prerevolutionary France.* NY, 1994.

Das, David. "History Writing and the Quest for Fame in Late Muscovy: Andrei Lyzlov's *History of the Scythians.*" *Russian Review* 51 (1992): 502–9.

Datsiuk, B. D. *Iurii Krizhanich: Ocherk politicheskikh i istoricheskikh vzgliadov.* M, 1946.

Derbov, L. A. *Istoricheskie vzgliady russkikh prosvetitelei vtoroi poloviny XVIII veka.* Saratov, 1987.

———. *Obshchestvenno-politicheskie i istoricheskie vzgliady N. I. Novikova.* Saratov, 1974.

Detstvo, vospitanie, i leta iunosti russkikh imperatorov. Spb, 1914.

D"iakonov, M. *Vlast' moskovskikh gosudarei: Ocherki iz istorii politicheskikh idei Drevnei Rusi do kontsa XVI veka.* Spb, 1889.

———. "Vydaiushchiisia russkii publitsist XVIII veka." *Vestnik prava* 7 (1904): 1–27.

Dickinson, Sara. "The Poetics of National Landscape in Radishchev's Journey." Paper delivered at the National Convention of the American Association for the Advancement of Slavic Studies, September 1998.

Ditiatin, I. I. "Verkhovnaia vlast' v Rossii XVIII stoletiia." In *Stat'i po istorii russkago prava,* by I. I. Ditiatin. Spb, 1895.

Dmitrieva, R. P. *Skazanie o kniaziakh vladimirskikh.* M, 1955.

Dostoevskii, F. M. "Nabroski i plany." *PSS.* Vol. 9:113–14. L, 1974.

Druzhinin, N. M., ed. *Absoliutizm v Rossii, XVII–XVIII vv.* M, 1964.

Duffy, Christopher, ed. *Russia's Military Way to the West: Origins and Nature of Russian Military Power, 1700–1800.* London, 1981.

Dufour, Alfred. "Pufendorf." In *The Cambridge History of Political Thought, 1450–1700,* edited by J. H. Burns. Cambridge, 1991.

Dukes, Paul. *Catherine the Great and the Russian Nobility: A Study Based on the Materials of the Legislative Commission of 1767.* Cambridge, 1967.

———, ed. and trans. *Russia under Catherine the Great.* Vol 1, *Select Documents on Government and Society.* Newtonville, Mass., 1978.

Dülmen, Richard van. *The Society of the Enlightenment: The Rise of the Middle Class and Enlightenment Culture in Germany,* translated by Anthony Williams. Cambridge, 1992.

Dunbabin, Jean. "Government, c. 1150–c. 1450." In *The Cambridge History of Medieval Political Thought, c. 350–c. 1450,* edited by J. H. Burns. Cambridge, 1988.

Duran, James A., Jr. "The Reform of Financial Administration in Russia During the Reign of Catherine II." *Canadian Slavic Studies* 4 (1970): 464–96.

Durin, P. N. *Istoriia Leib-gvardii Semenovskago polka.* Spb, 1883.

Dvornik, Francis. "Byzantium, Muscovite Autocracy, and the Church." In *Rediscovering Eastern Christendom,* edited by A. H. Armstrong and E. J. B. Fry. London, 1963.

———. *Early Christian and Byzantine Political Philosophy: Origin and Background.* 2 vols. Dumbarton Oaks, 1966.

——. "The Emperor Julian's 'Reactionary' Ideas on Kingship." In *Late Classical and Mediaeval Studies*, edited by Kurt Weitzmann. Princeton, 1955.

——. *The Slavs: Their Early History and Civilization*. Boston, 1956.

Edgerton, William B. "Ambivalence as the Key to Kniazhnin's Tragedy 'Vadim Novgorodskii.'" In *Russia and the World of the Eighteenth Century*, edited by R. P. Bartlett, A. G. Cross, and Karen Rasmussen. Columbus, Ohio, 1988.

Egorov, S. A. "M. M. Shcherbatov o preobrazovanii gosudarstvennogo stroia v Rossii." *Sovetskoe gosudarstvo i pravo* 1 (1985): 112–19.

Eidel'man, N. Ia. *Gran' vekov: Politicheskaia bor'ba v Rossii v kontse XVIII–nachale XIX stoletiia*. M, 1982.

Elias, Norbert. *The Court Society*. Translated by Edmund Jephcott. NY, 1983.

Eliseev, G. Z. "Nakaz Imperatritsy Ekateriny o sochinenii proekta novago ulozheniia." *Otechestvennye zapiski* 176 (1868): 78–80.

Elliott, J. H., and H. G. Koenigsberger, eds. *The Diversity of History*. Ithaca, 1970.

Elliott, J. H., and L. W. B. Brockliss, eds. *The World of the Favourite*. New Haven, 1999.

Ellis, Harold A. *Boulainvilliers and the French Monarchy: Aristocratic Politics in Early Eighteenth-Century France*. Ithaca, 1988.

Emerson, Caryl. *Boris Godunov: Transpositions of a Russian Theme*. Bloomington, Ind., 1986.

Endicott-West, Elizabeth. *Mongolian Rule in China*. Cambridge, Mass., 1989.

Engster, Daniel. *Divine Sovereignty: The Origins of Modern State Power*. DeKalb, 2001.

Epifanov, P. P. "'Uchenaia druzhina' i prosvetitel'stvo XVIII veka." *Voprosy istorii* 3 (1963): 37–53.

Ermolaev, L. "Kniga o postanovlenii blagochestivykh tsarei i velikikh kniazei na tsarstvo." In *Gosudarstvo i tserkov v ikh vsaimnykh otnosheniiakh v moskovskom gosudarstve*, edited by A. Ia. Shpakov. Kiev, 1904.

Eshevskii, S. V. "Ocherk tsarstvovaniia Elizavety Petrovny." *Otechestvennyia zapiski* (1868): no. 5, 17–58; no. 6, 337–419; no. 7, 9–62.

Esipov, G. *Raskol'nich'i dela*. 2 vols. Spb, 1863.

Etse, F. Kh. "Poezdka Imp. Elizavety Petrovny v estliandskuiu guberniiu." *Russkii arkhiv* (1895): 5–12.

Faggionato, Raffaella. "From a Society of the Enlightened to the Enlightenment of Society: The Russian Bible Society and Rosicrucianism in the Age of Alexander I." *Slavonic and East European Review* 79 (2001): 461–87.

Fedosov, I. A. *Iz istorii russkoi obshchestvennoi mysli XVIII stoletiia: M. M. Shcherbatov*. M, 1967.

Fedotov, George P. *Kievan Christianity: The Tenth to the Thirteenth Centuries*. NY, 1946.

Feinstein, S. C. "V. N. Tatishchev and the Development of the Concept of State Service in Petrine and Pre-Petrine Russia." Ph.D. diss., New York University, 1971.

Fennell, J. L. I. "The Dynastic Crisis of 1497–1502." *Slavonic and East European Review* 39 (1960–1961): 1–23.

Ferster, Judith. *Fictions of Advice: The Literature and Politics of Counsel in Late Medieval England*. Philadelphia, 1996.

Figgis, John Neville. *The Divine Right of Kings*. 1896. Reprint, Cambridge, 1967.

Filippov, A. N. "A. P. Volynskii, kak kabinet-ministr." *Istoricheskii vestnik* 84 (1901): 552–68.

——. *Istoriia senata v pravlenie Verkhovnago tainago soveta i kabineta*. Iu'rev, 1895.

Fine, John V. A., Jr. "The Muscovite Dynastic Crisis of 1497–1502." *Canadian Slavonic Papers* 8 (1966): 198–215.

Firsov, N. N. *Petr III i Ekaterina II: Pervye gody eia tsarstvovaniia: Opyt kharakteristiki.* Petrograd, 1915.

———. *Vstuplenie na prestol imperatritsy Elizavety Petrovny.* Kazan, 1888.

Fleischacker, H. "Porträt Peters III." *Jahrbücher für Geschichte Osteuropas* 5 (1957): 127–89.

Florinsky, Michael T. *Russia: A History and an Interpretation.* 2 vols. NY, 1961.

Florovskii, A. V. *Sostav zakonodatel'noi komissii.* Odessa, 1915.

Florovsky, Georges. "The Problem of Old Russian Culture." *Slavic Review* 21 (1962): 1–15.

Foucault, Michel. *The Archaeology of Knowledge and the Discourse on Language.* Translated by A. M. Sheridan Smith. NY, 1972.

———. *The History of Sexuality: An Introduction.* Vol. 2, *The Use of Pleasure.* Translated by R. Hurley. NY, 1990.

Fradenburg, Louise Olga, ed. *Women and Sovereignty.* Edinburgh, 1992.

Frančić, Mirosław. *Juraj Križanić, Idealog Absolutyzmu.* Warsaw, 1974.

François, Étienne, ed. *Sociabilité et société bourgeoise en France, en Allemagne, et en Suisse, 1750–1850.* Paris, 1986.

Franklin, Julian H. *Jean Bodin and the Rise of Absolutist Theory.* Cambridge, Mass., 1972.

Fuhrmann, Joseph T. *Tsar Alexis: His Reign and His Russia.* Gulf Breeze, Fla., 1981.

Fulbrook, Mary. "Religion, Revolution, and Absolutist Rule in Germany and in England." *European Studies Review* 12 (July 1982): 301–21.

Fuller, William C., Jr. *Strategy and Power in Russia, 1600–1914.* NY, 1992.

Garrard, J. G., ed. *The Eighteenth Century in Russia.* Oxford, 1973.

Geertz, Clifford. "Centers, Kings, and Charisma: Reflections on the Symbolics of Power." In *Culture and Its Creators: Essays in Honor of Edward Shils,* edited by Joseph Ben-David and Terry Nichols Clark. Chicago, 1977.

Gerhard, Dietrich. *Old Europe: A Study of Continuity, 1000–1800.* NY, 1981.

Giesey, Ralph E. "The King Imagined." In *The French Revolution and the Creation of Modern Political Culture.* Vol. 1, *The Political Culture of the Old Regime.* Edited by Keith Michael Baker. Oxford, 1987.

Gleason, Walter J. "The Course of Russian History According to an Eighteenth-Century Layman." *Laurentian University Review* 10 (1977): 17–29.

———. *Moral Idealists, Bureaucracy, and Catherine the Great.* New Brunswick, NJ, 1981.

———. "Political Ideals and Loyalties of Some Russian Writers of the Early 1760s." *Slavic Review* 34 (1975): 560–75.

———. "Pufendorf and Wolff in the Literature of Catherinian Russia." *Germano-Slavica* 2 (1978): 427–37.

———. "The Two Faces of the Monarch: Legal and Mythical Fictions in Lomonosov's Ruler Imagery." *Canadian-American Slavic Studies* 16 (1982): 388–409.

Glinskii, B. B. *Bor'ba za konstitutsiiu 1612–1861 gg.* Spb, 1908.

———. "K voprosu o titule 'samoderzhets.'" *Istoricheskii vestnik* 2 (1913): 567–603.

Golikov, I. *Zhizn' Leforta i Gordona.* M, 1800.

Golikova, N. B. *Politicheskie protsessy pri Petre I: Po materialam Preobrazhenskogo prikaza.* M, 1957.

Golitsyn, F. N. "Zhizn' ober-kamergera Ivana Ivanovicha Shuvalova." *Moskvitianin* 6 (1853): 87–98.

Golitsyn, N. V. "Feofan Prokopovich i votsarenie Imp. Anny Ioannovny." *Vestnik Evropy* 2 (1907): 519–43.

Gooch, G. P. *Catherine the Great and Other Studies.* Hamden, Conn., 1966.

———. *History and Historians in the Nineteenth Century.* Boston, 1959.

Goodenough, Edwin R. "The Political Philosophy of Hellenistic Kingship." *Yale Classical Studies* 1 (1928): 55–102.

Gordin, Ia. *Mezh rabstvom i svobodoi.* Spb, 1994.

Gordon, Daniel. "'Public Opinion' and the Civilizing Process in France: The Example of Morellet." *Eighteenth-Century Studies* 22 (1989): 303–28.

Gorskii, A. A., A. I. Kuprianov, and L. N. Pushkarev, eds. *Tsar' i tsarstvo v russkom obshchestvennom soznanii.* Vol. 2 of *Mirovospriiatie i samosoznanie russkogo obshchestva.* M, 1999.

Got'e, Iu. V. "Proekt o popravlenii gosudarstvennykh del Artemiia Petrovicha Volynskago." *Dela i dni* 3 (1922): 1–30.

Gratsianskii, P. S. *Politicheskaia i pravovaia mysl' v Rossii vtoroi poloviny XVIII v.* M, 1984.

Green, Richard Firth. *Poets and Princepleasers: Literature and the English Court in the Late Middle Ages.* Toronto, 1980.

Grey, Ian. *Ivan III and the Unification of Russia.* NY, 1964.

Griffiths, David. "Catherine II: The Republican Empress." *Jahrbücher für Geschichte Osteuropas* 21 (1973): 323–44.

———. "In Search of Enlightenment: Recent Soviet Interpretations of Eighteenth-Century Russian Intellectual History." *Canadian-American Slavic Studies* 16 (1982): 317–56.

———. "To Live Forever: Catherine II, Voltaire, and the Pursuit of Immortality." In *Russia and the World in the Eighteenth Century,* edited by R. P. Bartlett, A. G. Cross, and Karen Rasmussen. Columbus, Ohio, 1988.

Grigorovich, V. I. *Kantsler kniaz' A. A. Bezborodko v sviazi s sobytiiami ego vremeni.* 2 vols. Spb, 1879–1881.

Grot, Ia. K. "Bibliograficheskiia i istoricheskiia zametki: Proiskhozhdenie Ekateriny I." In *Sbornik otdeleniia russkago iazyka i slovesnosti Imperatorskoi Akademii nauk.* Vol. 18. Spb, 1877.

Gruder, Vivian R. "Bourbon Monarchy: Reforms and Propaganda at the End of the Old Regime." In *The French Revolution and the Creation of Modern Political Culture.* Vol. 1, *The Political Culture of the Old Regime,* edited by Keith Michael Baker. Oxford, 1987.

Gukovskii, G. A. *Ocherki po istorii russkoi literatury XVIII veka: Dvorianskaia fronda v literature 1750-kh–1760-kh godov.* M, 1936.

———. *Russkaia literatura XVIII veka.* M, 1939.

Gurvich, G. *"Pravda voli monarshei" Feofana Prokopovicha i eia zapadno-evropeiskie istochniki.* Iur'ev, 1915.

Habermas, Jürgen. *The Structural Transformation of the Public Sphere: An Inquiry into a Category of Bourgeois Society.* Translated by T. Burger. Cambridge, Mass., 1998.

Halperin, Charles. "The Concept of the Russian Land from the Ninth to the Fourteenth Centuries." *Russian History* 2 (1975): 29–38.

———. *Russia and the Golden Horde: The Mongol Impact on Medieval Russian History.* Bloomington, Ind., 1985.

———. "The Russian Land and the Russian Tsar: The Emergence of Muscovite Ideology, 1380–1408." Ph.D. diss., Columbia University, 1973.

Hara, Teruyuki, and Kimitaka Matsuzato, eds. *Empire and Society: New Approaches to Russian History.* Sapporo, Japan, 1997.

Haumant, Émile. *La Culture française en Russie.* Paris, 1910.

Hearn, Maxwell K. *Splendors of Imperial China.* NY, 1996.

Helbig, G. *Biographie Peters des Dritten.* 2 vols. Tübingen, 1809.

Hellie, Richard. *Enserfment and Military Change in Muscovy.* Chicago, 1971.

Hellmuth, Eckhart, ed. *The Transformation of Political Culture: England and Germany in the Late Eighteenth Century.* Oxford, 1990.

Henshall, Nicholas. *The Myth of Absolutism: Change and Continuity in Early Modern European Monarchy.* NY, 1992.

Herzen, Michael Von. "Catherine II—Editor of *Vsiakaia Vsiachina?* A Reappraisal." *Russian Review* 38 (1979): 283–97.

Hjärne, H. "Ryska konstitutionsproject år 1730 efter svenska förebilder." *Svensk historisk tidskrift* 4 (1884): 189–272.

Hocart, A. M. *Kings and Councillors: An Essay in the Comparative Anatomy of Human Society.* Chicago, 1936.

Hoffmann, P. "Lomonosov als Historiker." *Jahrbücher für Geschichte der UdSSR und Volksdemokratischen Länder Europas* 5 (1961): 361–73.

Hosking, Geoffrey. *Russia and the Russians: A History.* Cambridge, Mass., 2001.

Hughes, Lindsey A. J. "Courts at Moscow and St. Petersburg, c. 1547–1725." In *The Princely Courts of Europe: Ritual, Politics, and Culture under the Ancien Régime, 1500–1750,* edited by John Adamson. London, 1999.

———. *Russia and the West: The Life of a Seventeenth-Century Westernizer, Prince Vasily Vasil'evich Golitsyn (1643–1714).* Newtonville, Mass., 1984.

———. *Russia in the Age of Peter the Great.* New Haven, 1998.

———. *Sophia, Regent of Russia, 1657-1704.* New Haven, 1990.

Hunger, Herbert. *Die hochsprächliche profane Literatur der Byzantiner.* 2 vols. Vienna, 1978.

———. *Prooimion. Elemente der byzantinischen Kaiseridee in den Arengen der Urkunden.* Vienna, 1964.

Hurwitz, Ellen. "Andrei Bogoliubskii: An Image of the Prince." *Russian History* 2 (1975): 68–80.

———. "Metropolitan Hilarion's *Sermon on Law and Grace:* Historical Consciousness in Kievan Rus'." *Russian History* 7 (1980): 322–33.

Iakushkin, V. A. *Gosudarstvennaia vlast' i proekty gosudarstvennoi reformy v Rossii.* Spb, 1906.

Ignatieff, Leonid. "Rights and Obligations in Russia and the West." *Canadian Slavonic Papers* 2 (1957): 26–37.

Ikonnikov, V. S. "Boltin." In *Russkii biograficheskii slovar',* vol. Betankur-Biakster. Spb. Reprint, New York, 1962.

———. *Istoricheskie trudy Boltina.* Spb, 1902.

Ilovaiskii, D. I. "Graf Iakov Sivers." In *Sochineniia.* Vol. 1. M, 1884.

———. "Graf Iakov Sivers: Biograficheskii ocherk." *Russkii vestnik* 45 (1865): no. 1, 5–47; no. 2, 628–684; no. 3, 153–215.

Ingham, Norman W. "The Sovereign as Martyr, East and West." *Slavic and East European Journal* 17 (1973): 1–16.

Iukht, A. I. "V. N. Tatishchev o reformakh Petra I." In *Obshchestvo i gosudarstvo feodal'noi Rossii,* edited by V. T. Pashuto. M, 1975.

Iushkov, V. *Ocherk iz istorii russkago samosoznaniia XVIII-go veka. Obshchie istoricheskie vzgliady I. N. Boltina.* Kiev, 1912.

Izbekov, D. E. "Odin iz maloizvestnykh literaturnykh protivnikov Feofana Prokopovicha (Dmitrii Kantemir)." In *Pamiatniki novoi russkoi istorii,* edited by V. Kashpirev. Spb, 1871.

Jones, Gareth W. "Biography in Eighteenth-Century Russia." *Oxford Slavonic Papers, New Series* 22 (1989): 58–79.

———. *Nikolay Novikov: Enlightener of Russia.* Cambridge, 1984.

———. "Novikov's Naturalized *Spectator.*" In *The Eighteenth Century in Russia,* edited by J. G. Garrard. Oxford, 1973.

Jones, R. H. *The Royal Policy of Richard II: Absolutism in the Later Middle Ages.* London, 1968.

Jones, Robert E. "Catherine II and the Provincial Reform of 1775: A Question of Motivation." *Canadian Slavic Studies* 4 (1970): 497–512.

———. "The Polemics of the 1769 Journals: A Reappraisal." *Canadian-American Slavic Studies* 16 (1978): 432–43.

Kabuzan, V. M. "Naselenie Rossiiskoi imperii v XVIII veke." In *Issledovaniia po istorii Rossii XVI–XVIII vv.: Sbornik statei v chest' 70-letiia Ia. E. Vodarskogo.* M, 2000.

Kafengauz, B. B. *Ocherki istorii SSSR: Period feodalizma.* M, 1954.

———, ed. *I. T. Pososhkov: Zhizn' i deiatel'nost'.* M, 1940.

Kahan, Alan S. *Aristocratic Liberalism: The Social and Political Thought of Jacob Burckhardt, John Stuart Mill, and Alexis de Tocqueville.* Oxford, 1992.

Kahan, Arcadius. "Continuity in Economic Activity and Policy During the Post-Petrine Period in Russia." *Journal of Economic History* 25 (1965): 61–85.

Kamendrowsky, Victor. "Catherine II's Nakaz, State Finances, and the Encyclopédie." *Canadian-American Slavic Studies* 13 (1979): 545–54.

Kamenskii, A. B. "Akademik G.-F. Miller i russkaia istoricheskaia nauka XVIII veka." *Istoriia SSSR* 1 (1989): 144–59.

———. "Catherine the Great." In *The Emperors and Empresses of Russia,* edited by Donald J. Raleigh. Armonk, NY, 1996.

———. "Ekaterina II." *Voprosy istorii* 3 (1989): 62–88.

———. *'Pod seniiu Ekateriny . . .': Vtoraia polovina XVIII veka.* Spb, 1992.

———. "Reformy v Rossii XVIII veka v istoricheskoi retrospektive." In *Sosloviia i gosudarstvennaia vlast' v Rossii, XV–seredina XIX vv.* Vol. 1. M, 1994.

Kamenskii, Z. A. *Filosofskie idei russkogo prosveshcheniia.* M, 1971.

Kantorowicz, Ernst. *The King's Two Bodies: A Study in Medieval Political Theology.* Princeton, 1957.

Karpovich, E. "Zamysli verkhovnikov i chelobitchikov v 1730 godu." *Otechestvennyia zapiski* 1 (1872): 209–37.

Kashpirev, V., ed. *Pamiatniki novoi russkoi istorii.* Spb, 1871.

Kazanskaia istoriia. Edited by G. N. Moiseeva. M, 1954.

Keenan, Edward L. *The Kurbskii-Groznyi Apocrypha: The Seventeenth-Century Genesis of the Correspondence Attributed to Prince A. M. Kurbskii and Tsar Ivan IV.* Cambridge, 1971.

———. "Muscovite Political Folkways." *Russian Review* 45 (April 1986): 115–81.

———. "Muscovy and Kazan, 1445–1552: A Study in Steppe Politics." Ph.D. diss., Harvard University, 1965.

———. "The Trouble with Muscovy: Some Observations upon Problems of the Comparative Study of Form and Genre in Historical Writing." *Medievalia et Humanistica* 5 (1974): 103–25.

Keep, John L. H. "The Decline of the Zemsky Sobor." *Slavonic and East European Review* 36 (1957): 100–52.

———. "Paul I and the Militarization of Government." In *Paul I: A Reassessment of His Life and Reign,* edited by Hugh Ragsdale. Pittsburgh, 1979.

———. "The Secret Chancellery, the Guards, and the Dynastic Crisis of 1740–1741." *Forschungen zur Osteuropäischen Geschichte* 25 (1978): 169–93.

Kelly, Catriona. *Refining Russia: Advice Literature, Polite Culture, and Gender from Catherine to Yeltsin.* Oxford, 2001.

Kenney, James J., Jr. "Lord Whitworth and the Conspiracy Against Tsar Paul I: The New Evidence of the Kent Archive." *Slavic Review* 36 (1977): 205–19.

Khmyrov, M. D. *Grafinia E. I. Golovkina i ee vremia.* Spb, 1867.

Khudushina, I. F. *Tsar'. Bog. Rossiia. Samosoznanie russkogo dvorianstva (konets XVIII— pervaia tret' XIX vv.).* M, 1995.

Kirchner, Walther. "The Death of Catherine I." *American Historical Review* 5 (1946): 254–61.

Kisliagina, L. G. "Formirovanie idei samoderzhaviia v politicheskoi kontseptsii N. M. Karamzina." In *Voprosy metodologii i istorii istoricheskoi nauki.* M, 1977.

Kivelson, Valerie A. *Autocracy in the Provinces: The Muscovite Gentry and Political Culture in the Seventeenth Century.* Stanford, 1996.

———. "The Constitutional Crisis of 1730 and the Evolution of Noble Political Culture." In *Imperial Russia: New Histories for the Empire,* edited by Jane Burbank and David L. Ransel. Bloomington, Ind., 1998.

———. "Kinship Politics/Autocratic Politics: A Reconsideration of Early Eighteenth-Century Political Culture." In *Imperial Russia: New Histories for the Empire,* edited by Jane Burbank and David Ransel. Bloomington, Ind., 1998.

Kizevetter, A. A. "Russkaia utopiia XVIII veka." *Istoricheskie ocherki* (1912): 27–56.

Klaniczay, Gabor. "Representations of the Evil Ruler in the Middle Ages." In *European Monarchy,* edited by Heinz Duchhardt. Stuttgart, 1992.

Klippel, Diethelm. "The True Concept of Liberty: Political Theory in Germany in the Second Half of the Eighteenth Century." In *The Transformation of Political Culture: England and Germany in the Late Eighteenth Century,* edited by Eckhart Hellmuth. Oxford, 1990.

Kliuchevskii, V. O. *A Course in Russian History: The Seventeenth Century.* Translated by Natalie Duddington. Armonk, NY, 1994.

———. *Kurs russkoi istorii.* 4 vols. M, 1908.

———. *Peter the Great.* Translated by Liliana Archibald. NY, 1961.

———. "Petr Velikii sredi svoikh sotrudnikov." In *Ocherki i rechi.* M, n.d.

———. *Sochineniia.* 9 vols. M, 1958.

Klochkov, M. V. *Ocherki pravitel'stvennoi deiatel'nosti vremeni Pavla I.* Petrograd, 1916.

———. "Pososhkov o krest'ianakh." In *Velikaia reforma.* Vol. 1. Spb, 1911.

Kobeko, Dmitrii. *Tsesarevich Pavel Petrovich, 1754–1796.* Spb, 1883.

Kollmann, Nancy Shields. *By Honor Bound: State and Society in Early Modern Russia.* Ithaca, 1999.

———. *Kinship and Politics: The Making of the Muscovite Political System, 1345–1547.* Stanford, 1987.

Korf, M. *Braunshveigskoe semeistvo.* Spb, 1917. Reprint, M, 1993.

Korsakov, D. A. "Artemii Petrovich Volynskii: Biograficheskii ocherk." *Drevniaia i novaia Rossiia* 2 (1876): 45–60.

———. "Artemii Petrovich Volynskii i ego 'konfidenty'." *Russkaia starina* 48 (1885): 17–54.

———. *Votsarenie Imperatritsy Anny Ioannovny.* Kazan, 1880.

Koselleck, Reinhart. *Critique and Crisis: Enlightenment and the Pathogenesis of Modern Society.* Cambridge, Mass., 1988.

Kostomarov, N. "Ekaterina Alekseevna, pervaia russkaia imperatritsa." *Istoricheskiia monografii i izsledovaniia.* Vol. 14. Spb, 1881.

———. "Tsarevich Aleksei Petrovich." In *Istoricheskiia monografii i izsledovaniia.* Vol. 14. Spb, 1881.

Kovolenskii, M., ed. *Moskovskaia politicheskaia literatura XVI veka.* Spb, 1914.

Kozlov, O. F. "Delo Tsarevicha Alekseia." *Voprosy istorii* 9 (1969): 86–91.

———. "K voprosu o politicheskoi bor'be v Rossii v pervoi polovine XVIII v." *Ezhegodnik Gosudarstvennogo istoricheskogo muzeia* (1965–1966): 119–28.

Krieger, Leonard. *An Essay on the Theory of Enlightened Despotism.* Chicago, 1975.

———. *Kings and Philosophers, 1689–1789.* NY, 1970.

———. *The Politics of Discretion: Pufendorf and the Acceptance of Natural Law.* Chicago, 1965.

"Kriticheskiia zametki po istorii politicheskikh idei v Rossii." *Nauchnye trudy russkago narodnago universiteta v Prage.* Vol. 1. Prague, 1928.

Kruglyi, A. O. "I. P. Elagin: Biograficheskii ocherk." *Ezhegodnik Imperatorskikh teatrov* 2 (1893–1894): 96–118.

Kulakova, L. I. *Denis Ivanovich Fonvizin.* M, 1966.

———. "Ia. B. Kniazhnin." In *Russkie dramaturgi XVIII–XIX v.* Vol. 1. M, 1959.

Kunte, Heinrich, ed. *Glaube und Geschichte: Festschrift für Friedrich Gogarten.* Giessen, 1948.

Kurskov, Iu. V. *Vedushchie napravlenie obshchestvennoi mysli i proekty gosudarstvennykh preobrazovanii Rossii v 40–60kh godov XVII veka.* Chita, 1973.

Lakier, A. "Istoriia titula gosudarei Rossii." *Zhurnal Ministerstva narodnago prosveshcheniia* 56 (1847): 81–56.

Lappo-Danilevskii, A. S. "Ideia gosudarstva i glavneishie momenty eia razvitiia v Rossii so vremen smuty do epokhi preobrazovanii." *Golos minuvshago* 2 (1914): 5–38.

———. "L'Idée de l'état et son évolution en Russie depuis les troubles du XVIIe siècle jusqu'aux réformes du XVIIIe." In *Essays in Legal History,* edited by P. Vinogradoff. London, 1913.

La Vopa, Anthony J. "Conceiving a Public: Ideas and Society in Eighteenth-Century Europe." *Journal of Modern History* 64 (1992): 79–116.

Lawrence, E. "Catherine II." *Harper's Monthly* 38 (1869): 624–35.

LeDonne, John. *Absolutism and Ruling Class: The Formation of the Russian Political Order, 1700–1825.* Oxford, 1991.

———. "Frontier Governors General, 1772–1825." [pt. II] "The Southern Frontier." *Jahrbücher für Geschichte Osteuropas* 48 (2000): 321–40.

———. "The Provincial and Local Police under Catherine the Great, 1775–1796." *Canadian Slavic Studies* 4 (1970): 513–28.

Lentin, Antony. "Did Montesquieu Know *Pravda voli monarshei?*" *Study Group on Eighteenth-Century Russia Newsletter* 27 (1999): 18–25.

———. "Shcherbatov, Constitutionalism, and the 'Despotism' of Sweden's Gustav III." *Russia and the World of the Eighteenth Century.* Columbus, Ohio, 1986.

———. "Some Reflections on *Pravda voli monarshei.*" *Study Group on Eighteenth-Century Russia Newsletter* 24 (1996): 3–7.

———, ed. and trans. *Peter the Great: His Law on the Imperial Succession in Russia, 1772. The Official Commentary.* Oxford, 1996.

———, ed. and trans. *Prince M. M. Shcherbatov: On the Corruption of Morals in Russia.* Cambridge, 1969.

Leonard, Carol S. *Reform and Regicide: The Reign of Peter III of Russia.* Bloomington, Ind., 1993.

———. "The Reputation of Peter III." *Russian Review* 47 (1988): 263–92.

Leonard, G. I. "Novikov, Shcherbatov, Radishchev: The Intellectual in the Age of Catherine the Great." Ph.D. diss., SUNY Binghamton, 1980.

Leontovich, V. V. *Istoriia liberalizma v Rossii, 1762–1914.* Paris, 1980.

Lermontov, E. D. *Pokhval'noe slovo Likhudova Tsarevne Sof'e Alekseevne.* M, 1910.

Levin, Iu. D. "The English Novel in 18th-Century Russia." In *Literature, Lives, and Legality in Catherine's Russia,* edited by A. G. Cross and G. S. Smith. Nottingham, England, 1994.

Levitt, Marcus C. "An Antidote to Nervous Juice: Catherine the Great's Debate with Chappe d'Auteroche over Russian Culture." *Eighteenth-Century Studies* 32 (1998): 49–63.

———. "Sumarokov's Russianized Hamlet: Texts and Contexts." *Slavonic and East European Journal* 38 (1994): 319–41.

Lievan, Dominic. *Empire: The Russian Empire and Its Rivals.* New Haven, 2001.

Lipski, Alexander. "A Re-examination of the 'Dark Era' of Anna Ioannovna." *American Slavic and East European Review* 15 (1956): 477–88.

———. "Some Aspects of Russia's Westernization During the Reign of Anna Ioannovna." *American Slavic and East European Review* 18 (1959): 1–11.

Liubomirov, P. G. *Ocherk istorii nizhegorodskogo opolcheniia 1611–1613 gg.* M, 1939.

Liutsh, A. "Russkii absoliutizm XVIII veka." In *Itogi XVIII veka v Rossii.* M, 1910.

Lobacheva, G. V. *Samoderzhets i Rossiia: Obraz tsaria v massovom soznanii rossiian konets XIX–nachalo XX vekov.* Saratov, 1999.

Loewenson, Leo. "The Death of Paul I (1801) and the Memoirs of Count Bennigsen." *Slavonic and East European Review* 29 (1950–1951): 212–32.

Łojek, Jerzy. "Catherine II's Armed Intervention in Poland: Origins of the Political Decisions at the Russian Court in 1791 and 1792." *Canadian Slavic Studies* 4 (1970): 570–93.

Longinov, M. N. *Novikov i moskovskie martinisty.* M, 1867.

Lortholary, Albert. *Le Mirage russe en France au XVIIIe siècle.* Paris, 1951.

Lotman, Iu. M. "Agreement and Self-Giving as Archetypal Models of Culture." In *The Semiotics of Russian Culture,* by Iu. M. Lotman and B. A. Uspenskii, edited by Ann Shukman. Ann Arbor, 1984.

Lotman, Iu. M., and B. A. Uspenskii. "Myth-Name-Culture." In *Semiotics and Structuralism: Readings from the Soviet Union,* edited by Henryk Baran. White Plains, NY, 1976.

Lovejoy, Arthur O. *Reflections on Human Nature.* Baltimore, 1961.

Lucid, Daniel, ed. *Soviet Semiotics.* Baltimore, 1977.

Luppov, S. P. *Kniga v Rossii v pervoi chetverti XVIII veka.* L, 1973.

Luzhin, N. P. "Dva pamfleta vremen Anny Ioannovny." *Izvestiia Imperatorskoi Akademii nauk po otd. russkago iazyka i slovesnosti* 8 (1858): 49–64.

McArthur, Gilbert H. "Catherine II and the Masonic Circle of N. I. Novikov." *Canadian-American Slavic Studies* 4 (Fall 1970): 529–46.

McConnell, Allen. "The Autocrat and the Open Critic." In *Catherine the Great,* edited by Marc Raeff. NY, 1972.

———. "Radishchev and Classical Antiquity." *Canadian-American Slavic Studies* 16 (1982): 469–90.

McGrew, Roderick. *Paul I of Russia, 1754–1801.* Oxford, 1992.

———. "Political Portrait of Paul I from the Austrian and English Diplomatic Archives." *Jahrbücher für Geschichte Osteuropas* 18 (1970): 503–29.

Madariaga, Isabel de. *Politics and Culture in Eighteenth-Century Russia: Collected Essays by Isabel de Madariaga.* London, 1998.

———. *Russia in the Age of Catherine the Great.* New Haven, 1981.

Magids, Viktor. "Ego vysochestvo v originale i na portrete." *Tvorchestvo* 10 (1990): 31–32.

Maikov, L. N. *Ocherki iz istorii russkoi literatury XVII i XVIII stoletii.* Spb, 1889.

Majeska, George P. "The Moscow Coronation of 1498 Reconsidered." *Jahrbücher für Geschichte Osteuropas* 26 (1978): 353–61.

Makarov, A. N. *Uchenie ob osnovnykh zakonakh v russkoi iuridicheskoi literature XVIII–pervoi treti XIX veka.* Spb, 1913.

Makogonenko, G. P. *Nikolai Novikov i russkoe prosveshchenie XVIII v.* M, 1951.

Malia, Martin. *Russia under Western Eyes: From the Bronze Horseman to the Lenin Mausoleum.* Cambridge, 1999.

Malinin, V. *Starets Eleazarova Monastyria Filofei i ego poslaniia.* Kiev, 1901.

Manstein, Christoph H. von. *Contemporary Memoirs of Russia from the Year 1727 to 1744.* London, 1968.

Manz, Beatrice Forbes. "The Office of Darugha under Tamerlane." *Journal of Turkish Studies* 9 (1985): 59–69.

Marasinova, E. N. "Obraz imperatora v soznanii elity rossiiskogo dvorianstva poslednei treti XVIII veka (po materialam epistoliarnykh istochnikov." In *Tsar' i tsarstvo v russkom obshchestvennom soznanii. Mirovospriiatie i samosoznanie russkogo obshchestva,* edited by A. A. Gorskii et al. M, 1999.

———. *Psikhologiia elity rossiiskogo dvorianstva poslednei treti XVIII veka (Po materialam perepiski).* M, 1999.

Marker, Gary. *Publishing, Printing, and the Origins of Intellectual Life in Russia, 1700–1800.* Princeton, 1985.

Martysevich, I. D. *Voprosy gosudarstva i prava v trudakh M. V. Lomonosova.* M, 1861.

Masaryk, Thomas G. *The Spirit of Russia.* 3 vols. London, 1919.

Mavrodin, V. V. "Nekotorye voprosy evoliutsii russkogo samoderzhaviia v XVII–XVIII vv." In *Voprosy genezisa kapitalizma v Rossii: Sbornik statei.* L, 1960.

Medlin, William K. *Moscow and East Rome.* Geneva, 1952.

Medushevskii, A. N. *Utverzhdenie absoliutizma v Rossii.* M, 1994.

Meehan-Waters, Brenda. *Autocracy and Aristocracy: The Russian Service Elite of 1730.* New Brunswick, NJ, 1982.

———. "Catherine the Great and the Problem of Female Rule." *Russian Review* 34 (1975): 293–307.

———. "The Development and the Limits of Security of Noble Status, Person and Property in Eighteenth-Century Russia." In *Russia and the West in the Eighteenth Century,* edited by A. G. Cross. Newtonville, Mass., 1983.

———. "The Russian Aristocracy and the Reforms of Peter the Great." *Canadian-American Slavic Studies* 8 (1974): 288–303.

Melton, James van Horn. "From Enlightenment to Revolution: Hertzberg, Schlözer, and the Problem of Despotism in the Late *Aufklärung.*" *Central European History* 12 (1979): 103–23.

Mendelsohn, E., and M. Shatz, eds. *Imperial Russia, 1700–1917: State, Society, Opposition.* DeKalb, 1988.

Merguerian, Barbara J. "Political Ideas in Russia During the Reign of Peter the Great (1682–1739)." Ph.D. diss., Harvard University, 1970.

Meyendorff, John. *The Byzantine Legacy in the Orthodox Church.* Crestwood, NY, 1982.

———. *Byzantium and the Rise of Russia.* Crestwood, NY, 1989.

Miliukov, P. N. *Glavnyia techeniia russkoi istoricheskoi mysli.* M, 1897.

———. *Gosudarstvennoe khoziaistvo Rossii v pervoi chetverti XVIII stoletiia i reforma Petra Velikago.* Spb, 1905.

———. "Verkhovniki i shliakhetsvo." In *Iz istorii russkoi intelligentsii.* Spb, 1903.

Miliukov, P. N., et al., *Histoire de Russie.* 2 vols. Paris, 1932.

Miller, David. "The Coronation of Ivan IV of Moscow." *Jahrbücher für Geschichte Osteuropas* 15 (1967): 561–74.

Minaeva, N. V. *Pravitel'stvennyi konstitutsionalizm i peredovoe obshchestvennoe mnenie v Rossii v nachale XIX veka.* Saratov, 1982.

Mironenko, S. V. *Samoderzhavie i reformy: Politicheskaia bor'ba v Rossii v nachale XIX v.* M, 1989.

Mirovospriiatie i samoznanie russkogo obshchestva. Vol. 2, *Tsar' i tsarstvo v russkom obshchestvennom soznanii,* edited by A. A. Gorskii, A. I. Kuprianov, and L. N. Pushkarev. M, 1999.

Mohrenschildt, Dmitri von. *Russia in the Intellectual Life of Eighteenth-Century France.* NY, 1936.

Molloy, Fitzgerald. *The Russian Court in the Eighteenth Century.* NY, 1905.

Morozov, A. A. "M. V. Lomonosov i teleologiia Kristiana Vol'fa." *Literaturnoe tvorchestvo M. V. Lomonosova,* edited by P. N. Berkov and I. Serman. M, 1962.

Morozov, P. O. *Feofan Prokopovich kak pisatel'.* Spb, 1880.

———. "Russkii teatr pri Petre Velikom." *Ezhegodnik Imperatorskikh teatrov* 4 (1893–1894): 52–80.

Morrison, Kerry R. "Catherine II's Legislative Commission: An Administrative Interpretation." *Canadian Slavic Studies* 4 (1970): 464–84.

Mousnier, Roland E. *The Institutions of France under the Absolute Monarchy, 1598–1789,* Vol. 2, *The Organs of State and Society,* translated by Arthur Goldhammer. Chicago, 1984.

Muller, Alexander V., trans. and ed. *The Spiritual Regulation of Peter the Great.* Seattle, 1972.

Myers, Henry A. *Medieval Kingship.* Chicago, 1982.

Myl'nikov [Mylnikov], A. S. "Peter III." In *The Emperors and Empresses of Russia: Rediscovering the Romanovs,* edited by Donald J. Raleigh and compiled by A. A. Iskenderov. Armonk, NY, 1996.

———. "Petr III." *Voprosy istorii* 4–5 (1991): 43–58.

Nakane, Chie. *Japanese Society.* Berkeley, 1970.

Naumov, V. P. "Elizabeth I." In *The Emperors and Empresses of Russia: Rediscovering the Romanovs,* edited by Donald J. Raleigh and compiled by A. A. Iskenderov. Armonk, NY, 1996.

Nelson, Janet. "Kingship and Empire." In *The Cambridge History of Medieval Political Thought, c. 350–c. 1450,* edited by J. H. Burns. Cambridge, 1988.

Nezelenov, A. N. I. *Novikov, izdatel' zhurnalov, 1769–1785 gg.* Spb, 1875.

Nicol, D. M. "Byzantine Political Thought." In *The Cambridge History of Medieval Political Thought, c. 350–c. 1450,* edited by J. H. Burns. Cambridge, 1988.

Nørretranders, Bjarne. "Ivan Groznyj's Conception of Tsarist Authority." *Scando-Slavica* 9 (1963): 238–48.

————. *The Shaping of Czardom under Ivan Groznyi.* Copenhagen, 1964.

Obolensky, Dmitri. "Popular Religion in Medieval Russia." In *The Religious World of Russian Culture,* edited by Andrew Blane. Vol. 2. The Hague, 1975.

————. "Russia's Byzantine Heritage." In *Selection II,* edited by Cecily Hastings and Donald Nicholl. London, 1954.

O'Brien, Charles B. "Ivan Pososhkov: Russian Critic of Mercantilist Principles." *American Slavic and East European Review* 14 (1955): 503–11.

Ogg, David. *Louis XIV.* Oxford, 1967.

Olšr, G. "La Chiesa e lo Stato nel cerimoniale d'incoronazione degli ultimi sovrani Ririkidi." *Orientalia Christiana Periodica* 16 (1950): 268–79.

Omel'chenko, O. A. *"Zakonnaia monarkhiia" Ekateriny II.* M, 1993.

Orlov, A. S. "'Tilemakhida' V. K. Trediakovskogo." *XVIII vek* (1935): 5–11.

Ostrowski, Donald. *Muscovy and the Mongols: Cross-Cultural Influences on the Steppe Frontier, 1304–1589.* Cambridge, 1998.

Ozouf, M. "L'Opinion publique." In *The French Revolution and the Creation of Modern Political Culture.* Vol. 1, *The Political Culture of the Old Regime,* edited by Keith Michael Baker. Oxford, 1987.

————. "'Public Opinion' at the End of the Old Regime." In *The Rise and Fall of the French Revolution,* edited by T. C. W. Blanning. Chicago, 1996.

Papmehl, K. A. *Freedom of Expression in Eighteenth-Century Russia.* The Hague, 1971.

————. "Pososhkov as a Thinker." *Slavic and East European Studies* 6 (1961): 80–87.

————. "The Quest for the Nation's Cultural Roots in Russian Historiography Before Karamzin." In *Russia and the World of the Eighteenth Century,* edited by R. P. Bartlett, A. G. Cross, and Karen Rasmussen. Columbus, Ohio, 1988.

Pashuto, V. T., ed. *Obshchestvo i gosudarstvo feodal'noi Rossii.* M, 1975.

Pavlenko, N. I. "Petr I (K izucheniiu sotsial'no-politicheskikh vzgliadov)." In *Rossiia v period reform Petra I,* edited by N. I. Pavlenko. M, 1973.

————. *Ptentsy gnezda petrova.* M, 1984.

Pavlov-Sil'vanskii, N. P. "Mneniia verkhovnikov o reformakh Petra Velikogo." *Sochineniia.* Vol. 2. Spb, 1910.

————. *Proekty reform v zapiskakh sovremennikov Petra Velikago.* Spb, 1897.

Peirce, Leslie P. *The Imperial Harem: Women and Sovereignty in the Ottoman Empire.* Oxford, 1993.

Pekarskii, P. P. *Istoriia Imperatorskoi Akademii nauk v Peterburge.* 2 vols. Spb, 1870–1873.

————. *Nauka i literatura v Rossii pri Petre Velikom.* 2 vols. Spb, 1862. Reprint, Leipzig, 1972.

————. "Novye izvestiia o V. N. Tatishcheve." *Zapiski Imperatorskoi akademii nauk* 4 (1864): 478–514.

————. *Opisanie slaviano-russkikh knig i tipografii 1698–1725 godov.* Spb, 1862. Reprint, Leipzig, 1972.

————, ed. "Ukaz Ekateriny I." In *Istoricheskie bumagi sobrannyia K. I. Arsen'evym. Sbornik otd. russkago iazyka i slovesnosti Imperatorskoi Akademii nauk.* Vol. 9. Spb, 1872.

Perrie, Maureen. *The Image of Ivan the Terrible in Russian Folklore.* Cambridge, 1987.

————. "The Popular Image of Ivan the Terrible." *Slavonic and East European Review* 56 (1978): 275–86.

Peshtich, S. A. *Russkaia istoriografiia XVIII veka.* 3 parts. L, 1961–1971.

Petrov, L. A. *Obshchestvenno-politicheskie vzgliady Prokopovicha, Tatishcheva, i Kantemira.* Irkutsk, 1959.

Petrova, V. A. "Politicheskaia bor'ba vokrug senatskoi reformy 1763 goda." *Vestnik Leningradskogo universiteta* 14 (1967): 57–66.

Piatkovskii, A. P. "Osmnadtsatyi vek v russkoi istorii." In *Iz istorii nashago literaturnago i obshchestvennago razvitiia.* Vol. 1. Spb, 1889

Pipes, Richard. *Russia under the Old Regime.* NY, 1974.

Platonov, S. F. *Drevnerusskiia skazaniia i povesti o smutnom vremeni.* Spb, 1913.

———. *The Time of Troubles: A Historical Study of the Internal Crisis and Social Struggle in Sixteenth- and Seventeenth-Century Muscovy.* Translated by John T. Alexander. Lawrence, Kansas, 1970.

Plekhanov, G. V. *History of Russian Social Thought.* Translated by B. M. Bekkar. NY, 1967.

———. *Istoriia russkoi obshchestvennoi mysli.* M, 1914.

Poe, Marshall. "What Did Russians Mean When They Called Themselves 'Slaves of the Tsar'?" *Slavic Review* 57 (1998): 585–608.

Pogodin, M. P., ed., "Tsarevich Aleksei Petrovich po svidetel'stvam vnov' otkrytym." *Chteniia v Imp. Obshchestve istorii i drevnosti rossiiskikh pri Moskovskom universitete* 3 (1861): 1–374.

Pokrovskaia, A. K., ed. *Materialy po istorii russkoi detskoi literatury (1750–1855).* M, 1929.

Pokrovskii, S. A. *Politicheskie i pravovye vzgliady . . . Desnitskogo.* M, 1955.

Pokrovskii, V., ed. *A. D. Kantemir, ego zhizn' i sochineniia.* M, 1910.

Polosin, I. I. "Ivan Timofeev—russkii myslitel', istorik, i d"iak XVII v." In *Sotsial'no-politicheskaia istoriia Rossii XVI–nachala XVII v.* M, 1963.

Poole, Stanley B. R. "Peter III and Pugachev." In *Royal Mysteries and Pretenders.* London, 1969.

Priima, F. Ia. "Lomonosov i 'Istoriia rossiiskoi imperii pri Petre Velikom' Vol'tera." *XVIII vek* 3 (1958): 170–86.

Pritsak, Omelian. "The Invitation to the Varangians." *Harvard Ukrainian Studies* 1 (1977): 7–22.

———. *The Origin of Rus'.* Vol. 1. Cambridge, Mass., 1981.

Procopé, John. "Greek and Roman Political Theory." In *The Cambridge History of Medieval Political Theory, c. 350–c. 1450,* edited by J. H. Burns. Cambridge, 1988.

Prosina, A. B. "Teoreticheskoe obosnovanie F. Prokopovichem reform Petra I." *Vestnik Moskovskogo universiteta* 6 (1969): 63–71.

Protasov, N. A. "Dvorianskie proekty 1730 goda." *Istochnikovedcheskie raboty* 2 (1971): 61–102.

———. "'Konditsii' 1730 g. i ikh prodolzhenie." *Uchenye zapiski Tambovskogo gosudarstvennogo pedagogicheskogo instituta* 15 (1957): 211–29.

———. "Sushchestvoval li politicheskii plan D. M. Golitsyna?" *Istochnikovedcheskie raboty* 3 (1973): 90–107.

———. "Zapiska Tatishcheva o proizvol'nom rassuzhdenii dvorianstva v sobytiiakh 1730 g." *Problemy istochnikovedeniia* 11 (1963): 237–65.

Prozhogin, Nikolai. "Sud'ba odnogo portreta." *Nashe nasledie* 2 (1990): 34–35.

Pushkarev, I. "Gosudarstvo i vlast' v obshchestvenno-politicheskoi mysli kontsa XVII v." In *Obshchestvo i gosudarstvo feodal'noi Rossii,* edited by V. T. Pashuto. M, 1975.

———. *Istoriia Imperatorskoi Rossiiskoi gvardii.* Vol. 1. Spb, 1844.

———. *Iurii Krizhanich. Ocherk zhizni i tvorchestva.* M, 1984.

Pushkarev, L. N. "Bogoizbrannost' monarkha v mentalitete russkikh predbornykh deiatelei rubezha novogo vremeni." In *Tsar' i tsarstvo v russkom obshchestvennom soznanii,* edited by A. A. Gorskii, A. I. Kuprianov, and L. N. Pushkarev. M, 1999.

Putnyn', E. K . *Istoki russkoi istoriografii antichnosti: M. V. Lomonosov, A. N. Radishchev.* Saratov, 1968.

Pypin, A. N. "Istoricheskiia trudy Ekateriny II." *Vestnik Evropy* 5 (September 1901): 170–202; 6 (December 1901): 760–803.

———. "Kto byl avtorom 'Antidota'?" In *Sochineniia Imperatritsy Ekateriny II.* Vol. 7. Spb, 1901.

———. "Nachatki novago dvizheniia: Literatura vremen Petra Velikago." *Vestnik Evropy* 12 (1894): 732–80.

———. *Russkoe masonstvo XVIII i pervaia chetvert' XIX v.* Petrograd, 1916.

Raba, Joel. "The Authority of the Muscovite Ruler at the Dawn of the Modern Era." *Jahrbücher für Geschichte Osteuropas* 24 (1976): 321–44.

Raeff, Marc. "The Domestic Policies of Peter III and his Overthrow." *American Historical Review* 65 (1970): 1291–94

———. "An Early Theorist of Absolutism: Joseph of Volokolamsk." *American Slavic and East European Review* 8 (1949): 79–89.

———. "The Heterogeneity of the Eighteenth Century in Russia." In *Russia and the World of the Eighteenth Century,* edited by R. P. Bartlett, A. G. Cross, and Karen Rasmussen. Columbus, Ohio, 1988.

———. *Origins of the Russian Intelligentsia: The Eighteenth-Century Nobility.* NY, 1966.

———. "Review Article: Autocracy Tempered by Reform or by Regicide?" *American Historical Review* 98 (1993): 1143–58.

———. "Review of *The Spiritual Regulation of Peter the Great.* Translated and edited by Alexander Muller." *Canadian-American Slavic Studies* 8 (1974): 327–28.

———. "Seventeenth-Century Europe in Eighteenth-Century Russia? (Pour prendre congé du dix-huitième siècle russe)." *Slavic Review* 41 (1982): 611–19.

———. "State and Nobility in the Ideology of M. M. Shcherbatov." *American Slavic and East European Review* 19 (1960): 363–79.

———. *Understanding Imperial Russia: State and Society in the Old Regime.* Translated by Arthur Goldhammer. NY, 1984.

———. *The Well-Ordered Police State: Social and Institutional Change through Law in the Germanies and Russia, 1600–1800.* New Haven, 1983.

———, ed. *Catherine the Great.* NY, 1972.

———, ed. *Plans for Political Reform in Imperial Russia, 1730–1905.* Englewood Cliffs, NJ, 1966.

———, ed. *Russian Intellectual History: An Anthology.* NY, 1988.

Ragsdale, Hugh. *The Russian Tragedy: The Burden of History.* Armonk, NY, 1996.

———, ed. *Paul I: A Reassessent of His Life and Reign.* Pittsburgh, 1979.

Raleigh, Donald J., ed. *The Emperors and Empresses of Russia: Rediscovering the Romanovs.* Compiled by A. A. Iskenderov. Armonk, NY, 1996.

Ransel, David L. "Nikita Panin's Imperial Council Project and the Struggle of Hierarchy Groups at the Court of Catherine II." *Canadian Slavic Studies* 4 (1970): 443–63.

———. "Political Perceptions of the Russian Nobility: The Constitutional Crisis of 1730." *Laurentian University Review* 3 (1972): 20–38.

———. *The Politics of Catherinian Russia: The Panin Party.* New Haven, 1975.

Ransel, David L., and Jane Burbank, eds. *Imperial Russia: New Histories for the Empire.* Bloomington, Ind., 1998.

Rasmussen, Karen Malvey. "Catherine II and Peter I: The Idea of a Just Monarch. The Evolution of an Attitude in Catherinian Russia." Ph.D. diss., University of California, Berkeley, 1973.

Recke, W. "Die Verfassungspläne der russischen Oligarchen im Jahre 1730 und die Thronbesteigung der Kaiserin Anna Ivanovna." *Zeitschrift für Osteuropäische Geschichte* 2 (1911–1912): 11–64.

Reisman, Edward S. "The Cult of Boris and Gleb: Remnant of a Varangian Tradition?" *Russian Review* 37 (1978): 141–57.

Reisner, M. A. "Obshchestvennoe blago i absoliutnoe gosudarstvo." *Vestnik prava za 1902*, nos. 9–10: 1–128.

Renwick, J. "Marmontel, Voltaire, and the Bélisaire Affair." *Studies on Voltaire and the Eighteenth Century* 121 (1974): 397

Reyfman, Irina. *Vasilii Trediakovsky: The Fool of the "New" Russian Literature.* Stanford, 1990.

Riasanovsky, Nicholas V. *The Image of Peter the Great in Russian History and Thought.* Oxford, 1985.

———. "The Norman Theory of the Origin of the Russian State." *Russian Review* 7 (1947): 98–99.

———. *A Parting of the Ways: Government and the Educated Public in Russia, 1801–1825.* Oxford, 1976.

Rice, Tamara Talbot. *Elizabeth, Empress of Russia.* NY, 1970.

Robling, Franz Hubert. "Political Rhetoric in the German Enlightenment." In *The Transformation of Political Culture: England and Germany in the Late Eighteenth Century,* edited by Eckhart Hellmuth. Oxford, 1990.

Rogger, Hans. *National Consciousness in Eighteenth-Century Russia.* Cambridge, 1960.

Romanovy: Dinastiia v romanakh: Ioann Antonovich. M, 1994.

Ross, S. C. "Tatishchev's 'Joachim Chronicle.'" *University of Birmingham Historical Journal* 3 (1951): 53–54.

Rossiiskii tsartsvennyi dom Romanovykh. Spb, 1896.

Rothkrug, Lionel. *Opposition to Louis XIV: The Political and Social Origins of the French Revolution.* Princeton, 1965.

Rovinskii, D. A., comp. *Materialy dlia russkoi ikonografii.* 12 folios. Spb, 1884–1890.

Rowland, Daniel. "Did Muscovite Literary Ideology Place Limits on the Power of the Tsar (1540s–1660s)?" *Russian Review* 49 (1990): 125–55.

———. "The Problem of Advice in Muscovite Tales About the Time of Troubles." *Russian History* 6 (1979): 259–83.

Rozhkov, N. *Proiskhozhdenie samoderzhaviia v Rossii.* M, 1906.

Rule, John C., ed. *Louis XIV and the Craft of Kingship.* Columbus, Ohio, 1969.

Runciman, Steven. "Byzantium, Russia, and Caesaropapism." *Canadian Slavonic Papers* 2 (1957): 1–10.

Russkaia istoriografiia. M, 1941.

Russkaia zhivopis' v XVIII veke. Vol. 1, *D. G. Levitskii, 1735–1822,* compiled by S. P. Diagilev. Spb, 1902

Russkii biograficheskii slovar'. 25 vols. Spb, 1896–1918.

Russkii graver Chemesov. Spb, 1878.

Sabine, George H. *A History of Political Theory.* NY, 1937.

Safonov, M. M. *Problema reform v pravitel'stvennoi politike Rossii na rubezhe XVIII i XIX vv.* L, 1988.

Samarin, A. Iu. *Chitatel' v Rossii vo vtoroi polovine XVIII veka.* M, 2000.

Samarin, Iu. *Stefan Iavorskii i Feofan Prokopovich.* M, 1844.

Scattergood, V. J. *Politics and Poetry in the Fifteenth Century.* London, 1971.

Schaeder, Hildegard. *Moskau das dritte Rom.* Hamburg, 1929.

Schmitt, Carl. *The Leviathan in the State Theory of Thomas Hobbes: Meaning and Failure of a Political Symbol.* Westport, Conn., 1996.

Sciacca, Franklin. "In Imitation of Christ: Boris and Gleb and the Ritual Consecration of the Russian Land." *Slavic Review* 49 (1990): 253–60.

Scott, H. M., ed. *Enlightened Absolutism: Reform and Reformers in Later Eighteenth-Century Europe.* Ann Arbor, 1990.

Sedov, S. A. "Plany ogranicheniia samoderzhaviia v 1730 godu i pozitsiia dvorianstva." In *Sosloviia i gosudarstvennaia vlast' v Rossii, XV—seredina XIX vv. Chteniia pamiati Akad. L. V. Cherepnina. Tezisy dokladov.* Vol. 2. M, 1994.

Semennikov, V. P. *Sobranie . . . o perevode inostrannykh knig, uchrezhdennoe Ekaterinoi II, 1768–1783 gg. Istoriko-literaturnoe izsledovanie.* Spb, 1913.

Semevskii, M. I. *Slovo i delo, 1700–1725.* Spb, 1884.

———. *Tsaritsa Katerina Alekseevna, Anna, i Villem Mons, 1692–1724.* Spb, 1884.

Semevskii, V. I. *Krest'ianskii vopros v Rossii v XVIII i pervoi polovine XIX veka.* Vol. 1. Spb, 1888.

Šerech, J. "On Teofan [*sic*] Prokopovic as Writer and Preacher in his Kiev Period." *Harvard Slavic Studies* 2 (1954): 211–23.

———. "Stefan Yavorsky and the Conflict of Ideologies in the Age of Peter I." *Slavic and East European Review* 30 (1951): 40–62.

Sergeevich, V. I. *Lektsii i izsledovaniia po istorii russkago prava.* Spb, 1883.

Serman, I. "Vozmozhna li rekonstruktsiia zamysla Petridy Kantemira?" *Study Group on Eighteenth-Century Russia Newsletter* 21 (1993): 17–21.

Ševčenko, Ihor. "A Neglected Byzantine Source of Muscovite Ideology." *Harvard Slavic Studies* 2 (1954): 141–80.

———. *On a Kiev Edition of a Byzantine Mirror of Princes.* Cambridge, Mass., 1974.

Shampai, D. D. "O tirazhakh 'Kratkogo rossiiskogo letopistsa s rodosloviem.'" In *Literaturnoe tvorchestvo M. V. Lomonosova,* edited by P. N. Berkov and I. Serman. M, 1966.

Shchapov, Iu. N. "Dostoinstvo i titul tsaria na Rusi do XVI veka." In *Tsar' i tsarstvo v russkom obshchestvennom soznanii,* edited by A. A. Gorskii, A. I. Kuprianov, and L. N. Pushkarev. M, 1999.

Shchebal'skii, P. K. "Perepiska Ekateriny II s gr. N. I. Paninym." *Russkii vestnik* 45 (1863): 748–62.

Shchipanov, I. Ia., ed. *Izbrannye proizvedeniia russkikh myslitelei vtoroi poloviny XVIII v.* M, 1952.

Shevliakov, M., and Ia. Shchegolev, eds. *Petr Velikii v anekdotakh.* Spb, 1901.

Shils, Edward. *The Intellectuals and the Powers and Other Essays.* Chicago, 1972.

Shliapkin, I. A. "Sv. Dmitrii Rostovskii i ego vremia, 1651–1709." *Zapiski Istoriko-filologicheskogo fakulteta Imp. S-Peterburgskogo universiteta* 25 (1891).

Shmidt, S. O. "La Politique intérieure du tsarisme au milieu du XVIIIe siècle." *Annales, Economies, Sociétés, Civilisation* 21 (1966): 95–110.

———. "Vnutrenniaia politika Rossii serediny XVIII veka." *Voprosy istorii* (1987): 42–58.

Shmurlo, E. F. *Petr Velikii v otsenke sovremennikov i potomstva.* Spb, 1912.

Shpilevskii, S. M. *Vlast' moskovskikh gosudarei.* Spb, 1889.

Shtelin, Ia. Ia. "Zapiska." *Russkii arkhiv* 2 (1909): 527.

Shtrange, M. M. *Demokraticheskaia intelligentsiia v XVIII veke.* M, 1965.

Shukman, A., ed. *The Semiotics of Russian Culture.* Ann Arbor, 1984.

Shumigorskii, E. S. *Imperator Pavel I: Zhizn' i tsarstvovanie.* Spb, 1907.

Sipovskii, V. V. *Ocherki iz istorii russkago romana.* Spb, 1909.

———. *Politicheskiia nastroeniia v russkom romane XVIII v.* Spb, 1905.

Sivkov, K. V. "Samozvanstvo v Rossii v poslednei treti XVIII v." *Istoricheskie zapiski* 31 (1950): 88–135.

Skorobogatov, A. V. "Obraz monarkha v ofitsial'noi ideologii Rossii na rubezhe XVIII–XIX vekov." In *Filosofskii vek. Al'manakh 17: Istoriia idei kak metodologiia gumanitarnykh issledovanii,* edited by T. V. Artem'eva and M. I. Mikeshin. Vol. 1. Spb, 2001.

Skrynnikov, R. G. *Boris Godunov.* Translated by Hugh F. Graham. Gulf Breeze, Fla., 1982.

———. *Ivan the Terrible.* Translated by Hugh F. Graham. Gulf Breeze, Fla., 1981.

Slany, William. "Russian Central Governmental Institutions, 1725–1741." Ph.D. diss., Cornell University, 1958.

Sleptsov, A. *Bironovshchina.* Petrograd, n.d.

Smirnov, Iu. N. "Rol' gvardii v ukreplenii organov vlasti rossiiskago absoliutizma v pervoi polovine XVIII veka." In *Pravitel'stvennaia politika i klassovaia bor'ba v Rossii v period absoliutizma.* Kuibyshev, 1985.

Smith, Douglas. *Working the Rough Stone: Freemasonry and Society in Eighteenth-Century Russia.* DeKalb, 1999.

Smith, Preserved. *The Enlightenment, 1687–1776.* NY, 1962.

Smolitsch, I. "Zur Frage der Periodisierung der Geschichte der russischen Kirche." *Kyrios* 5 (1940–1941): 66–81.

Sokolova, V. K. *Russkie istoricheskie predaniia.* M, 1970.

Soloviev [Solov'ev], S. M. *History of Russia.* Vol. 25, *Rebellion and Reform: Fedor and Sophia, 1682–1689,* translated and edited by Lindsey A. J. Hughes. Gulf Breeze, Fla., 1989.

———. *History of Russia.* Vol. 34, *Empress Anna: Favorites, Policies, Campaigns,* translated by Walter J. Gleason, Jr. Gulf Breeze, Fla., 1984.

———. *History of Russia.* Vol. 42, *A New Empress: Peter III and Catherine II, 1761-1762,* translated by N. Lupinin. Gulf Breeze, Fla., 1990.

———. *Istoriia Rossii.* Vol. 9. M, 1963.

———. "Pisateli russkoi istorii XVIII veka." *Arkhiv istoriko-iuridicheskikh svedenii* 2 (1855): 3–146.

Sommerville, J. P. "Absolutism and Royalism." In *The Cambridge History of Political Thought, 1450–1700,* edited by J. H. Burns. Cambridge, 1991.

Sosloviia i gosudarstvennaia vlast' v Rossii, XV–seredina XIX vv. M, 1994.

Stafford, P. *Queens, Concubines, and Dowagers: The King's Wife in the Early Middle Ages.* Athens, Ga., 1981.

Stennik, Iu. V. "Ekaterina II—Polemist: Polemika v literaturnykh zaniatiakh imperatritsy Ekateriny II." In *Filosofskii vek. Al'manakh 11: Ekaterina i ee vremia. Sovremennyi vzgliad.* Spb, 1999.

Stolpianskii, P. "Odin iz nezametnykh deiatelei Ekaterinskoi epokhi: Iakov Pavlovich Kozel'skii." *Russkaia starina* 128 (1906): 567–84.

Stremooukhoff, Dmitri. "Moscow the Third Rome: Sources of the Doctrine." *Speculum* (1953): 84–101.

Stroev, V. *Bironovshchina i kabinet ministrov.* Vol. 1. M, 1909–1910.

Stupperich, R. "Feofan Prokopovich in Rom." *Zeitschrift für Osteuropäische Geschichte* 5 (1931): 327–39.

Sukhomlinov, M. I. "Lomonosov, student Marburgskago universiteta." *Russkii vestnik* 31 (1861): 127–65.

Sumner, B. H. *Peter the Great and the Emergence of Russia.* NY, 1962.

Sushintskii, F. "Iz literatury epokhi Petra Velikago: Starets Avraamii i ego poslanie Petru Velikomu." *Filologicheskiia zapiski* 1 (1914): 112–40.

Svodnyi katalog russkoi knigi grazhdanskoi pechati XVIII veka, 1725–1800. Edited by I. P. Kondakov et al. 6 vols. M, 1962–1975.

Syromiatnikov, B. I. *"Reguliarnoe" gosudarstvo Petra Pervogo i ego ideologiia.* M, 1943.

———. "S. E. Desnitskii—Osnovatel' nauki russkogo pravovedeniia." *Izvestiia Akademii nauk SSSR, otdeleniia ekonomiki i prava* 3 (1945): 33–40.

Szeftel, Marc. "L'Autocratie moscovite et l'absolutisme français au XVIIe siècle: Parallèles et divergences." *Canadian-American Slavic Studies* 16 (1982): 54–58.

———. "The Epithet 'Groznyi' in Historical Perspective." In *The Religious World of Russian Culture,* edited by Andrew Blane. The Hague, 1975.

———. "The Title of the Muscovite Monarch up to the End of the Seventeenth Century." *Canadian-American Slavic Studies* 13 (1979): 59–81.

Takenaka, Yutaka. "Land-Owning Nobles and Zemstvo Institutions: The Post-Reform Estate System in Political Perspective." In *Empire and Society: New Approaches to Russian History,* edited by Teruyuki Hara and Kimitaka Matsuzato. Sapporo, Japan, 1997.

Tanaka, Yoshihide. "Tsar and the Elite at the Beginning of the Eighteenth Century." *Slavic Studies* 46 (1999): 91–124.

Taranovskii, F. V. "Politicheskaia doktrina v Nakaze Imperatritsy Ekateriny II." *Sbornik statei po istorii prava, posviiashchennyi M. F. Vladimirskomu-Budanovu.* Kiev, 1904.

Tarnopol'skaia, I. O. "'Bozhestvennoe pravo korolei' i 'kontraktnaia teoriia': Monarkhicheskaia ideia na zapade i vostoke Evropy v XVI–XVII vekakh." In *Tsar' i tsarstvo v russkom obshchestvennom soznanii,* edited by A. A. Gorskii, A. I. Kuprianov, and L. N. Pushkarev. M, 1999.

Tartakovskii, A. G. *Russkaia memuaristika XVIII–pervoi poloviny XIX v.* M, 1991.

Tatarskii, I. *Simon Polotskii, ego zhizn' i deiatel'nost'.* M, 1886.

Tel'berg, G. *Istoricheskiia formy monarkhii v Rossii.* M, 1914.

Ternovskii, F. "Mitropolit Stefan Iavorskii: Biograficheskii ocherk." *Trudy Kievskoi dukhovnoi akademii* (1864): 237–90.

Terras, Victor, ed. *The Handbook of Russian Literature.* New Haven, 1985.

Thyrêt, Isolde. *Between God and Tsar: Religious Symbolism and the Royal Women of Muscovite Russia.* DeKalb, 2001.

Tikhomirov, M. N. "Soslovno-predstavitelnye uchrezhdeniia (zemskie sobory) v Rossii XVI veka." *Voprosy istorii* 5 (1958): 3–22.

———. *The Towns of Ancient Rus'.* M, 1959.

———, ed. *Ocherki istorii istoricheskoi nauki v SSSR.* M, 1955.

Tikhonravov, N. S. "Moskovskie vol'nodumtsy nachala XVIII veka i Stefan Iavorskii." In *Sochineniia.* Vol. 2. M, 1898.

Titlinov, B. "Feofan Prokopovich." In *Russkii biograficheskii slovar',* vol. Prituits-Reis. Spb, 1913.

Tolstoi, A. K. "Istoriia gosudarstva rossiiskago ot Gostomysla do Timasheva." In *Polnoe sobranie stikhotvorenii v dvukh tomakh.* Vol. 1. L, 1984.

Troitskii, S. M. "Istoriografiia 'dvortsovykh perevorotov' v Rossii XVIII v." *Voprosy istorii* 2 (1966): 38–53.

Tsarevskii, A. *Pososhkov i ego sochineniia*. M, 1883.

Tsarstvuiushchii dom Romanovykh. N.p.,1913.

"Tsesarevich Pavel Petrovich." *Russkaia starina* 9 (1874): 667–83.

Tucker, Robert C. "Culture, Political Culture, and Communist Society." *Political Science Quarterly* 88 (1973): 173–90.

Ullmann, Walter. *The Carolingian Renaissance and the Idea of Kingship*. London, 1969.

Urai, Yasuo, ed. *A Lemmatized Concordance to A Journey from Petersburg to Moscow of A. N. Radishchev*. Sapporo, 1998.

Usenko, O. G. "Ob otnoshenii narodnykh mass k tsariu Alekseiu Mikhailovichu." In *Tsar' i tsarstvo v russkom obshchestvennom soznanii*, edited by A. A. Gorskii, A. I. Kuprianov, and L. N. Pushkarev. M, 1999.

Uspenskii, B. A. "Historia sub specie semioticae." In *Soviet Semiotics*, edited by Daniel P. Lucid. Baltimore, 1977.

———. *Tsar' i patriarkh: Kharizma vlasti v Rossii*. M, 1998.

———, ed. *Iazyki, kul'tury, i problemy perevodimosti*. M, 1987.

Ustrialov, N. G. *Istoriia tsarstvovaniia Petra Velikago*. 6 vols. Spb, 1858–1863.

Val'denberg, V. *Drevnerusskiia ucheniia o predelakh tsarskoi vlasti*. Petrograd, 1916.

Valishevskii [Waliszewski], K. *Doch' Petra Velikago*. M, 1990.

———. *Le Fils de la grande Catherine: Paul I, empereur de Russie. Sa vie, son règne, et sa mort, 1754–1801*. Paris, 1912.

Valk, S. N. "V. N. Tatishchev i nachalo novoi russkoi istoricheskoi literatury." *XVIII vek* 7 (1966): 66–73.

Vandal, Albert. *Louis XV et Elisabeth de Russie*. Paris, 1896.

Vasetskii, G. A. "Filosofskie vzgliady Mikhaila Lomonosova." In *Iz istorii russkoi filosofii*. M, 1951.

Vasil'chikov, A. A. *Semeistvo Razumovskikh*. M, 1869.

Vasnetskii, G. M. *V. Lomonosov: Ego filosofskie i sotsial'no-politicheskie vzgliady*. M, 1954.

Venturi, Franco. *The End of the Old Regime in Europe, 1768–1776*, translated by R. Burr Litchfield. 2 vols. Princeton, 1989–1991.

———."History and Reform in the Middle of the Eighteenth Century." In *The Diversity of History: Essays in Honor of Sir Herbert Butterfield*, edited by John H. Elliott and Helmut G. Koenigsberger. Ithaca, 1970.

———. *Utopia and Reform in the Enlightenment*. Cambridge, 1971.

Vernadskii, George V. *Ancient Russia*. New Haven, 1943.

———. "Heresy of the Judaizers and the Policies of Ivan III of Moscow." *Speculum* 8 (1933): 436–54.

———. *Kievan Russia*. New Haven, 1947.

———. *Russkoe masonstvo v tsarstvovanii Ekateriny II*. Petrograd, 1917.

Veyne, Paul. *Les grecs, ont-ils cru à leurs mythes? Essai sur l'imagination constituante*. Paris, 1983.

Vierhaus, Rudolf. *Germany in the Age of Absolutism*. Cambridge, 1988.

Vilenskaia, E. S. "Ob osobennostiiakh formirovaniia russkoi osvoboditel'noi mysli v XVIII veke." *Voprosy filosofii* 2 (1951): 114–28.

Vinogradoff, P. *Essays in Legal History*. London, 1913.

Vodoff, W. "Remarques sur la valeur du terme 'tsar' appliqué aux princes russes avant le milieu du XVe siècle." *Oxford Slavonic Papers* 9 (1978): 1–41.

Voeikov, A. F. "Iz zapisok." In *Istoricheskii sbornik Vol'noi russkoi tipografii v Londone*. London, 1861.

Volkov, D. V. "Avtobiograficheskie zapiski." *Russkaia starina* 11 (1874): 481–87.

Volkov, M. Ia. "Monakh Avraamii i ego poslanie Petru I." In *Rossiia v period reform Petra I*, edited by N. I. Pavlenko. M, 1973.

Voprosy genezisa kapitalizma v Rossii: Sbornik statei. L, 1960.

Vovelle, Michel. "La représentation populaire de la monarchie." In *The French Revolution and the Creation of Modern Political Culture*. Vol. 1, *The Political Culture of the Old Regime*, edited by Michael Keith Baker. Oxford, 1987.

Vryonis, S., Jr., ed. *The Past in Medieval and Modern Greek Culture*. Malibu, 1978.

Vsevolodskii-Gerngross, V. N. *Russkii teatr vtoroi poloviny XVIII veka*. M, 1960.

Vstuplenie v nastoiashchuiu istoriiu o Rossii. M, 1847.

Vysotskii, N. G. "Zapreshchennyia pri Ekaterine Velikoi knigi." *Russkii arkhiv* 10 (1912): 252–55.

Warner, Richard H. "The Political Opposition to Tsar Paul I." Ph.D. diss., New York University, 1977.

Weber, Max. *Economy and Society: An Outline of Interpretive Sociology*, edited by Guenther Roth and Claus Wittich. Berkeley, 1978.

———. *The Theory of Social and Economic Organization*, translated by A. M. Henderson and Talcott Parsons. NY, 1947.

Weitzmann, Kurt, ed. *Late Classical and Mediaeval Studies*. Princeton, 1955.

Whittaker, Cynthia Hyla. "Chosen by 'All the Russian People': The Idea of an Elected Monarch in Eighteenth-Century Russia." *Acta Slavica Iaponica* 18 (2001): 1–18.

———."The Idea of Autocracy Among Eighteenth-Century Russian Historians." *Russian Review* 55 (1996): 149–71.

———. "The Reforming Tsar: The Redefinition of Autocratic Duty in Eighteenth-Century Russia." *Slavic Review* 51 (1992): 77–98.

Winter, Ernst. "Josefinismus und Petrinismus: Zur vergleichenden Geschichte der österreichischen und russischen Aufklärung." *Canadian-American Slavic Studies* 16 (1982): 357–68.

Wirtschafter, Elise. *Social Identity in Imperial Russia*. DeKalb, 1997.

Wittram, Reinhard. "Formen und Wandlungen des europäischen Absolutismus." In *Glaube und Geschichte: Festschrift für Friedrich Gogarten*, edited by Heinrich Kunte. Giessen, 1948.

———. *Peter I: Czar und Kaiser*. 2 vols. Göttingen, 1964.

Wolf, John B. *Louis XIV*. NY, 1968.

Wolf, Robert Lee. "The Three Romes: The Migration of an Ideology and the Making of an Autocrat." *Daedalus* 88 (1959): 291–311.

Wolff, Larry. *Inventing Eastern Europe: The Map of Civilization on the Mind of the Enlightenment*. Stanford, 1994.

Wortman, Richard S. *The Development of a Russian Legal Consciousness*. Chicago, 1976.

———. *Scenarios of Power: Myth and Ceremony in Russian Monarchy*. Vol. I, *From Peter the Great to the Death of Nicholas I*. Princeton, 1995.

Wren, Melvin. *The Western Impact upon Tsarist Russia*. Chicago, 1971.

Wuthnow, Robert. *Communities of Discourse: Ideology and Social Structure in the Reformation, the Enlightenment, and European Socialism*. Cambridge, Mass., 1989.

Yanov, Alexander. "Drama of the Time of Troubles, 1725–1730." *Canadian-American Slavic Studies* 12 (1978): 1–59.

———. *Origins of Autocracy: Ivan the Terrible in Russian History*. Berkeley, 1981.

Zagoskin, N. P. *Verkhovniki i shliakhetstvo 1730 goda*. Kazan, 1881.

Zagriatskov, M. D. "Obshchestvenno-politicheskie vzgliady S. E. Desnitskogo." *Voprosy istorii* 7 (1949): 101–12.

Zamyslovskii, E. *Tsartvovanie Fedora Alekseevicha.* Spb, 1871.

Zaozerskii, A. I. "A. R. Vorontsov: K istorii byta i nravov XVIII v." *Istoricheskie zapiski* 23 (1947): 120–25.

Zelensky, Elizabeth K. "'Sophia the Wisdom of God': The Function of Religious Imagery During the Regency of Sofiia Alekseevna of Muscovy." In *Women and Sovereignty,* edited by L. O. Fradenburg. Edinburgh, 1992.

Zheliabuzhskii, I. A. "Dnevnyia zapiski." *Russkii arkhiv* 3 (1910): 5–154.

Zhivov, V. M. *Iazyk i kul'tura v Rossii XVIII veka.* M, 1996.

Zhivov, V. M., and B. A. Uspenskii. "Tsar' i bog: Semioticheskie aspekty sakralizatsii monarkha v Rossii." In *Iazyki, kul'tury, i problemy perevodimosti,* edited by B. A. Uspenskii. M, 1987.

Zil'berman, I. *Politicheskie vzgliady Ivana Groznogo.* L, 1953.

Zimin, A. A. "O politicheskoi doktrine Iosifa Volotskogo." *Trudy otdela drevnerusskoi literatury* 9 (1953): 159–77.

Znamenskii, P. "Tatishchev i ego istoriia." *Trudy Kievskoi dukhovnoi akademii* 1 (1862): 197–228.

Zorin, Andrei. *Kormia dvuglavogo orla: Literatura i gosudarstvennaia ideologiia v Rossii v poslednei treti XVIII—pervoi treti XIX veka.* M, 2001.

INDEX

reform principle and, 33–58; repetitiveness of arguments in favor of, 14–20, 56; rule of law in Russia and, 3, 9, 22, 88–91, 102–18, 133–40, 173–75, 187–88; support of in Russia, 3–12; superiority of, over democracy or aristocracy, 11, 15–16, 20–21, 26, 111–12, 129–32, 149, 187; writing on, 13–20

Monarchy, Constitutional or Limited: absolute monarchy as preferable to, 73–74, 105; Alexander I and, 185–86, 189; conditions of 1730 limiting monarch, 59, 70–76

Monarchy, Divine Right, 18–19, 23–24, 29–31, 122, 182; versus divine duty for Peter I, 33–39

Monarchy, Elective, 16, 57 (*see also* Election); in Russian context, 59–90, 101

Monarchy, Enlightened Absolutist, 103, 104, 184, 230n75; Peter I as forerunner of, 39–49; Peter III and, 94–95; Catherine II and, 102–7

Monarchy, Hereditary, 57; heredity as basis for succession, 33, 52–58, 60; attempt of House of Braunschweig to replace Romanovs, 79–81; inheritance, dynastic, 3, 15–16, 21–22, 63, 125–29, 182

Montesquieu, Charles de Secondat, 108, 109, 235n158; influence on Catherine II, 111–13; on monarchy, 103, 115, 116, 135, 153; on succession, 55, 60

Monthly Essays (journal), 85

Morality tales, as advice literature, 143

Moscow Academy, 51

Moscow University, 87, 142; founding of, 85, 86

Müller, Gerhard, 126

Myl'nikov, Aleksandr, 93, 96

N

Nakaz. See Instructions

Napoleon Bonaparte, 18

Narva, Russian defeat at, 39

Naryshkin family, 31, 65

Natural law, 104–5

Naumov, Viktor, 84

Necker, Jacques, 8

Nero, Emperor of Rome, 138, 170

Netherlands, 11, 75

Nicocles (Isocrates), 19

Nikolev, Nikolai, 151, 165, 168

Nikon, Patriarch, 30

Nondespotic approach to Russian history, 125, 133–39

Normanist theory, 126

"Notebooks" (Avraamii), 47–48

"Notes Concerning Russian History" (Catherine II), 120, 134

Novels, 194n8; as advice literature, 5, 87, 144, 147–48, 151, 155, 157, 160, 169–70, 171–72, 176; emergence of, as vehicle for discussing political issues, 87–88

Novgorod, 125, 180; appointment of Sivers as governor of, 103; medieval, 136

Novikov, Nikolai, 120, 124, 148, 162, 179, 181

Numa Pompilius (Kheraskov), 144, 161

O

Odes (*see also* Poetry): as advice literature, 5, 85, 86, 94, 115, 144, 151, 154, 155, 161–62, 165, 167–69, 172–73, 178, 179, 181

"Ode to Slavery" (Kapnist), 172–73

Old Believers, 28; denial of Peter I's legitimacy by, 35; Peter III's toleration of, 94, 96

The Old Russian Library (journal), 153

Olearius, Adam, 91

Olga, Grand Princess of Kievan Rus', 24

On Crimes and Punishments (Beccaria), 109

"On the Corruption of Morals" (Shcherbatov), 175

Ophir (Shcherbatov), 148, 157, 161, 169–70

Orlov brothers, 165

Ottoman Empire, 11, 75

P

The Painter (journal), 158

Palitsyn, Avraamii, 27

Panin, Nikita, 88, 106, 107, 117, 137, 150, 174, 188–89, 231n93; biography of, 145

Panin, Petr, 117, 150, 165, 174

Panin party, 173

Paul, Grand Duke, 93, 98, 101, 117, 146, 158, 173. *See also* Paul I

Paul I, 11, 150, 181–85, **183** (*see also* Paul, Grand Duke); accession manifesto of, 182; assassination of, 185; as bad tsar, 166, 170, 182, 184–85, 189; Masons' overtures to, 179; name day odes, 167, 168–69; publications under, 184; as reforming tsar, 182–85; rule of law and, 183; succession law of, 182, 190

Peresvetov, Ivan, 24

Peter I the Great, 33–58, **35**, **37**, 87, 92, 174; abolition of the patriarchate by, 38–39; advice literature under, 36–38, 47–48, 49–50; Aleksei as heir to, 52–54; Catherine I and, 65–67; celebration of, 51–52, 209n36; as co-tsar with Ivan V, 32; death of, 65; despotism and, 44–48, 55, 103, 210n64; divine duty